WHOSE LIVES
ARE THEY ANYWAY?

WHOSE LIVES ARE THEY ANYWAY?

The Biopic as Contemporary Film Genre

Dennis Bingham

RUTGERS UNIVERSITY PRESS
NEW BRUNSWICK, NEW JERSEY, AND LONDON

Library of Congress Cataloging-in-Publication Data

Bingham, Dennis, 1954—Whose lives are they anyway? : the biopic as
contemporary film genre / Dennis Bingham.
p. cm.
Includes bibliographical references and index.
ISBN 978–0–8135–4657–5 (hardcover : alk. paper)
—ISBN 978–0–8135–4658–2 (pbk. : alk. paper)
1. Biographical films—History and criticism. I. Title.
PN1995.9.B55B56 2010
791.43′65—dc22
2009016183

A British Cataloging-in-Publication record for this book is available from
the British Library.

Visit our Web site: http://rutgerspress.rutgers.edu

Manufactured in the United States of America

"It is my very humane endeavor
To make to some extent
Each evil liver
A running river
of harmless merriment"
—W. S. Gilbert

CONTENTS

ACKNOWLEDGMENTS

The biopic is such an unappreciated genre that virtually everyone who allowed me to teach a course, make a presentation, or publish an article, usually after giving me a quizzical look that said, "Biopics? Why biopics?" deserves to be thanked. Such would include Robert Burgoyne at Wayne State University, where I taught my first of many courses on biopics back in 1991. Once my interest in biopics developed into the book stage, the project spanned the terms of five chairs of English at Indiana University Purdue University Indianapolis: Richard Turner, Ken Davis, the late Christian J. W. Kloesel, Susanmarie Harrington, and Thomas Upton, and the tenures of three deans of the IU School of Liberal Arts: Herman Saatkamp, Robert White, and William Blomquist, as well as Associate Dean David Ford. Each of the aforementioned chairs and deans was generous and understanding in meeting my requests for time and resources as the book wended its way toward completion. The project received extensive institutional support, including an Indiana University President's Arts and Humanities Initiative Fellowship, two IU School of Liberal Arts Research Summer Fellowships, one sabbatical travel grant, and a Grant-in-Aid from the Office for Professional Development.

An early version of Chapter 5 was published as "Oliver Stone's *Nixon* and the Unmanning of the Self-Made Man," in *Masculinity: Movies, Bodies, Culture*, ed. Peter Lehman (New York: Routledge, 2001), and appears here with permission. Chapter 12 was first published, in somewhat different form, as "I Do Want to Live!: Female Voices, Male Discourse, and Hollywood Biopics," in *Cinema Journal* 38.3 (1999): 3–26, and appears here with permission of the University of Texas Press. An excerpt from "Nixon on the Joys of Undressing a Woman" by Karen Kovacik, from her collection of poems entitled *Nixon and I* (1998), appears here with the kind permission of Kent State University Press.

During my research, the staff at the Performing Arts Special Collections at UCLA, Ned Comstock at the University of Southern California, and Barbara Hall at the Margaret Herrick Library of the Academy of Motion Picture Arts and Sciences were extremely helpful in preparing scripts and other papers for my perusal and making my research trips to Los Angeles extremely productive. For help with photographs, I am most grateful to Murray Pomerance and to Stephen LeBeau and Joy Kramer.

Many colleagues have shared suggestions and feedback on my work at Society for Cinema and Media Studies Conferences (SCMS) and other meetings over the years. Amy Lawrence came up and told me that my work on *I Want to Live!* sounded "unusually polished." Harriet Margolies, at an early version of my work on *An Angel at My Table*, set me straight on some of my suppositions about New Zealand and Jane Campion. Glenn Man graciously invited me onto a panel he constituted on biography in long-ago 1999–2000. Cynthia Baron, Frank Tomasulo, and Diane Carson coaxed me onto a workshop they would be presenting in eight months' time, and I gambled that I would be recovering from my then-impending stem cell transplant and ready to go to Washington, D.C., in what turned out to be the last pre-9/11 spring. Cynthia Erb and Zivah Perel helped with ideas and encouragement. Kevin Hagopian, Michelle Arrow, and Clare Connors were good enough to join me for a session on biopics at the 2008 SCMS conference in Philadelphia. I owe many thanks to the Department of Media Arts at the University of Arizona and the Center for Film, Media, and Popular Culture at Arizona State University, which invited me to share my work on biopics with large, appreciative audiences. I also wish to thank Marcia Landy and James Naremore for their invaluable encouragement and suggestions.

Leslie Mitchner at Rutgers University Press has been more than patient with me through the numerous delays, setbacks that have beset this book over a period of several years, as well as the creative riptides that drove it forward. Leslie has also been the most encouraging kind of editor, allowing the book to take shape as changes to the genre dictated. We agree that it's a better book now than if I had finished it circa 2002, my original target date.

Most writers I know look upon the copyediting stage of the publishing process with dread. However, Eric Schramm, an accomplished copyeditor whom the press and I were lucky to have work on my book, proved a great collaborator. Eric played the role of the objective outsider who came along after I was long past able to make clear judgments of my own writing and asked, "Did you really mean to say *this*?" Not only does the book have a lot fewer errors thanks to him, but the thoughtfulness of his comments and queries helped me to give the book a good final polish.

My good friend Kevin Sandler was a frequent sounding board who both kept my spirits high and kept me from taking myself too seriously. My professional partnership and personal friendship with Debra White-Stanley have been a bulwark of strength for me through the late stages of the book. As always, students at IUPUI, past and present, have helped me keep the faith, given me new ideas, and reminded me why I wanted to be a teacher of film studies in the first place. I owe much to Jon Knipp, Damien Belleveau, Katherine Ellison, the late Michael Coatney, Wes Felton, Tess Saunders, Shaun Ancelet, Anne Laker, Lisa Stamm, Julie Driscol, and Stephen Jones.

Finally, my wife Christine and I have, it seems, lived out most of the marriage vows. This book and its author have emerged in one piece because of Christine, who happens to be an astute critic, a splendid editor, and an all-around perfect partner. This book is much better than it would have been without her input and guidance; in fact, it might not have come to be at all without her. My son, Jerome, who grew from preschooler to eighth-grader during the years I worked on this book, is a constant wonder and delight. Christine and Jerome are my love and my lifeblood. This book, like everything I do, is for them.

WHOSE LIVES
ARE THEY ANYWAY?

Introduction

A Respectable Genre of Very Low Repute

[I] tried to stay human and true to this man [George W. Bush]. It's supposed to be a fair and true portrait. People get me confused with my outspoken citizen side, but I am a dramatist first and foremost.
—Oliver Stone, 2008

At the start of *Man on the Moon* (1999), light comes up on a young man, played by Jim Carrey, filmed in black and white, surrounded by darkness. Speaking in an indistinguishable "foreign" accent and high-pitched voice, he looks directly but nervously at the audience, his eyes shifting, like a child making a presentation at school. "Hello," he says. "I am Andy. And I would like to thank you for coming to my movie. I wish it was better, you know. But it is so stupid. It's terrible. I do not even like it. All of the most important things in my life are changed around and mixed up for, um, [really struggles to get out this next phrase] dramatic purposes." Announcing that he has "decided to cut out all the baloney," "Andy" tells the unheard, unseen audience, "Now the movie is much shorter. In fact, this is the end of the movie. Thank you very much." When the audience fails to leave, the man moves awkwardly to a child's suitcase phonograph from the 1950s, which plays the "The Theme from *Lassie*" while the film's actual end credits roll. Increasingly desperate, "Andy" tries playing the 45 RPM record over and over, until he gives up, shuts the lid on the "suitcase," and the screen goes black.

After several seconds go by, the man slowly pokes his head into the frame, and Andy, rather than "Andy," says, "Wow. You're still here. O-kaaay," he exclaims, bounding into the shot with exaggerated heartiness. "I hope you're not upset. I did that to get rid of those folks who just wouldn't understand me, and don't even want to try. Actually, the movie is really great," he says, overly enthusiastic. We can't be any surer about this Andy than we were about the one we saw before. Indeed, he says that the movie "is just filled with colorful characters, like the one I just did, and the one I'm doing now." "Our story begins," he says, in a sing-song tone, moving to a 16-millimeter projector, "back in Great Neck, Long Island." The light of the projector shines right on us, making us not only the audience, but also the screen.

Now acting as voiceover narrator, Andy introduces his childhood house, a suburban *Leave It to Beaver*–type home of the late 1950s. His father, sister, brother, and mother are all shown in small-screen color home movies, until the inevitable widening out into the color widescreen film. Andy Kaufman (1949–1984) is now our protagonist in a re-created past, not the stand-up performance artist conjured up out of eternity. "We," the audience, are ourselves, however, constituted from Andy's own transcendence of physical existence, and we meet him in a liminal space between an afterlife and what we think of as our actuality. Here is Kaufman, the film says, performing his routines by making audiences doubt what is real and what is part of the act, all the while forcing them to receive as entertainment feelings of discomfort and uncertainty. The 1992 R.E.M. song "Man on the Moon," itself a kind of index of the late comedian, starts playing as Andy says, "Our story begins . . ." and is yet another link from the extra-narrative Andy to the movie's story world itself.

This story world soon becomes loaded down with tropes of the classical biopic, many of which were identified by George F. Custen in his ground-breaking 1992 study, *Bio/pics: How Hollywood Constructed Public History*. These include the narrative told in flashback, the voiceover (although it never returns after the opening), and the opposition of the subject's family (the "Great Neck" scenes begin with Andy's father asking why Andy has to perform make-believe TV shows in his room and why he can't go outside and "play sports"). In good time, other tropes appear: the characters of The Sidekick, Bob Zmuda (Paul Giamatti), Kaufman's writer and frequent partner in mischief; and The Mentor, his manager, George Shapiro (Danny De Vito, who co-starred with Kaufman on the TV sitcom *Taxi*, and whose production company made the film). Another frequent character of the Great

Man film, the patient helpmeet-wife, is not here exactly because Kaufman never married. However, Lynne Margulies (Courtney Love), one of Kaufman's girlfriends, allowed her name to be used and thus a number of Andy's paramours are composited in her. The composite character, whether real (as here) or invented, as is usually the case, is a feature that few biopics of any type or era have done without. Finally, after the film's ethereal prologue, the brief childhood scenes climax with Andy performing a childhood rhyme to his sister. Cut and we're looking at the stage of a sparsely attended comedy club where a grown-up Andy sings the same rhyme to a puzzled looking audience. Now we're into the *in medias res* opening, which I define as beginning the story at the moment just before the subject begins to make his/her mark on the world. This is what the film's writers, Scott Alexander and Larry Karaszewski, call a strategy whereby they "get away with bizarro material by marrying it to Hollywood form" (*Man* xii).

This opening of *Man on the Moon,* one of a number of "biopic[s] of someone who doesn't deserve one," written by Alexander and Karaszewski, self-consciously confronts many of the objections made to the biographical film, or the biopic. Andy, acting like a critic objecting on grounds of historical accuracy, complains that his life has been "changed around and mixed up," for that ubiquitous justification, "dramatic purposes." Kaufman's "act" often involved destroying the scripted, illusory routines of show business, from polished stand-up acts and well-rehearsed TV skits to, most incredibly, professional wrestling. Thus it follows that he, or his earthly representatives, should open his biopic by disrupting the genre's operations and agreeing with its sharpest critics. Andy, having used some sort of celestial scissors, claims to have reduced the film to what many critics charge biopics and historical films would be without alteration, compression, invention, and metaphor: Nothing (Rosenstone *Visions* 73–75). When he returns to endorse "his" movie for being "filled with colorful characters, like . . . the one I'm doing now," the second character appears to be Andy as he "really is," fulfilling the aim of all biopics, to reveal the "real person" behind the public persona. Here the filmmakers self-consciously project their defense of a movie that turns Kaufman's life into a "story," one that combines much that is from, or of, actuality, with some that is invented and "changed around" for dramatic purposes.

To be sure, Andy Kaufman is in the realm of what Custen, taking off from Leo Lowenthal, referred to as the Idol of Consumption, an entertainer or sports figure who in effect is a consumer product and whose conspicuous

1. The subject and the sidekick. *Man on the Moon* (Milos Forman, Universal, 1999) parodies the inspired biographical subject as Andy Kaufman (Jim Carrey) watches wrestling on TV, transfixed. With Paul Giamatti as Bob Zmuda. Digital frame enlargement.

consumption the spectator can vicariously enjoy but also see the limitations of. Andy, without a doubt, was a product of such consumer forums as comedy clubs and commercial television, especially the sitcom *Taxi,* which he hated doing by all accounts. But he fought these institutions all the way; in fact, the film's opening is a reference to his ABC special "in which Andy claimed that he'd blown his budget, and said the entire show was just him in a chair, and he advised viewers to change the channel" (Alexander and Karaszewski *Man* 155).

Custen's counterpart to the Idol of Consumption, by way of Lowenthal, was the Idol of Production. This was the man, and sometimes the woman, who made great things for society. Statesmen like *Alexander Hamilton* (1931) and *Young Mr. Lincoln* (1939), soldiers like *Sergeant York* (1941) and blinded Marine Al Schmid in *The Pride of the Marines* (1945), as well as scientists such as Louis Pasteur (*The Story of Louis Pasteur* [1936]) and Thomas Edison (*Young Tom Edison* [1939] and *Edison the Man* [1940]) and even *Madame Curie* (1943) are examples of visionaries who made the world better, heroes from the past whose determination was meant as a tonic for audiences during the Great Depression and World War II. The Idol of Production gave way to increased curiosity about the famous with the onset of the consumer society. This figure came back, however, as part of the neoclassical biopic revival of the 2000s, but with a warts-and-all or *Citizen Kane*–like investigatory tinge, in such films as *Kinsey* (2004) and *The Aviator* (2004).

As *Man on the Moon* positions its biographical subject in a liminal place between life and death (appropriately, since many who knew Kaufman refused to believe that his cancer and death were not some kind of joke), between story and direct address, the biopic genre finds itself in a liminal space between fiction and actuality. Late in the screenwriters' research, they "realized something was off":

> We didn't know what the movie was about. We didn't know who Andy was. Panic set in. The thousands of anecdotes weren't coalescing into a character, a guy whom we understood. Andy was just a cipher moving through a series of episodes—our greatest fear. We struggled, reading and rereading the notes, looking for our Rosebud, our key to Andy Kaufman. It was hopeless. . . . In a funk, we rang up Lynne Margulies, Andy's girlfriend the last two years of his life. . . . We told her the problem. No matter how much we studied the material, we couldn't figure out the real Andy. Lynne responded simply, yet provocatively. "Guys, there *is* no real Andy." And that was it. Lynne had given us the secret to the movie. (*Man* xi–xii)

Every biopic is supposed to have a basis in reality. *Man on the Moon* subverts the genre by not insisting upon a reality for its subject, by not even maintaining that their subject was "real." Actual? Yes. Real? No. Alexander and Karaszewski, with Milos Forman's direction, pass their own dilemma on to the audience. The way to create a "true portrait" of Andy Kaufman is to accept that there is no real Andy Kaufman, no core that can be exposed, no "inner life" that explains him. The biopic subject, at least in the male Great Man variant, is usually posed as a visionary with a pure, one of a kind talent or idea who must overcome opposition to his idea or even just to himself. All of this is why the filmmakers put Kaufman in charge from the beginning, implying that he ultimately is in control of how much we can know about him; even the filmmakers are consigned to mere names on the credit roll that Andy switches on and off at will. Not for nothing then do Alexander and Karaszewski call *Man on the Moon* and their other biopics "anti–Great Man" films. Everything about the opening of this film recalls and also stands on its head a genre that in some way ends in emphasizing the success and the transcendently timeless importance of its protagonist.

As we see in such a counterexample, therefore, the biopic is by no means a simple recounting of the facts of someone's life. It is an attempt to discover biographical truth, in this case gathered through scores of interviews with people who knew Kaufman, viewings of every TV appearance he made, Lynne Margulies's documentary *I'm from Hollywood* (1989) about Kaufman's wrestling days, and audio recordings of many of his stage performances. Robert Rosenstone, a historian who has become a champion of historical drama in film, points out that in a visual medium history "must be fictional in order to be true" (*Visions* 70). By fiction, Rosenstone refers to the Latin meaning, "formed," but without ruling out "fiction" in "the more modern sense of 'an imaginative creation'" ("In Praise" 13).

If biopics partake of fiction in making their subjects' lives real to us, how is the biography a kind of history? In her study of literary biography Catherine Parke argues that historically a "tug of war" has taken place among fiction, biography, and history, "with biography in the middle" (xvi). This interconnection has not been well enough understood. Parke points out that in public libraries, the biography section is usually next to the fiction stacks. A librarian explained to Parke that "our users tend to think of these books together." She continued, "Both are, after all, studies of people's lives." Reference librarians, on the other hand, would prefer to have biography on the second floor next to history and near the telephone reference desk. When someone calls with a question about the Civil War, a librarian might want to turn to a biography of Ulysses S. Grant or Robert E. Lee. But, she concluded, "we shelve books with our patrons' reading habits in mind. That's why we put biography next to fiction" (Parke xv). Furthermore, the debate among fiction, biography, and history is not new. Plutarch, in his *Lives,* declared, "It is not Histories that I am writing, but Lives; and in the most illustrious deeds there is not always a manifestation of virtue or vice, nay a slight thing like a phrase or a jest often makes a greater revelation of character than battles where thousands fall, or the greatest armaments, or sieges of cities" (qtd. in Parke 15).

If, however, historians are overcoming their misgivings about the "invention" that dramatic film invariably brings to the visualization of histories, then those who deal with history might want to consider Rosenstone's idea that invention does not necessarily violate historical truth (*Visions* 67–69). Indeed, since historical fiction stems from the desire to see biographical and historical figures living before us, there are instances where the filmmakers see the need to "complete" history, to fill in what didn't happen with what a viewer might wish to see happen. To use a well-known example, Queen Elizabeth I so feared her cousin, Mary Stuart of Scotland, as a threat to her reign that she imprisoned her for nineteen years, then had her executed. In historical fact, Elizabeth and Mary never met. But in the films and plays that make drama out of the standoff between the two rivals, there is always a tense *tête-à-tête* confrontation between them, especially when they are embodied by powerful stars like Glenda Jackson and Vanessa Redgrave, who played Elizabeth and Mary, respectively, in *Mary Queen of Scots* (1971). Of course, we want these two powerful women to meet up. What would be gained in terms of realism (that is, a sense that things do not happen neatly or conveniently in life) would surely be lost in interest.

Films more interested in the imponderables of history than in high drama might leave actualities alone, as Mary Harron did in *The Notorious Bettie Page* (2006). Bettie Page the pinup model was subpoenaed to testify in 1955 before a Senate subcommittee that was investigating the effects of pornography on minors. Harron sets up the hearings as the film's framing device, flashing back to the story of Bettie's life from scenes of Bettie waiting for hours to be called before the senators. In the event Page was never called to testify; instead she was dismissed without explanation. Many a filmmaker would have been tempted to invent a dramatic climax between two Tennesseans, the pinup and bondage model and the subcommittee chairman, Senator Estes Kefauver, in the sort of courtroom scene that ended many biopics of the classical period. Harron is more interested in the effect of the hearings on Bettie, sacrificing dramatic fireworks for the inscrutability of real life.

Decisions like Harron's demonstrate that sometimes drama is capable of letting actualities be actualities. For instance, some biopics have been loath to supply character motivations where none were forthcoming in life. Why does Erin Brockovich wear low-cut leather tops, micro-minis, and stiletto heels in conservative business settings? Why did reporter Ed Montgomery change his attitude toward alleged murderer Barbara Graham, whose story is told in the film *I Want to Live!* (1958), from believing she was "guilty as hell" to championing her post-conviction claim of innocence? The real Montgomery never said why, and the film takes his about-face as a given, nothing more.

For Rosenstone, fiction and history differ in that "they both tell stories, but the latter is a true story." "Need this be a 'literal' truth," he asks, "an exact copy of what took place in the past? . . . In film, it can never be," he answers (*Visions* 69). A viewer, furthermore, must

> learn to judge the ways in which, through invention, film summarizes vast amounts of data or symbolizes complexities that otherwise could not be shown. We must recognize that film will always include images

that are at once invented and true; true in that they symbolize, condense, or summarize larger amounts of data; true in that they impart an overall meaning of the past that can be verified, documented, or reasonably argued. And how do we know what can be verified, documented, or reasonably argued? From the ongoing discourse of history; from the existing body of historical texts, from their data and arguments. (*Visions* 71)

The point is simply this: The biopic is a genuine, dynamic genre and an important one. The biopic narrates, exhibits, and celebrates the life of a subject in order to demonstrate, investigate, or question his or her importance in the world; to illuminate the fine points of a personality; and for both artist and spectator to discover what it would be like to be this person, or to be a certain type of person, or, as with Andy Kaufman, to be that person's audience. The appeal of the biopic lies in seeing an actual person who did something interesting in life, known mostly in public, transformed into a character. Private behaviors and actions and public events as they might have been in the person's time are formed together and interpreted dramatically. At the heart of the biopic is the urge to dramatize actuality and find in it the filmmaker's own version of truth. The function of the biopic subject is to live the spectator a story. The genre's charge, which dates back to its salad days in the Hollywood studio era, is to enter the biographical subject into the pantheon of cultural mythology, one way or another, and to show why he or she belongs there.

The biopic has evolved and gone through life-cycle changes and continues to do so, from the studio era to the present; these phases have sometimes themselves become subgenres. This book studies the evolution and life-cycle changes of the genre. It also sees biographies of men and women as essentially different genres, as criticism of literary biography has also tended to do. Films about men have gone from celebratory to warts-and-all to investigatory to postmodern and parodic. Biopics of women, on the other hand, are weighted down by myths of suffering, victimization, and failure perpetuated by a culture whose films reveal an acute fear of women in the public realm. Female biopics can be made empowering only by a conscious and deliberate application of a feminist point of view. Films such as *An Angel at My Table* (1990), *Center Stage* (1992), *Erin Brockovich* (2000), *The Notorious Bettie Page* (2006), and *Marie Antoinette* (2006) attempt to invent new ways of looking at the woman who occupies the public sphere, while critiquing the old conventions. The fact that there are so few recent examples of such films, however, shows how difficult it is to reinvent the female biopic.

Film studies has not recognized the biopic as a genre with its own conventions and historical stages of development, disintegration, investigation, parody, and revival. Indeed, before making my arguments, I need to show that film biography is even a genre. Not only has biography been left out of most genre studies of film, at least until very recently, but the term "biopic" is frequently used as a pejorative not much different from "oater" for westerns and "weepie" for the woman's film, and yet those hardly became the accepted terms for those genres. Furthermore, "biopic" has come to specify a genre of the Hollywood studio era, when biographies were staples of several of the major studios, especially Warner Bros., Twentieth Century Fox, and MGM. Custen's book, the only major study of the genre, is solely concerned with products of the Studio System.

The identification of film biography with the Studio Period, however, does not quite explain why the term "biopic" spurs an instantly negative reaction, nor why the film biography is so often thought of as tedious, pedestrian, and fraudulent. "I don't like those biographical things. I just don't believe them," said Robert Altman, while promoting *Vincent and Theo*, his 1990 anti-biopic of Van Gogh (Tibbetts 39). In their monograph on *Queen Christina* (1933) Marcia Landy and Amy Villarejo write that "critical cavils regarding the biopic are consonant with the view that Hollywood produced frivolous films that falsify 'reality,' wreaking havoc with history in favour of 'escapist' entertainment" (17). Mary Joannou and Steve McIntyre wrote in *Screen* about a 1983 symposium on biopics, "they follow a more or less unproblematic historical trajectory of the individual toward the achievement by which he or she is best known to the public. . . . Perhaps understandably, this simple narrative organisation left many people unsatisfied, and, together with the excessive length of some biopics, explained why many people said they do not 'like' biopics" (147). James Welsh, interviewing scholar John Tibbetts about his book on composer biopics, said, "The biopic is a mendacious genre that may have little to do with historical or biographical truth. Can you justify your interest in movies that exist mainly to tell entertaining lies?" (86). While that may come as close to a "When did you stop beating your wife?" presumption as one can get, it suffices to say that biography may be the most maligned of all film genres.

No less meticulous a scholar and film historian than David Bordwell, writing about genres that were "rehabilitated" in the New Hollywood, observed in 2006: "Most recently, the biography, long a stuffy prestige item (*Wilson*, 1944; *MacArthur*, 1977), has been revived with lesser-known eccentrics as the subject [sic]. So we get biopics about a pornographer (*The People vs. Larry Flynt,* 1996), a triple-X star (*Wonderland,* 2003), a world-class imposter (*Catch Me If You Can,* 2002), and a game-show host who may be a CIA hit man (*Confessions of a Dangerous Mind,* 2002)" (*The Way* 55). Bordwell's observation of the parodic strain in some contemporary biopics is correct, but he shows no understanding of how the genre got from stages A to R in its evolution. Fast-forwarding through nearly sixty years of the genre, Bordwell singles out the extremes. *Wilson,* Darryl F. Zanuck's pet project, a biography of Woodrow Wilson, has never been deemed a success, even if it did win five Academy Awards. It is a guilty pleasure of mine just for the misplaced passion of Zanuck as a producer that is extravagantly on display. *MacArthur* was an anachronistic dud attempting to cash in on the success of *Patton* (1970), with a badly miscast Gregory Peck. Pulling out these entries to represent all biopics is like mentioning overproduced misfires like *The Outlaw* (1946) and *Bite the Bullet* (1975) as examples of westerns or second-rate productions like *Cover Girl* (1944) or *The Wiz* (1978) to sum up musicals. Bordwell's uncharacteristically careless statement itself exemplifies the lack of serious thought, not to mention the knee-jerk condescension, given to this diverse genre in essentially all echelons of film criticism.

With the "biopic" as a term held until recent years at the level of a pejorative, two things tended to happen. First, filmmakers denied that they had made a "biopic." In a featurette on the DVD of *Topsy Turvy,* Mike Leigh's 1999 film about Gilbert and Sullivan, actor Allan Corduner expresses his hope that the film won't look like "some strange Victorian chocolate box biopic." At around the same time, in an interview with Milos Forman, Scott Alexander challenges the director when he tries to deny that *Man on the Moon* is a biopic. "Larry and I openly admit we like doing 'biopics.' We've written three. . . . We like that genre. But when you talk about it, you always sort of distance yourself. You don't talk about it as just a biopic. Yet when I think about your body of work, you've done a lot of movies with real historical figures. . . . So you don't like approaching it as a biopic, but there's something there you like" (Alexander and Karaszewski 198).

Second, there was no quicker way to pan a film than to brand it "a biopic." In their reviews of Lawrence Kasdan's 1994 film *Wyatt Earp,* which told Earp's story in the form of a biography rather than as the events leading up to the gunfight at the OK Corral, Richard Schickel of *Time* and David Ansen of *Newsweek* each called the movie "a solemn biopic," as if those two words just naturally went together. Schickel described the film as "grinding relentlessly, without selectivity or point of view, through a rootless and episodic life from adolescence to old age" (73). His criticism might have summarized the stereotypical reaction of many commentators and scholars to the entire genre.

Despite the pejorative odor of the term, I believe the word "biopic" should be embraced and appropriated by those who find the genre intriguing and worthwhile, not discarded in search of some more dignified term without the toxicity of "biopic." Rosenstone has attempted to bring the genre some respect by consigning the "biopic" historically to the Hollywood studio period and coining the term "biofilm" to cover all other types of biographical films, from contemporary dramatic films from all over the world to documentaries and experimental films ("In Praise" 15). Despite the best efforts of this respected scholar, "biofilm" sounds to me like a euphemism, and a colorless one at that. I believe those of us who take the genre seriously should reappropriate that tangy word "biopic" and unfurl it in the faces of all those who have treated the genre with the smugness they accuse the biopic of possessing in volumes.

Given this background, the critical reaction to the relative flood of biopics released since 2004, greenlighted in response to the box office triumphs of *Erin Brockovich, A Beautiful Mind* (2001), and *Catch Me If You Can,* showed a change in attitude toward the biopic as a genre, as did some of the ways the filmmakers chose to make and promote the films. Kenneth Turan in the *Los Angeles Times* called *Ray* (2004) "a proudly conventional film that . . . makes us not only forgive but actually almost relish how conventional the presentation is" (E1). The director Taylor Hackford, Turan writes, "believes passionately in the value of the well-worn conventions he's recapitulating . . . we're so conditioned to biopics being structured this way that we're more than comfortable with the approach" (E16).

David Ansen, interviewing Kevin Spacey ten years after joining the "solemn biopic" mantra and *still* not giving in, asks why Spacey made a movie about Bobby Darin (*Beyond the Sea,* 2004) when "it was an interesting life, but you are stuck with a lot of the rags-to-riches conventions that we've seen many times." Spacey replied, "The problem may never be solvable. I think people ought to stop searching for the biopic that solves all the problems. The truth is, you go see a Eugene O'Neill play, and *it* still has problems" ("Invading" 64).

Finally, David Edelstein, in a column on *Slate.com* in November 2004, wrote: "Reading through the hundreds of e-mails in response to my biopic challenge ('Name one good one, I dare you'), I was struck by my rashness in declaring the genre the most vacuous in cinema. The explanation, I think, is that when I see a clumsy, superficial biographical movie, I think, 'Ick . . . biopic.' But when I see a biographical film that has the depth and compression of fiction, I think, 'Hey, good movie!'" ("Readers' Picks").

There are reasons for the rocky reception the biopic has received, even if that reception is turning now into grudging acceptance. One, as I alluded to earlier, is the collision of actualities and dramatic fiction, which causes a lot of resistance. Another is that "genres construct the proper spectator for their own consumption," as Dudley Andrew wrote in what has become accepted wisdom. "They build the desire and then represent the satisfaction of what they have triggered" (110). However, biopics are presented as the stories of individual real people, not as the latest entry in a genre. Thus, the frequent consternation that results when a spectator finds him/herself confronted with generic conventions in a film about an actual person.

A humorous handling of the conflict between actualities and dramatic fiction is found in *American Splendor* (2003), about the comic book writer Harvey Pekar, a man accustomed to having his stories and dialogue interpreted by the artists who illustrate them. In one memorable section of the film, the courtship of Harvey (Paul Giamatti) and his third wife, Joyce Brabner (Hope Davis), is first shown in all the naturalism of a contemporary dramatic film. Joyce, who runs a comic book store in Wilmington, Delaware, first calls Harvey to order more comics. After striking up a friendship, the two decide to meet face-to-face. Joyce journeys to Cleveland, where Harvey takes her out to a corny "yuppie" restaurant. Back in his cluttered, filthy apartment, the couple kiss, but what sounds like Joyce's cries of pleasure turn into groans of nausea, as Joyce runs to the bathroom to vomit. Harvey, thinking he is seeing his dream date derailed, remembers Joyce drinking lots of chamomile tea during their phone chats, and offers her some. Joyce, visibly touched, thinks, decides, opens the bathroom door, and speaks the film's most devastating line, "Harvey, I think we should skip all the courtship stuff and just get married." This is later followed by various treatments and incarnations of the couple, including the courtship scene, which starts to take on the mythic quality of the oft-repeated legends that are part of the biopic's stock-in-trade.

Our tendency to accept film dramatizations as real is contested by all the different versions of the constitution of the Pekar-Brabner couple. Joyce as played by Davis turns into Joyce as drawn by several artists, representing Harvey's stories about her. The actual Joyce critiques the version of reality constructed by the actual Harvey, who is right next to her, as "leaving out the happy stuff," while the couple sits in director's chairs on a bare white soundstage that is supposed to stand for a movie set, but seems more like a comic book frame, waiting to be filled in. The couple is interviewed by an off-camera woman, actually Shari Springer Berman, the co-writer and co-director of the film (and like Joyce Brabner, a member of a husband-and-wife artist team). Then we go to a scene from *American Splendor,* the stage play, which looks like a dollhouse version of their lives compared to the cinematic reality we've previously seen with actors, Molly Shannon and Donal Logue, who don't look like either Brabner and Davis or Pekar and Giamatti. Moreover, while the film shows Harvey and Joyce as urban types, the play in Pasadena has "midwesternized" them, with Harvey in a flannel shirt and Joyce wearing a day-glo orange T-shirt and bib overalls, making her look like Peppermint Patty in *Peanuts,* decidedly the wrong comic.

This calls into question all the representations we've seen of the couple, including if not especially the appearance of the actual Joyce and Harvey themselves. The film even presents two versions of the real Harvey Pekar, Harvey in his early sixties as seen on Berman and Robert Pulcini's bare set and the forty-something Harvey who frequently appeared on *Late Night with David Letterman* in the 1980s. And both of these are different sorts of camera and formal interventions. It is Giamatti who enters the studio and Pekar who goes on the air in the actual broadcasts. As a spectator, I find myself scrutinizing the performances of Davis and Giamatti for meaning beyond the level of impersonation in their grimaces and raised eyebrows. Perhaps the actors and the dramatic world come closer to finding a human truth to Joyce and Harvey than what is revealed by the real Joyce and Harvey in the inscrutability of their pauses and silences. This is probably why, when the narrative enters its emotional turning point, the real Brabner and Pekar drop out of the film for a long while and the actors and the dramatization take over. The politically committed Joyce goes to Israel as a volunteer and to gather material for a comic book of her own. Harvey rebels against his role as Letterman's comic foil while fearing that the lump he finds on his right thigh might be cancer (it turned out to be lymphoma).

2. Bodies too much? In *American Splendor* (Robert Pulcini and Shari Springer Berman, Fine Line Features, 2003), Hope Davis and Paul Giamatti create naturalistic portrayals of Joyce Brabner and Harvey Pekar. Digital frame enlargement.

3. Brabner and Pekar, on the other hand, play stylized versions of themselves in *American Splendor*. Which rendition is more "real" than the other? Digital frame enlargement.

The film climaxes, with Giamatti as Pekar, recovering from his cancer, standing in a bare comic book frame, looking out at us and asking, "Who is Harvey Pekar?"

American Splendor shows how far things have come from the critical discourse of 1970s and 1980s film studies, when differences between dramatizations and representations of actuality were discussed as ruptures through which would show the ideological assumptions at the root of the fiction and its production. "A Body Too Much," Jean-Louis Comolli's 1978 concept whereby the actor playing an actual person becomes the only version of the person that we have as we watch the film, while those two bodies—the body of the actor and the body of the actual person—compete for the spectator's belief—"a body too much"—gets a workout in this film. To Comolli, the actor enacts as much as he can the stance and demeanor of the subject while in performance emphasizing his own separateness from him. "Here's me, or the guy playin' me," says the real Pekar in his voiceover, "even though he don't look nothin' like me. But whatever." Giamatti's Pekar is a little softer, a little less raw than the genuine article. The film may be reminding us that film fiction renders life with an idealizing touch that may be inevitable. We crave the sensitivity and expressiveness that good actors and a creative mise-en-scène can provide. Harvey Pekar just doesn't have the skills or the depth of emotional and mental projection to play Harvey Pekar. Don't call us, Harvey. We'll call you.

Illustrating the point even further, in 1988 Carolyn Anderson, in one of the few scholarly treatments of the biopic pre-Custen, wrote that *Pride of the Yankees* (1942) "featured [Lou] Gehrig's teammates (most notably Babe Ruth) playing themselves, a practice which lends a special credibility to the biopic, yet simultaneously introduces the awkwardness of clashing styles of presentation and highlights the artifice of the biographic project" (333). *American Splendor* confronts the problem of how to represent the reality of a subject's life in a staged, artificial form that looks real only thanks to "movie magic," by not treating it, as Kevin Spacey suggests, as a problem. The film puts the reality of Harvey Pekar and Joyce Brabner up for grabs. It is a *Citizen Kane* in which Xanadu is a pile of comic books and a stack of old three-quarter-inch videos of *Late Night with David Letterman,* the memories of Pekar and Brabner, the interpretations of Giamatti and Davis, and the filmmakers' attempt to create Harvey Pekar's Cleveland out of, well, Harvey Pekar's Cleveland.

Therefore, like any genre that dates back nearly to the beginning of narrative cinema, the biopic has gone through developmental stages, emerging from each of its historical cycles with certain modes that continue to be available to filmmakers working in the form. These are

- the classical, celebratory form (melodrama)
- warts-and-all (melodrama/realism)

- the transition of a producer's genre to an auteurist director's genre (Martin Scorsese, Spike Lee, Oliver Stone, Mary Harron, Julian Schnabel, etc.)
- critical investigation and atomization of the subject (or the *Citizen Kane* mode)
- parody (in terms of choice of biographical subject; what Alexander and Karaszewski call the "anti-biopic—a movie about somebody who doesn't deserve one" [*Man* vii], mocking the very notions of heroes and fame in a culture based on consumerism and celebrity rather than high culture values)
- minority appropriation (as in queer or feminist, African American or third world, whereby Janet Frame or Harvey Milk and Malcolm X or Patrice Lumumba own the conventional mythologizing form that once would have been used to marginalize or stigmatize them)
- since 2000, the neoclassical biopic, which integrates elements of all or most of these

Furthermore, existing models of generic development over time can be proved to apply just as well to the biopic as to any genre of comparable longevity. As Rick Altman points out, genre theorists have been drawn to two types of models for explaining genre change, a life-cycle model and an evolutionary model. The more influential of the two has been the concept of evolution from classicism to parody to contestation and critique (or, in the term I'll use most often, deconstruction). This was the sequence proposed by Christian Metz in *Language and Cinema*. Lesser known but still interesting is the life-cycle theory of genres put forth by Henri Focillon in his *The Life of Forms in Art* (1942). The stages (or "ages," as Focillon calls them) are experimental to classic to refinement to baroque (that is, self-reflexive).

Each of these models has a lot to offer in understanding the development of the biopic, Focillon's actually more so. In his brilliant study of 1930s biopics, Kevin Hagopian in effect pinpoints the genre's "experimental" stage, as a cycle of "exotic" melodramas taking place in mostly European courts. Such movies as *Voltaire* (1933), *The Affairs of Cellini* (1934), and *The Scarlet Empress* (1934), writes Hagopian, "created an impression of History as a remote and exotic European place" (184). The films we remember as the classical biopics are mostly those produced after the Production Code took full effect in July 1934. Idols of Production became the order of the day, teaching "the lessons of the past within a conservative politics as a way of proposing a social analysis of the . . . present" (Hagopian 185). Thus even an entertainer biopic like *Yankee Doodle Dandy* (1942) played like an Idol of Production film due to its emphasis on its subject, Broadway star and composer George M. Cohan, as a patriotic American whose songs give his fellow countrymen inspiration upon America's entry into World War II.

Focillon's refinement to the classical form is warts-and-all. The focus after the war and for many years to come on the private lives and travails of entertainers and athletes leads to some fascinating films in the 1950s, such as *Love Me or Leave Me* (1955), *The Joker Is Wild* (1957), and *I Want to Live!* (1958), but the subgenre's tendency toward the downward spiral is what led many to consider the entire genre as dreary and repetitive in later years. What Focillon calls "the baroque age" can be interpreted as one stage or more of self-reflexivity, deconstruction of the myth and form, parody and pastiche. Indeed, the key film in the parody and deconstruction cycle of the biopic is a film usually not acknowledged as a biopic at all: *Citizen Kane* (1941). We will see examples of all of these, including *Kane,* in my studies of particular movies.

As we apply development models like those of Focillon and Metz, we see that the genre seems to have been through the stages and cycles more than once! Other genres from the studio period, most notably the musical, the western, and the crime film, underwent their later evolutionary and life-cycle stages in discrete periods of the 1950s, 1960s, and 1970s. The biopic, unlike those genres, went into eclipse as a consistently produced popular genre in the 1960s.

The 1970s, when so many exciting things were happening in American cinema, was the low ebb of the biopic. Biography provided much fodder for television "movies of the week," while critically blasted biopics set in Old Hollywood, such as *Gable and Lombard* and *W. C. Fields and Me* (both 1976), continued to give the theatrical genre a bad name. Biopics did not receive a full revival until the 1980s for a panoply of reasons. Chief among these were the rise of the auteur and the film school generation and the attendant shift of the biopic from the producer's genre of Custen's study to the director's medium of *Raging Bull* (Martin Scorsese, 1980), *The Last Emperor* (Bernardo Bertolucci, 1987), *Tucker: A Man and His Dream* (Francis Ford Coppola, 1988), *Malcolm X* (Spike Lee, 1992), and many others. Thus the biopic's parodic and self-reflexive phases have been held up and interrupted, and restarted more than once. It is the number of films in the 2000s, such as *Ray, The Aviator,* and the two Truman Capote films, *Capote* (2005) and

Infamous (2006), among others, which synthesize the classical celebratory form with elements of warts-and-all and the deconstructive mode, that convince me that the life cycle may be starting over. Meanwhile, films of parody, pastiche, and deconstruction such as *American Splendor* and *I'm Not There* (2007) continue to redefine the genre and to shake it up.

As a "director's film," the contemporary biopic continues to develop dynamically. As Custen demonstrates, the studio biopic was a producer's medium. Any screening survey of studio biopics soon makes clear that the films were almost never made by the directors from the era who were singled out later as auteurs. When a distinctive director made a biopic, the result was usually an odd clash of genre and style, such as Preston Sturges's *The Great Moment* (1943) or a film devoid of the director's signature touches, such as Billy Wilder's *The Spirit of St. Louis* (1957). *La politque des auteurs,* Film Studies' "return of the repressed," which never remains dead no matter how many obituaries are written for it, may be the factor more than any other that doomed the biography to our field's "dustbin of history." Biographies are now often the work of culturally prestigious directors, such as Oliver Stone, Martin Scorsese, Spike Lee, Jane Campion, Milos Forman, Warren Beatty, Mike Leigh, Gus Van Sant, Roman Polanski, and Bill Condon. Biographies now are frequently experimental and formally adventurous, in contrast to the formulaic genres of the present period. They give off an aura of auteurism and artistic ambition that the industry both eyes warily and realizes it needs in order to win Oscars and retain its tenuous claims to respectability.

The sea change that resulted in the emergence of the biopic as an auteurist genre can best be seen by contrasting two of the outstanding figures of the two ends of the historical spectrum: Darryl F. Zanuck in the studio era and Todd Haynes in the twenty-first century. Custen centered his research on the hands-on studio head, Darryl F. Zanuck, later the subject of a biography by Custen. Zanuck was an indefatigable showman and storyteller with an eighth-grade education; for much of his career, he had unerring instincts for what the mass public wanted to see. Todd Haynes is an auteur drawn to the biopic form in postmodern times. Haynes graduated with a B.A. in semiotics from Brown University. After Haynes became a famous director, one of his professors, Mary Ann Doane, wrote critical essays about his films. While it is difficult to find opposites more polar than Zanuck and Haynes, they are not such extreme examples when it comes to the biopics of the classic era versus biopics of postmodernity. There were classic-era producers more erudite than Zanuck—Walter Wanger, for example—but they didn't specialize in biopics. However, when Wanger did make a biopic, it stood out as remarkably intelligent and circumspect for its era: *Queen Christina* in the 1930s and *I Want to Live!* a quarter-century later. Furthermore, the list of contemporary directors with academic credentials and a knowledge of film history and signification is long indeed—Scorsese, Lee, Campion, Stone, Condon; these people, and others, have made biopics that interrogate, deconstruct, reinvent, and reinvigorate the genre.

There is, moreover, a glaring disconnect, especially since 1980, between the genre's withering critical and academic reception and its enduring success with the voters of the Academy of Motion Picture Arts and Sciences and other award-giving bodies. Evidence abounds that biography has been a more prestigious genre since 1980 than it was in the studio period. This is despite the obvious fact that biography first became a "prestige" item when Adolph Zukor presented Sarah Bernhardt as Queen Elizabeth as movie bait for middle-class audiences in 1912. For instance, *Raging Bull* was voted the best film of the 1980s in a poll of film reviewers and scholars conducted by *American Film*. The 1980s began and ended with thunderously successful revivals of restored epic biographies, the 1927 *Napoléon vu par Abel Gance* in 1981 and the 1962 *Lawrence of Arabia* in 1989. The intense publicity that surrounded these restorations and the excitement they stirred increased the viability of biography as a film genre. In the hotly debated list of the one hundred greatest American films released by the American Film Institute in June 1998, the only film from the 1990s to make the top ten was a biography, *Schindler's List* (1993). In the tenth anniversary AFI list, issued in 2007, *Raging Bull* had climbed into the top ten, at four, where it joined *Lawrence* (eight) and *Schindler* (nine).

A comparison of the Academy Award lists for the years 1980 through 2007 with those of the 1940s and 1950s tells the same story. Scores of biographies were made in the two earlier decades. However, among the Best Picture nominees from 1944 through 1960—the first seventeen years after the annual number of nominees was lowered from ten to five—were only four biographies, *Wilson, Moulin Rouge* (1952), *The Diary of Anne Frank* (1959), and *The Nun's Story* (1959); none of these won. On the other hand, three biographies were nominated for Best Picture in 1980 alone: *Coal Miner's Daughter, The Elephant Man,* and *Raging Bull*. A generation later, the trend was similar, with three biopics up for Best Picture of 2004: *Ray, The Aviator,* and *Finding Neverland*. Twenty-eight more were among the nominees from 1981 through 2008, and seven won: *Gandhi* (1982), *Amadeus* (1984), *Out of Africa* (1985), *The Last Emperor, Schindler's List, Braveheart* (1995), and *A Beautiful Mind.*

These major changes suggest, first, that in the 1940s and 1950s even Hollywood insiders considered biographies formulaic, run-of-the-mill fare. As the industry and its audience became more fragmented, however, biographies were often received as attempts to communicate with an adult audience, to do something risky and out of the ordinary. The Oscar winners are not necessarily the most interesting biopics of the contemporary era; in fact, among the films I discuss at length, *Lawrence of Arabia* is the only Best Picture winner.

For my methodology in this book, I attempt to put into action the aims, stated or inferred, of many of the makers of biopics: to lead the spectator to want to know more about the lives and times of their subjects. My approach to each movie in this book blends research into the subject's life and circumstances, some history of the film's making, some assessment of the filmmakers' aims, an analysis of the results in terms of cinema, ideology, and the truth of the subject's life, and finally what the film means in the context of the genre's development. It is, I hope the reader will find, a painstaking approach, and one that will help lead the way to future research, rather than close it off by reaffirming preconceived notions about the biopic, as I feel earlier studies of the genre have done. My purpose is to challenge the many misconceptions that exist about the biopic, beginning with the impression that the genre has been static and unchanging. I take the reader on a critical tour through the development of film biography with the hopes of leaving little doubt that the biopic is a genre in its own right, one that has evolved dramatically, and which continues to change through its long history. It is essential, moreover, to look at the male "Great Man" biopic and biographies of women as practically separate genres, with their own "patterns of development" (Custen's phrase), ideologies, and conventions, and with their own distinct alternatives to the classical paradigms of the biography.

This is not a sweeping survey, but an extended discussion of the evolution of the genre since the classical Hollywood period. In the case of the Great Man, I start out discussing the parallel legacy of the British literary biographer Lytton Strachey and the biopic using the 1936 *Rembrandt* as an example. I then move to *Citizen Kane,* assessing it as both a parody/revision of the genre as it was in the 1930s and as an almost incalculable influence on later biographies. I study *Lawrence of Arabia* (1962) as a brilliant example of *Kane*'s investigatory approach. The subject, T. E. Lawrence, presents director David Lean and screenwriter Robert Bolt with an opportunity to critique the British Empire by limning the life of a famous but deeply flawed individual at an early post-imperial moment when Empire could be questioned in entertainment.

From the postmodern era, the book looks at two quite different mid-1990s films, Oliver Stone's *Nixon* (1995), which uses a multi-perspectived cinematic approach to try to understand a deeply unknowable politician whose motives are often nonetheless and perhaps rightly taken for granted. François Girard's Canadian film *Thirty Two Short Films About Glenn Gould* (1993), like *American Splendor,* mixes multiple modes, including documentary and animation, with drama. Girard's film, however, deals with a high-art figure, the classical pianist Glenn Gould, literally fragmenting him into thirty-two separate films, each with its own style. The film, unlike *Kane* and most of the other films following in its wake, is nonetheless finally a celebration of the subject, not a critique of him. However, Girard and his screenwriter Don McKellar are not afraid of bringing up such facets of their subject as his prescription drug dependencies and his ambiguous sexuality. The classical, studio-era Great Man biopic also gets renovated in the postmodern period and taken in surprising directions, in the "biopic of someone who doesn't deserve one," which, as we've already seen, was pioneered by Scott Alexander and Larry Karaszewski. The book studies this subgenre in depth in a chapter focusing on *Ed Wood.*

The minority appropriation poses the question of whether it is actually possible for a filmmaker and subject matter that historically were marginalized to take up the classical celebratory majoritarian form without being assimilated by it. This is the topic in chapters on *Malcolm X* (1992) and the international production *Lumumba* (2000), which is about the abortive term of Patrice Lumumba, the first prime minister of newly independent Congo. The co-writer-director Raoul Peck had made an earlier, very personal documentary on Lumumba. Peck's two films pose intriguing questions as to why drama is often necessary in an artist's pursuit of the biographical subject's character.

Biopics of women are structured so differently from male biopics as to constitute their own genre, and they are studied as such in Book Two. The conventions of the female biopic, as I have mentioned, have proved much more intractable than those of the male biopic. This is due to the culture's difficulty with the very issue of women in the public sphere. The stars of the studio era were kept emotively busy playing queens, be they Greta Garbo as

Queen Christina or Katharine Hepburn as *Mary of Scotland* (1936), powerful women either born or married to the throne. It was the warts-and-all mode that began in the mid-1950s that proved perfect for patriarchy's concept of public women, trapping them for decades in a cycle of failure, victimization, and the downward trajectory.

Todd Haynes is probably the most perspicacious artist working in the biopic as I write this. The female biopic section begins with an essay on the "outlaw film" *Superstar: The Karen Carpenter Story* (1987), a forty-three-minute experimental film by the twenty-six-year-old Haynes. I find it a perfect critical crystallization of the tropes of the female biopic. Haynes develops the theme of objectification by using objects—Barbie dolls—as the characters. He moves us to care about them at the same time that we are made aware by various means, including documentary intrusions, of the social constructs that drove Karen Carpenter to her death by anorexia. One of Haynes's models for his pastiche of mother-daughter friction is *I'll Cry Tomorrow* (1955), the biography of Lillian Roth as she descends through alcoholism; this was one of the films that confirmed the warts-and-all biopic as the dominant form and from which "Susan Hayward emerged as the genre's female icon" (Casper 173).

Next is Hayward's apotheosis, *I Want to Live!*, about executed murderess Barbara Graham. Like Robert Wise's other biopics (*Somebody Up There Likes Me* [1956], *Star!* [1968]), the film does not define or judge its protagonist, but displays as many facets of her character as possible. Moreover, *I Want to Live!*, remarkably, is a film made by men that, in order to expose the system that put Barbara Graham in the gas chamber, details how her guilt in a murder case was left in doubt, while she was in effect found guilty of being female. Rather than wallow in Graham's suffering, the film, led by Hayward's dynamic performance, is more of a critique of the female biopic. At the same time, it serves as one of the great female star turns, and an Oscar-winning one at that, as Hayward's melodramatic style rubs up against Wise's unblinking realism. I'm interested in two female musical biopics that opened in the same season in the maelstrom year of 1968, *Star!* and *Funny Girl*. These spectacular musicals, *Star!* especially, led to the demise of the biopic as female star vehicle, for myriad complex reasons that are well worth exploring. Skipping the 1970s, the decade that is paradoxically the strongest period for American films after the "Golden Age" and the weakest for biopics, I go to the 1980s. This decade saw a surge in new female stars from Meryl Streep to Sigourney Weaver, and an attendant rise in the number of female biopics. The resulting cycle offers up some of the most despairing films ever made about the potential of women in public roles. After a brief general discussion of these biopics of the 1980s, I focus on *Gorillas in the Mist* (1988), with Weaver as Dian Fossey. Future filmmakers who want to give their female biographical subjects voice and subjectivity can see in this film practically every convention to avoid.

Feminist interventions in the biopic, which must set out with a consciousness of the sexist conventions of the form, begin with *An Angel at My Table,* Jane Campion's 1990 New Zealand–made biography of the novelist Janet Frame, who lived eight years of her life in an asylum. Frame had been pronounced a schizophrenic before she was released to pursue her writing and find her way in the world. Without a male gaze, intervening male character, or point of view, Frame's subjectivity is allowed to rise out of the material.

A commercial Hollywood film, *Erin Brockovich,* provides Julia Roberts a dominating (and Oscar-winning) role that recalls the days of Susan Hayward. *Erin Brockovich* makes an interesting study of whether or not contemporary Hollywood cinema, and a sensitive male director, Steven Soderbergh, can produce a female biopic that does not simply rehearse all the conventions. Granted, it is easier for a megastar like Roberts to play Brockovich when the latter was unknown. The movie made Erin Brockovich herself into a celebrity, but when it was new, there was no "body too much" issue to contend with. Does this cross between biopic and social problem drama (like *I Want to Live!*) merely find new ways to redirect the male gaze at the female subject's expense? The question seems especially pertinent since there were so few attempts after *Erin* to make female biopics at major studios. This was despite the commercial, critical, and awards success of the film, and despite the plethora of male biopics made in the same period.

Book Two ends with a study of two small films of female subjects by women filmmakers, which take back the gaze and the woman's story in quietly emphatic ways. *The Notorious Bettie Page* and *Marie Antoinette* (both 2006) take as their subjects infamous women, Bettie Page, the pinup queen and bondage model of the 1950s who has become a camp Internet icon decades later, and the French queen popularly remembered as heedless, extravagant, and callous toward the people. Both films, like Campion's, are steadfast in their avoidance of the genre's usual melodrama, or of incidents that explain the protagonist or that fix her in a particular ideology. Bettie Page and Marie Antoinette both look back at the spectator, not challengingly— as if Barbara Graham had looked back at the men who crowded around the gas chamber to watch her die—but matter-of-factly, as if to ask, "What's so special about me?" It's a question that the entire genre, with its intense focus on individual persons, may well ask.

One resounding answer to that question comes from *I'm Not There* (2007), Todd Haynes's tour-de-force exploration of Bob Dylan and a film that may be the definitive statement on film biography for a long time to come. Although he had full permissions from Dylan, Haynes treats his biopic as if he needed to make a veiled film-à-clef like *Citizen Kane;* everything is fictionalized, as if to prove Rosenstone's axiom that only in fiction can dramatic film tell historical truths. Not only does it seem that Dylan, whose real name is never heard in the film, is looked at differently by everyone who knows him, but he becomes six different personae, or characters, played by different actors, including an African American child and a woman. This endlessly brainy, nearly obsessive film concludes that only by *not* attempting to portray a famous person as a unitary subject can one find coherence in human personality.

An undeniable peculiarity of this book is that I see the genre whole, without a lot of discrimination among types of subjects or the fields in which they work. Therefore, I segue from artists to sports figures to monarchs to show business personalities to criminals. I don't see a lot of distinction among these divisions because I don't feel the genre does. This has much to do with the biopic's tendency to intersect with other genres. For example, Kirk Douglas would not have played Van Gogh in *Lust for Life* (1956), a part he was clearly meant to play, if he hadn't first portrayed flamboyant anti-heroes in such films as *Champion* (1949), *Young Man with a Horn* (1950), *Ace in the Hole* (1951), and *The Bad and the Beautiful* (1952). The biopic is an "impure" genre in the way it overlaps with other genres. Another peculiarity about the book is that it doesn't stick strictly to Hollywood, considering as it does films from Canada, Great Britain, New Zealand, and Africa (by way of Haiti), along with studio and indie Hollywood product. I confess to being drawn to certain films without a lot of concern for what national cinemas they represent. This book is not a representation of biographical films from around the world. Nor is it strictly a study of a genre from post-studio Hollywood, although it is mostly that.

I have tried to write in clear standard English, which some have found to be in short supply in film studies scholarship. Jargon-laden, if-it's-clear-it-can't-be-scholarly discourse in film studies gets a deserved pen-lashing from historian Robert Brent Toplin (see *Reel History* 172–173). I myself have been rightly chided for gratuitous theory-speak (see Goldstein 701–702). Here I have tried to steer clear of it, or at least to use it judiciously.

Inevitably, I'm afraid, there are omissions. A section on queer appropriations, in which I planned to discuss *Gods and Monsters* (1998) and *Before Night Falls* (2000), fell out of the book due to time and space restraints. I will certainly discuss queer biopics at another time and place. I didn't seriously consider *Boys Don't Cry* (1999), an important film that qualifies as *both* a female biography and a queer biopic, by a female director and screenwriter *and* with a corresponding documentary (*The Brandon Teena Story* [1998]), to which it is far superior. *Boys Don't Cry*, an instant classic with many admirers, is the film that comes up more often than any other in question sessions when I've spoken on the biopic at forums or conferences. It would seem to be a bonanza for discussions of gender, sexuality, and sexual identity in the biopic. It also partakes of the genre's gravitation to female victimology while standing it on its head in interesting ways. Why then do I omit it? The reason might be that my categories are limited; the story of Brandon Teena (née Teena Brandon), a young woman who masqueraded as a boy in rural Nebraska and was raped and murdered, fell outside them. I myself was so convinced by Brandon/Teena's masquerade, as flawlessly acted by Hilary Swank, that the film didn't come to mind when I thought of female biopics. Overall, however, *Boys Don't Cry* has received much more critical attention than most of the films I cover here, except probably *Malcolm X* (and *Citizen Kane*, about which there are always new things to be discovered). Given the choice between *Boys* and *Erin Brockovich*, a vastly interesting biopic to my mind but one that is often dismissed as "just" a Julia Roberts commercial vehicle, the decision wasn't hard. And there are other omissions, even *Raging Bull*, one of the towering landmarks of the genre. Consideration of these films, and others, can be taken up in future articles, by me and others. The omissions alone could fill a book.

The biopic is an endlessly fascinating genre. Even its neglect raises issues about the values and preferences of scholars and journalists who dismiss the importance of the genre, as compared to the continued enthusiasm for biopics shown by the film artists who keep making them. This book explores a genre that examines and reflects upon its own cinematic and narrative traditions. Despite the fact that the world runs on the work of vast organizational systems—or perhaps because of this—the individual and his/her media-beamed likeness, the celebrity, have never been more central to our sense of public and personal life. It follows, then, that filmmakers would want to explore the meaning of celebrity and fame, the definitions of greatness and success by which cultures measure themselves. The questions that many recent biographies ask in the life stories they tell and the ways they tell them are the same ones we can ask of the films themselves. What do we learn about our culture by the heroes who rise, the leaders who emerge? Have film biographies begun questioning what is knowable, even what is coherent, in a human subject? Has film biography taken up the issue of the fragmented human subject—the subject as a series of roles—that has held so much thought about identity in thrall since the 1960s? These, and more, are the questions that this book sets out to answer.

BOOK ONE

THE GREAT (WHITE) MAN BIOPIC AND ITS DISCONTENTS

1

Strachey's Way,
or All's Well That Ends Welles

The biopic has its foundations in popular forms that range from the lives of saints, national myths, and legends to melodramas and revues (as were, in part, some musical biopics such as *The Great Ziegfeld* [1936] and *Yankee Doodle Dandy* [1942]). In the genre's evolution, however, two figures cast their eccentric and outsize shadows over the biopic's destiny. With vastly different artistic orientations and influences, they had one quality in common: audacity. They were Lytton Strachey and Orson Welles.

Lytton Strachey (1879–1932) was a writer in the bohemian London Bloomsbury circle that also included Virginia Woolf and E. M. Forster. Strachey was an obscure author of some essays and poems when his book *Eminent Victorians* appeared at the beginning of 1918, in the final year of the Great War. *Eminent Victorians* was a slim volume comprising biographical portraits of icons, well remembered or not, of the Victorian era: Roman Catholic Cardinal Henry Manning, educator Thomas Arnold, pioneering nurse Florence Nightingale, and the most colorful figure of the four, Charles Gordon, the general who died in 1885 defending the city of Khartoum, in the Sudan, for British interests. An immediate sensation, Strachey's book did for biography what the works of his Bloomsbury friends were doing for the novel—bringing a literary genre into the new century, helping to define modernism.

Victorian biographies duly set out the public deeds of prominent people, without looking into their private histories, probing their personal motives, or questioning the larger social purposes their accomplishments served

(Hamilton 126). *Eminent Victorians* did all of these, and in a fast-paced style that appropriated more than a few techniques from fiction. That fictional style, ironically, owed more to Dickens and Trollope than to Woolf and Joyce. Strachey's point of view combined omniscience with an approach to personal motivation and emotional reaction that goes as far as biography can when the writer has only letters and the works of others to go on. As biographies, Strachey's accounts are pretty cheeky, comprising as they do only material from published sources, with no original research conducted.

Strachey's largest influence on literary biography, on journalism, and, eventually, on the biopic stems from the author-narrator's point of view, which is implicitly critical, dismissive, often scornful, and, in a term from a later time, countercultural. "The tone was officer-class," wrote Ian Hamilton, "[but] the sentiment was other rank" (qtd. in Holroyd 428). Strachey was adept at avoiding the facile, superior attitude that often besets "minority" treatments of "majority" topics. At times the author displays real sympathy for his subjects, such as Nightingale, a figure whose unthreatening Victorian reputation as the saintly "lady with the lamp" conceals the frustrated independence of a feminist pioneer. "For all Strachey's irony," writes Samuel Hynes, "admiration for those Victorian great ones keeps creeping in" (42). This is because Strachey, again like a good novelist, discovers his characters as he writes. Furthermore, while his accounts are narratives, they are also commentaries on their subjects. Discoursing upon General Gordon's soul, he writes "there were intertwining contradictions: intricate recesses where egoism and renunciation muted into one another, where the flesh lost itself in the spirit, and the spirit in the flesh" (Strachey 197).

Strachey's evident influence on film biography is far-reaching. The hagiographic, formulaic biopics of the studio era may seem analogous to the stodgy, impersonal Victorian form that Strachey's "New Biography," in Woolf's triumphant term, displaced. The Hollywood biopics, concerned as they were with proving the social responsibility of the studios in the early years of the Production Code Administration and during World War II, glorified scientists, inventors, writers, and statesmen. A common theme was that these greats created the progressive, capitalist, liberal-humanist modern world that the spectator was having the good fortune to inhabit. The lives of Strachey's eminences might have been based on virtues "which the modern world is too wise and too disenchanted to share" (Hynes 43). The bourgeois, capitalist, democratic America the movie studios strove to represent, however, wished very much to share them. Whereas later biopics, like Strachey's accounts, not only in *Eminent Victorians* but in his 1922 biography of Victoria herself, set out to demythologize and to scrutinize their subjects, the studio biopic, like the Victorian biography, made myths.

Each of the four sections in *Eminent Victorians* is of its own distinct type. The first section is devoted to the type of subject hardly any biopic of any sort would touch. Cardinal Manning is the kind of ambitious, gray functionary who makes great systems run, but who is without inspiration or innovation. Biopics celebrate groundbreaking individualists, not organization people. The marketers of *Patton* (1970), for example, desperate to sell an expensive epic about a military superhawk in the midst of the Vietnam morass, promoted the film at first as "*Patton: Salute to a Rebel.*" General Omar Bradley (Karl Malden) is portrayed as an unimaginative bureaucrat, comparable to Manning, though without his cunning. On the other hand, although he was temperamentally a "company man," Manning did summon up the integrity and gumption to leave the Church of England and join the minority Roman Catholic Church. Yet readers of *Eminent Victorians,* especially Americans, may grow restless wondering why Strachey focuses on the staid, officious Manning and not the renowned and institutionally oppressed Cardinal John Henry Newman, whose life Manning helped make miserable. Newman is precisely the sort of struggling visionary about whom biographies are usually written and biopics usually produced. Imagine *A Man for All Seasons* (1966) with Master Secretary Cromwell as the protagonist rather than Saint Thomas More.

Given Strachey's interest in establishment figures, however, people who actually made the Victorian world turn, Cardinal Manning is a logical choice. Manning exemplifies the politic climber, compared to Newman, a figure of destiny, who suffers the humiliations the organization doles out to mavericks, but whose brilliance the system ultimately cannot ignore and must assimilate. Newman's work at Oxford for the Church resulted in the Paulist Fathers' construction of Newman Centers at universities around the English-speaking world. No one has founded any Manning Centers, but at all times in all institutions there are many Mannings and few if any Newmans. The only film with a similar approach is *Amadeus* (1984). It doesn't take a great stretch of mind to imagine Manning as Salieri to Newman's Mozart.

The Florence Nightingale chapter is organized the way most biopics, in the United States and Great Britain, have been pitched. The restless young subject defies her family; it would be easy and, nay, natural to follow the ways of her "extremely well-to-do" family, which would find her "marrying, after a fitting number of dances and dinner-parties, an eligible gentleman, and living happily every afterwards" (Strachey 101). Having denied the pressures to marry, she found herself a post as a nurse—even though "'it was as if,' she herself said afterwards, 'I had wanted to be a kitchen-maid'" (103), a job from which a family like the Nightingales would not have seen much difference. Then, writes Strachey, "Miss Nightingale had been a year in her nursing home on Harley Street when Fate knocked on the door" (106). The subject having answered Fate's call, Strachey shows next a scene of rank disorder, which the subject enters in order to clean up. Nightingale first gained fame for taking over and reforming the military hospitals at Scutari, Constantinople, during the Crimean War. Strachey devotes nearly three pages to detailing the conditions that existed at the hospital prior to her arrival.

> The structural defects were equalled by the deficiencies in the commonest objects of hospital use. There were not enough bedsteads; the sheets were of canvas, and so coarse that the wounded men recoiled from them, begging to be left in their blankets; there was no bedroom furniture of any kind, and empty beer-bottles were used for candlesticks. There were no basins, no towels, no soap, no brooms, no mops, no trays, no plates; there were neither slippers nor scissors, neither shoebrushes nor blacking; there were no knives or forks or spoons. The supply of fuel was constantly deficient. The cooking arrangements were preposterously inadequate, and the laundry was a farce. As for purely medical materials, the tale was no better. Stretchers, splints, bandages: all were lacking; and so were the most ordinary drugs. (110)

We can compare this descriptive preparation for the heroine's intervention to the introduction of the narrative in *Patton*, following the famous semi-diegetic prelude in which the general delivers a fiery address in front of a screen-filling American flag. The film proper, following the credits, and a subtitle, "Kasserine Pass, Tunisia, 1943," opens on the dead body of an American soldier, with scorpions crawling on his back. A Tunisian woman struggles to get a ring off the dead man's finger. As the camera dollies back, this sight is revealed as part of a larger scene in which poor people strip the dead and pile the clothing onto the backs of camels and mules. The military command, led by General Omar Bradley, moves in to survey the apparently total defeat. The hooded faces, with the poverty-stricken Tunisians shown in long shot and from behind, give the scene the same build-up of objective detail, the same tone of anonymous omniscience, and of authenticity sketched calmly and distantly, that we read in Strachey's account. The assessment of the defeat at Kasserine, grimly voiced by General Bradley—"Looks like the reports were pretty accurate" and later, "For the American Army to take a licking like that the first time at bat against the Germans"—serves the purpose of Strachey's assessment at the end of his objective cataloguing ("preposterously inadequate"; "a farce").

Additionally, Strachey's narration carries a tone of historical consensus. Perhaps because he knew he was, in a real sense, rehashing published accounts of events more than two generations in the past, there is a feeling of reciting stories already known and interpretations already agreed upon, in order to put a new gloss upon them. This is what many biographies do except in instances where the author has discovered or gained access to new information about a subject or when a biographer is, in effect, introducing an unfamiliar subject to the audience. Film biographies, however, almost always deal with a subject and events the audience knows a little something about. The audience for *Patton* in 1970 could be assumed to include a large number of middle-aged World War II veterans who remembered at least something of the stories of Kasserine Pass and Patton's battles against the German's General Rommel. The same feeling of historical consensus, or simple hindsight, is essential to the narration of the biopic, especially one made for mass audiences.

A key to Strachey's style is the way his narration takes the point of view of his subjects, as well as of those who oppose them. Consider the following passage:

> . . . unto what state of life *had* it pleased God to call her? That was the question. God's calls are many, and they are strange. What was that secret voice in her ear, if it was not a call? Why had she felt, from her earliest years, those mysterious promptings towards . . . she hardly knew what but certainly toward something very different from anything around her? Why, as a child in the nursery, when her sister had shown a healthy pleasure in tearing her dolls to pieces, had *she* shown an almost morbid one in sewing them up again? Why was she driven now to minister to the poor in their cottages, to watch by sick-beds, to put her dog's wounded paw into elaborate splints as if it was a human being? Why was her head filled with queer imaginations of the country house at Embley turned, by some enchantment, into a hospital, with

herself as matron moving about among the beds? Why was even her vision of heaven itself filled with suffering patients to whom she was being useful? So she dreamed and wondered, and, taking out her diary, she poured into it the agitations of her soul. And then the bell rang, and it was time to go and dress for dinner. (102)

Strachey characterizes his heroine as "different," a word without which the biopic, in all eras, simply could not exist. Biographical subjects are defined as different from the prevailing norms. What makes them different are their talent and their "calling," what Strachey describes here as "mysterious promptings." An inevitable conflict is set up between the protagonist, marching to her different drummer, and the ordinary world that goes on about its timetables and routines as if in a parallel universe so far as the subject is concerned. A reader or spectator is made to feel the frustration of the subject of destiny who has to forget her inner compulsions and "go and dress for dinner."

By this convention, however, the subject is judged by the world s/he inhabits as at best "peculiar" and at worst "half-witted," "mad," "crazy," more words the biopic could not do without. As Strachey does here, however, the biopic poses the question about which is more mad, the subject who cannot live in the world as it is or the world that she is called to go beyond. Indeed, we can judge what kind of biopic we're watching by the way it handles that question. The studio-era biopic sides with the subject, who must prove to the world that he (and it usually is a he) is right—that the earth is round, that voices can be sent over wires, that painting needn't be strictly representational, and so on—and that the stances of inertia, convention, and the status quo are wrong. This is why the biopic, from 1935 on, lends itself so well to prevailing melodramatic conventions. "Biographical motion pictures," wrote Kevin Hagopian, "recreated history itself as a melodrama, in which a charismatic character, following his personal lights of service to humankind or scientific/technological innovation, struggles against philistinism and greed" (192).

The biopic in the studio era, moreover, takes any opportunity to align difference in the biopic subject with the ordinariness of the spectator. World War II provided some unusual occasions for this approach. In *The Story of G.I. Joe* (1945) young ordinary soldiers ask Ernie Pyle (Burgess Meredith), the war correspondent who gathers their personal stories for his syndicated newspaper column, why a middle-aged civilian like him would be on the front lines with a bunch of lowly G.I.'s. The film stemmed from "his . . .

praise and devotion for the common foot soldier. 'I love the infantry because they are the mud-rain-frost-and-wind boys. They have no comforts, and they even learn to live without the necessities. And in the end they are the guys wars cannot be won without'" ("Ernie Pyle"). Pyle's attitudes, in a film made while the war was still raging, result in a biopic that attempts to displace its subject, who is so self-effacing he is shown not even turning away from his reporting on the G.I.'s to celebrate the news that he had won a Pulitzer Prize. Pyle is usually in compositions in which he is off to the side in group shots of the company he is covering, emphasizing that the film is about them, not him. This displacement culminates in the film's title, with its collective subject—all U.S. fighting men as composite characters—and the film's biographical subject relegated to space, in newspaper lingo, below the fold. The very fact of Pyle's actual death, amid an ambush in Okinawa, after the film's production but before its release, underlines the heroism of his service to the soldiers, making what is already an elegiac film all the more poignant and bittersweet.

There is also the idea of "calling," with its spiritual connotations. Strachey, for all his supposed iconoclasm, produces a mystical quality of destiny in his biographies, and neither his "irony" nor his tone of world-weary mockery can save him from it. Destiny and vocation bestow the work of God upon certain people. They suggest powerful belief systems and explain why the biopic, and most literary biography too, is usually not palatable to skeptics. Ideas of "destiny" help biographers pose mysteries of human personality: Why are certain human beings exceptional while the rest of us live in obscurity, more or less? "Destiny" becomes not just an idea, but a separate place inhabited by great people. Such people are of more than just this world, and their stories hearken back to saints' lives and to the nineteenth-century melodramatic convention of the hero too good, too pure, to inhabit the rough-and-tumble physical world. This is why ambition is found too grubby and human a vice for visionaries to exhibit; it therefore must be displaced onto characters who take care of the messy details of climbing up the ladder. "Destiny" also takes form as a powerfully convenient convention; how easy it is to say Alexander the Great and Napoleon did what they did because of destiny. Destiny also refers to the fulfillment of religious prophecy and most of all to Judeo-Christian myths of a Messiah who will come to fulfill the scriptures.

In General Gordon, finally, Strachey finds his most dramatic subject: the "glorious" military hero, a martyr to the Empire, who just might have been a little deranged. Gordon is easily used by the military-political establish-ment, which sends him on a suicidal mission no sane man—or at least no ordinary man—would accept. Soon after he does accept it and departs, to the great acclaim of the English press and public, the government finds it-self in the awkward position of having to rescue the great man from Islamic radicals, led by the fanatic Mahdi, an 1880s Osama bin Laden. The massacre of Gordon by the Mahdi's forces in January 1885, an event creatively re-ferred to in *Topsy Turvy* (1999), Mike Leigh's revisionist Gilbert and Sullivan biopic, is the British Empire's equivalent of Custer's Last Stand, which had occurred just seven years earlier. Both were military debacles, humiliating for the first-world nations that sustained them. Both, however, eventually brought fierce retribution onto the rebels. Despite Gordon's eccentricities, or more likely because of them, he demonstrates the reach and power of the Empire and the paternalistic attitude (at best) of the first world toward the third world. Strachey's treatment of Gordon illuminates a fascinatingly odd individual who believes wholeheartedly and spiritually in the rightness of his cause. This belief allows him to be caught willingly in the gears of a complex and irreversible machine as well as in between two ferociously powerful systems of belief.

Some of the studio-era biopics are Stracheyan in other important ways. They are cinematic the way Strachey's stories were novelistic. They employ the materials of the art form for the telling of the famous life. They may even be permitted to expose those materials more than most films of the period—for instance, in *Edison the Man* (1940), the sunspot on the camera lens reflecting Thomas Edison's newly invented light bulb as it blazes away for hours on its test run. This might be the only pre-1960s use of an ef-fect that cinematographers and directors of the old school had considered a "mistake" that could never be allowed into the release version of a film.

More important, in the canny spectator positioning that made Hollywood films so successful, studio biopics play the biographical subject against the sorts of rigid bureaucracies, greedy self-interests, warped value systems, and unimaginatively opposed families that Strachey depicted most of all in his Nightingale section. The Nightingale chapter sets some imposing guide-lines for the studio biopic. Not only is the conflict between the subject and the established order more clear-cut than in the other three stories, but it permits its heroine to clash, out of principle, with inert and unthinking hu-man obstacles. Nightingale not only represents compassion and reform that are beyond debate—who can object to clean, well-equipped hospitals and thorough, caring medical practices?—she is also the bringer of that commodity most prized by the studio biopic: Progress.

Even the obstreperous determination and relentless drive of Strachey's Nightingale show up in the subjects of studio biopics. Strachey characterizes his fiery nurse as "a Demon"; the biopic always preferred to relegate excessive ambition and talent to the realm of the otherworldly. Some of the Fox subjects pushed onto the screen by Darryl F. Zanuck, whom Custen credits with originating the genre, come off as kooks and misfits who might have qualified for the post of village idiot had the world not presented them with outlets for their eccentric energies. This description applies to figures as estimable as Alexander Graham Bell, Abraham Lincoln, and Woodrow Wilson. Warner Bros. subjects, as befits the lean toughness projected in the products of that company, are obstinate and unyielding to the point where they usually alienate, at least temporarily, people who once supported them. At Warners, scientists, such as Paul Muni's Louis Pasteur and Edward G. Robinson's Paul Ehrlich, seem determined to save lives even if it kills them and everyone who stands in their way. Fledgling entertainers like James Cagney's George M. Cohan throw themselves so hard against the stage doors of Broadway that their talent nearly spins into Tasmanian Devils of egotism. It shouldn't be too surprising, then, that *The White Angel* (1936), a biopic about Nightingale depicting mostly her period in the Crimea and starring Kay Francis, was rushed into production at Warner Bros. as William Dieterle's next film after *The Story of Louis Pasteur*. Frank S. Nugent of the *New York Times* found it "dismayingly pompous," "a treatment [that] becomes all the more incomprehensible when we realize that the film was suggested not by the more reverent biographies but by Lytton Strachey's extremely human sketch of Miss Nightingale in his *Eminent Victorians*" (24).

Some studio films even took up elements of Strachey's social observations, although never when doing so would reflect negatively on the heroic subject him or herself. Such films as *Dr. Ehrlich's Magic Bullet* (1940) and *The Story of Alexander Graham Bell* (1939) are presented as if there were only one way to understand their subjects. It is in films of the uneven, unsteady British film industry that we more often and much earlier find films that regard their subjects and, more important, the worlds and cultures around them with the ambivalence and the irony of Strachey's writing. I want to look first at a British film that shows a Stracheyan perspective influenced primarily by the development of the film medium, Alexander Korda's *Rembrandt* (1936). I then examine how the end of the British Empire after World

War II brought in its wake the ambivalent view of the romance of heroism and the sweep of Empire seen in *Lawrence of Arabia,* a film that on close examination appears as one of the most important biographies ever made. Intervening in historical order, however, will be an exploration of a certain film by Orson Welles that has had a continuing influence on biographies up to the time of this writing.

2

Rembrandt (1936)

Patricia: "What is your greatest ambition?"
The Poet (after a thoughtful pause): "To become immortal, and then to die."
    —À BOUT DE SOUFFLE (JEAN-LUC GODARD, 1960)

If the biopic is a genre based on destiny, then the narrative action of the subject would seem to be the act of dying, for only after death can the great one's immortality and impact on the world really begin. As I mentioned in the introduction, the affinity of the genre for the story of Christ seems unmistakable. This is complicated, however. Take a film such as *Gandhi* (1982), which begins with the subject's death and funeral and invites us to witness his life less *as a life* (not a mean trick in the case of Gandhi, who did seventy-eight years of living) but as a series of phases leading to immortality. There are, on the other hand, any number of films that bring a subject to life and want us to feel what it might have been like to be that person. There's no evading the sense given by a film such as *Bound for Glory* (1976), which seems finally relieved to hustle its subject, Woody Guthrie (David Carradine), off the screen so that it can be the songs that live, and not the unpleasant, restless, unhappy man that Hal Ashby's film has been honest enough to portray. Todd Haynes's great film *I'm Not There* (2007), about Woody Guthrie disciple Bob Dylan, treats its subject finally as a ghostly figure haunting the landscape with indelible poetry and shape-shifting humanity. It's hard to imagine Haynes's ending being any different if his very much living subject had been no longer with us. Biopics often appear to be of two minds: Is the idea to demonstrate how to live (or in a few cases, how not to) or how to *leave*? That is, how to leave a legacy that makes the life itself of small importance.

This is the conundrum to which the British film *Rembrandt* (1936) gives dramatic life. It was directed by Alexander Korda, the Hungarian-born film producer-director whose *The Private Life of Henry VIII* (1933) proved "a milestone in the English cinema, a movie that could stand comparison with the best—and the most commercial—Hollywood had to offer" (Korda 100). For the film about Rembrandt van Rijn (1606–1669), Korda reunited with his *Henry VIII* star Charles Laughton. Laughton had won an Oscar for the earlier film, the first player in a British movie to do so, and rapidly became a Hollywood star. In the mid-thirties he was considered the exemplar of great film acting.

Rembrandt is a loose and languid string of vignettes, a character sketch, and a study in visual style. The production design by Vincent Korda, the producer-director's brother, and the cinematography by Georges Perinal closely approximate the look of Rembrandt's paintings. The narrative does not make *Rembrandt* the type of goal-oriented biopic in which Hollywood specialized. Dramatizing and indeed exaggerating the penury and scorn in which the Amsterdam painter supposedly dwelt, the film has Rembrandt muttering, "I can't behave properly. I can't paint properly. But I can live my life properly." Accordingly, Rembrandt is shown cooking, drinking, eating simple food, enjoying the company of women, and taking part in a lusty tavern fight. As played by Laughton, who often employed his own corpulence to convey the singularity and isolation of his characters, Rembrandt is more physical, more sensual, and more alive than the "gentlemen of rank and position" to whom he must constantly subjugate himself in order to gain commissions. The advantage in experience and spirit that the poor fancifully hold over the rich is an international theme in films of the Depression era, seen in movies as different from each other as *Boudu sauvé des eaux* (Jean Renoir, 1932) and *It Happened One Night* (Frank Capra, 1934). However, Rembrandt is shown as significant not just for the paintings that render him truly immortal, but for his life, lived as it is in spite of a heedless world that cares not whether he lives or dies. After all, and I don't mean this glibly, not everybody gets to be played by Charles Laughton. In a genre known for its great performances, *Rembrandt* epitomizes the centrality of star performance in showing the life of a "Great Man."

Laughton was an unusual actor for his era, a player who appeared to project his characters from within himself, rather than construct them on the

outside, out of his physical and vocal equipment. This was significant because in the early thirties film acting was rapidly coming through the transition from both mimetic silent film styles and rhetorical, Delsartean stage
acting. Both styles, whipped as they were through the Hollywood studio
system of production that demanded thorough preparation and quick results, emphasized crisply rendered but relaxed performance codes and, in
general, a clipped dialogue delivery. Laughton's performance style, on the
other hand, seemed the product of an elaborate interior process. "He was
an intellectual among actors," writes Michael Korda, "a clever man who enjoyed talking and thought out his performances as members of the Actors
Studio were to do twenty years later" (99). Laughton's performances seemed
to work from a psychological and emotional concept of the character, which
then informed posture, facial expression, and gesture—the character's entire external affect. In the mid-1930s, a period that made up the peak of
Laughton's career, his specialty, writes his biographer Simon Callow, was the
vision "of a soul trapped by itself" (*Laughton* 91).

Unquestionably, there is a Janus-faced quality to Laughton that comes
from his seeming regard of acting not just as display but also as a conversation with the audience. When Callow quotes Laughton as saying that
hateful "parts like [Captain Bligh in *Mutiny on the Bounty* (1935)] make me
physically sick," he is getting at Laughton's practice of commenting on the
role in the playing of it (*Laughton* 98). A relentless tyrant like Captain Bligh
becomes not simply a heartless villain but an ailing soul; Laughton's suggestion of illness behind the mask leads one to wonder how this character got
that way, indeed if there is something about being a captain on the high seas
for years that might make anyone curdle and die inwardly. Laughton's tendency to move from the specific character to the general condition he represents perfectly prepared him to work with Bertolt Brecht in the stage debut
of *Galileo* in Los Angeles in 1947. If Laughton's Bligh gives off an inkling
of something profoundly inhuman at the core of humanity, his Rembrandt
does the opposite, becoming the whole of genuine humanity, a biographical subject who does not constitute a miracle brought forth onto the earth,
but an earthly soul bound to live in the face of the world's indifference. If
this sounds like the description of any number of artist-biopics, the theme
plays very differently in *Rembrandt,* partly because the film's loose, unhur-
ried structure allows Laughton to take it over in a way that more tightly constructed narratives would not. Moreover, the film puts contradictions at its
heart. A title crawl at the start of the film declares Rembrandt to be Holland's

"greatest glory," but the next line announces that he "died in obscurity, his belongings worth no more than a few shillings."

When Orson Welles made *Citizen Kane,* the idea of a Great Man being defined by contradictions was treated as a novelty; the film's advertising even capitalized on it. One of the tasks of the conventional American biopic was to banish contradictions and ambiguities. A biographical subject whose virtue (or on rare occasions, vice) was not abundantly clear did not merit a biopic. Most of Strachey's biographical narratives, however, hinged on the question of whether or not the contradictions in his subjects could be reconciled. The Gordon chapter, for instance, begins in piety and humility and ends in a blaze of glory (albeit ambiguous glory, since it has never been known whether the general went to his death compliantly or defiantly).

As with Strachey's Nightingale, Korda and Laughton's Rembrandt is defined by the contradiction between the way he was treated in life and the way his works are prized into perpetuity. Music and art are media with potential lives of their own far past the mortals who created them. These forms can progress by challenging the accepted norms and eventually replacing them. Thus, the biographies of artists often become either melodramas of suffering and rejection, with the artist victimized by the cruel world he or she must live in, or ironic meditations on a world too dulled by routine to recognize the presence of brilliance in its midst. American films, placing a high value on success, throw their luckless artists into paroxysms of agony (for example, Kirk Douglas's Van Gogh in *Lust for Life* [Vincente Minnelli, 1956]). So do more recent European artist bios, such as the French *Camille Claudel* (1989), made in the postmodern climate of global industrialism. Such is even true of the British film *Carrington* (1995), whose eponymous painter, Nora Carrington (Emma Thompson), suffers fatally for the love of, of all people, Lytton Strachey (Jonathan Pryce)!

However, it is Strachey the cool-eyed modernist who watches over 1930s British films like *Rembrandt.* Korda's film could be named *Eminent Dutchmen* and capture a double irony of those who set themselves up as the betters of the lowly painter and the artist whose name is synonymous with artistic immortality (and with classical filmmaking, as in the term "Rembrandt lighting"). The title prologue concludes, "Today no millionaire is worth the money the works of Rembrandt would realize if ever offered for sale." Much later, after Rembrandt's forced bankruptcy and auction of all his property in 1656, when the artist was fifty, a bystander declares, "A man without money is a vagabond and a rogue." The theme of money, especially when stated at the very start, risks placing the film in "the *Gandhi* trap." Richard Attenborough's film opens with Gandhi's death. The scene of his massive funeral parade is accompanied by a radio report in voiceover. It quotes Albert Einstein, no less, as saying of Gandhi, "Generations to come will scarce believe that such a one as this ever in flesh and blood walked upon this earth." When the narrative itself begins a minute later (but more than forty years earlier), the characters all look like unaccountable clods for failing to recognize this saint in their midst. British biopics generally, in their understatement as compared to melodramatic Hollywood, make an almost comical habit of depicting calm, steady protagonists who keep their wits in the face of a "normality" that appears to be off its rocker (see *A Man for All Seasons,* as well as *Becket* [1964], for prime examples).

Laughton keeps *Rembrandt* out of these traps. His painter is much too restless and broody to be anything but human; he can't stand still or keep his hands from waving about, except when he puts a brush into one of them. Laughton's van Rijn is more human than the rest of sheeplike humanity. His Rembrandt's inability ever to keep still suits the idea of the vagabond; even this man's feet and hands wander aimlessly. And his Rembrandt is capable of acting roguishly; after the destitute painter promises to spend some newly acquired money on food, the next thing he does is buy brushes. Rather than this appearing, as it would in a Hollywood biopic, the action of an ethereal being driven to fulfill his destiny, here it looks obsessive-compulsive. Laughton plays the painter as such an eccentric ragamuffin that even we in the audience forget momentarily that this is the immortal painter Rembrandt and not a dotty local curiosity, the nut case of a Twentieth Century Fox biopic but without a destiny to fulfill.

However, there may be a reason besides Laughton that the movie falls back so heavily upon the painter's humanity. With one exception, we don't see Rembrandt's paintings. No doubt the reason was that Korda had neither the budget nor the research staff to comb the world's museums for the paintings and permission to film them (and in black and white; Technicolor, which producer Korda would first put to spectacular use in *The Thief of Bagdad* [1940], was still in the impresario's future). Without the paintings, which in artist biopics shift the subject's humanity onto his/her transcendent genius, we are left with a flawed man forced to flail his way around an unfeeling world.

All of this is why I was surprised when students in one of my biopics courses savored such Hollywood bio-romances as *The Story of Alexander*

Graham Bell and *Madame Curie* while loathing the British film. They found *Rembrandt* a dull movie that turned the genius artist into a clownish beast. The failure to show Rembrandt's works was, to them, unforgivable. They couldn't believe that anyone would even want to make a film about a great artist without displaying his works. These reactions show us two things. First, a biopic pays a price for not integrating the subject's quirks and foibles into a goal-oriented story with a beginning, middle, and end. The other is that biopic audiences expect results—artworks painted, songs written, battles won, scientific breakthroughs made—in short, accomplishments that justify the film's production. (Class discussions of *The Aviator* [2004] came down to the same point: What exactly did Howard Hughes *do,* anyway?) To show only a great man's struggles is to humiliate him; indeed, when Robert Altman made a point not to show Van Gogh's works in *Vincent and Theo* (1990) (like Korda, trying to make an aesthetic virtue out of budgetary necessity), he seemed intent on subverting the genre and making a movie about a grubby painter's cruel humiliations. But while the point of Altman's film is to show the pure artist ground under the heel of crass commercial establishments (with obvious reference to Altman's own grudges at that time toward the film industry), Korda's movie aims to reveal Rembrandt's complex and indomitable humanity. In a materialist world, however, that is not enough. We need to see those enduring artworks, those paintings worth countless millions. Show us the money.

Rembrandt approximates Strachey's ambivalence toward his subjects. Strachey cannot quite condemn his subjects, not even repressive churchmen like Manning and rampant imperialists like Gordon. The bohemian rebel, however, recognizes in these people the values that led to the current disastrous war. Conversely, *Rembrandt* cannot quite embrace its protagonist. He might have been a genius (although he appears too human and vital for that label, which always seems to me to have an embalming effect), but he was also a Demon, "difficult" in the same way that Charles Laughton was "a difficult actor." In a sense, then, the Laughton film anticipates by two decades the warts-and-all film that became an enduring biopic subtype in the 1950s. The 2004 Hollywood biopic *Ray,* which insists on deepening the flaws in a man whom audiences would probably be happy going on believing was simply a "genius," takes a remarkably similar approach. Along with Callow, however, I see Laughton's Rembrandt as "an idealized self-portrait," designed to celebrate the actor's "own love of beauty, his creative aspirations, his sense of humanity" (*Laughton* 107).

The theme set out at the beginning puts the value of Rembrandt's work beyond money, and since money is the term by which worldly worth is measured, then Rembrandt's worth is beyond the world. Carl Zuckmayer's script has Rembrandt calling the world "a narrow cage enclosed on four sides by iron bars. You can beat your head against those bars until you're sick. But you'll never get out. Never as long as you live." But after the toil that is worldly existence ends with death, the film hints, the life of a great artist truly begins, a kind of resurrection that elevates the artist to a plane usually reserved for deities and saints, and that shows the influence of the story of Christ on the biopic. This is no doubt because for many of those left on earth, art is a near-religious experience, affording an uplift that seems to carry us momentarily beyond this world.

Rembrandt, however, still charged with living, cites King Solomon from the Book of Ecclesiastes, "Vanity of vanities! All is vanity. . . . There is nothing better than that a man should rejoice in his own works. For that is his portion." Korda and Laughton keep up their vision of the artist as isolated and misunderstood by having Rembrandt speak these words as a wizened old man, his head wrapped in a turban, being treated to a drink in a tavern by a crowd of reveling young lords and ladies who take him for a foolish old coot wandering the streets. As he speaks, his rowdy companions roar with thoughtless laughter at the incoherent mutterings of a doddering "grandpa." Thus what profundity the film has to give us we must make our way toward through the annoying clamor of the "vain" world. (Some modern translations of the Bible, such as the *Protestant New International Version* [1973], render Solomon's lines as "Everything is meaningless," losing the vital double denotation of "vanity" as both pointlessness and narcissism.) When the proprietor recognizes Rembrandt and calls his name, the merrymakers abruptly halt. Do they stop out of respect for the locally known painter? Or out of pity for a troubled misfit artist? (The same Solomonic lines from *Ecclesiastes* flow through a much later and far different artist biography, Andrei Tarkovsky's *Andrei Rublev,* made in and suppressed by the Soviet Union in 1966.)

Either way, the film makes clear the vanity of reputation, of the meanings the world attaches to people. *Rembrandt* ends with the painter, outfitted with new oils and brushes, checking his mirror image for a self-portrait. In what will be the last words of the film, he repeats "All is vanity," as he looks at his own reflection and then turns to work. I wish Korda had faded out on this shot, instead of signifying the painter's death by craning up for a hackneyed image of light first streaming in through a high window and then dimming. The mirror shot conveys the essence of Rembrandt's life and character, the idea that work—and the love that goes into the work and that the work expresses—is what gives life meaning, and that all else—title, money, position—is fleeting and, well, vain. This is one Great Man film in which the man can't possibly know he's great; what he sees when he looks in the mirror is his own subjectivity, the material for his painting, and his drive, his compulsion to paint. The shot anticipates many final shots of biopics. These include *Lawrence of Arabia,* leaving a clouded past and heading into an equally clouded future, as we see him through a dusty windshield. The mirror shot of Jake LaMotta at the end of *Raging Bull* shows him shadowboxing after having rehearsed "I coulda been a contender," *his* version of "All is vanity." In the words of Solomon, a certifiable Great Man brought in as final authority, meaning rests only in one's own works.

Such an idea, as expressed in this early biopic, one without the certitude and sense of destination of the Warner Bros. and Twentieth Century Fox biopics of the same era, nonetheless lends itself to individualist myths. American biopics value these highly even as they contradict them with their

4. Charles Laughton in the title role of *Rembrandt* (Alexander Korda, United Artists, 1936). "All is vanity," he murmurs, checking the mirror for a self-portrait, an activity the world sees as vain in the moment, but whose product lasts through the centuries. Digital frame enlargement.

insistence that the importance of the subject is weighed in relation to his/ her contribution to society. In Britain, where desire for individual worth is severely constrained by the class system, the achievements of people whose worth is in their works rather than in their status are attained at great personal cost. Self-determination is a lonely endeavor, for which the world will regard one as mad and which may actually *make* one mad. I think of *Lawrence of Arabia* and Sherif Ali's line incredulously praising the singular man "for whom nothing is written unless he writes it," and of how that film makes its protagonist choke on those words. The vain world is a torment to the one who recognizes that "one must rejoice in his own works."

There is no point to a biopic, the conventional thinking goes, unless it shows why the world must rejoice in the subject's works. By refusing the audience transcendence, perhaps inadvertently, and by refusing more than fleeting looks at the paintings themselves, *Rembrandt* makes the audience dwell on the poor painter's life as it may well have been in actuality. The film catches us up in another of the genre's contradictions. We say we want to know who the subject was, not just what he did, to allude to a somewhat later, hugely pivotal faux-biopic. When confronted with a film that shows only who the subject was, however, even as a way of demonstrating how he did what he did, we're dissatisfied. We want legacy, transcendence, justification, even as we scoff at films that deliver those to us. Nevertheless, Rembrandt's works and what he went through to make them are cause for rejoicing. But what about the successful man whose life and works give no such cause even when he is a looming cultural figure to whom attention must be paid?

3

Citizen Kane and the Biopic

Citizen Kane (1941) has been rarely discussed as a biopic, either in terms of how Orson Welles's film uses the genre, or of *Kane*'s influence on the development of the biopic decades later. Because it fictionalizes its story, *Citizen Kane* is usually not considered a biography at all. It falls outside George Custen's designation of the biopic, which is "minimally composed of the life, or the portion of a life, of a real person whose name is used" (6). This definition might seem devised to exclude *Kane*. If that was Custen's aim, one can hardly blame him, since his purpose was to study the typical biopic and the typical Hollywood product. *Citizen Kane,* as has been well documented, is the studio era's outstanding anomaly, the work that subverts the system in almost every way while taking full advantage of the resources of the studio—the first American mainstream art film.

There has been much research into the film's basis in the life of the publishing magnate William Randolph Hearst (1863–1951), around which controversy began to rage almost as soon as the film was finished. It has been shown, by Laura Mulvey, Robert Carringer, Simon Callow, and Louis Pizzitola, among others, that *Kane* was inspired partly by Welles and Herman J. Mankiewicz's desire to make a coy investigation into the life, career, and politics of Hearst, and so to dramatize the relations among capitalism, power, sex, and modern mass media in America. As the film that almost all agree is the greatest ever made, *Citizen Kane* stands at a crossroads with one road leading back toward films and culture that went before it and to which it is reacting. The other road, as we know from retrospect, reaches toward much that comes after it both in

terms of cinema and of how cinema looks out at the world. Morris Dickstein writes:

> Like many daringly innovative works of the early modern period from
> *Les demoiselles d'Avignon* (1907) to *The Rite of Spring* (1913), *Kane* has
> begun to look more traditional, more familiar, appearing less like a
> rupture, a sharp break with the past, and more like a culmination, a
> synthesis of what preceded it. . . . In Welles's case critics still seem pre-
> occupied with his originality. They see *Kane* through the lens of what
> followed it; instead, I began to wonder about the books and films that
> had shaped it. (83)

In order to understand *Kane* as the central, genre-changing event in the
history of the biopic, we need to look both forward and back. One critic at
the time of the film's release, Tangye Lean (brother of director David Lean),
described the film as "technically . . . perhaps a decade ahead of its contem-
poraries" (Dickstein 83). *Kane*'s influence on biopics did not even begin to
be seen until *two* decades after its release and was really not felt en masse
until forty or fifty years later. However long it took due to the vagaries of the
genre, we cannot appreciate how *Kane* would model a new type of biopic
without first analyzing the ways in which Welles worked with conventions
of the biopic as the genre had developed by 1941.

Is "a sharp break with the past," as Dickstein puts it, ever feasible? Startlingly different works like *Kane,* while stretching the formal envelope,
also respond to what came before. As these are, with few exceptions, the
works of young people, they are retorts to the world of the artists' parents
and grandparents. In *Kane* this world is embodied by one of the powerful men who helped make it, Hearst. Implicit in the approach of Welles
and Herman Mankiewicz to Hearst was satire of the sensationalism and
excess of "Great Yellow Journalist" and his descent from Progressive Era
reformism to New Deal isolationism, fascist sympathy, hysterical anticommunism, and refusal to acknowledge the causes and extent of the Great
Depression. It has not been documented that Welles and Mankiewicz had
their minds on the biopic. They did end up, however, including nearly every convention and character type the genre had developed by 1940. In its
disguised satire of Hearst, *Citizen Kane* fragments, objectifies, and, so to
speak, psychoanalyzes the prototypical biopic subject of the 1930s. It also

questions the worth of the world he created, and the motives behind his creations.

Citizen Kane asks whether in the mechanized world there are works to rejoice in, or if all is vanity, with modern media hype, hucksterism, and fleeting messages that are emblazoned in newsprint and literally not worth the paper they are printed on. The saving grace of premodern artists from Rembrandt in the seventeenth century to Van Gogh in the late nineteenth might be that they created their works as self-expressions and not as the commodities they later came to be. Even the famous inventors and entrepreneurs Alexander Graham Bell and Thomas Edison, men whose works led to industrial empires, were reshaped at Twentieth Century Fox and MGM, respectively, into selfless visionaries whose innovations would be a "benefit," not a commodity. The myth of noncommodification pervades the thirties biopic in most countries. The creator—the artist, the inventor, the life scientist—is ensconced in a myth of helpless destiny, of a natural drive to create, a myth about creativity that dies hard. "Being an artist is about no choice!" bellows Lionel Dobie, the leonine painter played by Nick Nolte in "Life Lessons," Martin Scorsese's gemlike segment of *New York Stories* (1989), "No choice but to do it." The myths of noncommodification and helpless destiny are constant presences in studio biopics as the genre moves from idols of production to idols of consumption, to the emphasis on the private life, and ultimately to people who weren't idols at all, as well as to figures in cultures where the success myth is unattainable or undesirable.

George Custen based much of his treatment of the biopic on a 1944 article by Leo Lowenthal of the Frankfort School, "Biographies in Popular Magazines." In his survey of some one thousand issues of *Collier's* and the *Saturday Evening Post* Lowenthal found that

> while magazines of the first decades of the century had focused their attention on the biographies of what he called "idols of production" (captains of industry, the military, and other members of conventional ruling elites), later magazines, inspired by the new media, radio, and the motion picture, chose to highlight what Lowenthal called "idols of consumption." In this change . . . he detected a shift in American values and a shift in the morality lessons—"lessons of history"—that readers might derive. . . . Power through the making of the world had been replaced by power through ownership of its coveted items. Consumerism

had replaced community as a way of life. This new power was attained through the appropriation of a proper and glamorous appearance. (33)

Custen never marks a clear historical dividing line between "idol of production" biopics and those that celebrate "idols of consumption." Evidently the shift occurs shortly after World War II, as shown, for instance, by a quadrupling of the number of films about entertainers between the 1930s and the 1950s. Conversely, the number of movies depicting scientists, medical researchers, and inventors—plentiful in the 1930s—dwindles to nearly none in the 1950s (Custen 248–255). A clear shift from lessons about those who built the modern world to the more vicarious cinematic experience of those who gain success in the world, who reap its material rewards, and who produce not beneficial advances but products for sale, takes place in the classical biopic after the war.

Custen proposes, however, that such a dividing line would not be simple, because even the most public-minded biopic presents its subject in the form of a movie star, a commodity with whom the spectator pleasurably identifies. An exception is the biggest studio biopic of all, *Wilson,* produced by Darryl F. Zanuck at Twentieth Century Fox, in 1944 after his return from service in the war. The most expensive film ($5.2 million) made until that time, *Wilson* eschews the use of stars, casting a little-known Canadian actor, Alexander Knox, so as to distract a spectator neither from the "lesson of history" being taught nor from the unitary point of view, almost palpably Zanuck's, that does the teaching, through his dutiful teaching assistants, studio screenwriter Lamar Trotti and longtime contract director Henry King. In this, Zanuck anticipates such notable post-studio epics as *Lawrence of Arabia* (1962) and *Gandhi* (1982), which cast unknown stage actors in the title roles, with results more sensational than *Wilson*'s. Such films come decked out in the glamorous production values and the cogent, satisfying dramatic narratives of Hollywood movies—in short, in the raiments of a commodity, or what Zanuck called "the glittering robes of entertainment" (Custen *Twentieth* 257).

In a larger sense, however, the classical biopic is about values and endorsement—a free pass to the cultural pantheon. *Citizen Kane* parts company from this mode of biography by selecting an actual person, Hearst, and dissecting both the man and what he has meant in American culture. To do this, Welles and his collaborators had to change the subject's name and create a fictional tycoon. Like Frank Capra, who directed the writers of *Mr. Smith Goes to Washington* (1939) and *Meet John Doe* (1941) to invent American fascists out of political bosses who owned communication empires, Welles understood that in twentieth-century America, power is wielded not just by government but through control of mass media that by the 1930s reached almost every American. Kane, unlike the studios' idols of production, does not produce new technologies or medicines; he produces ideas. He communicates ideology in a bold and literal way, one nickel newspaper at a time. In this, he seems more like, say, Al Jolson, the subject of *The Jolson Story* (1946), the highest grossing biopic of the 1940s, than Thomas Edison. Jolson sells records and sheet music and, finally, talking pictures; Kane sells papers. Both make contributions that seem fleeting compared to those of, say, the comparatively obscure Paul Ehrlich, whose crucial advances in the development of antibodies, vaccines, and chemotherapy still provide the foundations for much medical science of today. Yet people flocked to *The Jolson Story* in such numbers that Columbia Pictures made a rare biopic sequel, *Jolson Sings Again* (1949). There is no question that Jolson was more vital to audiences of his day. Ehrlich, whose worth had to be elaborately demonstrated, merely helped keep those audiences alive.

Citizen Kane blurs the distinction between consumption and production by presenting its fabulously wealthy protagonist as one of history's most prodigious consumers. In this the film connects Kane to a level of excess, decadence, and waste seldom hinted at in films, with an occasional exception such as Sternberg's *The Scarlet Empress* (1934), which used its mise-en-scène to evoke the moral squalor of the Russian court of Catherine the Great and of the tsars' oppression of the people. Welles's use of lighting and composition to convey the dominance of Kane's ego over those around him seems to have a precedent in Sternberg. Wealth in late-thirties films either created vicarious fantasy, as in the Astaire-Rogers cycle and the screwball comedies, or senseless greed for money and power, as in the Capra movies. Few films actually showed conspicuous consumption and its consequences, without either excusing or condemning them.

On the other hand, the "News on the March" newsreel that famously opens the nonlinear timeline of Kane's life leads off with Xanadu, "a collection of everything, so big it can never be catalogued or appraised." This ordering assumes that the newsreel's spectator will be more interested in the big man's possessions than in the newspaper empire he produced. But where the classical biopic celebrates the great work, the living legacy left by

The Great One to the rest of us, "News on the March" connects the man's possessions to his physical death: "Like the pharaohs, Xanadu's landlord leaves many stones to mark his grave."

Imagine that an exemplary biopic such as *The Story of Louis Pasteur* (1936) or *The Story of Alexander Graham Bell* (1939), each made through Cosmopolitan Pictures, William Randolph Hearst's production company, had been prefaced by a newsreel. Pasteur's development of a vaccine for anthrax, or Bell's movement from scholar in elocution to the explorer of ways to transmit voices over a wire, would be the big story, just as it is, in dramatic form, in each of the films themselves. The ending montage of *Edison the Man,* in which Edison marches forward, in double exposure, amidst a medley of inventions—including the motion picture apparatus through which we watch his inventions that seem to come at us, like Kane's gold, "in a never-ending stream"—fundamentally serves the purpose that *Kane*'s newsreel subverts. A newsreel preface to these movies would simply be redundant. The point of view and purpose of the films themselves just do not differ enough from those of the newsreel for the contrast between them to have any point. Dickstein writes that "the bio-pic view of Charles Foster Kane is the sonorous, fragmentary history we get in the opening newsreel—the superficial public traces of the private personality" (87).

This is not strictly true, however, because *Kane*'s newsreel does precisely what the Great Man biopic of the 1930s would never do. It covers a downward trajectory, tracing an outline of obsolescence, self-indulgence, and eventual irrelevance that Welles's film will elaborately fill out. The final line of the Xanadu section—"Since the Pyramids, Xanadu is the costliest monument a man has built to himself"—describes flamboyant selfishness. This is the antithesis of the selfless subject of classical biopics. The montage of newspaper headlines announcing his death finds an even more damning statement, in Kane's rival paper, the *Chronicle:* "Always Thought Only of Self."

In *Kane,* moreover, the all-knowing, all-knowable Great Man of the studio films is not knowable by anyone, least of all himself. *Kane* may be the first American film, outside some gangster films of the early 1930s, such as *Scarface* (1932) and *Public Enemy* (1931), to depict an unexamined life. But in 1930s Hollywood only outlaws (who occasionally became the subjects of biopics, for example, *Jesse James* [1939]) and the heroines of melodramas such as *Stella Dallas* (1937) were held capable of bringing themselves low. And *Citizen Kane* has key elements in common with them both. Like the heroines, Kane as a youth is a victim of class-motivated decisions made by those in power; in consequence, as an older man, he unconsciously inherits the patterns and habits of the victimizer. Like the movie gangster, Kane revels to excess in the trappings of wealth and power; in doing so, he isolates himself, becoming vulnerable to his many enemies. Unlike the gangsters, Kane is not a criminal, although in many ways he appears so powerful as to be above the law, as in the whispers about Hearst being the murderer of Thomas Ince aboard Hearst's yacht, the *Oneida,* in 1924, a story with which Welles was said to have been fascinated. As with the criminals, however, Kane's story—both in the newsreel and in the horror film–like prelude/death scene that precedes it—ends with him alone in his "hideout," all avenues of escape closed off. Kane's life ends as *Scarface* would have if the cops hadn't even cared enough about Tony Camonte to show up and shoot him.

One reason for the lack of knowability in *Kane* and the fractured film styles it inspires is that the unitary point of view of the biopic is fragmented, indicating that the many sides of a story lead to the crackup of a clear, understandable narrative—and of a coherent biographical subject, much less of a figure with whom an audience could ever identify. The newsreel stands as the official public story, which the film both can and cannot flesh out and move beyond. It also stands as the conventional wisdom. "It's not enough to tell us what a man did," says Rawlston, the newsreel editor, to the reporter; "You've got to tell us who he was," echoing Plutarch's belief that "history describes what people do . . . while biography reveals who they are" (Parke 6). The editor's charge also resonates, as Louis Pizzitola demonstrates in his book, *Hearst over Hollywood,* with Hearstian yellow journalism's drive toward the sensational "angle" on a story, one that will grab readers. Thus the newsreel has to personalize the man's life, making it not a story of stones and statues but one of love and longing.

The newsreel is a *downer,* soaked in uninvolving facts. In rejecting it, the editor behaves like Zanuck, who urged his writers to find the "rooting interest," as seen in his responses to an early script draft for the Bell biopic in 1938: "Dull, flat, undramatic. Lost all punch because it is so swamped with boring scientific babble. . . . Get to the human story and comedy" (Custen 134). Elsewhere Zanuck advised that "a man who devotes all time to deaf and dumb can be a freak if we don't make him so real, so human, so down to earth and such a regular guy" (Custen 132). In a theatrical and perverse way, the more "human" Welles makes Kane—that is, the more psychological and emotional complexities he finds in him—the more of a "freak" he seems, especially compared to the exemplary Pasteurs, Edisons, and Bells who had populated Hollywood biopics. Kane, moreover, unlike Laughton's Rembrandt, could never be a "regular guy." Even when Kane indulges in simple pleasures, like the shadow plays he puts on for Susan when he first meets her, he asserts their exceptionalism: "The fellow who taught me that is now the president of Venezuela."

Furthermore, the newsreel is narrated with the "already seen" attitude found in Strachey. The "I know you've heard this before, but . . ." manner of address allowed the biographer of Bloomsbury to drop the first names from initial mentions of historical figures and to allude to events such as the Crimean War with minimal explanation. A similar approach permits Welles to make furtive references to the Spanish American and First World Wars. Furthermore, just as "Mr. Gladstone" needs no introduction for readers of Strachey's Victoriana, "News on the March" can portray historical personages of the past and present, from Teddy Roosevelt to Adolf Hitler, with no identification. Overall, as Alexander Korda's films assume a weary familiarity with European class structure and economic immobility, *Kane* makes contact with the touchstones and archetypes of American myth, but does so in a way that reappropriates them. Kane, like Hearst, hails from the West. But while Hearst was born of a wealthy, influential family whose head, George Hearst, W.R.'s father, was a U.S. senator, Kane is born poor. The newsreel narrator describes "Kane's humble beginnings in this ramshackle boarding house," as we see a scrapbook-style photograph of a log cabin. This is such a cliché that a frequent *New York Times* crossword puzzle clue, "humble beginning," has "log cabin" as its answer. When I toured the historic Morris-Butler House, which was built by a well-to-do Indianapolis lawyer in the 1880s in the neighborhood where *The Magnificent Ambersons* (1942) is set, a turn-of-the-century family dinner table setting had as its centerpiece a log cabin, a replica of which was commonly displayed in such homes as totems of a family's "humble beginnings."

Kane's late-frontier family serendipitously hits the mother lode. This plot stroke smacks simultaneously of Dickensian coincidence, the *bildungsroman,* American '49er fantasy, and the Bunyanesque tall tale. Kane's mother unloads young Charlie onto an Eastern banker, Mr. Thatcher, a man with the moniker of a Mark Twain character and the manner of a Wall Street financier such as J. P. Morgan. While Mary Kane's signing over of young Charlie seems the bafflingly ambiguous action of a character in a modernist work, a Camus novel, say, or an Antonioni film, it is also a reference to and reversal of nineteenth-century melodrama: the top-hatted banker forecloses on the homesteaders, taking even their first-born! In addition, Jed Leland seems the disillusioned yet still romantic observer-narrator of many an American novel, from Ishmael to Nick Carraway. The significance of names in the Mankiewicz script (which John Houseman contributed to and Welles appended) is also striking. Kane, as has been much remarked upon, seems a play on the biblical Cain, but it also alludes to sugar cane (a valuable natural resource, like the tycoon's gold) and the cane that a wounded person, say, an Oedipus with the mythical "swollen foot," would lean on. The fact that "cane/Cain" in all these senses is misspelled, and in the commercial manner that turns Cs to Ks ("Rice Krispies," "Kleenex," "Kool Aid"), gives Kane himself the quality of an artificial creation. Emily Monroe Norton—who is such a trophy wife that just after announcing his engagement to her, Kane runs to join her carrying a trophy he has hurriedly received from his staff—has the first name of a singular American poet, the middle name of a U.S. president, and the surname of a prominent publishing house (Freud's American publisher, no less). Susan Alexander, more ironically, also has a noble name, one shared with a youthful Greek conqueror and no fewer than three Zanuck heroes of the 1930s: *Alexander Hamilton* (1931), *The Story of Alexander Graham Bell*, and *Alexander's Ragtime Band* (1939).

In all of these respects, *Citizen Kane* seems a deliberate and subtle negation of the values and tropes of the 1930s biopic. It has the dynamic, visionary young man who succeeds without really trying over the opposition of his Wall Street guardian. However, where the biopic subject is driven by vision and principle, Kane's motivation is whimsical: "I think it would be fun to run a newspaper." Thatcher represents the end of a class-based and unbending nineteenth-century Eastern establishment. Kane's trust-busting crusades against Thatcher's business interests establish him as possessing the conviction and courage of the conventional biographical hero, but are later revealed to have stemmed from deeper psychological motivations.

Kane even redefines at their foundations cinematic tropes without which the 1930s Warners-Fox strain of storytelling, in the biopic and other genres, couldn't function. The newspaper headline as source of new narrative information is turned on its head in *Kane*. For example, in *The Maltese Falcon* (1941), the newspaper headline serves as a democratic equalizer to deliver objective information about incidents that affect the characters, and does so from a source almost as omniscient as the film's own storytelling apparatus. In *Kane* the protagonist has taken omniscience and objectivity unto himself. In the montage in which Thatcher reads the series of headlines bearing down on his interests, Kane uses the newspaper headlines, delivered by Welles as the conventional montage, as Oedipal torture for his hated guardian. In this, as in montages heralding Susan Alexander's operatic debut or the *Inquirer*'s titanic circulation figures, the headlines are not about Kane; he is about them. He owns them. The best analogy is to montages in musical biopics, say, in *Love Me or Leave Me* when the star's climb up the record charts or up the heights of Broadway are indicated by a few bars of a song accompanied by a shot of its sheet music, a record single, a theater marquee, or a line on the Billboard chart. There, the subjects earn those spots, that success; here Kane buys it.

Kane includes many more of the character types found in biopics. Indeed, a possible knock on *Kane* is that it contains not one character except for Kane himself who is not a stock type. There tend to be two types of supporting male characters in the genre, the folksy comic sidekick, such as Watson in *Bell* (a young Henry Fonda) or Bunt in *Edison the Man* (Lynne Overman), and the collaborator with whom the protagonist later parts ways, usually to reconcile in the end (Emile von Behring in *Ehrlich*). The sidekick as wry observer/philosopher/mirror, after the fools in Shakespeare, was such a staple of the genre that films invented such figures, very often as composite characters, like the sportswriter played by Walter Brennan in *Pride of the Yankees* (1942), who pinch-hits for all the newspapermen who covered Lou Gehrig. (Even today, rare is the biopic that does not concoct at least one composite or invented character.) The sidekick could be a character simply inserted into the story, such as the economics professor pal (Charles Coburn) that Fox screenwriter Lamar Trotti dropped into *Wilson* to enliven Woodrow Wilson's journey from Princeton to the White House, dispensing nuggets of Will Rogers–style folk wisdom along the way.

Citizen Kane splits the sidekick into two characters, Bernstein and Leland. Bernstein (Everett Sloane), Kane's comic loyalist, represents an unquestioning submission to the Great Man that tends toward blindness (Kael "Raising Kane" 65). His ethnicity was broadly emphasized, claimed Pauline Kael, in order to give Hearst credit for not being antisemitic in his hiring practices, unlike most establishment New York businesses of the late nineteenth century. At that, Bernstein is given moments of rare lucidity, such as the daydream he relates to the "kinda young" Mr. Thompson about the image of a young woman getting off a ferry, which has entered his mind every day for fifty years. The elder Bernstein also comes closer than anyone to nailing the identity of Rosebud as "maybe . . . something [Kane] had or some-

5. The dual sidekicks of *Citizen Kane* (Orson Welles, RKO-Radio Pictures, 1941): Leland (Joseph Cotten, left), the moral barometer, and Bernstein (Everett Sloane, far right), the loyal employee. Both are dominated visually and every other way by Kane (Orson Welles). Digital frame enlargement.

thing he lost." Indeed, Bernstein in his old age appears to have acquired a wisdom and understanding not seen in the obedient underling shown in the flashbacks. In this young person's movie, Bernstein and Leland both appear to have grown different personalities in old age, unless one allows that Bernstein now feels free to express himself as he could not when he was at Mr. Kane's beck and call and that near senility has made the formerly repressed Leland garrulous and lusty. As the younger Kane's best friend, Leland is a moral barometer. He becomes disenchanted with Kane and functions as a critical guide, pointing out for us Kane's decline from forceful young turk to half-mad tyrant who embodies all he once opposed.

The film also turns the biopic convention of the blissful marriage inside out. In Great Man films, the wife is an endlessly supportive helpmate, running the house and raising the children while the husband drives himself to make his discoveries and reach his breakthroughs. At female-spectator-oriented studios like MGM and Fox, the films depict courtships, even going so far in the Bell biopic as to contrive the partial deafness of Bell's wife as a major motivation for work with the voice and elocution. Fox-Cosmopolitan's

Young Mr. Lincoln (1939) suffuses with romance Lincoln's infatuation with the doomed Ann Rutledge and downplays his relationship to Mary Todd, with whom Lincoln lived out a famously troubled marriage. In the following year's *Abe Lincoln in Illinois,* made at the always less focused and less consistent RKO, Lincoln's travails with Mary are made into one of the Pulitzer Prize play-turned-film's central conflicts. In the dominant Fox-Warners-MGM biopic constellation, however, Mary Todd Lincoln would not have qualified as a good wife, the kind who lives to help, inspire, and support her remarkable husband.

The wife in the biopics is secondary to her husband, but she assists him in myriad ways. Woodrow Wilson's first wife gives what sounds like a passable political speech as she urges her husband to enter politics as a candidate for New Jersey governor. The widowed president's second wife steadies his hand as he leads the nation in the Great War and (although the film plays this down) essentially runs the country after Wilson is felled by a stroke. Bell's wife arrives at his lawsuit trial, eight and a half months pregnant but still insistent upon reading a private letter that incidentally proves that Bell invented the telephone before the corporate defendant claims to have done so. Mrs. Ehrlich lights the stove that heats the slide which inadvertently but finally proves her husband's contested hypothesis.

In contrast, the first Mrs. Kane wonders why her husband has to work such long hours, doesn't understand his newspaper business, objects to his paper's stands on issues ("Attacking the president," she scolds; "You mean Uncle John," he retorts, in the film's allusion to the Hearst papers' attacks on President William McKinley, which had been so fierce that many blamed Hearst for McKinley's assassination in 1901 [Pizzitola 92]); she also objects to the idea of Mr. Bernstein's visiting their son, exposing an antisemitic streak in the blueblood wife. All this is shown in one of the film's most celebrated sequences, a three-minute montage in Leland's narrative, made up of scenes with the couple at breakfast over the years, with the vignettes connected by means of whip pans. The montage is introduced by Leland's line, "It was a marriage like any other marriage." This is one of several lines in *Kane* that has always stuck with me because of its ambiguity. Are we to conclude from it that all marriages are marked by suspicion and lack of communication? If so, that sentiment certainly overturns biopic convention; one also wonders how it got by the stringently pro-marriage Production Code. Is the line such a throwaway that no one paid it much mind? Or are we to take it as merely the cynical expression of a lifelong bachelor? By the time of Kane's second marriage, moreover, the spectator gets the impression that the wife is deliberately kept from any understanding of her husband's work, as even he himself seems separate from it, living in a castle, two thousand miles from his empire's center of operations.

Like the sidekick figure, the biopic wife in *Kane* is split into two characters, and in a way that reflects Kane's trajectory from idealism to tyranny and from worldly ambition to near madness. Laura Mulvey identifies a division in the film's narrative progression between a first half that deals with Kane's Oedipal struggle against the surrogate father, Thatcher, in chasing after the bitch-goddess, success; and a second half, in which Kane gravitates toward the unfinished business of his early childhood, in his choice of a "down to earth" mother substitute, Susan Alexander (45–49). It is with Susan that Kane's road to delusion begins. For a director whose style is often described as expressionistic, quasi-Brechtian, and "narrative rather than dramatic" (Naremore "Director" 279), Welles treats his key motif, the snow globe, in the most understated way imaginable, embedding it in his mise-en-scène, making Rosebud almost as difficult for the spectator to spot as it is for the reporter.

It takes quite a few viewings of *Kane* for most spectators to realize that the snow globe—with its reminders of the 1871 Colorado winter and of the last time, apparently, that Kane saw his mother—makes its first appearance in the chronicle of Kane's life only half in focus (in a film renowned for its deep focus) on Susan's vanity table. Indeed, Kane's boldly competitive, baldly masculine behaviors, such as his buying whatever and whomever he wants and cruelly one-upping his competition, are undermined by "Rosebud," his search for the mother, which, symbolized by the snow globe, is found twice in a woman's boudoir. Kane's chance encounter with Susan interrupts his "sentimental journey" to the westside warehouse to look at his mother's effects, which would bring him face to face with Rosebud. This possible jolt into consciousness is prevented from happening. In its place comes Kane's pursuit of Susan, which soon leads to his isolation from those such as Leland, who will "tell me when I do something wrong." Cut off from a symbolic reconciliation with his mother, Kane uses the absolute power that his money affords him to carry out idle wishes of Susan's mother for her daughter. "Well, you know what mothers are like," Susan says to Kane. "Yes," he replies wistfully but curtly.

Kane will attempt to do to Susan what his mother did to him; that is, to put her in the hands of those who will change her from citizen to exception, and from New World low culture to European high culture, and will do so against her will. Thus in sending her from the world with which she is familiar, he will be her Mr. Thatcher. Unlike Thatcher, however, who keeps his wits about him and judges Kane by his own (rigid) standards, Kane loses touch with any standards. Moreover, latter-day accounts of the film's making, namely the documentary *The Battle over "Citizen Kane"* (1995) and *RKO 281* (1999), the HBO film based upon it, take the Hearstian-sensationalist line toward the origins of "Rosebud," that it came from Hearst's rumored name for Marion Davies's clitoris. A more intriguing and plausible explanation is that "Rosebud" was the nickname of Phoebe Hearst, the publisher's mother (Pizzitola 181).

One persistent criticism of W. R. Hearst and his brand of yellow journalism is that he built his empire through the slanting and the selection of stories in highly subjective directions, while presenting them with the objectivity and the authority of newsprint. Thus in keeping with the implicit criticism and satire of Hearst, Kane and his newspapers perfectly mirror one another—in the same way that David Thomson and others argue that *Citizen Kane* and Orson Welles reflect each other. Furthermore, most 1930s biopics build to a conflict with a major adversary, whom the subject climactically confronts in an open forum (such as a courtroom), a scene whose purpose is to expose "The Truth." Kane's campaign against his opponent, Governor Jim Gettys, however, seems opportunistic and vindictive from the start. The politician is more vulnerable to irresponsible attacks than a wealthy newspaper publisher. This is because the media mogul has tighter control over the symbolism that defines politicians. Kane's initial downfall comes in his inability to see that by carrying on an affair with Susan Alexander, he has permitted his opponents to conflate his public persona and his private life. Ironically, though Gettys has the objective evidence on him, Kane's defiance of him constitutes the same empty gesture as little Charlie's attack on Mr. Thatcher with the sled. The yellow journalist has yellow journalism used against him.

To illustrate this turnabout, Welles and his production designer Perry Ferguson employ the classical convention of visual symmetry—whereby scenes and motifs displayed at the beginning of a film return later—to drive home many of the ironies of Kane's life, and to chart, as the entire film does, his general decline. Some examples: The shot ending the Thatcher "headline montage," in which Thatcher puts down his copy of the *Inquirer* to reveal for the first time the young Kane, is rhymed later. The foreground figure when

Depression-era foreclosure papers are being read in an elderly Thatcher's office moves to show a middle-aged Kane signing over his empire to his guardian's bank. This also rhymes with the shot in which Mrs. Kane signs over Charlie himself to Thatcher. The décor in the apartment of Susan, the kept woman, is rhymed by the décor in her room at Xanadu, the room that Kane destroys. The elderly Kane's vehement destruction of his second wife's personal effects (a scene so violent and emotional that when Welles finished performing it, he said, "I really felt it. I really felt it" as he left the set [Callow *Welles* 514]) ends with his discovery of the "Rosebud" snow globe. The moment can be understood as a reprise of the original scene, in which he attacked Thatcher with Rosebud as the banker was about to snatch him from the bosom of his mother. In the rhyming scene the mother-substitute, Susan, finally withdraws herself from his presence.

In yet another rhyme, the famous crane shot in which Kane towers amid stacks and stacks of the first edition of the *Inquirer* with the Declaration of Principles included, has its equivalent late in the film in the long shot of the endless crates and boxes at Xanadu, a perfect summation of the degradation of Kane, from master publisher to a man distinguished by the mountains of possessions he leaves behind. The idol of production, after he returns to the dust from which he came, is remembered in a morass of consumer items for very rich consumers, "the junk as well as the art." Along the lines of Mulvey's two-part division of the film's dramatic progression is the scene in which Boss Gettys, with Kane's wife Emily present, gives Kane the choice of withdrawing from the gubernatorial race or dragging the tycoon's candidacy down along with the rest of his reputation. At this point, Kane passes over from resolve and purpose to obsession and delusion, as the film itself lopes over a line that the thirties biopic does not cross.

Obsession is the hobgoblin of the classical biopic, the trait that controls the subject's drive and makes him exceptional but that must be held in check lest the protagonist look like, in Zanuck's term, "a freak." In the classical films the character's obsession—the pursuit of his goal in disregard of all else—helps portray him as noble and heroic. Thus Ehrlich, working to stain the tuberculosis cells without concern for himself, succeeds but contracts the disease. Then, on his "cure" in Egypt, he observes an immunity to snake venom in the locals that leads him to his next great project and medical breakthrough. Even Don Ameche's Bell, showing a comic flair that would serve the actor well in Ernst Lubitsch's *Heaven Can Wait* (1943), is allowed moments of near-manic obsession as he brushes aside the skepticism of

6. Kane's newspaper empire makes him the perfect Idol of Production. Digital frame enlargement.

7. After his death, his reduction to meaningless consumption is signified by the endless pile of rubble at Xanadu, much of it personally meaningful, such as the Rosebud sled being taken away. Digital frame enlargement.

others with a distracted certainty that, very briefly, suggests delusion. But that's as far as it goes.

The obsession is always (a) strictly selfless and almost altruistic in its aim, and (b) always free of self-aggrandizement and ego. The latter motives are reserved for antagonists, such as Dr. Charbonnet, chief nemesis of Paul Muni's Louis Pasteur. The actor, Fritz Leiber, in a beautiful bit of Delsartean gesturing, codes Charbonnet's complacency and arrogance by cocking his head back and grinning as he confidently dismisses the audacious Pasteur's latest challenge to accepted medical practice.

The saving grace of the Great Man, therefore, is his self-possession. The biopic subject knows himself, knows his limitations, and in pushing himself past them, displays both his human weakness and his surpassing strength. The subject shows doubts, displayed usually in a private scene with his wife. Nearly every film in the genre has a "Marie, I've failed" moment that establishes the hero as reassuringly human and humble, gives the wife a chance to show how wonderfully supportive she is, and more often than not serves as a prelude to some greater triumph. But while Pasteur, Ehrlich, Bell, and the rest toil for causes much greater than they are, Kane is always bigger than his cause, a point made by the famous shots of the crusading candidate Kane speechifying about justice and reform while a giant image of himself looms all around him. In the shot that follows, moreover, Kane's self-importance is indescribably belittled. The imposing platform is seen as the miniature that, as a piece of cinematic stagecraft, it actually is. A portly top-coated man who looks down upon the scene as though he could pick it up and crumple it turns and moves off. Even a first-time viewer knows this is Gettys and also senses that Kane has arranged his own ruin. The oft-noted radio-style sound sequence begins with the line, "All right. Let's go to the parlor," and ends as Kane's shouted threats to send Gettys to Sing Sing aurally blur into the din of a distant car's horn. Visually, too, the sequence starts with "parlor" and lands on "love nest." All of the seven scenes in the montage build to a sense that Kane's blind self-deception and self-destruction have become his destiny. "You're making an even bigger fool of yourself than I thought you would," his opponent exclaims. The obstinacy and resolve of the biopic subject in reaching his goal have become the goal itself.

Citizen Kane exposes the fact that the Great Man biopic is about nothing more than the vindication of the ego. Thus, *Kane* is the film behind all films that demystify in some way their biopic subjects or the worlds around them. In the scene in which Gettys goads Kane to admit that "you're licked,"

8. "I'm not a gentleman, Mrs. Kane. I wouldn't know what a gentleman is": Boss Gettys (Ray Collins, far right) takes the moral high ground that Kane formerly identified with himself. With Ruth Warwick (far left), Dorothy Comingore, and Orson Welles. Digital frame enlargement.

Kane mistakes his opponent for the bullheaded nemeses of 1930s biopics. It is Kane himself who exhibits stiff-necked pride and egotistical inflexibility, while Gettys, like a Pasteur or a Lincoln, is blessed with self-knowledge: "I'm not a gentleman, Mrs. Kane. Your husband's only trying to be funny calling me one. I don't even know what a gentleman is."

It has become commonplace in writings on this film to point out the similarities between the character of Kane and Welles himself. Such criticism benefits from hindsight. It ends up ironically echoing George Custen's thesis that in making biopics idealizing Great Men, the men who ran the studios—producers, rather than the directors celebrated by *la politique des auteurs* and its followers, who lionized Welles among others—were actually celebrating themselves. It is somewhat of a surprise, therefore, to see that in RKO's press materials for the film's release, Welles *was* the promotional campaign. The opening night program reminds the reader of Welles's quadruple credits on *Kane,* celebrating him as a "man of many faces" (*Citizen Kane* DVD). It literally is about nothing else. Prevented by the Hearst empire from capitalizing on the film's provocative subject matter and unaccustomed to selling a film for its formal excellence, the RKO promotion department had little to work with except the Boy Wonder, despite the widespread hostility that Welles's unprecedented carte blanche at the studio had already elicited from the Hollywood press (Carringer 2).

In celebrating the omni-talented Orson, RKO oddly misses the point of the film, in which overweening ego ensures a man's downfall. The publicity does to Welles what Kane does to himself, completing the repetition compulsion played out so thoroughly in the film's narrative. Just as every mention of *Citizen Kane* at that year's Academy Awards drew scattered boos from the crowd (Callow *Welles* 577), so excessive attention to the one-man show risks a one-man-clapping effect similar to that dramatized in the sequence depicting Susan's operatic debut. Welles himself came to such a realization, endeavoring to make the film's ending credits the height of humility, even if some of it, such as the writing credit shared with Herman Mankiewicz, was arrived at reluctantly (Callow *Welles* 518). For the classical biopic subject, however, greatness is not a role to be played but a mantle to be bestowed by the film and its spectators. The subject himself is humble.

Nothing is exactly humble about *Citizen Kane* itself, but nothing is exactly flashy about it, either. In its now instantly recognizable techniques—deep focus, high contrast, low angle; inventive associative editing, sound that only someone who developed his/her creativity in the heyday of radio could have designed, the maze-like narrative; the story that seems not to want to be told—the film, like its protagonist, retains a recessive mystery that seems new and makes it a different movie practically each time one sees it. This mystery also sends artists back to it as a kind of well of inspiration.

In Kane's drive for self-aggrandizement, the film strikes directly against the motivations and purposes of the biographical subject. He is far from the intrepid crusader who follows his dream to the betterment of humanity. His lofty principles, like Hearst's, are doomed to fail because they are wrapped up in a contradiction—professing to champion the common people while appealing to their basest instincts and manipulating their emotions in order to create popular support for private enthusiasms like the Spanish-American War. Once Kane seizes upon the untalented Susan's operatic career as vindication for his failed political aspirations, his only motivation is his ego, and it drives him to monumental abuses of his power while pressing those who receive paychecks from him or send him invoices to almost absurd depths of obsequiousness.

All this is what ultimately makes *Kane* an essential work of modernism.

The film itself takes the form of the narrative's action—the content—and makes its own storytelling methods a concern of the spectator. Through the arts of cinema, theater, radio, music, and, as Welles famously conceded, a touch of "dollar-book Freud," *Citizen Kane* becomes everything Thompson's newsreel tries to be, until in a final bit of paradoxical futility, with the revelation of the Rosebud sled, Welles's film itself reaches the limits of what the world can know about a person. In myriad ways the film is about its own artifice, a perpetual inspiration to young filmmakers for what director Robert Rodriguez calls "big movies made cheap" ("Big Movies"). Its matte paintings and miniatures often make little effort to look like anything other than theatrical conceits. See, for example, the opening shots leading up to Xanadu or the establishing shots of the political rally, which look like sets in a wealthy child's puppet theater or, as Welles famously put it, in an electric train set.

In its narrative structure, which breaks up the linear chronology of the great one's life in order to put the pieces back in several different places in telling and retelling, *Kane*, as Jorge Luis Borges said, amounts to "a labyrinth without a center" (qtd. in Mulvey 9). Rosebud is planted into the center of the film in order to send the Great Man off into the most childish regression conceivable. Utilizing the device of "Rosebud," Welles and his collaborators engage in an undermining of the public, political self by means of private, sexual secrets. Such undermining is at the heart of yellow journalism: it is motivated by curiosity about those who control modern media and are presented to us through them, and it is a convention for breaking past the constructed imagery and through to what we take for the truth. *Kane*'s truth as symbolized by Rosebud is slippery at best. It is brought onstage, as it were, for our observation before it too disintegrates, and we are left, like Kane, with our memories. Most of the studio biopics about American subjects played heavily on nostalgia for a premodern past even as they celebrated people who, like the heroes of westerns, would help ensure the demise of their worlds. Kane himself evaporates into nostalgia for ways of life his success has helped to destroy.

The various tellings of Kane's story both are and are not satisfying. They satisfy because they show what each character knew about the great man, but finally we have to question whether Leland, Thatcher, Bernstein, or Susan really did know Kane, and conclude that each was sorely limited in what he or she knew of him. Nor would Kane's own version of his story likely enlighten us more. The truth about a subject, especially one presented through the filters of time, memory, subjectivity, image, and representation, can never be captured, but neither can curiosity about the people our world isolates and magnifies ever be quenched. From the vantage point of *Kane*'s release in 1941, this play with relentless curiosity, unknowability, and lack of self-recognition is what would reanimate the biopic in decades to come. However, the inquisitiveness of the artist about the human form inside the artistic form alienates the ordinary spectator and turns the biopic from a majority genre to a minority one. Describing *Kane* as a "manifestation of anti-Hollywood spirit," Laura Mulvey writes that the film

> defies normal processes of identification, and confounds the implicit moral judgments they depend on, leaving critics [despite the nearly rapturous reception with which mainstream reviewers greeted the film on its first screenings] and the general public stripped of the dramatic reassurance which a straight moral binary opposition between villain and victim provides. Within a popular culture tradition (still today, almost as much as in 1941), this narrative strategy comes across as anti-heroic and anti-Hollywood. (22)

It is hard to know just how "anti-Hollywood" any of the collaborators set out to be. RKO hired Orson Welles, the *cause célèbre* of the Halloween 1938 *War of the Worlds* broadcast, to *be* Orson Welles. In this, the studio anticipated the auteur contracts of much later eras of independent production. George J. Schaefer, the RKO studio head, "set out to add a more artistically prestigious component to the studio's product line by making a series of independent production deals involving quality talent and literary properties." According to Robert Carringer, "Schaefer believed that Welles was going to pull off something really big almost as much as Welles did himself" (2). Therefore, he was willing to take the heat in the industry for violating "one of [its] most sacred canons. . . . In granting Welles the right of final cut, he allowed creative considerations to take priority over the studio's means of protecting its financial investment" (2). Moreover, when Herman Mankiewicz was shown footage, with the film still in production, "he was impressed but startled: He had not imagined this kind of photography. He thought it was 'magnificent' aesthetically, but he did wonder if the public would understand it. Mankiewicz had never imagined they were embarked on anything other than a mainstream picture" (Thomson 178). In summarizing the film's disappointing box office outside the major cities, Carringer concludes that "*Citizen Kane* is simply not a film for an ordinary commercial audience" (117).

RKO finally reintroduced *Citizen Kane* to a public that had not seen it, by and large, in over a decade, cementing its reputation as the greatest film ever made. Welles's film was re-released on 20 February 1956, as the opening attraction of the 57th Street Playhouse, a small Manhattan art theater. (*The Benny Goodman Story*, a conventional though new biopic, opened in New York the same day.) *Kane* has been the province of art museum film series, revival houses, and of course classrooms ever since. *Citizen Kane's* journey from the movie palace to the art house is mirrored eventually by the transformation of the biopic from mass entertainment to auteurist testing ground.

To Laura Mulvey, who in her article "Visual Pleasure and Narrative Cinema" advocated the elimination of pleasure from movies, "anti-Hollywood" amounts to a badge of honor. However, what "anti-Hollywood" actually means is "anti-audience" or at least "anti-mass audience." Forever after *Citizen Kane*, the observation that a biopic subject appears empty and hollow at the center will, in the last analysis, be taken as praise, but praise that is double-edged. Even to say that a subject is hollow is to suggest the expectation and the hope for some tangible, definitive meaning. Eventually, the mystery and the demons that belie the subject will replace accomplishment and public-mindedness as the genre's raison d'être even before the mass audience completely fades out.

4

Lawrence of Arabia

"But does he really deserve a place in *here?*"

Lawrence of Arabia (1962) is significant in the early postclassical development of the biopic. A mostly British-made film with a Hollywood independent producer and backing from Columbia Pictures, *Lawrence of Arabia* shows the influence of everything from the British "Angry Young Man" school, the Hollywood warts-and-all biopic with its antihero (although this time eschewing star casting), and, most important, *Citizen Kane*. Like *Kane, Lawrence* questions cultural definitions of individuality and accomplishment and the purposes to which a culture puts its great ones. Unlike *Kane,* it does so in a way that, as the decades have shown, satisfies mainstream audiences' desire for identification, adventure, spectacle, and narrative sweep while leading them down a trajectory into contradiction and psychological complexity. In doing this, *Lawrence* breaks through the boundaries of the biopic.

In a peculiar start for a biopic of epic sweep, *Lawrence of Arabia* opens with a static shot taken in 70-millimeter Super Panavision from an eighteen-foot platform looking straight down. On the right of the frame we see plain gray pavement, which provides a "screen" for the credits. On the left, a man prepares a motorcycle for riding, twice crossing the screen to fetch oil and a cleaning cloth. Thus T. E. Lawrence prepares for the ride that will take him to his accidental death. To viewers in Britain and the Middle East who are familiar with Lawrence, David Lean's film sets the mythohistoric figure instantly on the stage where legend, enigma, and perhaps even history may play out. Lawrence is known after his retirement from the officer ranks to have tried twice to disappear into the identity of an ordinary soldier. He lived in obscurity even after the 1926 publication of his memoirs, *Seven Pillars of Wisdom,* which was more widely known in its time in an abridged version, titled *Revolt in the Desert.* The book established his fame, mystique, and place in history.

The motorcycle sequence already satisfies the expectations set by the 1960s "roadshow spectacle" for "you-are-there" visceral sensation. Lawrence's face is obscured by goggles and the only sounds are those of the cycle's engine and the wind whistling past the cyclist. The rider, swerving to avoid two bicyclists scarcely seen by the spectator, loses control and sails off the road. In a sound bridge we hear organ music, and the film cuts to a bust of "T. E. Lawrence 1888–1935," which was unveiled at a memorial service in January 1936, more than eight months after Lawrence's death. The reverse shot shows a priest, with a man we later learn is "Colonel Brighton," a composite character comprising a number of army officers with whom Lawrence served in Arabia. "He was the most extraordinary man I ever knew," says Brighton, setting off a scene in which forms of the word "know" are spoken twelve times by numerous characters within ninety-six seconds, all to the effect that the world either did not know Lawrence or wished to disavow knowledge of him, while still going through the motions of celebrating him as a national hero.

Brighton's remark is challenged by the priest: "Well, *nil nisi bonum*" (the end of a Latin axiom, "Of the dead say nothing unless it is kind"), "but does he really deserve a place in *here*?" This first injection of skepticism is followed by the exposition of "here": a spire-to-pavement establishing shot of the front of Saint Paul's Cathedral. A reporter asking General Allenby about "Lawrence, himself" is rebuffed, "No, I didn't know him well, you know." Another prominent character, Jackson Bentley, a journalist based on Lowell Thomas, issues a pompous statement for the record, then mutters to a companion that Lawrence was "also the most shameless exhibitionist since Barnum and Bailey." A bystander indignantly objects; when Bentley asks if he knew Lawrence, the man states that he "once had the honor to shake his hand in Damascus." This is followed by a cut to another departing mourner, General Murray. With Murray, we don't even hear a question asked, just his demurral. "Knew him? I never knew him," he says as he becomes isolated from the background and walks into close-up range. "He had some minor function on my staff in Cairo." This cues a flashback, and we cut to a hand meticulously painting a map. A cut to a full medium shot reveals Lawrence and his story at last begins.

Criticism on *Lawrence of Arabia* has well noted that each of these speakers is shown in the narrative to have been mendacious, on Allenby's part, or unfair, in Bentley's case, or the victim either of faulty memory (Murray) or plain ignorance (the man who takes offense at Bentley's remark). The opening, particularly the Saint Paul's sequence, could be called awkward in its expectation that a spectator will be able to connect up these unreliable statements with the characters as they're revealed over the film's three and a half-plus hours. Discovery, however, rather than simple exposition, is what this film is about; in this respect the film is like *Citizen Kane*. A pattern of obscurity and partial revelation followed by more obscurity is established, beginning with the title sequence. A man is seen from above, as if from some omniscient source, his face and identity not shown. When he is viewed up close, in present reality, we see first his foot, as he kicks his cycle into motion. Then we see his face, but it is mostly covered by goggles. When his full face is finally shown completely, it is literally monumental, cast in stone. The respect paid by his country is instantly questioned, and knowledge of him either disclaimed or held suspect, casting aspersions on the motives of official culture in nearly deifying a controversial hero of World War I in the mid-thirties, by which time that war was scorned and discredited in most of the nations that fought in it.

In *Lawrence of Arabia,* or at least in the film's 135-minute first act, which climaxes in the Arab army's capture of Aqaba and Lawrence's triumphant return to Cairo, director David Lean reverses classical conventions of exposition, playing with closeness and distance in a way that subordinates his characters—and especially his subject—to the vastness of the world. Only in the second act, when Lawrence becomes engulfed by the enormity of the role he has created for himself and by the false hopes of independence he has encouraged among the Arabs, does Lean begin sequences with long shots of vast landscapes. The great "El 'Aurens," as his followers come to know him, is presented as equal to the enormity of the desert, similar to the way John Wayne is visually on a par with Monument Valley in John Ford's westerns. This visual presentation is used, however, to reflect Lawrence's hubris and delusions of mastery. In general the film presents its great man in terms of conventional heroism, only to undercut and interrogate those terms methodically.

The film's direction creates an ambivalent aesthetic, a postcolonial meditation on a historical moment of High Empire: the heroism of Lawrence of Arabia amid a war that had precious little heroic about it. British sociologist Jonathan Rutherford, writing of the success at Covent Garden of "With Allenby in Palestine and Lawrence in Arabia," the illustrated lecture by American journalist and showman Lowell Thomas, called Thomas's story "a powerful and regenerative myth for a disenchanted age. . . . [Lawrence] remained untainted by any association with the older military caste of failed, walrus-moustached father figures who had caused so much needless death." This was in spite of the fact that Lawrence was the cause of needless deaths himself, as he openly admitted in his account in *Seven Pillars of Wisdom* of the massacre of the Turkish column during the Arab Revolt's climactic drive to Damascus. He had appeal nonetheless across the range of British culture, particularly to "young men who had rejected the manly stoicism of their father's generation" (Rutherford 72–73). Such young men are the sort who made *Eminent Victorians* a success and found Lawrence a suitably modern hero. However, knowing the ideological freight he carried, Lawrence wrote to a friend in 1927, "Dimly behind my mind lay the certainty that some Lytton Strachey of the future would attempt a life of me" (Wilson 359). However, Stracheyan irony applied to Lawrence of Arabia, whom Strachey himself is said to have considered "a 'tawdry' figure and writer" (Holroyd 538), lay far ahead in the future.

The narrative of Lawrence's sojourn to the Middle East begins by giving the character the steely determination, idiosyncratic magnetism, and breezy self-confidence of the young classical biopic figure. The screenplay eventually undermines Lawrence, however, gradually returning to and confirming the doubts expressed in the prologue. By this time, the film's premise itself has come into question: Is Lawrence not the man for the job or is the job ultimately too dubious, deceptive, controversial, uncontrollable, and indefinable to be done? Is the job the construction of the government or of Lawrence? The film explores an array of neuroses in Lawrence: sadistic enjoyment in violence, masochistic pleasure in being physically punished, narcissism, and exhibitionism. Often these aspects are shown in frank contradiction of one another, as in the portrayal, evidently accurate, of Lawrence as both loving the limelight and craving anonymity.

However, to say that the film concentrates largely on these personal traits is to distort it. Lawrence is seen in the context of a modern media machine that blows public people up into larger-than-life "extraordinary" beings and later condemns them as "shameless exhibitionists." He is shown as a tool of an American establishment that is looking to build popular support for the nation's intervention in the Great War. Furthermore, the film shows its roots in post-imperial Britain by its portrayal of the British military hierarchy, deviously appearing to serve other cultures while actually concentrated solely on its own interests. These are the "fat country, fat people" that Lawrence tells his Bedouin guide Tafas "I'm different" from.

The nearly epigrammatic dialogue Robert Bolt created characterizes Lawrence in the vocabulary of the biopic. At the start of his journey, at least, he is presented—and, as he did in life, presents himself—as one who sees beyond boundaries of race, class, nationality, gender, and religious doctrine. For instance, the historical Lawrence was critical of any attempts by Britain and France to use the outcome of the war to expand their empires. As such, it is difficult to define Lawrence as simply a "stalking horse of imperialism" (Bolt 16).

Lawrence of Arabia portrays a subject steeped in ambivalence. The filmmakers are ambivalent about him; he's tortuously ambivalent about himself. The film takes a perspective on him that is certainly not unitary, but neither is it fragmented in the manner of *Citizen Kane*. It begins, like *Kane*, after the protagonist's death; however, the flashback brought on by the reporter's questions outside the memorial service takes the shape of a conventional "objective" narrative. Even *Citizen Kane*, however, like the studio biopics, had an agenda, a set of points it wanted to make about the subject, and a destination it wanted to go to with him. *Lawrence of Arabia*, on the other hand, could be blasted, as it was by A. W. Lawrence, the colonel's brother, in terms that seem to describe a 1950s Hammer horror film: "take an ounce of narcissism, a pound of exhibitionism, a pint of sadism, a gallon of blood-lust and a sprinkle of other aberrations and stir well" (qtd. in Hodson 122).

Newsweek's uncredited reviewer, on the other hand, found the film "so faithful . . . to the truth of Thomas Edward Lawrence that a viewer leaves the picture with no idea whatever of what Lawrence was really like" (qtd. in Morris and Raskin 179). The film seems to want to say *everything* it can about Lawrence, leaving out almost nothing. This makes Lean and Bolt's project very unlike the script written for a Lawrence biopic Alexander Korda wanted to produce in 1938. That unmade movie, which of course would have come out in High Empire times, omits Lawrence's forever shadowy account of what happened to him at the hands of the Turkish general in Deraa and also less accountably leaves out one of the key dramatic passages of both *Seven Pillars* and of Lean's film, the rescue of Gasim. "Lean's direction, in its objectivity and detachment," writes Michael Anderegg, "allows conflicting view-points to speak for themselves, establishing an ironic, ambivalent tone that pervades all aspects of the film" (92). Even though Anderegg is talking here about Lean's previous film, *The Bridge on the River Kwai* (1957), his remarks apply perfectly to *Lawrence*.

Lawrence deconstructs the conventions of the heroic Great Man biopic as surely as *Kane* did by showing its subject to be too contradictory finally to make sense of him. One salient plot thrust that it has in common with *Kane* is that its subject ends up betraying all his initial ideals and aspirations. Kane takes a lifetime to do this. Lawrence does it in a couple of years of war. Part of what makes *Kane* more modernist than *Lawrence,* moreover, is that Kane completely lacks self-knowledge; he becomes a kind of existential sketch of psychological blindness and emotional failure. Lawrence, on the other hand, hardly requires a "Rosebud," although Steven C. Caton suggests that the shot of the goggles following Lawrence's fatal crash serves as a clue, one of a number of "masks" the spectator must see behind in order to "know" Lawrence. However, in comparison to Kane, Lawrence knows himself; he suffers because of it. The conflicts and contradictions are not expressed here in multiple perspectives. Rather, Lawrence's contradictions are presented in the deceptively unitary style of "objectivity."

This is what makes the film difficult to analyze; no one could ever charge *Lawrence* with presenting its view of the subject as the *only* view. On the other hand, most viewers seem to take the film as a definitive treatment. In the years since its release, and especially since 1989, when the film was restored to its proper length and to its director's specifications, *Lawrence of Arabia* has been almost universally received as one of two films that put the format of the 1950s and 1960s roadshow superproduction to its most intelligent and creative use (the other being *2001: A Space Odyssey* [1968]). Caton, a Middle East scholar, who wrote a remarkable book, *"Lawrence of Arabia": A Film's Anthropology* (1999), calls the film dialectical in its attitudes toward imperialism, Orientalism, military masculinity, the relationship of Lawrence's military triumphs to his personal defeats, and even the film's own style as a psychological spectacle.

What is most striking about *Lawrence* as a biopic is the way the tropes of the genre, including some of the more dubious ones, are used not only to set Lawrence's adventure into motion, but also to call those devices, and their underlying assumptions, into question. "Not many people have a destiny," Allenby tells Lawrence; "it's a terrible thing for a man to flunk it if he has."

The dialogue deals centrally with "any man," with the ordinary versus the extraordinary, and with the liberal-humanist ideals of individuality and self-determination and the religious principle that people's fates are "in God's hands." Once such ideas, which are conventionally confined to the cultural unconscious, come to awareness, as they do to Bolt and Lean's Lawrence, a few things result.

First, they contradict each other: How can a person determine the course of his own life and also be predestined for particular things? One of the central myths of biography is that self-determination and destiny absolutely do go together, and that following the crowd and denying one's dreams lead the great one away from both his/her destiny and the things that make a singular personality. Allenby, however, uses Lawrence's myth of self in order to manipulate his fragile young major into working the will of the British Army. This suggests that myths of destiny are less cultural ideals to be appealed to than delusions to be cynically exploited. Allenby displays his actual opinion of Lawrence when, earlier, Brighton tells him that the Arabs think of Lawrence "as a kind of prophet," and the general snaps, "They do, or he does?"

Second, Lawrence's awareness of having the weight of the world on his shoulders, knowledge that is kept from the "regular guy" great men of classical biopics, leads him to the verge of madness. This consciousness moves Caton to find Brechtian "alienation" techniques at work in the film. He sees these techniques at moments when Lawrence, or the audience, or both, is made aware that the character is performing (124). For instance, Auda abu Tayi (Anthony Quinn) catches Lawrence preening in the white robes of a Harith. I would argue that the director's illusionist style immerses us in the world of Lawrence in a sensuous manner that is the antithesis of Brecht. However, the film can be seen as a Brechtian biopic to the extent that its points about the effects of power, fame, and adulation might apply to celebrities of the modern media age in general, not just to T. E. Lawrence. The film, moreover, causes us to think about such issues as the intervention of the "first world" in the "third world," and the myths of the White Man's Burden. Since the film depicts events that led to the formation of the Middle Eastern nations as we now know them, including Iraq, it has been cited second only to *Battle of Algiers* (1966) as a metaphor for the U.S. war in Iraq. However, it is not clear how critical the film means for us to be of such interventions.

Third, *Lawrence* sends its hero on the idealist path traditional to a male biopic subject, only to complicate his journey to an extent unprecedented for its time. When we first see Peter O'Toole as Lawrence, he is a twenty-six-year-old visionary misfit. "You seem unable to perform your present duties properly," the exasperated General Murray (Donald Wolfit) sputters at him, as Lawrence is "seconded" from the army to the Arab Bureau. The diplomat who requests him, Dryden (a composite character played by Claude Rains), expresses his own doubts about him. According to revisionist biographers, especially Richard Aldington, in a hostile "debunking" biography, *Lawrence of Arabia: A Biographical Inquiry* (1955), there was much tension between newly inducted scholars like Lawrence with expertise on the Middle East and the army regulars assigned to Cairo. The film presents the conflict as the generic antagonism in biopics between the visionary misfit and the hidebound status quo. The young lieutenant bursts with talent and smarts, a tantalizing combination of predestination and caprice. "I cannot fiddle," he quotes Themisticles to the unappreciative General Murray, "but I can make a great state out of a little city." However, he gives the impression of skipping off on a "rather vague" mission without fully comprehending the hazards. "It's going to be fun," he tells Dryden, recalling Kane at the "I think it would be fun to run a newspaper" stage. After Dryden jocularly warns him that "only two kinds of creatures get fun from the desert, Bedouins and gods, and you're neither," Lawrence reiterates "it's going to be fun," forcing Dryden to concede, "It is recognized . . . you have a funny sense of fun," presaging Lawrence's eventual reputation as a "funny" sort of officer. In one of the film's best-known moments, Lawrence in close-up holds a match to his fingers just until it burns him, in a trick that turns masochism into a controllable game. Lawrence blows it out, motivating the film's entry into the desert.

Whereas the first major sequences present Lawrence as there for us to find, what follows the blowing out of the match is a landscape much larger and grander than Lawrence. We watch the Saharan sun rise and then dissolve to two figures on camelback riding over a desert that can only be described as luscious and sensuous. It has been said that Lean wants us to see the attraction of the desert for his protagonist, but if that were all the director planned for us to do, he could have shown the desert from Lawrence's point of view and then returned to a reaction shot of him. Such an approach would have been too "ordinary" for the format of the widescreen spectacle, which was expected to sweep the spectator into a larger-than-life and presumably larger-than-humanity experience. Thus, when Hollis Alpert wrote in 1962 that *Lawrence of Arabia* "belongs in Super Panavision; it justifies the use of that huge screen and at times overpowering sound, because it has a fit sub-ject" (29), the history of the spectacular film as the medium of imperialist romance would appear to have come full circle. Lean, who was more suc-cessful than any other director of this era in fusing dramatic narrative with the latter-day cinema of attractions, separates visually the audience's point of view from Lawrence's. Lean invites us to feel the thrill and sense of chal-lenge and adventure Lawrence must have gotten from the desert, while not rendering his view of the desert and ours as the same.

In a way that Lawrence in his time could not have understood, he was one of the first figures to lead, if that's the right word, the "first world" out of colonialism and into a confused and hubristic era in which Europe and/or America paternalistically set out to "give" third-world people their freedom, as the film's Lawrence messianically vows to do. Thus, what Lawrence began in 1921 by helping to install Prince Feisal and the Hussein royal family at the head of Mesopotamia (then renamed Iraq) continued more than eighty years later in the determination of the George W. Bush administration to bestow its particular conception of American democracy on the former dic-tator state of Iraq (Kifner 4:1).

However, it is unclear to many what Lawrence was up to, just as he him-self believed he had failed and betrayed his Arab compatriots. As Bolt re-ported in 1962, material published about Lawrence amounted to "a tangle of contradictory facts" (16). Today, it is hard to know who is more accurate (or fanciful): the actor Leslie Howard, who planned to star in Korda's film, tell-ing an interviewer in 1937 (with a diplomatic tact suitable to his times) that a film on Lawrence should "take on the shape of a tragedy: the ultimate defeat of all Lawrence's ideals by the well-meaning, uncompromising machine of British government" (27); or the historian Niall Ferguson in 2003 describ-ing Lawrence as a calculating "chameleon" whose pitch to the Arab Bureau and the British generals was that "the Arabs had to feel they were fighting for their own freedom . . . not for the privilege of being ruled by the British instead of by the Turks" (308–309).

Even Howard, the script for whose aborted film walks the same line be-tween independent thought and Empire that Lawrence had to tread (and that had mostly but not entirely evaporated by the time Bolt and Lean took their turn), would have ended his film with the hero "riding to his death along a country lane on his powerful motor cycle. Then some sort of quick shot back to Palestine with its intrigues and insurrections—a tormented stretch of land which, if only Lawrence had had his way, might have been a more peaceful and united country" (27). The nature of Howard's "tragedy" can be characterized as perhaps more "political" and certainly less "personal" than the Bolt/Lean/O'Toole version. The ending Howard described, which is not in the Korda-commissioned 1938 script by Miles Malleson, Brian Desmond Hurst, and Duncan Guthrie, would have put his Lawrence film into the "if only we had listened" realm of wartime historical biography that Darryl F. Zanuck epitomized in his paean to Wilson and the League of Nations, and which expressed the rueful post–Great War tone that predominated in most countries in the thirties. I can picture a Korda Lawrence much like his Rembrandt, an eccentric individualist more attuned to spiritual and earthy kinds of life—both epitomized by the Arab Revolt—than to "the well-meaning, uncompromising machine of British government."

Mixed up in the "enigma" of Lawrence, then, is an essential disagreement over the nature of his "tragedy": Is it the geopolitical tragedy of a man who feels he has led his followers not to freedom but into subjugation—a leader who learns too late that idealism and the imperial (or superpower) national interest do not mix? Or is his a racist tragedy—the one about the "white negro"—the white man who wants to live in a black, or "brown" world, and who belongs in neither place? Lawrence wrote of himself in exactly this way:

> In my case, the effort . . . to live in the dress of Arabs, and to imitate their mental foundation, quitted me of my English self, and let me look at the West and its conventions with new eyes: they destroyed it all for me. At the same time I could not sincerely take on the Arab skin. . . . I had dropped one form and not taken on the other . . . with a resultant feeling of intense loneliness in life, and a contempt, not for other men, but for all they do. . . . Sometimes these selves would converse in the void; and then madness was very near, as I believe it would be near the man who could see things through the veils at once of two customs, two educations, two environments. (31–32)

How could Lawrence have spent several years with Arabs without imagining that the person of color in a colonial diaspora must see through the "two veils" as a way of life? One is reminded of the discourse on "two-ness" in *The Souls of Black Folk,* written by the African American W.E.B. Du Bois and published a quarter-century before *Seven Pillars of Wisdom.* American audiences in the civil rights–aware year of 1963 would have been struck by the scene in which the fair-complected O'Toole grabs a lump of his own flesh and tells Omar Sharif, "A man may do what he wants, but he can't want what he wants. *This* is the stuff that decides what he wants."

Lawrence's line precisely describes the condition that activists like Martin Luther King Jr. were striving to change. Spoken by a white male, the line alludes to discrimination, whether it means to or not, but in the bizarre reverse way that occurs only in discourses controlled by white men. A white man (or a white gentile, anyway) is free to make his way with Arabs, be accepted by them, and even be acclaimed as a kind of prince. But the reverse certainly is not so, as the film points out in scenes that show the bigotry of the British military toward the "bloody wogs." Lean and Spiegel's own racial presumption in casting the film is worth bringing up here. The director and producer settled on Lawrence for their next picture after the idea for a film about Gandhi starring Alec Guinness in the title role (!) was scrapped by Lean, who was heard to declare that "the Indians can't act" (Brownlow 393). For *Lawrence,* Lean and Spiegel offered the role of Sherif Ali to a German actor, Horst Bucholz, and two Frenchmen, Alain Delon and Maurice Ronet, before Lean, after assuming that there wouldn't be Arab actors available who could handle such a demanding English-language part, seized upon the Egyptian film star Omar Sharif for Ali, having already tested him for a much smaller role (Brownlow 427).

Near this same time, Lean and Spiegel hired Michael Wilson, the American writer who, along with fellow blacklistee Carl Foreman, had penned *The Bridge on the River Kwai* uncredited. The incompatibility of Wilson's and Lean's viewpoints led, after numerous drafts, to Wilson's walking off the film after more than a year of work. Spiegel replaced him with British playwright Robert Bolt (*A Man for All Seasons*) (Brownlow 420–422). In Wilson's first treatment, entitled "Elements and Facets of the Theme," he wrote, "In trying to serve two masters, Lawrence betrayed them both. Part of Lawrence's tragedy was his intellectualism. With his inheritance of western culture, he could never really hope to submerge himself in an alien and primitive culture. . . . Did he not serve to introduce into the Arab world the very evils from which he had fled? . . . He was a man who, fleeing blindly from a deadly disease to a healthy land, himself afflicts it with the plague" (qtd. in Brownlow 408).

The peerless racism of this passage is actually typical of many white liberal Hollywood intellectuals in the 1950s. Michael Wilson, though blacklisted for communist ties, bases his script on racist assumptions about the "inheritance of western culture" and "an alien and primitive culture." Lawrence may well have been "fleeing" the "disease" of British Empire. But to say that he afflicts a "healthy land" with the plague is to pretend that the Arab cultures Lawrence encounters are innocent of their own political struggles and social histories. Robert Bolt's eventual screenplay, ironically coming from an English writer, makes Lawrence more of the traditional idealistic Hollywood biopic subject and less the 1950s Hollywood antihero (Sam Spiegel, after all, once had Marlon Brando signed for the part of Lawrence). Lawrence, therefore, becomes more of a sympathetic figure, whose chief flaw is his instinctive malleability. This allows Bolt and Lean to turn the focus, subtly, to the machinations of the British Empire, as embodied mostly in one actual personage, General Allenby, and two invented composites, Dryden and Brighton. It also renders Lawrence more of an identifiable figure for a general, international audience. Peter O'Toole's performance makes Lawrence both larger than life and barely in control of himself at any one moment. This Lawrence's indescribable indulgence in his own ego makes him both intoxicating and intoxicated. O'Toole's acting, Lean's direction, and Freddie Young's camerawork take us so far into Lawrence that we never feel outside, judging him.

The Lawrence that makes it onto the screen is neither Leslie Howard's concept of the deceived hero nor Michael Wilson's deceptive antihero. He is a self-deluded dreamer. His dreams are derailed, however, by his narcissism and exhibitionism, negative flip sides of what in the biopic are transformed into positive traits. Narcissism is the underside of self-confidence, which is viewed as productive so long as it is directed outward toward worthy goals and is not turned back onto the self. Like narcissism, exhibitionism is a perversion that the classical biopic represses. Acclaim and adulation must come to the biopic subject in order to settle his conflicts with his opponents, vindicate him in the eyes of official culture, and bring him the kind of transcendence that, say, a memorial in Saint Paul's Cathedral is supposed to ensure. Narcissism and exhibitionism lead to a self-obsession that renders Lawrence's motives questionable.

In the scene in which he meets Allenby after the taking of Aqaba, wearing his Harith robes, Lawrence delights in parading otherness before the British establishment, while at the same time slumped in a chair and seemingly wishing to be somewhere or something else. While we get the unflattering assessment of Lawrence by the military, however, we also see Lawrence the ultra-competent visionary, displaying that he has both anticipated Allenby's moves and thought out the general's strategy perhaps better than the general himself has. Most portrayals of this scene, such as the one in Terence Rattigan's play, *Ross* (1960), after one of the names Lawrence used after the war while trying to enter the RAF as an obscure aircraftman, show Allenby manipulated as much by Lawrence as vice versa. At their meeting, Lawrence wrote, Allenby "could not make out how much was genuine performer and how much was charlatan" (322). O'Toole's body language and the slightly high camera angles on him most of the time make him appear vulnerable, wishing to flout authority while at the same time submitting to it; that is, to submit to punishment at the hand of the father, as in Freud's scenario of male masochism. This wish is made explicit in the second half of the film when the film enacts the mysterious possible rape at the hands of the Turks, as Lawrence cryptically described it in *Seven Pillars*. While in Rattigan's play, the Turks at Deraa know Lawrence's identity, in Lean's film they don't appear to, leaving Lawrence to imagine that he is being punished for things that go far beyond the war, starting with his status as an illegitimate child. Indescribable depths are intimated by O'Toole's devastating reading of the line in which he confesses to Allenby that his execution of a man with his pistol in order to restore peace among tribes greatly disturbed him because "I *enjoyed* it."

Lean cuts to close-ups for the only time in this sequence on that line and the reaction of Allenby (Jack Hawkins) to it. Allenby drops his eyes, like a Victorian who has happened onto something unimaginably private, something that the cinema in 1962 itself can just barely allow. Brownlow quotes Bolt as saying that the director read this scene in Bolt's script, which stopped at the point where Allenby backs off from pressing Lawrence on the point that he felt "something else" rather than guilt. "David said, 'What is something else, Robert?' I said, 'Well, he sort of enjoyed it.' David's script went up in the air. 'For heaven's sake, why don't you put it in?'" (429).

This is a Lawrence more manipulable than manipulating, with megalomaniacal dreams that horrify him and seduce him in turn. This is the internal Jekyll-Hyde conflict that according to Rick Altman occurs when genre films focus on a single protagonist rather than on a straightforward good-versus-evil conflict (24). For all Lawrence's talents, he is undercut by his flaws and is willingly used by his military superiors. Lean does not break the intimacy of the scene, playing it as a match between the general and his strange lieutenant. He cuts neither to Dryden, the Claude Rains character, nor to Brighton, the Anthony Quayle character, keeping them in deep space rather than cutting to them on their lines, as would be expected. Instead

9. "I enjoyed it." Lawrence (Peter O'Toole), dismayed by his bloodlust, confesses to General Allenby in *Lawrence of Arabia* (David Lean, Columbia, 1962). Digital frame enlargement.

10. General Allenby (Jack Hawkins) hoods his eyes in deep embarrassment and repression. Seconds later, Allenby intuits how to appeal to Lawrence's ego, because "I know a good thing when I see one." Digital frame enlargement.

they are called on like students in a master class or played to like audience members who can be counted on to applaud on cue. When Lawrence, realizing that the general's shrewdness has gotten the better of his own egotism, concedes "You're a clever man," he signals his own willingness to be played to, and acquiesces to his own victimization.

Various versions of the Lawrence saga have handled differently the secret Sykes-Picot agreement of February 1916. This pact between Britain and France, as Anthony Nutting explains, "in theory provided that, after the Ottoman Empire had been destroyed, independent Arab states should be set up and based in Damascus, Aleppo, and Mosul" (40). In fact, however, the agreement assured that Arabia would be divided between Britain, France, and (tsarist) Russia. "These arrangements were in complete contradiction of the pledges" made by the British High Commissioner in Cairo "to the Grand Sherif before the start of the Arab Revolt and which the Sherif, his family, and his followers, as Lawrence had discovered in his talks with Abdullah and Feisal, interpreted as promising freedom and unity to all Arabia, once the Turks had been driven out" (Nutting 40–41).

Lawrence's knowledge of this agreement even before his posting to Feisal had much to do with why he felt like a phony and a liar during much of his time with the Arabs. "Rumours of the fraud," wrote Lawrence, "reached Arab ears, from Turkey," during the drive to Aqaba (275). "I could see," he continued, "that if we won the war the promises to the Arabs were dead paper. Had I been an honorable advisor I would have sent my men home, and not let them risk their lives for such stuff. Yet the Arab inspiration was our main tool in winning the Eastern war. So I assured them that England kept her word in letter and spirit. In this comfort they performed their fine things: but, of course, instead of being proud of what we did together, I was continually and bitterly ashamed" (275–276).

Previous treatments of the story appear to have chosen different parts of passages like this one. The Korda script has Lawrence responding to the discovery by Feisal and Auda of Sykes-Picot with a passionate speech about how truly England keeps her word. Rattigan's utterly sour play depicts a dispirited Lawrence who tells Allenby upon their first meeting in Cairo that the man who leads the Arab Revolt

LAWRENCE: . . . must forget that he's ever heard of the Sykes-Picot Agreement.
ALLENBY: What agreement?
LAWRENCE: (*impatiently*) The secret treaty partitioning post-war Arabia between the French and us.
ALLENBY: I've never heard of it.
LAWRENCE: No? Nor, for the moment, has Feisal, but if he finds out there'll be hell to pay. So it's essential that he and his people should be fed, from now on, the right kinds of lies by the right kind of liar. Therefore, this man of yours has to be a very senior officer. Then his lies will have real weight.
ALLENBY: I thought you didn't approve of senior officers.
LAWRENCE: I don't approve of the man I've just described. And, nor, I suspect, do you. But it's the man you want for the job. Not me. (48)

And yet, later in this scene, Lawrence says, "This job is for a Messiah. For a visionary with real faith—not for an intellectual misfit" (49).

Lean's film depicts a more innocent and idealistic Lawrence, and then, typically, picks apart that initial impression. The film's Lawrence doesn't learn of the secret pact until February 1918, on his post-Deraa visit to Allenby after the British have taken Jerusalem. This comes at the 176-minute mark of a 217-minute movie. The filmmakers invent a scene in which Lawrence enters the general's office to encounter Feisal, after the latter has learned of the agreement. After the emir leaves, Allenby and Dryden confront Lawrence about the treaty, the existence of which the general assumes is Lawrence's reason for asking not to be reassigned to Arabia. Lawrence's reaction to the news is indignation, prompting an upbraiding from Dryden. "You may not have known, but you certainly had suspicions. If we've told lies, you've told half-lies. And a man who tells lies, like me, merely hides the truth. But a man who tells half-lies has forgotten where he put it."

Bolt's dialogue here pithily sums up the film's approach to its hero. Rather than posit a man, as Lawrence was, caught between his ideals and the realities of a political world, the film's Lawrence, for most of its running time, is free to lead from his idealism, and the audience is free to "root" for him, as Zanuck would say. He hears about the treacherous agreement from authority figures, who pull all the strings. In fact, Allenby, who went to Cairo from the European trenches and had been in command for less than two weeks when Lawrence returned from Aqaba (another actuality the film omits), was new to Arabia and probably didn't know about Sykes-Picot when Lawrence did, as in Rattigan's play.

While Lawrence in his memoirs portrays himself as a peddler of false hopes, this self-portrait seems exaggerated because, as he also makes clear, his leadership from the beginning was calculated to turn Sykes-Picot itself into "dead paper." The Arabs at large didn't know about the agreement; they found out, incredibly enough, after the October 1917 revolution in Russia, when the Bolsheviks discovered a copy of it in the Kremlin and, eager to disrupt the Great War in any way they could, leaked it to Auda abu Tayi and other Arab leaders. However, Lawrence told Feisal about it early on. Lawrence believed that "the vigour of the Arab Movement would prevent the creation—by us or others—in Western Asia of unduly 'colonial' schemes of exploitation" (Lawrence 131–132). He convinced Feisal "that his escape was to help the British so much that after peace they would not be able, for shame, to shoot him down in its fulfillment. . . . I begged him not to trust in our promises, like his father, but in his own strong performance" (555).

That last sentence distills the aspect of Lawrence that Lean and Bolt choose to play up; in writing it, Lawrence projects his own philosophy onto his Arab counterpart. In the film Sherif Ali pronounces the Nefud desert "the worst place God created," and Lawrence replies with calm confidence, "I can't answer for the place, only for myself." The belief in self, rather than in institutions or deities, marks Lawrence as a secular, modern type and unquestionably as a conventional biopic subject. But it was also crucial to Lawrence; in a real sense, his self was all he had. In his massive Lawrence biography, published in 1990, Jeremy Wilson explains,

> He was not a professional soldier. He had no habit of unquestioning obedience to help him cope with his predicament. Instead, he had been brought up to believe in uncompromising standards of personal conduct, and these now conflicted with a patriotism he felt no less deeply. The manner in which Britain was prepared to treat the Arabs bore no relation to the chivalrous kind of warfare Lawrence had imagined and admired during his childhood. He was being forced to play a role that undermined the whole basis of his self-esteem. As an illegitimate child, he had inherited no sense of security or social position from his family. His future public status, no less than his self-respect, would depend on what he made of himself. (410)

Thus, Lawrence relied upon himself to an extent that both the British and the Arabs found exotic and eccentric. And this tension between Lawrence's way of seeing himself and the two very different cultures' ways of seeing him becomes prime dramatic material. However, the filmmakers also show a Lawrence who is less torn between the aims to which he led the Arabs and the purposes to which he knew the Allies planned to subjugate the Arab Revolt than he is shaken by his own neuroses.

The scripts by Wilson and Bolt boiled down the unwieldy cast of characters in Lawrence's career in the desert into streamlined composites. The several commanders under whom Lawrence served are reduced to two actual figures: General Archibald Murray, who commanded the British Army against the Turks until defeats in two major battles caused him to be recalled in June 1917, just before Lawrence took Aqaba; and General Edmund Allenby, his much more successful replacement. Dryden, the diplomat who heads the Arab Bureau, and Brighton, Feisal's military advisor and apparent adjutant to Allenby, are composites. Other actual figures are Auda abu Tayi, leader of the Howeitat tribe, Prince Feisal of Mecca, and Sherif Ali of the Harith tribe. Jackson Bentley stands in for Lowell Thomas, who was still living in 1962 and presumably did not want his name associated with the cynical, vulgar opportunist Arthur Kennedy plays in the film.

All these characters have complex functions and bear subtle similarities to familiar biopic types. None of them can be talked about simply in terms of his function in the narrative. For instance, Dryden and Allenby each contain elements of the mentor figure; Lawrence even characterizes Hogarth, one of the models for Dryden, as a *Mentor* in the Homeric sense (58). However, both are devious and manipulative toward Lawrence, so they cannot be seen as benign father figures, but they are not antagonists either. Similarly, Colonel Brighton enters the film as an extension of the inept General Murray; he is a rigid, unimaginative trooper who would force imperial values and methods on the Arabs. Even he, however, comes to admire Lawrence after the taking of Aqaba and in the film's second half becomes sympathetic to, though still skeptical of, Lawrence's actions, while serving as a go-between from Lawrence to Allenby.

Conversely, Sherif Ali, an actual person largely fictionalized here, starts out antagonistic toward Lawrence. When it is clear they will have to work together, on the expedition to Aqaba, the tension between them provides much of the drama. After Lawrence's rescue of Gasim, Ali and his kinsmen acclaim Lawrence as a courageous leader who does care more about them than he does about the British. This new function as friend and sidekick leads Ali to become sounding board and critic to the protagonist. Sherif Ali passes through a number of functions or phases:

1. Cocky young challenger to Lawrence, beginning with Ali's stunning appearance out of the distance (the famous deep-focus shot in which Ali rides on horseback out of the void of the desert from the vanishing point up to the foreground of the shot, aiming at and killing Tafas, Lawrence's guide). This stage climaxes in the chance meeting of the two young men in Prince Feisal's tent.
2. Reluctant and skeptical partner on the "impossible" landward attack on Aqaba.
3. Admiring friend and advisor following Lawrence's rescue of Gasim, an event that goes against everything that to the Muslim mind is "written."

4. A critical commentator on Lawrence, often to third parties such as Bentley or Auda. This begins at the raid on the Turkish train, which is the
   first we see of Ali in act two. In the rhetoric of the roadshow spectacular,
   this provides a starting-over point. It is he who anxiously awaits outside
   at Deraa, who berates him when he appears to be abandoning the Arab
   Revolt and when he hires mercenaries for the final push on Damascus—
   anytime that Lawrence appears to abandon principle for contingency,
   the main risk of rebelling against belief systems.
5. A politician in a new nation. When he puts away the weapons of war and
   stays in Damascus "to learn politics," he becomes part of a hopeful (and
   hopelessly vague) future of Arab self-determination that (as Lean suggests but hardly details) will be betrayed by European chicanery.

These are a lot of functions for one character to play, a lot of phases for
one character to evolve through. The film doesn't always demonstrate these
transformations gracefully, and Omar Sharif, who as Lean had famously
noted was performing in his first major English-language role, made a charismatic and magnetic screen presence. But he didn't quite yet possess the
skill to carry off the role's more awkward transitions.

In the Bolt screenplay events and conditions are pithily condensed in
scenes dense with biographical subtext. The film's depiction of Feisal exemplifies the aspects of omission and selection in the biopic. The most influential Arab leader during the waning days of the Ottoman Empire was Sherif
Hussein, the Emir of Mecca, "guardian of the Holy Places . . . a religious

11. Sherif Ali (Omar Sharif) plays many functions; here he is the skeptical and reluctant partner on Lawrence's
"impossible" attack on Aqaba. Digital frame enlargement.

leader revered . . . throughout the Moslem world" (Wilson 164). After the outbreak of war, in which Turkey was allied with Germany, Hussein followed a careful path of resistance to the Turks and furtive favoritism toward the British. This resistance began when Hussein in effect ignored the call for an Islamic jihad against the Allies, issued in November 1914 by the Sultan of Turkey in his role as Caliph (Wilson 166). By June 1916, the Arab Revolt was under way, initiated, as the film mentions, by the not-shown emir, then sixty-one. Hussein had four sons; the film eliminates out of existence the two eldest, Ali and Abdullah, and the youngest, Zeid, and concentrates on the third son, Feisal. In justification, the filmmakers get much help from Lawrence himself. Lawrence extols Feisal, writing, "I felt at first glance that this was the man I had come to Arabia to seek—the leader who would bring the Arab Revolt to full glory" (91).

The scene in Feisal's tent involving Brighton, Ali, Lawrence, and Feisal dramatizes the impatience and condescension with which most of the British officers in the Hejaz regarded the Arabs. Anthony Quayle's performance as Brighton embodies what Lawrence biographer Jeremy Wilson calls the "attitude towards natives prevalent" in British colonies such as India, Egypt, and the Sudan and which "was inappropriate for work in Arabia, where the British were acting as advisors, not masters" (357). Lawrence, on the other hand, had vast experience in the region and knowledge both of the various tribes and nationalities and of the relations to them of their Turkish masters. This comes out early in the scene when Lawrence completes a passage from the Quran that he knows by heart. Again, while the actual Lawrence's knowledge of Arab cultures and of Islam came from experience and study, the film, like most biopics, makes this look like a special talent, if not a mystical connection.

Feisal, as portrayed by Alec Guinness, is a stately, careful man who keeps his own counsel. Feisal is willing to trust Lawrence, not realizing at first that he is in effect putting the Arab Revolt in his hands; however, he continues to regard Lawrence with skeptical bemusement. The first scene between them ends with Feisal telling Lawrence that he needs "something no man can provide. . . . We need a miracle." Lean then shows Lawrence outside the tent, entranced, facing into the darkness and wind. But there is a curious cut back to Feisal inside the tent, as he wonders about their exchange. The cut may suggest that Feisal somehow knows that by telling Lawrence of his need, he has presented him with a challenge. Lawrence journeys to the desert only to emerge determined to take Aqaba and then sets off to do so.

However, when Lawrence, as the confident young biopic subject, tells Feisal that he is off "to work your miracle, my lord," Feisal lightly scolds him for his "blasphemy." Lawrence's taking upon himself a role worthy only of God shows that he belongs neither to the Muslim culture of the emir's followers nor to the British military environment. This idea is developed when Feisal confronts Lawrence after the latter has organized fifty of Feisal's men into a party bound for Aqaba. "We can claim to ride in the name of Feisal of Mecca?" asks Lawrence. "You may claim it," Feisal replies. "But in whose name *do* you ride?"

That last question becomes crucial. Feisal seems never to understand how Lawrence can be an Englishman acting as an Arab in an Arab cause. Even much later when he refers to Lawrence as "almost an Arab," irony is behind the words. Distrust mingled with gratitude is subtly portrayed both by Bolt's delicate dialogue and Guinness's performance. The cautious distance Feisal keeps between himself and Lawrence is seen in the decision to make Feisal an older man, with numerous references in the dialogue to his age and Lawrence's youth. This plays off the real-life ages of Guinness and O'Toole, forty-seven and twenty-nine, respectively. The actual Feisal, however, was thirty-three at the start of the Arab Revolt, only six years Lawrence's senior. The resulting characterization of Feisal virtually transfers to him Lawrence's own ambivalence, described in his writings. It projects that ambivalence for the audience, with "In whose name do you ride?" becoming one of the film's two salient spoken questions (the other being the shouted "Who are you?" issued by a motorcyclist from across the Suez Canal as Lawrence arrives outside Cairo, the cyclist's voice dubbed by David Lean). Guinness's performance is enriched by the fact that scarcely more than a year before filming began on *Lawrence,* the actor had played the lead in *Ross,* which Terence Rattigan converted from his script for an aborted Lawrence film that J. Arthur Rank had tried to launch in the 1950s.

Furthermore, the ambivalence reflects the iconoclastic Aldington's claim "that neither of the two heroes in fact thought very highly of the other. [Ronald] Storrs has expressed resentment at the 'good-natured tolerance' with which Feisal spoke of Lawrence after the war" (163). The "resentment" not only seems justified, but demonstrates the sensitivity of the film toward Arab reaction to the perception, promulgated by the Allied propaganda machine, that an Englishman unified the Arabs and liberated them from the Turkish Empire, and that European powers would simply allow Arab nations their freedom following the war. Finally, then, the film's Feisal regards

Lawrence with a combination of admiration, fascination, skepticism, mild resentment, and, finally, cynicism. Neither a mentor nor a sidekick, Feisal is characterized in a way befitting long-exploited people emerging from a war between empires with some modicum of autonomy.

As the drama shapes the events, Lawrence suddenly wants to be delivered from his role as leader of the Arab Revolt after a horrific episode in the Turkish-occupied city of Deraa. There, as he describes it in *Seven Pillars,* he is captured, taken to the general in charge, apparently to supply sexual favors. When he refuses, he is beaten and tortured; he describes this ordeal in terms that border closely on the sexual (445). Although homosexuality was still largely undepictable in mainstream film in 1962, the floodgates were opening; this made suggestions of homosexuality (in such films as *The Children's Hour* [1961] and *Advise and Consent* [1962]) tantalizing to audiences, although always in a homophobic context. The sequence, with José Ferrer playing the Bey, is written and staged in a style that is either highly coded and subtle or incomprehensible, depending upon one's point of view. No less sexually minded a spectator than Billy Wilder told Lean that he "didn't understand anything that happened to Lawrence [in the Bey scene] apart from the beating" (Brownlow 483). Some commentators, such as Jonathan Rutherford and Kaja Silverman, have seen Lawrence's description as practically a textbook account of masochism as described in Freud's classic article "A Child Is Being Beaten." Moreover, recent biographers have uncovered evidence that in the postwar years the asexual though probably homosexual Lawrence actually had himself beaten in order to sublimate his sexual urges. Overall, however, many commentators, led by Aldington, found so many inconsistencies in Lawrence's Deraa chapter as to leave what happened to Lawrence there forever open to question. Lean, not caring to interpret the episode strongly one way or the other, acts out all the episode's uncertainties.

In the aftermath of Deraa, the film plays Lawrence's neuroses against each other in an extreme dramatic stylization of what we would now call bipolar disorder. Deeply traumatized, he meets Allenby and the British in the newly taken Jerusalem. Lawrence asks to be reassigned to "a job any man can do," while Allenby, realizing what a talented leader he has on his hands, is determined to have him "lead the big push on Damascus." Lawrence sounds like an insecure young person fishing for compliments; he challenges Allenby's characterization of him as a man of destiny: "Suppose you're wrong" about that, he says. "Why suppose that?" asks Allenby. "We both know I'm right." The two men face each other on either side of the shot with a doorway between them. "Yes," Lawrence says as he gets up. He doesn't say it, so the spectator must complete it for him. *Yes, I'm a man of destiny.*

Anyone who would say this about himself, even when goaded, has gone into something beyond mere egotism. Lawrence therefore is fully in mythic "Lawrence of Arabia" mode. As we said about *Citizen Kane,* destiny is granted to a biopic subject by cultural acclamation, not by self-appointment. Lawrence is now shown with his back to the camera, making his motivation inscrutable. He asks in a voice that has gone from cowering to commanding within a half-dozen lines, "The sixteenth [of the month]?" The two already know what they are talking about. It is as if a switch has been flicked. The dialogue makes clear that Lawrence's messianic narcissism is on at full power. "I'm going to give them Damascus," he says; "It's going to happen," fully in his role as a figure of destiny. O'Toole walks into a half-light (matching Dryden's charge in the previous scene of Lawrence as the teller of half-lies), and his eyes take on a dead, glazed quality achieved by both the actor and the cinematographer. As if there were any doubt that Lawrence fully gives in to delusions of grandeur, O'Toole bestrides the set, stopping in front of an etching showing a clash of the gods. "They'll come for *me,*" intones Lawrence. Crowds he has assembled for the campaign can already be heard chanting "'Aurens, 'Aurens," which we already know is the Arabic honorific for his surname. The voices cry out first in his head and then in actuality. His ability to turn his desires into reality outweighs his power to control them.

The march to Damascus proves to be the orgiastic culmination of all his neuroses, something Lawrence has feared all along, which is why he had

12. "Man of destiny" shadowed in ambivalence. Digital frame enlargement.

13. Lawrence in the full grip of messianic delusion; the artwork behind him foretells the destiny of him and his followers. Digital frame enlargement.

turned down reassignments after the execution of Gasim. In the gratuitous massacre of the Turkish column that Lawrence and his army find in retreat outside the ruined village of Tafas, Lawrence's megalomania, narcissism, and bloodlusting sadism act themselves out to the extreme. Certainly no biopic prior to this time—and few mainstream films of any kind—included shots like the ones in which *the hero* shoots down men approaching him with their hands up. The military establishment has failed to save Lawrence from himself, but Lawrence is shown to have been naïve ever to hope that it would. One wonders whether the "destiny" Allenby speaks of to Lawrence is to chase the Turks out of Arabia or to become completely unhinged.

The European generals and diplomats are equally callous toward the Arab Revolt, which fact Lawrence does know and which motivates *him* to want to save the Arabs. This desire, on its face, makes Lawrence seem heroic, according to a concept of heroism based on religious savior myths. After his very first meeting with Feisal, Lawrence leaves Feisal's tent in the kind of purposeful and inspirational trance familiar from biopics. He spends the night and part of the next day in the desert, lost in thought, emerging after determining that he must invade the Turkish-held seaport of Aqaba, from the desert-backed landward side, an idea dismissed as impossible by all concerned. The teenagers Daud (John Dimech) and Farraj (Michel Ray) witness this desert meditation and keep vigil with him, becoming his first disciples and beginning the myth of "El 'Aurens." This scene is in keeping with the biopic's secular myth of the divinely inspired subject.

However, Lawrence's early epiphany in the desert also evinces the self-consciousness of the director. "You don't know what it's like living out in the desert," said David Lean. "It's something unbelievable, the loneliness of it, the majesty of it, the wonder of the sky at night . . . When you're in the desert, you look into infinity. It's no wonder that nearly all the great founders of religion came out of the desert. It makes you feel terribly small and also in a strange way, quite big" (qtd. in Brownlow 433).

Two persistent traits of the biopic, the subject's secular spiritualism and the identification of the film's creator—producer or director—with the subject, come together in *Lawrence* at the very same point. I've said earlier that the nature of biopics changes when the genre begins to move from being a producer's forum and becomes more of a director's medium in the post-studio age of independent international production. *Lawrence of Arabia* marks one of the first instances where we truly see a melding of directorial conception and biographical subject in a biopic. On the occasion of the film's election as "best British film of all time" in a 2004 poll of British "technicians, writers, and directors" taken by the *London Sunday Telegraph,* Sandra Lean, the director's widow, remarked that "he worked best when he could relate to the characters on the screen, when they were a mirror image of him. David was Peter O'Toole in *Lawrence of Arabia*" (Hastings and Govan).

The film was the product of a tense collaboration between the director and Sam Spiegel, one of the shrewdest independent producers in film history. Lean had directed such well-regarded British films as *Brief Encounter* (1946), *Great Expectations* (1947), and *Summertime* (1955), receiving Oscar nominations for Best Director for all three. However, he was still seen as an English filmmaker until he teamed with Spiegel on Lean's first large-scale international success, *The Bridge on the River Kwai,* which won seven Oscars.

Lean and Spiegel appear to have decided jointly to use their new prestige to plunge in where so many before them had failed and attempt a film about Lawrence. Spiegel used his persuasive powers, which were said to be considerable, to secure the rights to *Seven Pillars of Wisdom* from Lawrence's brother. A Jew from a part of Austria that is now in Poland, Spiegel had fled Hitler's Berlin in 1933. In 1961 he found that he had dealt himself into a situation where he was producing a film in Arab countries while still working out of his London offices and keeping his distance from Lean's operation in Jordan. Lean filmed and lived in some of the very spots that the film's protagonist had inhabited and evidently came to experience the desert much as Lawrence did. Anthony Nutting, a former British cabinet minister with extensive connections in the Arab world, was hired by Spiegel to act as a kind of ambassador for him. Nutting told Brownlow that he once visited Lean's location in the midst of a sandstorm. "When I arrived at the camp, the first person I saw was David . . . he was caked with dust. It looked as if he'd been with a make-up artist who'd really laid it on thick. So I said, 'What do you think of my desert now?' I thought there was going to be an almighty explosion. He said, 'Anthony, everything you said was an understatement.' I thought, Oh God, here's another Englishman going potty in this bloody desert" (Brownlow 438).

The film's intense ambivalence and fascinated objectivity are matched by the sensuous cinema of Lean and his cinematographer Freddie Young. So much does the desert become the mindscape of the biographical subject that after the film's intermission, when Lawrence dominates the landscape and despoils it with brutal train derailments and massacres, the feeling of the film grows colder and more confined. There are two reasons for this; one is that the narrative calls for it. The other relates to the film's production: Sam Spiegel forced a hiatus, moving the film out of Jordan and arranging for most of the second half—including the interiors set in Cairo, Jerusalem, and Damascus, as well as the taking of Aqaba—to be shot in Spain. An exception was the final bloodbath at Tafas, which was filmed at the very end of shooting, in Morocco. Spiegel's worries are said to have ranged from concerns about the slow pace of shooting in the desert, to the advice of production designer John Box that he would be unable to build the major sets for the second half in Jordan, to reports that large numbers of the mostly British cast and crew were becoming exhausted and demoralized in the desert heat, and to Lean's surmises that Spiegel was getting pressure from fellow Jews about all the money the production was pouring into Arab economies (Brownlow 456).

Until the end of his life, Lean characterized his relationship with Spiegel in the poisonous terms of the Auteur Theory and, indeed, of the biopic: the driven visionary artist against the predatory philistine businessman. The contentiousness of Lean and Spiegel did not even end with the completion of *Lawrence,* although they never worked together again. Over the years, Spiegel, Lean, and/or Columbia Pictures cut away at *Lawrence.* It was 222 minutes upon its premieres in December 1962, 202 minutes on wide release in early 1963, and 187 minutes for a reissue in 1971 (Brownlow 706). Not until the film's combination restoration and director's cut in 1989 did Lean get the final say. Spiegel had died in 1986.

Lean's forced march to Spain for the second half of the film, however, coincides with Lawrence's successive losses of innocence. As his idealism is overtaken by myriad actualities—the political intrigues in which he is unknowingly ensnared, the Islamic religion for which he both professes respect while also blaspheming it, the gold in Aqaba he rashly promised Auda abu Tayi, even quicksand—Lawrence loses control, first over events, then finally over himself. At the same time, the film fills up with frame-to-frame décor, cities, crowds, and action, contrasting with the compositional spaciousness and visual quietude of the first two hours.

Those critics over the years who have found Lawrence to be an androgynous and even feminine hero might get that impression not just because Lawrence in his flowing Arab robes resembles a bride (Caton 208), but because the narrative itself takes on the trajectory of the female biopic. As we see in Book Two, female biopics, by and large, fetishize victimization. The female subject is either victimized because of her position in society or implicitly punished for her presumption and ambition in trying to make a life outside it. Madness is a frequent destination in these films. Tellingly, *Lawrence* qualifies in all these areas. Lawrence's illegitimacy, his status as an outsider in the military, and his inability to be an Arab, to "want what he wants," all make him a victim of his place in society. He is punished, at least in his own mind, for his ambition to lead the Arabs, for having made promises to them that he knows he cannot keep and for a modern standard of individualism and self-invention ("Nothing is written") of which he repeatedly and disastrously falls short. This plot trajectory marks something new in male biopics, reenacting a scenario seen in biopics about women who haven't stayed in their place.

While *Lawrence of Arabia* takes on much of the suffering and pain of the female biopic, its protagonist falls victim to male hubris of various sorts. This is where the film both harks back to the self-destruction of the subject that we see in *Citizen Kane* and also departs from it. Lawrence, very unlike Kane, is tortured by self-knowledge. He is caught between his myriad ambiguous desires and the rigors of British patriarchy, conflicted with both but directly confronted by neither. Moreover, *Citizen Kane* takes a single word, a signifier, and demonstrates its unknowability and that of its speaker. *Lawrence* takes that *sine qua non* of the biopic, the valedictory tribute and monument, moves them from the climax of the film to the exposition, and interrogates their worth and meaning for the nation. By giving him a spot in St. Paul's, the cathedral of the Empire, as it were, the film implicitly questions the values of that Empire. Instead of a monument, the film's actual ending leaves Lawrence in the dust and wind of the desert and the debris he leaves behind. Reaping the whirlwind indeed.

In its sprawling, elaborate way, the film portrays Lawrence as unknowable. Meanwhile, it presents the aspects of his personality that are known. As the film ends with Lawrence fading out into the self-willed obscurity from which he is drawn at the beginning of the film, *Lawrence of Arabia* has worked as good drama, transporting the spectator subjectively to the world of its subject. But as historical biography, the film is an early example of the biopic as a self-conscious deconstruction of its subject, a concession to the irrecoverability of the past.

5

Nixon, Oliver Stone, and
the Unmaking of the Self-Made Man

He wrote a bad notice. The way you wanted it. I guess that'll show you.
—BERNSTEIN TO LELAND IN *CITIZEN KANE*

Susan: You don't know what it's like to know the whole audience just doesn't want you.
Kane: That's when you gotta fight 'em.
—*CITIZEN KANE*

Of all the remarkable dialogue in *Citizen Kane,* these two exchanges, commented on nowhere I know of in the vast literature on Welles's film, have always stood out for me. They are nonsensical and confounding. Yet they express a certain pathology in American life, one that Richard M. Nixon embodied for many Americans. I have always associated Kane's delusion with Nixon's because just after seeing *Citizen Kane* for the first time in my twenty-year-old life in an Introduction to Film class early in the evening of 1 May 1974, I returned to my dorm room. I turned on my TV to hear what I expected would be the latest installment in the seemingly interminable Watergate melodrama. President Nixon was explaining in his unique tone of voice, both guilty and sanctimonious, why and how, after numerous court orders, he was finally releasing impressively bound transcripts of conversations secretly recorded in the Oval Office during his presidency. These were not the tapes themselves, mind you, but transcripts heavily edited by White

House aides no less pitiful and obsequious than the assistants who groveled before Kane. These aides—or somebody; perhaps it was Nixon himself—used the attempt to make these often barroom-level conversations dignified, contributing the colorful phrase "expletive deleted" to the American lexicon.

On top of the delusional Charles Foster Kane, therefore, the maddened Richard Nixon seemed confirmation that one man could make the United States of America into his own personal psychodrama. And Nixon did it with far fewer advantages than the fictional Kane. No fiction writer or filmmaker could have invented Richard Nixon; indeed, much of his appeal during his political career and his continuing resonance as an American icon, whether one likes the sound of that or not, is what his success and downfall say about the possibilities and the limitations of self-invention in America.

Fast-forward, as Stone's not exactly linear biopic might have done, to a sequel made three years after Nixon's resignation. Movie critics might have termed this "an unnecessary sequel." "I let down my friends," ex-President Richard Nixon told David Frost in the 1977 television interviews that have now themselves been the subject matter of *Frost/Nixon,* a play (2006) by Peter Morgan that was the basis of a film version (2008) directed by Ron Howard. "I let down the country. I let down our system of government . . . I let the American people down and I have to carry that burden with me for the rest of my life." In such a carefully phrased apology, Nixon in 1977 only just approaches the emotional point where Oliver Stone begins his drama of the disgraced president's journey into self-understanding. While *Nixon* (1995) begins with the president eight months before his resignation listening to his tapes and trying to comprehend how he lost his hold on the country, David Frost's Nixon is out, but not down. "Let down" is a curious, noncommittal phrase meaning not much more than that Nixon disappointed his supporters. Morgan and Howard's drama treats the words themselves as key parts of a cathartic confession to which David Frost's heroic and heretofore dubious journalistic powers push an obstinate Nixon. However, this "confession" confesses nothing. The Nixon of the Frost interviews is but a New Old Nixon, embattled, struggling as always to salvage his identity and his reputation. Nixon told Frost, "I brought myself down. I gave them the sword. And they stuck it in. And they twisted it with relish. And, I guess, if I'd been in their position, I'd have done the same thing."

Elsewhere in the same interview, he blamed his downfall on his *softness:*

If only he hadn't sought to protect Haldeman, Ehrlichman, Mitchell, and others (i.e., the "real" culprits), he would have let *them* have them sooner and there would have been no cover-up. Very late in his life, he told a sympathetic young biographer, Monica Crowley, that he was brought down because *they* changed the rules. Wiretapping and political skullduggery that were permissible when Democratic presidents engaged in them suddenly became criminalized when Nixon practiced them (Crowley 287). *They* are the special prosecutor, the press, Congress; in short and in general, *they* are "Franklins," named for their founding father, FDR, those handsome, Ivy League, liberal types against whom Nixon carried a lifelong resentment (Perlstein 22). To the end of his life, Nixon, who consistently worked football metaphors into his public remarks, needed to believe that Watergate was a rigged Super Bowl in which the opposing team stole the ball, kept his side illegally bottled up, got all the calls to go in their favor, and won the game by a point. "Nixon never did admit final defeat because he never believed that he was finally defeated, only temporarily set back" (Volkan et al. 105).

The classical biopic subject also believes himself to be only temporarily set back. Nixon's tragedy, more so than Kane's, is that he either fails to understand or simply refuses to see that he has no moral grounding from which to make a stand. Nixon himself represented a breakdown in certain American belief systems, at a time when so many mythologies were being rethought and debunked. As a biopic protagonist, he is purely a postmodernist hollow man; Stone even states this at the start of the film as the Watergate burglars sit in a conference room in the hotel, awaiting the "Go" signal via walkie-talkie. A black-and-white motivational film from the Department of Labor is being projected on a screen, more for the film's audience than for the characters. This is an obvious contrivance, but it works too well for the director to have left it unused. An insecure salesman on the screen asks his superconfident mentor, "You mean it doesn't matter what I say; it's how I say it?" Stone understands that the combination of self-invention and television image-making in the Land of Opportunity creates a situation where a symbol, such as the presidential seal, outweighs or at least can be easily confused with reality. "If the president does it," Nixon said in one of the more famously jaw-dropping moments of the David Frost interviews, "that means it's not illegal." The obstinacy of the man who always gets up when he is knocked down, a trait the culture is conditioned to admire, is hardened in Nixon to a seemingly impenetrable façade. Nixon, however, tried too hard. As Watergate churned on, the denial and the hysteria showed through.

Although Nixon actually asked Monica Crowley, upon hearing she had gone to see *JFK* (1991), "Why would you give Oliver Stone seven dollars of your money?" (Feeney 327), the director and the ex-president might have been better suited to each other than Nixon thought. About Stone's *Nixon,* which came out a mere twenty months after Nixon's death in April 1994, Mark Feeney said, "There's something very nearly psychotic about Stone's film-making. This keeps it exciting, unpredictable, electric, but also, well, nutty" (331). On the other hand, "looking and listening to [Nixon]," wrote Stanley Kauffmann, "I used to wonder if everyone else thought he was as mentally ill as I thought him" (26).

While I'm not always a fan of his films (*The Doors* [1991] and *Alexander* [2004] are serious missteps), I don't take issue with the mental soundness of Oliver Stone. He even generously portrays Nixon as being possessed of a bit more rationality in his final year in the White House than he actually might have been. Stone's Nixon is already defeated, undone, and unmanned; his White House is a hall of horrors. He's down but not out (of office) as the film begins. When he is first shown, it is from the point of view of his chief of staff, Alexander Haig (Powers Boothe), a former general who manages to be at once obsequious and swaggering. It is this ambivalent figure—half-symbolic father, half-servant—whom Nixon sees as a "whole man" compared to himself. Nixon in the opening scenes cannot master the small-est physical competencies; he fumbles with the child-proof cap on a bottle of pills and needs help disentangling a reel-to-reel tape. Haig stands over him holding incriminating tapes, the "sword" for which the enemies are clamor-ing. Nixon jokes that if Haig had wanted to be considerate to his employer, he might have brought him a pistol and then left him alone with it.

Nixon asks to be seen as a dissection, an examination of the continuity and coherence of Nixon's self-identity. The film does not demonize or vilify him, as many expected, and as many probably would still expect years later of an Oliver Stone film. Rather, it tries to understand the systems, ambitions, and ideologies that drove Richard Nixon. Stone makes a biopic that connects the inner man to his external reactions and decisions. The film involves Nixon trying to understand what he has done to bring him to the point of resig-nation. The real process of understanding, of course, is undergone by the spectator, as s/he sorts out the life of a leader who looms too importantly in American life to be forgotten. Rick Perlstein goes so far as to call his 2008 book about the nature of American politics since 1968 *Nixonland,* a phrase first coined by Adlai Stevenson in a 1956 campaign speech. The film takes

Nixon to a deeper point of consciousness than he ever allowed himself to go. This Nixon is divested of his power, his prestige, and he spends the film trying to understand where it went. Stone's film, writes Feeney, is "*Citizen Kane* without Rosebud" (332).

Anthony Hopkins, who plays Stone's version of the thirty-seventh president, is very different from Nixon physically; he is stout and bull-necked with heavy features and a jutting jaw. Stone and Hopkins forget, probably deliberately, that after 1960, Nixon learned about the damage a wan appearance can do to a candidate in the television age and cultivated an impressively dignified look. In the 1968 campaign and as president, Nixon wore well-tailored deep-blue suits, blindingly white shirts, and neat-patterned ties that made him appear more than sufficiently presidential on the new medium of color TV. Hopkins, by contrast, wears ill-fitting dark brown and black suits that make Nixon look as unworthy of his place in the world as the script shows him to feel. It's not clear how this man ever won a single vote. But there are many "Nixons," and Nixon the successful politician is not this film's concern. In discussing the casting, Stone points out that Hopkins is not English but Welsh, and brings to the role a lonely isolation that fits his conception of Nixon as a person whose ambition is driven by shortcomings and slights. Never does this Nixon believe that anything in life will be "fun." Never is he cocky or complacent. Stone's Nixon has swallowed his father's dictum that "struggle is what gives life meaning." The Stone-Hopkins Nixon is a graceless, sulking man who has already lost, not one who struggles against failure. This conception of Nixon is not even inconsistent with the view of the man prevalent in much of the popular culture of his era. A 1969 comedy record album by impressionist David Frye, whose popularity was tied strictly to Nixon's tenure in office, had Nixon receiving the news he'd been elected with "Well, you can't lose them all."

Like the historical Nixon, Stone's Nixon is defined by anger and pugnacity. Indeed, Nixon's self-image as "a fighter" was the face he most often tried to show his "enemies." The difference again is of kind. The cinematic Nixon exudes helpless rage, whereas the actual Nixon indulged his vengeful, vindictive rages. These were based more in impotence than he knew. When ex-President Nixon initially refused to go into the hospital in the fall of 1974 after a renewed flareup of the phlebitis that plagued him the year of his resignation, he told an aide in his San Clemente exile, "You've got to be tough. You can't break, my boy, even when there is nothing left. You don't admit, even to yourself, that it is gone" (Volkan et al. 105). Stone has Nixon say these lines to Haig and Ron Ziegler in the White House just before the firing of special prosecutor Archibald Cox in October 1973, demonstrating Nixon's misplaced, pathetic "fighting spirit." "A man doesn't cry," he adds. "I don't cry. You don't cry. You fight."

The film dramatizes what Volkan and his associates write about Watergate: "It demonstrates how the internal world of a political figure can intrude into his conscious world, intermingling with external factors . . . to affect a historical process" (4). Stone's complex editing style, and a spiraling narrative structure that never places a spectator either entirely inside or outside Nixon's point of view, creates an intricate stacking-doll experience. Nixon may have dominated the period from the late 1940s to the early 1970s, but he never made it look easy. In fact, Nixon's success often looked excruciating and compulsive. Even President Lyndon Johnson, a fellow overachiever out to prove his manhood, dubbed him "a chronic campaigner" (Wicker 457).

Stone's *Nixon* would appear to represent the apogee of the American male biopic to the point when it was made, a three-hour, twelve-minute *Citizen Kane*–mode investigatory biopic. *Nixon* fragments the man into multifarious points of view, most of them Nixon's own. The difference is that Stone's style is so thesis driven that, unlike in *Lawrence of Arabia* especially, the filmmaker has his own ideas about who Richard Nixon is. Nixon is too earthy, too real, and too self-evident, at least to Stone, to be mysterious. Nixon is to be explained or just plain reenacted, by the many books, plays, and films about him, not deciphered. The question is how a man so undiscovered, if not loathed, by himself could become the dominant political personality of an era in which America confidently bestrode the world as it never had before and perhaps never will again.

Nixon represents the epitome of the self-made man, the logical product of American democracy, a figure who, according to Michael Kimmel, "derives identity entirely from [his] activities in the public sphere, measured by accumulated wealth and status, by geographic and social mobility" (17). The self-made man makes his own way in life on a path defined by constant self-betterment and self-control. His "success must be earned. Manhood must be proved—and proved constantly" (Kimmel 23). Nixon embodies the self-made man's determination never to fall below his own studied image of what he must become. We see this in young Nixon's self-abasement in the interests of "toughness," for instance, his persistence in staying on his college football team when the only position for him was that of "tackling dummy" against whom the "real" football players practiced. He attended hometown Whittier College because the family could not afford to send him to Yale or Harvard, where he had been invited to apply for scholarships.

Garry Wills, in *Nixon Agonistes: The Crisis of the Self-Made Man,* published in the second year of Nixon's presidency, tied Nixon's visible resentments and noisy strivings to the ubiquitous self-made man archetype. Such men are "the Joneses we try to keep up with, whom we envy but imitate. We are told that it is easy to join their ranks—but that means it is easy, also, for them to slip down to our level, a fact that gives them their oppressively *scrambling* air. They are all runners who can never win the race, long distance runners, well-fed worriers; and they went to Miami [the site of the 1968 GOP convention] to choose their very archetype, the longest-distance runner of them all" (584).

Nixon's emotional and psychological baggage became his political calling card. He presented himself as a man who had a love-hate relationship with his humble background and with the obstacles, real and perceived, that he had overcome. Many voters identified with these struggles. Theodore H. White wrote that after his defeats for president in 1960 and California governor in 1962, Nixon still "retained an invisible nationwide base. There were millions who admired him for his tenacity, pluck, and conservative politics, as well as for the stigmata of poverty and bitterness they shared with him" (76). This polarizing personality was not the president the already divided social climate called for, but perhaps no one of his generation who could have been elected in that passionate time would have been. Moreover, Rick Perlstein argues that the polarization that Nixon opened up and exploited from the mid-1960s on is with us still.

Nixon completed a ten-year Oliver Stone cycle that included *Salvador* and *Platoon* (both 1986), the Vietnam films *Born on the Fourth of July* (1989) and *Heaven and Earth* (1993), and *The Doors* and *JFK* (both 1991). These films weave a mammoth, multiperspectived story of American anticommunism; the Vietnam War; the American government's response to Marxist regimes in our hemisphere, especially Cuba; the military-industrial complex and national security state; the assassinations of the Kennedy brothers and Martin Luther King Jr.; and the youth culture that coalesced around Vietnam protest. Stone's cycle dramatizes the consequences of the entire U.S. postwar, Cold War philosophy, its attendant economic boom, and its burgeoning popular culture. This gigantic historical saga, culminating in the Nixon story and its all-too-human anticlimax of Watergate, gives cinematic meaning to a comment by George McGovern: "Vietnam will loom as the major tragedy, and

Watergate—and the paranoia behind it—was one of the spin-offs from that. I have always thought the two were part and parcel of the same scenario" (Strober 525).

While Watergate is most often seen as a conspiracy spun from the paranoia of Richard Nixon, McGovern suggests that America's entire postwar policy was based on suspicion, secrecy, and distrust: there's always a story we don't know, a conspiracy we can't see. Communism, by this logic, must be behind domestic disputes, such as the civil rights movement and protests against the Vietnam War. Behind the international communist conspiracy, furthermore, must be a web of American treason. And the inverse of this was thought to be true: only America can save the world from the spread of communism. Furthermore, it is hard not to see the American experience in Vietnam as a widespread effort to salvage America's manhood, as it were. To do this theme full justice would probably require the Stanley Kubrick of *Dr. Strangelove* (1964) and *Full Metal Jacket* (1987), films that depict U.S. Cold War policies in satirical images in which male sexuality is displaced onto the desire to wage war and in which military preparedness calls for the obliteration of anything that smacks of "femininity." Stone's depiction of an emasculated Nixon is consistent with Susan Jeffords's thesis that the loss in Vietnam left the country "demasculinized." However, *Nixon* depicts the condition of demasculinization and "explains" it as a motivation for the Watergate scandal. In ending Nixon's story with his resignation, and declining to depict his "comebacks" in the last twenty years of his life, Stone makes no effort to recover Nixon's lost masculinity, but leaves him and the audience to ponder the mad scramble for a sense of masculinity as a cause of his downfall.

Nixon was a part of systems that determined his responses as powerfully as his personality did. Stone connects his antihero to a confederation referred to in *Nixon* as the beast. In a January 1997 appearance before the American Historical Association, on a panel that included McGovern and Arthur Schlesinger Jr., Stone described "the beast" as "a system . . . of the way things work. The system requires money, requires media, requires power and the perception of power." The military-industrial complex, the permanent government, the national security state: all are synonyms for "the Beast."

Stone's two Vietnam biopics, *Born on the Fourth of July*, about the American veteran Ron Kovic, and *Heaven and Earth*, about a South Vietnamese woman, Li Haislip, take the form of maturation stories in which a young person, through harrowing experience, learns the truth about the Vietnam War and develops a mature attitude toward the experience. Nonbiographical Stone films, such as *Platoon* and *Wall Street,* take similar tacks. Clearly, a *bildungsfilm* with a naïve young protagonist would not work for *Nixon.* However, the idea of a young man led out into the world by the drive to go out and achieve *something* is swirled up within the spiral narrative structure that Stone employs.

Stone is drawn to Oedipal narrative structures. In *Platoon* and *Wall Street* the young male protagonists, played in both films by Charlie Sheen, are confronted by a choice of fathers: a flashy, self-absorbed primal father who represents discredited ideals—murderous, warlike xenophobia in *Platoon,* unabashed greed in *Wall Street*—and quiet, sensible symbolic fathers. Stone even goes so far in *Wall Street* to cast Sheen's own father, Martin, as the blue-collar good dad. While *Wall Street* was received in 1987 as part of a backlash against the get-rich-by-all-means ethic that dominated America during the Reagan administration, the film can also be seen as a working out of the director's relationship with his father, a Wall Street stockbroker. Louis Stone was no Gordon Gekko, the omnivorous tycoon of Stone's film; indeed, Stone's parents' divorce when he was sixteen revealed his upper-middle-class family to be awash in debt and launched Stone on a young adulthood of rootless wandering. According to Frank Beaver,

> Stone's masculine sensibilities resulted from deep-seated psychological ties to his Father. . . . Lou Stone had chastised his son for dropping out of college, going to Vietnam as a soldier, and returning a drug-ridden, uneducated "bum." The elder Stone (who died in 1985, before *Salvador* and *Platoon*) reportedly never recognized his son's experience as a Vietnam soldier as valid. This refusal remained a painful gesture because, according to those closest to him, Oliver Stone had gone to Vietnam partly to prove himself to his father, a World War II veteran. (14)

Most of Stone's films can be seen, then, as resulting from what his wife Elizabeth called his "father complex," as his male protagonists feel "nagged on by a distant father" (Beaver 14). Even when films depict weak fathers, such as *Born on the Fourth of July,* in which the protagonist's ineffectual father has little advice for his son as he unpacks cartons of toilet paper at the supermarket he manages, they portray the son as molded instead by formidable "national fathers" such as the Marine Corps, or, in *JFK,* by the dead personage of President Kennedy, a national symbolic father of whose leadership the country has been robbed by the brutal primal fathers who may have had him assassinated. Thus even the conspiracy theorizing with which Stone's name became synonymous in 1990s popular culture is wrapped up with his "father complex."

Nixon, like *Wall Street* eight years earlier, is dedicated to Louis Stone. The director said that his memories of his father gave him

> a way of getting into the shoes of Richard Nixon, because I felt they were very similar. They both had suffered as young men coming out of college in the Depression and had felt in a sense screwed by the Roosevelt Administration. . . . My father was never wrong; he was never wrong about Vietnam; he was never wrong about the Cold War, about the Russians, and eventually he turned around on almost every issue. He was different from Nixon . . . in that he was able to call himself wrong. I never saw Richard Nixon do that and that was what was almost the Greek [tragic] figure of Richard Nixon. He was so stubborn and strong and he never doubted himself, or pretended not to anyway. . . . So I could not have [made the film] without having been Lou Stone's son. (*Nixon* DVD commentary)

Nixon thus is portrayed as a failed national father who cannot "call himself wrong"—he even lies to his daughter Julie when she asks him about the Watergate cover-up, then tries to compensate with the language of the David Frost interviews: "I just hope I haven't let you down, kid." For the Stone who assesses these two father figures, Lou Stone and Nixon, the president is damned by his inability to admit his mistakes, to stop his lying to himself, his family, and the country. His fate is assured by the inability to alter his firmly held determination to "act like a man," making him for Stone "a Greek figure." As a son himself, however, Nixon is depicted as scornful of his own failed father. Unlike Stone's other characters, Nixon is unable to relegate his own angry, ineffectual father to the back of his mind; Frank Nixon is more of an influence on him than Richard would ever admit. In speeches and in his writings it was Nixon's mother whom he revered as a source of strength. This Nixon carries around with him wildly confused lessons from his parents.

Hannah Nixon (Mary Steenburgen) is shown as a sternly religious symbol of repression and self-denial. Drowning in Watergate, Nixon comes to grips with his profanity of mind when he madly rushes to cross out the "expletives" peppering the transcripts of the White House tapes, shouting that the world cannot hear that Mrs. Nixon's son has a filthy mouth. The film points out the lingering influence of Nixon's bitter father, a midwesterner for whom the promise of a golden life in California never panned out and the initial source of Nixon's hatred of those he imagined "had things handed to them." While the mother represents rigid ideals that Nixon would betray, the father is the font of a liquid fear of failure and a loathing of those who succeed. In Richard, the film shows, the diatribes of the father hide out from the disapproving judgments of the mother. Both father and mother, at bottom, are patriarchal. The father illustrates the dark underside of the American Dream of the self-made man; the mother stands in for stiffly judgmental church fathers.

On election night 1960, Dick tells Pat that his defeat makes him think of his "old man. . . . He was a failure too. Do you know how much money he had in the bank when he died? Nothing." Frank Nixon (Tom Bower) has an angry tirade in front of his sons about work and struggle as the only reasons for living. "Maybe a trip to the woodshed will straighten you out," he tells seventeen-year-old Harold, stressing that no one gets "something for nothing." The lesson is shown to have been learned–and misapplied—when President Nixon, in infamous remarks days before the Kent State shootings, is seen calling student protesters "bums. . . . They call themselves 'flower children.' I call them spoiled rotten. And I tell you what would cure them—a good old-fashioned trip to my Ohio father's woodshed." Later in the film, however, Stone segues out of a childhood flashback with a Nixon stump speech, heard only in voiceover: "My old man struggled his whole life. You could call him a little man, a poor man, but they never beat him. I always tried to remember that when things didn't go my way."

This is a peculiar lesson. By biographical accounts, Frank Nixon was "an angry and essentially mean-spirited individual [whose] life, in fact, consisted of hardships, bad luck, and losses, leading him to know great frustration, discouragement, and humiliation" (Volkan et al., 25). Exactly how Frank Nixon went "unbeaten," who "they" are who never beat him, or why the son should remember this when things didn't go his way is not clear and Stone lets the line hang there for us to consider. (Nixon shouldn't let "them beat him" either.)

Apparently one of those Nixon wouldn't let beat him was his own wife, the former Thelma Patricia Ryan, whom Nixon pursued doggedly and largely unsuccessfully for two years. After she gave in and married him, in 1940, he repaid her elusiveness with coldness and distance. He could sometimes be seen in highly public situations, even when he accepted the vice presidential nomination in 1952, moving away from his wife on podiums when she tried to kiss or embrace him (Volkan et al. 49). "Nixon's fear of strong women and his desire to keep them in their place is suggested by his intense dislike of pant-wearing, opinionated women." For Nixon, "uncontrolled and uncontained, women are a potential source of shame and humiliation for men. Their job is to reflect their husband's glory, not to take away from it" (Volkan et al. 50). However, Stone and Joan Allen, who plays Pat, move "plastic Pat" out of the background and give her a voice and an attitude, making her Nixon's last reality checkpoint, the person who knows best how cut off from human contact and how obsessed with winning and maintaining control he has become. For Stone, who himself is known for treating women as little more than mannequins in his films, the portrayal of Pat Nixon as a woman who knows her husband better than anyone, including himself, is a breakthrough of sorts. It becomes clear that the rigid Hannah Nixon and a culture in which women are put on pedestals and kept out of the way have left Nixon unprepared for real women. There were few times that Nixon publicly referred to his mother without calling her "a saint." Allen's deep-voiced Pat, who has run out of the patience political wives are supposed to possess in abundance, makes a compelling foil.

As a man, Richard Nixon invites psychological probing because of the glimpses he shared of his pain and hostility. Stone's Nixon, as played by Hopkins, is brooding, introverted, and etched in sorrow. He is confused in the midst of a downfall that is both of his own making and wrought by forces that go far beyond him. Ironically, it was the long-sought presidency that took Nixon out of his element, so accustomed was he to running for things, scrambling toward a future position, rather than managing one in the present. The achievements for which Nixon's administration is remembered positively, particularly the strategy to thaw the Cold War by making overtures to both of the opposing communist superpowers, China and the Soviet Union, did involve the active pursuit of clear, linear goals. However, the dissent and unrest of the time, the no-win Vietnam War, and his status as a minority president continually placed him in passive, reactive, and directionless positions. Nixon's response was to fight, to hit back. With events like the Ellsberg psychiatrist break-in, the results were self-inflicted hits that Nixon experienced as blows from his enemies.

The film begins—outside Nixon, but really inside his soul—with the break-in at the Watergate; it then elides eighteen months to December 1973. It's a rainy night; the White House looks like The Old Dark House of horror films. A John Williams orchestral coda clashes away. Alexander Haig, who had replaced H. R. Haldeman as chief of staff, makes his way through darkened hallways. This credit sequence is punctuated by a drumbeat of authoritative news reports on the sound track and newspaper headlines, most of them from the *New York Times*. The scandal, as announced by the news media Nixon so despised, appears to grow closer to Nixon's door, as Haig does. The stentorian voiceovers signify *them,* Nixon's media enemies, coming to get him, proclaiming his criminality as gospel truth.

Haig, and the camera, find Nixon, a small, crumpled figure in retreat, huddled in a dark corner of the Lincoln Sitting Room. Haig comes bearing tapes. Nixon, in the film's version, then sits alone listening to the tape of the conversation of 23 June 1972, in which he directed Haldeman to order the FBI and the CIA not to investigate Watergate. This tape became the "smoking gun." It forced Nixon's resignation over seven months later when the Supreme Court ruled that Nixon had no right to withhold it and it became public, withering even his Republican support in Congress.

The film's spiral structure begins here. Feeling buffeted from outside, Nixon looks inside, as Stone begins a revelatory dramatic process that is alternately external and internal. The camera appears to track through the mechanism of the tape recorder itself into Nixon's office in the Executive Office Building on that sunny June day. In this way, this biopic of Nixon is

14. Anthony Hopkins as Richard Nixon in Oliver Stone's *Nixon* (Hollywood Pictures, 1995). A desperate, brooding man, alone with his tapes, his conscience, and his privacy made public. Digital frame enlargement.

removed from the Great Man archetype, by which a man's great talent and vision drive him on to great accomplishments. Nixon's vision is obscured. He doesn't know what has brought him to this precipice and he doesn't know what is causing him to topple. The "encounters" with the tapes are played as a continuing session with an analyst. Little wonder that Pat Nixon, who is portrayed as the conscience Nixon is determined to ignore, says of the tapes, "They're not yours. They *are* you." The film becomes, through this framing device, a conflict between Nixon and himself.

This is where Stone's evolving editing style becomes indispensable. "I don't know what to call this editing," Stone says:

> Some have called it vertical editing, in so far as we stop, and we go into a moment; we expand a moment by going into internal and external editing. . . . [A character] will say something on an external idea, but we will cut to a completely contrary look or feel, be it black and white or color. It comments on what's being said. . . . So I call it exterior/interior. Sometimes we will go to five or six images that will completely contradict or perhaps supplement the external action. (*Nixon* DVD commentary)

This technique might be seen as a new form of Eisensteinian juxtaposition, an expansion of cinematic "reality" that goes beyond the linking of cause-and-effect events, as photographed by an "objective" camera. In *Nixon* this jagged, freeform style lends itself to a whirlpool of torturing memories. It serves well to illustrate a man, as Martha Mitchell (Madeleine Kahn) says to Nixon, whose smile and face "are never in the same place at the same time." As Stanley Kauffmann wrote, "*Nixon* assumes that a film biography cannot rightly be linear because everyone carries his entire life with him all the time. The backpack, ever present and always growing, is invisible in life but need not be so in film" (Kauffmann 26). Biography balances the public realm, which is already familiar in the case of someone like Nixon, with the private. The long-standing appeal of biography lies in its promise to juxtapose the public and private selves, completing a full and satisfying impression of the subject's personality and motivations. This promise has sometimes led the biopic to extremes—either to sanitize a subject's personal life, as biopics of the studio era were often accused of doing—or to "expose" a sensational and sordid personal life.

Even if a biopic hews to one of these extremes, however, it will probably

15. Shades of Abel Gance. Stone employs double exposure to reveal Nixon's inner doubts and insecurity, even at his happiest moment, as he accepts the 1968 GOP nomination for president. Digital frame enlargement.

do so through the essentially objective and linear structure of mainstream cinema. *Nixon*'s editing elongates time, showing the feelings, thoughts, and associations behind Nixon's statements. It also breaks into the carefully controlled facade that was both Nixon's modus operandi and his biggest problem as a public figure, as well as what makes him continually fascinating to us now—the surface that invites us to peer beneath it while it forbids entrance. For example, in the sequence depicting Nixon's acceptance of the Republican nomination in 1968, Nixon's forceful delivery of his speech and the ecstatic response of the convention to it are both filmed in color. Superimposed on these images, however, is a shot showing Nixon, in black and white, looking uncertain, not knowing if he should smile, as if the "two-time loser," as my dad referred to Nixon throughout 1968, wondered if this moment of triumph would evaporate as others had. This device, double exposure, is almost as old as cinema; it recalls Abel Gance's extensive use of it in *Napoléon* to keep the private personality present even in the most historic public moments.

It's worthwhile to study the entire sequence that includes this moment because it shows Stone's associative, thematic method and how it welds the personal and the historical. As the sequence opens, a subtitle tells us we are in "1972: the President's Private Office," even though the previous sequence showed the run-up to the nomination in 1968. In 1972 Nixon, wearing a red smoking jacket and sipping a Scotch, tells Haldeman about Track Two, which was a conspiracy to assassinate Fidel Castro, conceived in the last months of the Eisenhower administration in 1960. It involved the then-vice president, the Mafia, Cuban counterrevolutionaries, and, most significantly for Nixon in 1972, CIA men, including Howard Hunt and Frank Sturgis, who were among those just arrested as Watergate burglars.

John Kennedy's ignorance of Track Two in his early days as president is, in Stone's version, one of the reasons for the botched Bay of Pigs invasion in May 1961. "I didn't want him to get the credit," Stone has Nixon saying, but only after Nixon says that the CIA didn't tell JFK either, "they just kept it going," stressing the theme of the "beast," the "permanent government" that operates independently of presidents. Nixon recounts how Kennedy called him to his office, "said I stabbed him in the back, called me a two-bit grocery clerk from Whittier." (This is a fictional conceit, consistent with Stone's dramatic concept of a put-upon Nixon; a White House meeting with Kennedy did take place, but by Nixon's own account it was very cordial [Nixon 233].) A black-and-white cutaway to the same moment has Nixon stopped, pondering, as if JFK's remark continued to sting. A color reaction shot of Haldeman shows him obviously moved. All the while, there are cutaways to mob members (played by actors), stock shots of actual Cuban guerrillas, Castro, and atrocities, as well as a cut to Hopkins and Allen as Dick and Pat Nixon in the backseat of the car during the 1958 Caracas riots. All of these, plus what the script calls "a Rum and Coca-Cola song" on the sound track, take us well out of the 1972 diegesis and into the conspiratorial world Nixon describes (Rivele et al. 180). Moreover, early in the sequence, the late-1973 Nixon is shown in the Lincoln Sitting Room hideaway listening to this conversation on tape.

Thus, when Nixon, in his talk with Haldeman, turns to the window and away from his interlocutor, Stone is ready with the thematic thread that unites the entire sequence. "When I saw Bobby lying there on the floor"— shots and sounds of RFK's assassination—"his arms stretched out, his eyes staring, I knew then I'd be president." Nixon stands at the window, fingers the lace curtains. "His death paved the way, didn't it? Vietnam, the Kennedys, cleared a path through the wilderness just for me." In black and white, Nixon is shown saying "over the bodies. Four bodies." A cut to a longer shot has Nixon on the left and Haldeman out of focus on the right. Fade to color and rack focus on Haldeman, who says, "You mean, two." Rack focus back to Nixon as Haldeman continues: "Two bodies."

"Four," answers Nixon in 1973, also at the window, drinking. He moves to a painting of Lincoln. "How many did you have? Hundreds of thousands? Where would we be without death, Abe," he asks. "Who's helping us? Is it God, or is it death?" Cut to a black-and-white shot of TB microbes under a microscope; then dissolve to an aerial view of a desert landscape. The eye requires a few seconds to perceive the difference. A subtitle reads: "1933. Arizona." This is the TB sanitorium where Harold Nixon spent his last days. (Earlier, the film cut from the death of JFK to the death in 1925 of Nixon's brother Arthur.) This scene, which plays in black and white, has Harold, in death throes, telling Dick that their parents will now have the money to send him to law school. Harold, scanning the desert, longs for death as Dick replies, "You're not gonna quit on me, are you?" echoing Nixonian rhetoric; even in his resignation speech, Nixon maintained that he had never been "a quitter." The sound mix includes a distant train whistle, an image Nixon used in his speeches to evoke the American Dream that beckons the humblest youngsters in remote places (like Whittier, California) to follow their ambitions.

Stone then cuts from trains to a toy plane that one of Nixon's two surviving younger brothers plays with following Harold's funeral. Richard will soon be leaving for Duke Law School. Hannah tells her son Richard, "God has chosen thee to survive," sounding a familiar theme of biopics, the idea that the Great Man "does not choose his way," as we have earlier heard Dick tell Pat to justify why he "had to" run in '68. The notion that the Great Man himself is a mere servant to his role in history and his significance as an icon—like Jesus the man in comparison to God the Son—becomes in Stone's rendering a delusion. It accounts for why as president, Nixon begins to refer to himself in third person. He tells John Mitchell, "I'd like to offer my condolences" to the families of the students killed at Kent State. "But Nixon can't." It is as if the man Richard Nixon has to wall himself off from feelings that the tough, masculine "Nixon" can't be shown betraying. And once "Nixon" the icon cuts himself off from feeling, Nixon the man does too.

Hannah admonishes Richard that he must seek "strength in this life, happiness in the next." The mother's words are often echoed ironically in Pat's. Pat speaks the word "happy" in two key scenes, first when Nixon tells Pat of his decision to run in '68 because he knows he can win. "Do you really want this, Dick? . . . And then you'll be happy?" Later, when as president amid the turmoil of Vietnam Nixon is too consumed with his enemies to want to make love to Pat, she says flatly, "It took a long time for me to fall in love with you, Dick. But I did. And if it doesn't make you happy . . ." From his mother's admonition, Nixon is next shown against a dark background, with random flashing lights and distorted sound. This is revealed to be the triumphant moment of his appearance before the 1968 GOP convention as its presi-

16. The voices Nixon hears: His mother, Hannah (Mary Steenburgen): "Strength in this life, happiness in the next." Digital frame enlargement.

17. Pat (Joan Allen): "It took me a long time to fall in love with you, Dick. But I did. And if it doesn't make you happy . . ." Digital frame enlargement.

dential nominee. As the hall turns up the lights, the candidate turns on his smile. However, what Nixon describes in his acceptance speech—illustrated by Stone in a cascading montage of stock shots in which the tumult of the late 1960s builds to a frightening crescendo—is a country where hard work and sacrifice have not brought "happiness"; they have not been rewarded by any sense of contentment or stability.

Thus, Stone's style of montage conveys the Nixonian conviction that in the absence of happiness one must be strong. Stone's montage then establishes this conviction as the foundation of Nixon's rhetoric and his policies as president. Nixon sees the absence of happiness everywhere. The cut to an uncertain Nixon during one of the great moments of his life is steeped in the theme of Nixon as a beneficiary of death, and in the concept of a man who can't allow himself to enjoy his success, to feel secure in it, or to feel that he deserves it.

The logic of the cut that follows this is clear. Stone elides such details as Hubert Humphrey's near-upset in the 1968 election and waits to show Nixon in the White House until he had been president for fifteen months, in April and May 1970, the time of Cambodia and Kent State. More bodies. The president is shown overruling his secretary of state in pursuing a policy of terror in Vietnam designed to make his enemies, as Kissinger (Paul Sorvino) puts it, "fear the madman Richard Nixon." Thus when Stone says that Nixon "lied all his life" but "would never have identified it as such," he is referring, for instance, to Nixon's notion that a leader can achieve peace by becoming more warlike (*Nixon* DVD supplement). Anthony Hopkins said, "Stalin told Churchill, 'If you're ruling a country like the Soviet Union, you can't waste time on Christian ethics. You have to be brutal.' And I think Nixon must have taken a lot from Stalin; in order to achieve things, you have to be tough. And he was a tough man" (Pickle I-4). For many, Nixon's downfall was that once he attained his tough posture, he could not drop it when he needed to, even after it became self-parody. John Ehrlichman says in the film, "Dick Nixon say 'I'm sorry'? That'll be the day. His whole suit of armor would fall off."

More dangerously, the Hopkins quote reflects the film's depiction of a man whose thinking could slip too easily from that of a president in a democracy to that of a leader with a far less discriminating sense of power. When the president feels plagued by news leaks from within his administration, he declares (while standing under a painting of George Washington), "A leak happens, the whole damn place should be fired. Really. You do it like the Germans in World War II. If they went through these towns and a sniper hit them, they'd line the whole goddamned town up and say, 'Now until you talk, you're all getting shot.'" When Ehrlichman, whom the film poses as a kind of good angel, whispering intermittently in the president's ear, says, "We're not Germans," Nixon mutters, "Yeah," as he often does when dismissing inconvenient data.

Stone stages the meeting between Nixon and Mao Tse-tung as a cauldron in which the Chinese communist leader and the Leader of the Free World melt together into one great, shapeless hunger for power. Stone suggests that while Nixon demonized Stalin, Khrushchev, Ho Chi Minh, Mao, Castro, and the rest, he also internalized them and emulated them. While this may make *Nixon* sound like a remake of *The Searchers,* it provides the film's ultimate juxtaposition, not the "bad Nixon" of break-ins and cover-ups with the "good Nixon" who made peace with China and the Soviets (Scheer xi), but Nixon the insecure, self-made man with Nixon the unconstitutional megalomaniac.

In this way, the film's introspective aspect, letting Nixon search for and discover the truth about himself, leaving him to stew in his own juice, as it were, creates a vast tableau. It shows him as a product of failed American assumptions about political success and the wielding of power. I think Stone has been overly apologetic for making Nixon a "sympathetic" figure, which he isn't here, exactly. "We went so far," Stone says, "as to give this sad figure a consciousness of what he had missed. I don't think we were right in doing that, but we did it for movie reasons. We empathized with him and made him better than he was, which film tends to do because we [want] an audience to care about the protagonist" (Stone). On the contrary, it's a brave thing Stone has done, identifying with the Other, adopting the point of view of someone who signifies for so many in the generations born since World War II everything sick and dangerous about the systems that drive us as Americans. The film makes this point early. In the Labor Department film the Watergate burglars watch, a counselor bucks up a salesman who has become unsure of himself. After saying, "I don't mean to pry, but is everything all right at home?" the man adds, "Remember what you're really selling—yourself." "You mean," says the salesman, "it doesn't matter what I say, but how I say it?" The counselor tells him, "Always look 'em in the eye. Nothing sells," he says, smiling at the camera, "like sincerity."

This hackneyed training film with its cluster of Chamber of Commerce clichés sets out a thematic agenda for the film. The Watergate scandal itself symbolizes a desperation beneath the American drive for success through persuasion and salesmanship, the "oppressively scrambling" air of the self-made man. "Everything" will be shown not to be "all right at home," whether the "home" is that of Hannah and Frank in the 1920s, the repressed household of Dick and Pat, protests and division "on the domestic front" in America, or the psyche of Richard Nixon that is "home" to all these traumas. As president, Nixon made policy out of the idea that it didn't matter what he said, because Nixon was saying it. He can desegregate schools and bargain with communists because of his image as a conservative and an anticommunist. "Don't worry about what we say; it's what we do," John Mitchell liked to tell reporters (Strober 108). Conservative Howard Phillips groused, "The conservatives got the rhetoric and the liberals got the government"

(Strober 108). The flip side was that in practicing "politics as the art of compromise," as Nixon says in the film, he gets little credit. "People have forgotten," the Nixon of late 1973 tells Haig in their first scene. "Such violence. The tear gas, the riots, burning the draft cards, the Black Panthers. . . . We fixed it, Al, and they hate me for it. Because it's Nixon. They've always hated Nixon."

As the Watergate burglars wait and the Labor Department film unspools, the title "Nixon" appears over the projector beam, as if to cue the audience that what it's about to see is a series of projections both from and onto its tortured protagonist and that much of what he projects will disturb even him. The man who boasts of "fixing" the violence will wince when his taped conversation reminds him of violence he perpetrated, such as the Ellsberg break-in ("I approved that?"), and violence from which he benefitted, such as the shootings of George Wallace and the Kennedys. The man who takes offense when Nelson Rockefeller (Edward Herrmann), his chief Republican rival, needles him at a 1963 party about the title of his book, *Six Crises* ("Sounds like you've got a crisis syndrome. Aren't you exaggerating a bit, Dick? Call it three and a half, maybe four . . .") is capable of telling John Dean during Watergate, "Everything is a crisis to the upper intellectual types, the softheads. The average people don't think it's much of a crisis." Such contradictions dramatize Stone's belief that Nixon was "unconscious" of much about what he did. The projector is a metaphor for the public man as a projection, with the actual man an assemblage of a million fragments, most of them, in the media age, electronic, multiplied by six thousand hours of White House tapes. This charge to find the man behind the image is one of Stone's many indirect references to *Citizen Kane*. Moreover, the projector also symbolizes the beam whose object is never just interior or exterior. For Stone, the personal story is also the larger political and historical story. And for Nixon, the political is always the personal.

On the trip back from China, Nixon tells Pat, "Think of the life Mao's led. In '52, I called him a monster. Now he could be our most important ally. Only Nixon could have done that." The dialogue winds up being not about Mao at all, but about Nixon himself. In a rage following a stormy news conference Nixon thunders, "I did everything the *New York Times* editorial page said I should do. . . . So why are these assholes turning on me? Because they don't like the way I look. They don't like where I went to school," and ultimately these slights turn into a slam on America itself: "They don't—they don't trust America!" Even the film's Ehrlichman picks up this thread: "You think this is about politics," he asks Haldeman. "This is about Richard Nixon. You got people dying because he didn't make the varsity football team. You got the Constitution hanging by a thread because he went to Whittier and not to Yale." This is perhaps the most troubling revelation the film makes: that systems of government on which millions of lives depend turn finally on individual subjectivities, on men, mostly, who take vast systems personally and who are really incapable of understanding the large implications of what they do.

> . . . Some mornings I linger
> in Pat's closet, among all the incompatible species
> of fox and alligator, ostrich and lamb.
> And I'm reminded of my Russian stacking dolls:
> how the smallest is absolutely empty
> but for silence, longing, a residue of perfume.
>
> —FROM "NIXON ON THE PLEASURES OF UNDRESSING A WOMAN"
> BY KAREN KOVACIK

Nixon fascinates because he is simultaneously a figure of dogmatic rigidity, and yet he appears so insecure. He lied extravagantly and everyone seemed to know it but he. He appeared to be trapped by the limitations of his era, his ethnicity and family background. He had aspirations as a national leader that went beyond his capacity to imagine many kinds of Americans other than himself. (Oddly, as a foreign policy enthusiast, he seemed to have less trouble with people of other nationalities.) He aimed for unifying, Lincolnesque rhetoric, choosing the slogan "Bring Us Together" as his administration's motto. Even if he believed in the idea, it was not in his nature to be capable of anything of the sort. Similarly, when he ventured out to the Lincoln Memorial in the middle of the night of 9 May 1970 to meet with protesting students, he was utterly unable to connect. To submit Nixon, as Stone does, to a combination of psychoanalysis and the kind of political reeducation that the protagonists of *Platoon* and *Born on the Fourth of July* undergo is to subvert his memory. However, it's also to stretch ourselves, to imagine possibilities beyond our own ideologically conditioned identities. This may well be why Nixon, the most willfully unmade, and remade, of self-made men, seems such an essential icon. Oliver Stone has shown that the way to approach this male product of Atomic Age fear is to atomize him. And why not? We're still living with the fallout.

P.S.: W.

It seems too easy to see *W.* (2008), Oliver Stone's second biography of a Republican president, only through the keenly focused lens of the Stone "father complex." To do so would be to cast Stone a bit too true to auteurist type. Shot in forty-six days with a script by Stanley Weiser (who wrote *Wall Street,* another plot about a son in the shadow of a disapproving father), *W.* was released three months before the end of George W. Bush's presidential term and three weeks before the 2008 election. It is fair to say that the film never establishes a tone. However, *W.* is in the investigative mode. "Who is George W. Bush?" is its question, and that may be enough to accommodate empathetic drama, satire, anthropological observation, and tragedy (the nation's), all at once.

Although the film was made too much on the fly to accommodate the dense "vertical editing" and "inside-outside" point of view of *Nixon,* Stone tries for a modified version. From key meetings and events of the run-up to and aftermath of the Iraq War—from January 2002 to April 2004—the film cuts to the story of Bush's past, from his student days at Yale to his decision to run for president. The flashbacks begin in the primal ooze, as it were, as young George W. stands in a steel tub being doused with gin at a Delta Kappa hazing at Yale, where it is not clear whether he passes the ritual because he knows how to play the initiation game or because he is a "legacy," "going back to my great, great grandfather" (one of whom may well have cued him into the ritual; this guy had *every* advantage, the film seems to say).

The flashbacks end with two vignettes. On the morning of W.'s inauguration as governor of Texas in 1995, his father (James Cromwell), now a defeated ex-president, gives him the cufflinks that his father, Senator Prescott Bush, had given to him. W., trying to get dressed, struggles with his pants the whole time; he never gets to appear dignified around his father. The other shows Bush in 1999 stating that he "has heard the call" to run for president in 2000. Significantly, he makes this announcement to a clergyman, Earle Hudd (Stacy Keach), "a composite character based on a number of Bush's evangelical minister friends, among them, James Robison" (Wyles 62). Stone portrays Bush's strong Christian faith as informing his entire presidency. At the end of the film's opening scene, a meeting of President George W. Bush and his national security team in the Oval Office, the president leads the group in silent prayer. In the meeting, held to debate whether to include language naming Iraq, Iran, and North Korea as the "Axis of Evil" in the 2002 State of the Union address, several of the advisors appear reluctant, not to rattle sabres but to find themselves part of a prayer group.

As usual, Stone's selection of events makes clear his priorities—his agenda. There is no 2000 campaign; no "compassionate conservatism"; no Florida recount; no 9/11, although that event is of course the pretext for all the administration's national security policies that follow. Moreover, there is no Abu Ghraib; no 2004 Swift Boating; no Hurricane Katrina; no Terri Schiavo. There is no Harriet Miers, no Valerie Plame, no Alberto Gonzales. The potentials for those later disasters, errors in judgment, and exercises in misplaced loyalty are all clearly planted by the character of Bush as Stone presents it, not unsympathetically. Stone, however, is focused on the character traits that led the nation into the invasion of Iraq in March 2003.

Bush, an alcoholic ne'er-do-well, successfully swears off alcohol and becomes a born-again Christian at the age of forty in 1986, a time that coincides with the start of then–Vice President Bush's campaign for president in 1988, which W.'s father asks him to help run. Bush's religion does not stop him from proposing to his father the infamous "Willie Horton ad," which so openly appealed to the basest instincts of white voters that the campaign ran it through Roger Ailes's political action committee external to the campaign (a ruse that fooled no one). "Poppy" Bush congratulates his son on his ingenuity and "Willie Horton" becomes the catalyst for bringing father and "black sheep" son closer together. Obviously, this passage is befuddling. Are we to take it as satire through irony, or as the appalling axiom of the Bush "family business" that politics, as opposed to other sides of life, is a low calling where "anything goes"? George Sr. got himself into "deep doo doo" in 1992 when he told a reporter matter-of-factly that he would "do whatever it takes" to get reelected and when he referred to running for office as "getting into campaign mode," as if asking the people for their votes were somehow beneath him. By contrast, George Jr., who, as the film has it, seemed constantly out to "show" his father by doing the opposite of what "Poppy" would do, ran his entire presidency in "campaign mode." The neocons Dick Cheney and Donald Rumsfeld became willing bedfellows of Karl Rove, the electoral "architect."

By weaving past and present together almost invisibly, Stone shows what a fake-folksy patrician Bush is, masking his Ivy League–permanent government connections with a Texas accent and manner, which paradoxically to him are genuine. The Bush story is not one that resonates with American myths; Nixon would consider W. a Franklin, except that the younger Bush would never see himself that way. When he decides to run for Texas governor in 1994 after his father's defeat by Bill Clinton, W. meets with the biopic's conventional family opposition; George Sr. and Barbara want their favored son, Jeb, to make his successful run for governor of Florida first, and the story threatens to turn into *East of Eden* (with Jeb an offscreen presence except for one brief scene). As it happened, both Bushes ran in 1994, against incumbents. While George W. defeated Ann Richards, Jeb lost to Lawton Chiles. Jeb Bush was elected Florida's governor four years later.

George W. is a strong believer in destiny. According to Stephen Mansfield's book *The Faith of George W. Bush,* Bush told his friend James Robison, in words that Stone and Weiser put into the mouth of the film's Bush, "I believe God wants me to run for president . . . I can't explain it, but . . . Something is going to happen, and, at that time, my country is going to need me" (qtd. in Wyles 62). Stone's most estimable achievement may be that we don't automatically laugh at such lines. Bush believes this, we sense (Josh Brolin's convincing performance helps), and the consequences have been, alas, enormous.

Bush's faith and his unshakable conviction that he is doing God's will, wrapped up with his "father complex," make him easy prey for the Machiavellian Rove (Toby Jones), the war-loving Cheney (Richard Dreyfuss), and the irrepressible Rumsfeld (Scott Glenn), whom the film portrays as the definitive loose cannon. Dreyfuss's Cheney gives the film's most truthful speech in every sense when he performs in front of an interactive map of the Middle East and makes it clear that war in Iraq is about oil. More than that, however, it is about consolidating American Empire. There is no exit strategy from Iraq, Cheney asserts, because there'll be "no exit." At this point, Bush springs from his seat, rubs his head, and exclaims, "Wow, Vice, big thoughts!" He then adds that "average Joe Voter" doesn't want to hear about oil or empire. "Joe Voter" responds to things like "Axis of Evil" and "9/11" and "weapons of mass destruction."

Bush is advocating rhetoric that is downright mendacious, but he's also practicing the family business, making the political pitch—whatever it takes. Stone leaves it to the viewer whether Bush is actually being devious or if he is projecting himself onto "Joe Voter"; does W. himself prefer not to go beyond the level of simplicities? Is he deceptive or is he dumb? Is he General Jack D. Ripper (as Stone suggests in one extreme low-angle shot borrowed from *Dr. Strangelove* [1964]), or is he Chauncey Gardiner, the simpleton onto whom others project political greatness in *Being There* (1979)? "You've got the touch, Mr. President," Cheney flatters him, "not me." Cheney, Rumsfeld, and then–National Security Advisor Condoleezza Rice (Thandie Newton) believe the intelligence they want to believe, while Secretary of State Colin Powell (Jeffrey Wright), though the voice of reason and reality, gives in like a good soldier (as the cliché goes) and obeys. Two days after this film opened on 17 October 2008, Powell, who left office after Bush's first term, went on *Meet the Press,* endorsed Barack Obama for president, and renounced the current tactics of his Republican Party. Thus it appears that by means of this biopic, it is not Bush who is vindicated but Powell.

Even more troubling is a scene where Bush tells his war council, "Americans don't like seeing dead boys in caskets, military funerals either." Moments like these make it harder to buy that Bush has been manipulated by the true believers, especially Cheney. The vice president appears to slip under Bush's nose a military order, which Bush signs, by which, according to *Washington Post* journalists Barton Gellman and Jo Becker, "foreign terrorism suspects held by the United States were stripped of access to any court—civilian or military, domestic or foreign. They could be confined indefinitely without charges and would be tried, if at all, in closed 'military commissions'" (qtd. in Wyles 16). It is clear that Bush knows what he is doing and is not a tool of Cheney and Rumsfeld and the Beast (which need not speak its name in this film), but rather an instrument of God. The film has Bush make to Rice the famous remark he had made to Bob Woodward when the reporter asked if Bush ever went to his father for advice on the war: "There is a higher father I appeal to" (Woodward 421). Rice, who is portrayed as little more than a "yes-woman," answers "Amen."

One surmises that Stone wanted to go on the record in the last year of Bush's presidency, sensing perhaps that a George W. Bush biopic after his term in office would be about as viable as one on Herbert Hoover after 1932. Stone depicts Bush almost as if he's making an Alexander-Karaszewski "biopic about someone who doesn't deserve one," an accidental president, or a Frank Capra or Preston Sturges comedy about a nobody who has greatness thrust upon him. Of course, Bush was none of these things; however, even more than *Nixon, W.* asks its spectator to consider the psychological makeup and personal motives of the people Americans elect to run the national government. Stone, the cinematic poet of the Vietnam War, presents the story of Bush and Iraq with the attitude that history plays out the first time as tragedy and the second time as farce. Whether Bush knowingly presented false intelligence as justification for the war or whether he "bought in," as Woodward puts it and as Stone stages it, doesn't matter. It's chilling either way.

In the film's coda, Bush is stunned and demoralized when David Kay, head of the Iraq Study Group, which CIA director George Tenet had charged with finding WMDs after the invasion, has to report that none were found, and that apparently there never were any. In this, Stone gives Bush the benefit of the doubt, allowing him the dramatic recognition that he led the nation into war under false pretenses, unbeknownst to him. While Cheney without blinking goes to work on a different rationale for the war, Bush fumbles into the primetime news conference on 14 April 2004, in which he unforgettably couldn't think of a single mistake he had made since September 11. I heard this performance (the actual one) while driving and I thought Bush sounded arrogant. Stone, in an article published before the film's release, seemed to have the same impression. "'Ever notice how impatient Bush is at press conferences, like, 'What right do you have to ask me a question?'" (Breznican 2D). However, when he enacts this scene dramatically, Stone handles Bush the way he did Nixon. He projects the public perception of the president, if not as a tragic figure, then as a failed, pathetic one. Josh Brolin's highly engaging performance, as a man constantly frustrated and angered by his father's disapproval and by his own failures, supports either reading.

In a dream sequence late in the film, George Sr., in a lighted up Oval Office devoid of all décor except for a portrait of John Quincy Adams, beats up his son on the presidential seal carpet, shouting, "You've wrecked it— the Bush name," not that Poppy's record was much to be proud of. This is George Jr.'s own fear and perhaps the spectator's cathartic pleasure, but, again, to believe that W. would actually think this way is to give him the benefit of the doubt. Early in W. Bush Sr. says that when he was captain of the Yale baseball team, he could field but he couldn't hit. The team played the University of California in the very first College World Series in 1947, but lost three games to none ("Bush Sr."). In the final scene of the film W. is watching a Yale baseball game on television. Yale leads 3–0 when, in a device Stone has used before in the film, W. fantasizes that he himself is in the outfield of an empty stadium, diving for the ball with his glove extended. Suddenly, the ball disappears. This is how Stone ends a story that not only has no ending in mid-2008 when he made the film, but whose historical perspective is a long way from being reached. "I think Bush is going to be accountable to history in a big way," Stone told an interviewer. "His policies are going to be still paying off 20 years from now. He's not gone, baby" (Breznican 2D). When Bush himself was asked about how he would look in history, he answered, in a line the film quotes, "History? We won't know. We'll all be dead" (Woodward 443).

As for *W.*, there is no clearer example of the concept that biopics are not history. They are attempts of individual artists to understand public people through drama. This movie has some second-rate elements, notably the musical score, which uses old recordings of songs such as "Yellow Rose of Texas," "What a Wonderful World," and "Robin Hood" for cheap ironic effect. *W.* is much less polished than most of the films I discuss in this book, including *Nixon*. But the lack of careful organization may make the questioning, exploratory purpose of the film easier to see and to appreciate. Stone seems loath to act too sure of himself in his depiction of the forty-third president. His caution may have resulted in a picture of an uncertain chief executive, when in actuality Bush's excess of self-certainty seems at the root of many of his failures. Nonetheless, Stone asserts his prerogative not to make a statement for the ages, but to pose questions that come out of the moment. The film may well prove its value, however, as a filmmaker's parting impressions from George W. Bush's last year as president. Imagine if we had such films from the final year of other presidencies. This seemingly minor film may mark as innovative a move for the biopic, and even as valuable a public service, as anything Stone could have done.

6

Thirty Two Short Films About Glenn Gould

Ghost Picture

In theory, the structure is taken from the *Goldberg Variations,* but that's really just a gimmick; outside the number, there is no similarity. In fact, Girard's technique has more to do with *Citizen Kane* or *A Coffin for Dimitrios* or Lawrence Durrell—trying to capture a subject by presenting a variety of partial glimpses or reflections.

> —ANDY KLEIN, *L.A. READER,* 14 APRIL 1994

Gould is in the black between the films. There you can find the ghost picture of Gould, much more than inside the film.

> —FRANÇOIS GIRARD

The protagonist of a 1993 biopic made by some of his fellow Canadians, Glenn Gould (1932–1982) is in many ways the perfect subject for a sympathetic postmodern biography. Gould was a prodigious pianist who had mastered all of Bach's *Well-Tempered Clavier* by the time he was ten and maintained a professional concert career before he was out of high school. He emerged, as if by magic, from a stable though ordinary middle-class upbringing in the then-quiescent town of Toronto. Gould burst onto the international music scene in 1956 with his first release for Columbia Records, a recording of the then-rarely heard Bach *Goldberg Variations* that unexpectedly became CBS's best-selling classical album to that time and has never been out of print; even the mature Gould's 1981 re-recording of the *Variations* didn't replace it. He impressed practically all who heard him by the technique, delicacy, and emotional intensity of his playing, as well as by the uncompromising nature of a repertoire that favored the baroque and the modern and eschewed for the most part the Romantic works that were and still are the mainstays of most piano soloists. At the same time, Gould emerged before a delighted press as an eccentric's eccentric; floppy-haired and unkempt, he sang and hummed his way through his performances, waving like a conductor whenever he had a free hand. He bundled up in scarf, gloves, and overcoat during the heat of summer and carried a brief-case full of medications to ward off every ailment, real or imagined. He would play only while seated on a chair, made for him by his father, which had the legs sawed off by four inches, making the seat only fourteen inches from the floor and giving the pianist the appearance of practically lying on the keyboard as he played (Bazzana 109).

Gould chafed, if not rebelled, against the tradition of the concert per-former who appears in white tie and tails and is hailed as an artist while living a laborious if luxurious life on the road. Gould attacked the cosmetic fineries first, making his entrances dressed in a business suit and tie rather than in a tux. His delicate constitution and undenied hypochondria earned him notoriety as an avoider of germs and canceller of concerts. Eventually, in a well-considered and scrupulously philosophized decision, one he docu-mented in many of the numerous magazine think pieces he wrote and inter-views he gave, Gould, at the age of thirty-one, walked away from the concert stage, never to return. What followed his last concert, in Los Angeles on 10 April 1964, and continued until his death from a stroke on 4 October 1982, was a successful career played out entirely through mass communica-tions media, on records, radio, and television.

Gould thought that the phonograph record, which decentered the per-former and put the listener in control over the conditions of listening, cre-ated the correct "artist-to-public relationship" for the late twentieth century; many would call this a properly postmodern attitude. Gould's post-concert-career recordings, unlike the albums of most classical artists, were not just the programs of current concerts and recitals laid down on wax. Rather, they featured performances specifically conceived as recordings. Given Gould's unorthodox approach to works in the standard repertoire (he hated Mozart, for example), this could be good or bad. The controversy stirred up by his interpretations brought them attention, in the form of split reviews—Gould was a love-him or hate-him type of performer—and in spirited album sales that more than made up financially for the pianist's absence from the touring circuit. Furthermore, Gould became in Canada, where he now lived, a fixture of radio and television. On the networks of the Canadian Broadcasting Corporation (CBC), Gould was a frequently seen television performer, familiar not only as a classical pianist but (again for good or ill) something of a sketch comedian, creating a small and bizarre menagerie of characters including the effete and senile conductor Sir Nigel Twitt-Thornwaite and the actor Myron Chianti (a parody of Marlon Brando, to whom Gould was sometimes compared early in his career, as a charismatic young 1950s "rebel").

However, it was radio where, besides on his recordings, Gould did his most distinctive work. For CBC Radio, Gould became producer, director, writer, interviewer, emcee, editor, sound engineer, and mixer. He created a series of documentaries, some of which could be more properly called radio essays or even aural montages, on topics ranging from the Canadian North (the famed 1967 broadcast "The Idea of North"); Newfoundland ("The Latecomers" [1968]); and the Mennonites ("The Quiet of the Land" [1977]). These formed a "Solitude Trilogy," the ideas of which had an obvious influence on *Thirty Two Short Films About Glenn Gould*. Other radio "mood-pieces" included one on the pop singer Petula Clark ("In Search of Petula Clark" [1968]), and "Portraits for Radio" on Leopold Stokowski (1971) and Pablo Casals (1974) (Bazzana 306).

Gould never married; his sexuality, like many aspects of his life, is misted in ambiguity. Like other artists who disconnected themselves from the customary celebrity circuitry—Stanley Kubrick comes to mind—Gould acquired an undeserved reputation as an enigmatic recluse, perhaps half-mad. A sympathetic 2004 biography by Kevin Bazzana, a Canadian music historian whose UC-Berkeley doctoral thesis was on Gould, noted "that the image of Gould as a misanthropic, paranoid hermit, perhaps autistic or mentally ill, is remarkably widespread" (316). A 1997 Gould biography by Peter Ostwald, published after the death of the author, who claimed to have been a personal friend of the subject as well as his psychiatrist for a number of years, speculated that Gould was a victim of Asperger's Syndrome (42). Asperger's is a strain of high-functioning autism; its symptoms include "deficiency in social skills, obsessive rituals and routines, unusual sensitivity to sensory stimuli, and (sometimes) extraordinary gifts in a particular area" (Bazzana 5). People with Asperger's are unable to feel empathy and to recognize conversational cues, such as boredom or offense, in interactions with others. Other symptoms, such as exceptional facility with numbers, are also frequently seen. It is difficult and perhaps unfair to ascribe to Gould an illness that was not officially recognized until 1995. However, since the publication of Ostwald's book, mentions of Gould have become standard in descriptions of Asperger's, along with those of other artists, including, ironically, Béla Bartók, a composer whose work Gould denounced to anyone who would listen (Bazzana 100; Friedrich 141). The possibility that Gould had the disorder has become part of what Bazzana reports as the bustling "posthumous life" that his memory now enjoys, but Asperger's has also perhaps become too easy a way of "explaining" the pianist's peculiarities.

Explanation is an area where *Thirty Two Short Films About Glenn Gould* falls decidedly short. Made in Canada in 1993, the film, directed by François Girard and written by Girard and Don McKellar, may qualify as less of a conventional biopic than any other film I'm considering in this book. However, Bazzana criticizes it for "elevating rather than humanizing" its subject, an objection frequently voiced about the biopic itself (7). Indeed, the Gould I've described above qualifies, I'd say, as a classic biopic subject—the possessor of an astonishing, unique talent of seemingly mystical origins; a personality that besides being kooky, quirky, and odd is independent-minded and rebellious; the bearer of a legacy destined to transcend all physicality, including national origin, earthly circumstances, and even the piano itself.

Perhaps most important, this bizarre personality came from, lived in, and indeed seems intrinsic to Canada, a country sometimes regarded as bland by the rest of the world. The film is unquestionably a nationalist production, befitting a subject whom one of the film's producers called "a great Canadian hero." Here a Quebeçois director collaborates with an English-Canadian co-writer to tell the story of an Anglophone public figure. (In one of the film's wryest segments, the well-elaborated interview questions of an earnest French-speaking academic are hilariously mistranslated by an incompetent English interpreter.) This cultural collaboration was rewarded with Genies, the Canadian equivalents of Oscars, for Best Picture and Director. In an article entitled "32 Thoughts about 32 Short Films," Douglas Coupland writes that "Canada is a cold country; its relatively sparse humanity is separated by vast distances. . . . Much of the Canadian identity seems to stem from having to define empirically the essence of self inside a sparse landscape." Coupland continues, "The movie features a few shots of Gould brooding his way across a frozen lake, which do, only briefly, make one pine for a fast-forward button. But isn't that what the Canadian winter is all about?" (2:1).

The film begins with a shot reminiscent of Sherif Ali's emergence from deep desert space in *Lawrence of Arabia*. Here in an expanse of frozen tundra—a northern desert—a tiny figure walks nonchalantly out of the vanishing point, nearing closer to us as we hear ever louder the opening aria from the 1956 recording of the *Goldberg Variations*. Glenn Gould approaches us, as if returning across the distances of death and time to join us mortals once again, and in his favored, barren meeting place, a locale that somehow matches the austere beauty of his playing; call it chilly warmth. Appropriately, references to otherworldliness are often made with respect to Gould. Elizabeth Fox, a CBC producer, likened the Gould home of Glenn's youth to E. B. White's book *Stuart Little,* "about these people who have a mouse as a child. And he's dressed up as a human being, but he goes up and down drains and all the rest. Well, when you were at the Goulds' house, you'd think, these people have produced something that is not of them. He's dressed *somewhat* like a human being, and he plays the piano, but it was—they were constantly in awe" (Friedrich 23–24). Similarly, Gould's father wrote about a phone call he received after a recital Glenn gave when he was fifteen. The caller said that her son told her, "'Mom, you've been telling me that there was such a thing as a hereafter and a life eternal. I never really believed it until I heard Glenn Gould play tonight'" (Bazzana 12).

For whatever national unity the production unit may express, *Thirty Two Short Films About Glenn Gould* achieves all sorts of aesthetic disunity. Eschewing narrative continuity, the film presents itself, like the Bach fugues and variations on which Gould largely built his career, as a collection of variations on a theme. (Thirty-two is also the number of piano sonatas that Ludwig van Beethoven wrote; the *Goldberg Variations*, Gould's signature performance piece, number 30, not 32.) The "32 films" are made in various formats. Some are unified scenes with Gould played by an actor, Colm Feore, who is a veteran of the Stratford, Ontario, Shakespeare Festival, an event that Gould himself helped institute in the 1950s and early 1960s. Some are briskly compressed montage narratives, such as "The Tip," which portrays Gould's propensity for playing the stock market. Some have the actor playing Gould in voiceover, as we see a conventionally photographed scene, such as an account of his childhood. Others are unconventional, such as "Pills," in which close-up after close-up of prescription drugs taken by

Gould is shown as he disinterestedly describes them in voiceover, or "CD 318," which is about Gould's favorite Steinway piano (even though it was replaced, toward the end of his life, by a Japanese import, a Yamaha). Some are documentary interviews with actual people who knew Gould, some famous, like Yehudi Menuhin, some not, like his piano tuner and his housecleaner. Some of the pieces enact Gould's writings in some way. "Gould Meets Gould," for instance, was written as a magazine article. Here it's performed. And some are not even directed by François Girard, such as "Gould Meets McLaren," a piece, reminiscent of some of Disney's *Fantasia,* originally entitled "Spheres," made in 1969 by Canada's best-known animator, Norman McLaren. The film's one major nod to biography tradition is that it stays within the chronology of its subject's life.

In most ways, however, *Thirty Two Short Films* fits the disconnected contours of postmodernism. A postmodern biopic would present the subject as a series of performances or roles, on which continuity, coherence, or meaning cannot be imposed. A postmodern biography would call attention to its own operations, as a series of cues and influences from its culture. A postmodern biography would problematize its own ability to re-create the life of its subject; it might also speak in a variety of styles and formats, again denying unity to the overall work. It may present its life in fragments, defying final conclusion or coherence. It would be without apparent point or agenda, although one might be pieced together out of the various patches and fragments. A postmodern biopic would not insist upon its own reality by banishing images of the actual subject in order to press as its reality the images of the actors playing the actual personages. A postmodern biography might mix drama and documentary, fictional and actual forms. While it does all this, Girard's film also reaches back to high modernism, particularly to Brechtian form, *presenting* its subject and *showing* events of his life, rather than *embodying* him and *representing* scenes.

More fundamentally, the term postmodern biopic, at least where it applies to famous subjects, may be redundant. As we've seen, the biopic usually concerns a subject who in some way brought modernity to society. Almost any subject worth making a biopic about, famous or not, produced something new and unique. That new and unique thing is now in the past or at least lives now in the present as something that is by definition no longer new. The subject, likewise, is familiar, already seen. "Why try to describe it," writes John Frow. "It's been written already. . . . Postmodern writing comes late, the postmodern sunset is another sunset, an event within a series, never an originating moment but mass-produced as much by the cosmological system as by the system of writing" (13). What we might call the "postmodern shrug," the acknowledgment that there's nothing new under the sun (or in it either) is knowledge that the biopic must fight. Gould's awareness that he was the latest in a system of virtuoso pianists caused him to opt out of what he saw as an exhausted system that kept on requiring tuxedoed "geniuses" to come and sit on interchangeable benches at interchangeable keyboards, banging out the standard repertoire. If he were to be mass-produced, it would be on his terms.

Unlike the classical record buyer who probably looks first for a record of, say, Beethoven's Seventh and thinks secondarily about considerations such as performer, label, etc., the person who wanted Bach on piano had probably been introduced to it by Gould. The consumer bought Glenn Gould's albums not because they would sound like other pianists' but because they probably wouldn't. To this extent, Gould exercised a modernist mastery over the elements of his art. On the other hand, what Gould offered was not the authenticity promised by the "live" concert performer, but a simulacrum. There is a paradox here. When Gould said that what he disliked about live performing was "the non-take-twoness" of it (Johnston), he seemed to be desiring the mastery that moved, say, a Hollywood director to work in the studio rather than shoot on location. And yet, as one of the journalists depicted in "Questions with No Answers" demands to know, why then does Gould allow the sound of his squeaky chair or his own singing to go out on the record as part of the finished product? Was this Gould's signature, his way of undercutting the system of mass production that he had chosen over the system of mass production he could not abide? In any event, unlike the concertgoer who bought a ticket to hear Gould in a set place and time, the record buyer bought Gould's absence, a disk that stands in for Gould, a dispersal of his talent to the far corners. In this, Gould foreswore the possibility of a modernist art and gave himself over to postmodernity, which for him did not constitute giving himself over at all.

In a similar way, while a biopic subject is re-created by an actor, even the public figure known repeatedly through the media can be said to be a copy of itself; the question of what or who is the original is itself the mystique that makes the biopic necessary and appealing. Thus a "postmodern biopic" would present the subject and the form as simulacra, copies with no originals. The film presents so many "Glenn Goulds" as to make the idea of an original personality by that name almost more elusive than he would have been if the film had not been made. Yet if Gould does not remain in the viewer's consciousness as a vivid personality, at least he is a vivid idea, a vibrant shadow.

If Gould is to be found in the black leader between the short films, as Girard suggests, then this is a film that finds in Gould the essence of a postmodern performer. In performance, classical music, like film in some significant ways, is a form that skipped a modernist period. Except for the discovery by the fifties auteur critics of personal authorship within the classical style, "Modernist Hollywood" is a contradiction in terms, an entity that cannot be located, until the so-called "Silver Age" of 1967–1976, decades after the modernist periods of literature and art had passed. Similarly, "modernist classical performance" (itself an oxymoron) really did not exist; the concert hall, the formal attire, the bows, and the reverential atmosphere were conventions of the eighteenth and nineteenth centuries rigorously adhered to in the twentieth. The concerts of the twentieth and twenty-first centuries are modern only to the extent that they take place in city centers made reachable by modern means of transportation; the formality, which itself started to wear away in the last quarter of the twentieth century, becomes a mark of upward mobility and/or the democratic availability to the many forms that were originally intended for the privileged few. The music of the moderns, from Stravinsky, Ives, and Hindemith to Gershwin, Berg, Bartók, and Schoenberg, was performed in the idiom of the high Romantics and Victorians. Gould, at least for himself, yanked classical music from the European-style concert hall and installed it in living rooms and car radios. In so doing, he made himself into a purchasable commodity without having to be present at the moment of consumption. The scene in which Gould, in a hotel room in Hamburg, cancels a concert, then proceeds to watch a cleaning woman as she listens to one of his new records as it plays on a phonograph, expresses perfectly Gould's postmodern gesture, the dispersal of the moment and the site of performance to the four winds of multitudinous consumption and, he assumes, appreciation.

The makers of *Thirty Two Short Films* deserve credit for not only understanding Gould's aspirations as a performer, but for finding a style that matches them. Looking at literary theorist Ihab Hassan's "synoptic chart" of the turn from modernism to postmodernism, which I excerpt below, we can recognize not only Gould's approach to performance but especially the difference between the classical biopic and Girard's approach and style (if not his ultimate aim).

MODERNISM	POSTMODERNISM
Form (conjunctive, closed)	Antiform (disjunctive, open)
Purpose	Play
Design	Chance
Mastery/Logos	Exhaustion/Silence
Creation/Totalization	Decreation/Deconstruction
Presence	Absence
Centering	Dispersal
Genre/Boundary	Text/Intertext
Metaphor	Metonymy
Selection	Combination
Root/Depth	Rhisome/Surface
Narrative/*Grande Histoire*	Anti-narrative/*Petite Histoire*
Master Code	Idiolect
Origin/Cause	Difference–*Différence*/Trace
Determinacy	Indeterminacy
Transcendence	Immanence

(Qtd. in Frow 16–17)

More than just set out to make a postmodernist biography, writes the historian Laura Mason, Girard's film "is able to appropriate Gouldian technique so effectively because the heart of the film lies in its engagement with Gould's philosophy of art" (337). This philosophy involves, Gould wrote, "the gradual, life-long construction of a state of wonder and serenity" (246). For Mason, "Girard's film brings Gould's philosophy to life in two ways: by illustrating the director's and others' engagement with Gould's work, and by becoming a new invitation to the introspection that Gould celebrated" (337). Mason's analysis, which works hard to relate Gould's ideas about performance, recording, and the ideal of the role of the listener, does not consider Gould himself. Conversely, those who have studied Gould's work most closely, such as Kevin Bazzana, who has spent the greater part of his life as a scholar researching the artist, don't have much use for the film. Bazzana dismisses the film's style as "trying too hard to make an artistic movie" (while seeming to consider the last term oxymoronic). While Gould's aspirations themselves can be thought of as contributions to musical, technological, and media postmodernism, Girard's film gathers all the pieces of Gould's life and career, leaving it to the spectator what those elements should mean, at least for the most part.

Thirty Two Short Films presents its subject as untouched and untouchable by reality in several ways. Gould appears to us across a great distance, his reemergence is as that of a ghost, and his interactions are at one remove at least. He is separate from the sound he produces. Many of the films are indeed *about* him rather than directly *of* him—interviews of actual people who knew him, letters he wrote or personal ads he dictated without sending, segments that represent him by means of metonymy, as in the film "Pills" in which Gould *is* the medicine he takes, or "Diary of One Day" in which he is signified by his X-ray. Gould is literally the film's structuring absence; in exact opposition to the biopic whose subject is in nearly every scene, Glenn Gould as played by Colm Feore is present in exactly half the films, and is heard as a disembodied voice in three others.

What is more, although the spectator of this film is immersed in an environment of constant Glenn Gould music, the playing does not seem to issue from him. Gould, as played by Feore, never touches a piano; he scarcely even goes near one. The director and actor refuse to unify sound and image by having the actor pretend to play the piano. Girard's explanation for this is simplicity itself: "You don't ask an actor to play like Glenn Gould" (Schultz 11). Girard told an interviewer that he knew there would come "a moment where you have to get your actor to give a great performance and play like Glenn Gould at the same time. Have you seen those old TV pictures? He's so intense. You try to reproduce that, you're dead" (Johnston). This in itself doesn't satisfy, because drama is verisimilitude. Biopic history is full of just such transformations as the ones Girard rules out: James Stewart learning to play the trombone like Glenn Miller at least well enough to mimic him; Robert De Niro and Will Smith training with Jake LaMotta and Muhammad Ali, respectively, in order to box like they did; Jamie Foxx, a trained pianist, auditioning for Ray Charles in order to win the title role in *Ray*. Indeed, the latter is an example of a film that might not have been made had an improbable combination of musical and acting talent not happened along. Yet however much a biopic refers to its genre, as a number of reviewers argued that *Ray* does, films in the Hollywood tradition do demand embodiment. While I don't mean to argue that *Thirty Two Short Films* can discard the formula just because it's an independently made Canadian film, I do think it stands as an exception that proves the rule. It can also be said to have found a different way to do what the "elevating" biopic has always done.

If readers of the biographies by Ostwald, Bazzana, or Otto Friedrich tried to imagine Gould's story as a biopic, they would find a life that resists drama

18. "Practice." *Thirty Two Short Films About Glenn Gould* (François Girard, Rhombus Media, 1993) depicts the "mystical transcendence" the pianist (Colm Feore) tried to achieve, without ever showing his hands touching the keys of a piano. Digital frame enlargement.

at almost every turn. Here was a solitary life for the most part. The only conflict—that between the world's expectations that a brilliant pianist like Gould would give concerts and Gould's desire not to—gets resolved pretty early in the narrative. Gould's story is that of an extraordinary man whose time on this earth made a difference to a great many people. One could even say that Gould would make the perfect biopic protagonist because narrative films hate to stop and display the hard work of solitary creation, and with Gould there is not much behind-the-scenes labor to show. To the astonishment of many who knew him, Gould rarely practiced and sometimes went days without playing, and yet could sit down (after his fashion) and play immaculately. And immaculate is a good word, for Gould abhorred the heavy pedaling and rich tonal color that is the hallmark of virtuoso Romantic playing, which is to say of most pianism of the twentieth century (itself a carryover from nineteenth-century playing). For years Gould dogged Steinway & Sons, the makers of most concert pianos, to find him an instrument with a cleaner sound, a light touch, low reverberation; Gould's impossible demand was for a twentieth-century piano that would be as close as possible to a keyboard instrument of Bach's day, which is to say a harpsichord.

Just as Gould's exacting, uncompromising personality makes him, in his very lack of conventionality, a conventional subject for a biopic, his struggles with the expectations of the musical establishment and the high excitement he inspired in the early years of his career might have made for a dramatic biopic. The near-comic glee of New York journalists and CBS publicists over Gould's initial recording sessions at the 30th Street studio in June 1955 (Friedrich 50–51; Bazzana 151–153) or the near-rapture over his tour of the Soviet Union in May 1957—the first by a North American pianist in the post-Stalin era—could be turned into wonderful film sequences. He was often in conflict with Steinway, suing the company in 1961 over a too-hearty slap on the back from one of its tuners. He tangled with promoters, hotels, and with the tight little world of music critics over the increasing unconventionality of his performances. An exceptionally slow rendition of the First Brahms Concerto with the New York Philharmonic in April 1962, one less "heroic and competitive," in Gould's words, than the norm, prompted conductor Leonard Bernstein to speak before the performance and offer a disclaimer to the audience about what they were going to hear. Gould's interpretation drew withering, even insulting reviews from the New York press, probably quickening his determination to get off the concert merry-go-round (Friedrich 101–107; Ostwald 210–213; Bazzana 204–208). Most of all, Gould was in conflict with himself over the realities of touring.

All this might make for scintillating drama (and would probably hoist a film to the big-budget, epic level with which biopics are often identified). But just about all of this "conflict" takes place in the first thirty-one years of Gould's life, before he ended the concert phase of it. Most Gould admirers believe that it was his last eighteen and a half years that made him unique and sealed his legacy. Just compare, for instance, the amount of space that Gould's biographers spend on the pre-concert retirement and post-retirement phases. Ostwald, an American writing after the release of Girard's film, whose book seems consumed by the traumatic aspects of Gould (his subtitle is *The Ecstasy and Tragedy of Genius*), takes 213 pages for the period leading up to the retirement, and only 117 pages for the years from 1964 to 1982. By contrast, in Friedrich, the only biography that predated the film, the emphasis is reversed; Gould retires on page 109 of a 330-page book. Bazzana, whose work aspires to be definitive and who spends much space trying to clear up the legends and clichés surrounding the artist's life, achieves more of a balance. However, he, like Friedrich, devotes more pages, 268 versus 230, to Gould's post-concert life.

For all his exceptional talent, however, and for all his eccentricity, Gould led a fairly routine and uneventful life. When he quit concertizing, Gould simply left one routine and took up another. Moreover, while Gould's pre-1964 life contains conflict, his post-retirement years really do not, and to play up the conflicted period at the expense of the years of serenity would produce a grossly distorted view. Simply put, Glenn Gould led the quiet everyday life of a genius. The serenity is precisely what Girard's film sets out to examine. Thus Gould gives his final concert in film number 9, twenty-seven minutes into Girard's ninety-four-minute movie.

Thirty Two Short Films is unusual, if not to say perverse, in that it is so non-interactive. Gould interacts with his fellow humans in few of the episodes; in those in which he does, his exchanges are usually cursory affairs with people he does not know, such as waitresses or chambermaids; are conducted through plates of glass or over the phone; or are presented as surreal affairs, such as a scene ("Solitude") in which Gould appears to conduct a press conference at the edge of the same frozen tundra with which the film opens and closes (without his breath showing; the "tundra" is evidently on a soundstage). Moreover, the segment is different from the beginning and ending in that Gould's discussion places it at a fairly definite point in time; in terms of the radio programs he says he has finished, is editing, and is planning, the segment takes place around 1973. Thus spatial abstraction and temporal realism cancel each other out. The film's most profound interaction (in "Gould Meets Gould") is between the pianist and himself. Otherwise there are phone calls to and from stockbrokers (the film's second most meaningful interaction), orders to uncomprehending telegraph operators (communications on top of communications), love letters and personal ads never sent (actual ones found and catalogued at the Glenn Gould Archive in the Canadian National Museum in Ottawa), and questions asked by hapless and flustered interviewers to replies of silence ("Questions with No Answers").

The film employs a more direct form of audience address than would a conventional dramatic film. Very often the film plays with point of view. The short film "Solitude" puts the spectator in the position of an unseen interviewer who questions Gould about his work for radio and his interest in the north. It is followed by "Questions with No Answers," in which the spectator is put in the position of Gould, making us know what it felt like to be him as he was peppered by annoying, often inane questions (even though biographies do not report Gould having been as irritated by questions from the public as the filmmakers imagine he was).

In these ways, *Thirty Two Short Films* at times resembles a one-man-show biography, a form made popular in the 1960s by *Mark Twain Tonight,* which starred Hal Holbrook, and continued in later years with James Whitmore as

19. "Solitude." An odd title for an interview with an unseen questioner taking place in the North Canadian tundra, or at least a studio mockup of same. Digital frame enlargement.

Harry Truman, Pat Carroll as Gertrude Stein, Henry Fonda as Clarence Darrow, and many others. A non-piano-playing Glenn Gould probably wouldn't sustain interest over the length of an evening's show onstage. Most of Feore's scenes, on the other hand, played with no one else on the screen with him, often showing him conducting or seeming to channel the music, not to play it, convey the theatrical, stylized sense of the one-man show. However, putting Glenn Gould, even a fictionalized Gould, onstage where he hated to be would constitute an abuse of his memory. Alone in the television or film studio, where he could achieve his favored "one to zero" relationship with the viewer, Gould would have felt at home.

Overall the absence of human interaction divests the film of drama; in the film's lack of interaction between musician and instrument, the customary illusion of reality refuses to adhere. This is a film, then, in which the elements do not unite. We fail to appreciate the abundance of music because of the paucity of the imagery. The producer of the sound in life, Gould, does not produce the musical sounds of the film. The real Glenn Gould speaks to us, insistently and distinctly, in his playing. Unlike his visual image in the film, Gould's aural representation is ubiquitous, heard in twenty-seven of the short films, twenty-eight if one counts "The Idea of North" as one of Gould's sound productions. Because the film spectator is so conditioned to regard "background music" as dramatic punctuation, we may not appreciate how constant Gould's presence is here. Because we are primed to take film sound for granted as the synchronized partner of the visual image, we not know how really how to comprehend the playing on the sound track as a kind of autonomous communication, independent of the film but somehow parallel to it.

The lack of interaction, of all sorts, means that the film is not dramatic, as it never purports to be. It is made up of various parts—film genres, styles— that do not cohere. And yet the film does stick to at least one convention of the biopic. It takes place in sequence and builds to the death of a man, part of whose fascination is that he died young. Such conventions as the downward trajectory, the subject's running down of his health through drugs and overwork, his premonitory apprehensions about death, and the mounting concerns of friends and family are here, they're nodded to, the spectator is aware of them, but they are *shown* to the audience; the spectator doesn't live them. Moreover, the film contains the stuff of enactment, of embodiment, but in little bits. As in other biopics, the mise-en-scène is composed out of the artifacts of Gould's environment. The old Chickering piano from the Gould home that the pianist kept with him his whole life is shown as the instrument on which Glenn's mother taught her little son to play. The abandoned Presbyterian church that Columbia Records converted into its 30th Street studio in Manhattan is represented without introduction; it is just given as an environment, as is even the Petula Clark song playing in the truck stop where Gould stops for breakfast and to take in the local color. But these bits of authenticity are just that; they are dropped into the film in intervals. They are like quotations from Glenn Gould's life, not as the continuous, unbroken diegesis in which the film lives.

Often the documentary form, the film's use of which is as intermittent and fragmentary as the other forms it partakes of, contributes to the sense of disconnection. Four individuals are each interviewed in one of the thirty-two films. Significantly, all these people were on good terms with Gould at the time of his death; some of those who weren't, such as Walter Homburger, his business manager from 1948 to 1968, are lumped into the interview montage, "Crossed Paths." The four given special treatment are professional collaborators Bruno Monsaingeon, a filmmaker and musician; Yehudi Menuhin; Gould's cousin Jessie Greig; and Margaret Pacsu, a radio producer and personality. These interviews, along with those of a number of Gould's acquaintances in "Crossed Paths," do some of the work of characterization. Monsaingeon's interview is short film 4, even though the Parisian filmmaker and violinist, who made a series of TV programs with Gould and became one of his most valued collaborators, did not meet him until 1972.

Monsaingeon describes getting to know the famous pianist, who showed up for their first meeting, in mid-July, covered from head to foot in winter clothing; he extols Gould's inexhaustible intensity as a conversationalist. Homburger describes the Soviet tour as well as Gould's decision to perform wearing a business suit.

Many if not most of the interviews touch on Gould's eccentricities. Megan Smith, who cleaned Gould's apartment, describes a room littered with bottles of ketchup and boxes of arrowroot cookies. Others talk about being on the receiving end of his one-sided telephone conversations. Keeping up the theme of characterization-by-metonymy, Verne Endquist, his longtime piano tuner, discusses the nostalgic thrill of tuning CD 318 for the Gould exhibit at the Ottawa Conservatory; he also praises Gould for trivial things, such as requesting tunings with two or three months' notice. Endquist, whose relationship with Gould is the subject of a 2008 book by Katie Hafner, makes these pronouncements with pomp and sentimentality, as if he'd watched a bunch of triumphant final scenes of classical biopics just before facing the cameras.

The montage of impressions displayed in "Crossed Paths" leaves a strange taste. While the sequence seems to present itself as a tribute, its parts add up to a disconnected gaggle of cross-eyed sketches. Each of the interviews was filmed in the same room, on the same chair, in front of a silk-curtained bay window. One can envision all the participants lined up off camera, like children on picture day at grade school, each waiting for his or her turn. For the parallel music, Girard picks the grandiloquent Adagio from the Sonata in B Minor by Richard Strauss, a work with a feeling of valedictory, although a dissonant piece by one of Gould's modernist favorites, Schoenberg or Hindemith, say, would seem more fitting (if obvious). Even the segment's title is strange. Yes, these are people who "crossed paths" with Gould and, thus, perhaps with each other. However, other senses of "crossed," as in "cross to bear," "crossed wires," "crossed up," or "crossed off" (as a few of these people actually were by Gould, a tendency that the film does not explicitly go into), give the title more than first meets the ear. Again, what is conveyed is a sense of missed connections, of furtive or indirect contact.

The four extended interviews (which actually run no more than a few minutes each) appear to take place in the interviewees' own surroundings, without music, thus emphasizing the "reality" of it all. Besides Monsaingeon's expository interview, the other three wonder over Gould's choices and habits. Menuhin calls the pianist's decision to work only in studios, never facing audiences, "too artificial for me"; Pacsu professes her bafflement at his drug-taking; and Jessie Greig, whose interview is placed just before Gould's death, remembers conversations a week before her cousin's fatal stroke in which he imagined a funeral to which no one came.

Greig asserts that their conversations had never before touched on death and were usually "light banter." However, her segment is preceded—and contradicted—by "Forty-nine." In this sequence, which takes place a year before Gould's death, he is parked at a pay phone telling Jessie about Arnold Schoenberg's death at the age of seventy-six, a number whose digits add up to thirteen. "I can't help it. I'm forty-nine tomorrow [forty-nine is a number whose digits amount to thirteen; what's more, the composer died on the thirteenth of the month] and Schoenberg's still talking to me" (and to us, coursing in his halting way through Gould's fingertips, as we hear the "Leicht zart" from *Six Little Pieces for Piano*). Hardly "light banter" this, and so we wonder some more about the accuracy of the varying accounts we hear, and about the overall account of Gould that the film affords us.

Girard's film ends in a coda that, conventionally for a film so unconventional, refers back to its beginning. Gould strolls through his tundra, back to the distances from which he came, just after we've been shown footage, unaccompanied by explanation, of the launching of the U.S. spaceship *Voyager*. As Gould walks, a voiceover by Colm Feore explains that *Voyagers* I and II took off in 1977, exited our solar system in 1987 and 1989, and are headed for the end of our galaxy. The spacecrafts were loaded with evidence "of the existence of an intelligent creature living on a planet called Earth," evidence that included a short Bach Prelude performed by Glenn Gould.

This ending does several things, typical of the film's treatment of Gould and not atypical of biopic convention. It keeps with the vague but persistent visitor-from-another-planet theme of much of the discourse on Gould. Shown in sequence just after Gould's death, it trusts the viewer to place the artist's earthly demise as occurring about five years after the ships took off and five years before they left our system, as if his soul met them somewhere en route. It is an honor, a tribute (like, say, Louis Pasteur being honored by the French medical establishment at the end of his biopic), but also an assertion. Gould's music is meant to outlast not just him, but also our planet and our species! Girard told an interviewer that in Gould's later years, "he disintegrated as a human being, but, at some point, there was a transformation. At the end of his life, Gould was pure music. . . . The whole journey of Glenn Gould was to leave more and more the dimension of his own ego.

His dream was to disappear and let the music take off. And this is what happened" (Schultz 14).

Thus, while Girard's tribute promises transcendence, it does so in a cosmic, metaphysical way, a way that cannot be proved. Will anyone ever hear this representation of the genius of which the human race was capable? Will future beings have any means of listening to this artifact? This is a highly contingent transcendence; it can blow away, like the snows of the frozen wasteland into which Gould disappears. And yet the film has more faith in this than in the many more earthbound and tangible tributes that already in 1993 it could have pointed to. As a tribute, the inclusion of Gould on *Voyager* is rather ambiguous; at the same time, it's eternal. What better way to summarize an artist and a life that dwell just outside our grasp? On the other hand, Girard's brand of postmodernism solves a problem of how to celebrate a great person without falling back on generic convention. But what about films that choose as their great men men who weren't so great?

7

Ed Wood

The Biopic of Someone Undeserving

It was untraditional: a biography of someone who didn't deserve a biography. A Z-grade hack notable for his failures. But we identified with his passion. Our challenge was to take an Anti–Great Man, someone who screwed up everything and angered everyone around him—and create empathy.

—Scott Alexander and Larry Karaszewski on *Ed Wood*

In his review of *Ed Wood* (1994), the first of a series of biopics on unlikely or disreputable subjects written by Scott Alexander and Larry Karaszewski, Jonathan Rosenbaum reminds his readers that the Grade-Z *Plan 9 from Outer Space* (made in 1956, released in 1959) never played in Los Angeles. However, the biopic of Edward D. Wood, directed by Tim Burton, climaxes with a gala premiere of Wood's movie, which became a cult classic in the 1980s, at the Pantages Theater, the famous Hollywood Boulevard movie palace where Academy Awards ceremonies were held for several years in the 1950s. Rosenbaum reports Burton as saying "with no irony whatsoever" that "he preferred to show us this event as Wood would have imagined it." The film's ending and Burton's comments push Rosenbaum to make the standard It-didn't-really-happen-that-way type of protest, evincing the historical literalism that detractors of the biopic have always wielded against it. Rosenbaum caps his disapproval by marveling "that Burton can claim with such confidence that he knows the inside of Ed Wood's head" ("Allusion Profusion" 175). Therefore, for this critic, biopics are capable only of documenting;

they cannot create or imagine like other forms of dramatic film. From this viewpoint, the biopic subject is strictly an actual person, portrayal of whom is limited to what can be known from the objective record. With a bias like this laid bare by a leading American film critic, it is little wonder that misunderstandings of the genre have run as wide and deep as they have.

The biopic subject, on the other hand, has to become a character if writers, directors, actors, cinematographers, designers, and costumers are to create dramatic cinema out of the stuff of actuality. *Ed Wood*'s triumphant ending is indeed an ironic reimagining of the event, not only as Wood would have desired it in his wildest dreams, but also as the classical biopic might have portrayed it—which just might amount to the same thing. The final touches made to "the worst film ever made," as it embarks on its way to ignominious immortality, play out as the biopic hero's inevitable and triumphant march into myth. *Ed Wood* presents a comic paradox: a biopic hero who has everything—enthusiasm, optimism, compassion in his befriending of the faded star Bela Lugosi (who by the 1950s was a penniless morphine addict), loyalty to his friends and co-workers, tenacity, and something he wanted to say in films. He has everything, that is, except talent. Thus the biopic dovetails with the self-reflexive Hollywood-on-Hollywood genre, and more successfully than numerous films from *Man of a Thousand Faces* (about Lon Chaney, 1957) to *Gable and Lombard* (1976). In casting an affectionate look at a passionate failure, the film parodies the biopic genre, not by imitating the genre in order to ridicule it, but by inverting the values on which it is based. For this reason, Alexander and Karaszewski have referred to the kind of films they write as the "anti–Great Man biopic," or "biopics of people who don't deserve one" (*Man on the Moon* vii).

Alexander and Karaszewski's other films in this vein include *Man on the Moon* (Milos Forman, 1999), about the singular comic/performance artist/wrestler Andy Kaufman, who died at thirty-five of a rare lung cancer; *Auto Focus* (Paul Schrader, 2002), which they produced to their specifications but did not write, about the actor Bob Crane, best known from TV's *Hogan's Heroes;* and *The People vs. Larry Flynt* (Milos Forman, 1996), one project on which I feel they mistook offensiveness for oddity. Each of the duo's protagonists, however, push hard at the limits of taste and acceptability, some willfully (Flynt, Kaufman), some with seemingly no consciousness that they are flouting convention (Wood, Crane).

Starting with *Ed Wood* in 1994, biopics of people who don't deserve them tend to be about artists working in low forms—off-the-radar exploitation movies (*Ed Wood*), weird comedy (Andy Kaufman in *Man on the Moon*), stars of sitcoms in questionable taste (Bob Crane in *Auto Focus*), stupid game shows (Chuck Barris in *Confessions of a Dangerous Mind* [2002], written by Charlie Kaufman, directed by George Clooney), cranky underground comics (Harvey Pekar in *American Splendor* [2003], directed by Shari Springer Berman and Robert Pulcini, from a script they wrote with Pekar). Farther yet down the food chain are films, curios really, about marginal figures who settle like fleas on the coats of famous personalities—*The Assassination of Richard Nixon* (2004), about Samuel Bicke (Sean Penn), an unhappy soul who died trying to shoot the president in 1973; *Color Me Kubrick* (Brian Cook, 2005), about a man named Alan Conway (John Malkovich) who mooched his way around London in the early 1990s by claiming to be Stanley Kubrick; and *I Shot Andy Warhol* (Mary Harron, 1996), on Valerie Solanas, a Warhol hanger-on who did indeed pop the pop artist in 1968. Two subjects whom Alexander and Karaszewski thought about for films but rejected, Bettie Page and Superman TV actor George Reeves, eventually wound up in biopics made by others, *The Notorious Bettie Page* (Mary Harron, 2006) and *Hollywoodland* (Allen Coulter, 2006).

These denizens of the lower depths, these bottom feeders, are elevated by becoming the subjects of major films, many of which have been well received. Moreover, it helps the subgenre's lust for quirkiness, as well as the larger genre's quest for drama, when the subject has a defining complication on the side. These include bondage model Page's ardent devotion to Jesus Christ, middlebrow sitcom actor Crane's sex-on-video addiction, and game show producer Barris's claim of living a double life as an undercover CIA operative. Many of the biopics from this period of people who do seem to deserve them, for example, *Nixon,* often question and explore the motives of their biographical subjects and the value of what they leave behind. Thus, *Ed Wood* takes a far more sanguine view of its subject than, say, *The Aviator* (Martin Scorsese, 2004) or *The Life and Death of Peter Sellers* (Stephen Hopkins, 2004). Indeed, two films made a generation apart about little figures on the periphery of the life of Howard Hughes—*Melvin and Howard* (Jonathan Demme, 1980), about Melvin Dummar, a would-be claimant of the batty billionaire's will shortly after the great aviator's death in 1976, and *The Hoax* (Lasse Hallstrom, 2007), about Clifford Irving, the huckster who nearly got away with getting a major press to publish a bogus autobiography of Hughes in 1972—regard their scruffy subjects with more empathy than Scorsese's full-blown Hughes biopic regards the billionaire himself.

Some of the "insignificant" figures, moreover, share ruinous traits with the "significant" ones; for instance, Crane's unexamined life leads to a tawdry tragedy that somehow echoes the unexamined male culture that brings down Richard Nixon. Indeed, the moment when the biopic begins to question its own values and ideologies comes in *Lawrence of Arabia* when the priest asks if Lawrence deserves a place in Saint Paul's. Biopics, which conventionally dramatize the validation of figures by majority culture, assert, by the very fact of their having been made, the "deserving" virtues of their subjects. Even the warts-and-all films of the fifties assume that the subject, faults and all, is somebody worthy of having his or her story told.

Accordingly, Tony Williams, in a post to the SCREEN-L listserv, criticized *Ed Wood* for "its problematic blurring of the relevant boundaries between Wood and [Orson] Welles." The director of the "worst" movie has a chance meeting with the maker of the "best" picture in a scene whose humor lies in Wood's identification of himself with his directorial hero. The scene can also be taken as a wry acknowledgment of Welles's shabby treatment by a business that has often failed to appreciate its own artistic riches. Moreover, as Rudolph Grey reports in his 1992 book, *A Nightmare of Ecstasy,* Wood idolized Welles, a poignant if not pathetic reminder that a director known for ineptitude, and largely devoid of talent, loved movies and dreamed of greatness, and on the flip side, that a director appreciated for his genius, then and now, often was shoved to the margins of the movie business as much as a figure like Wood. Williams, however, sees *Ed Wood* as "an ideal conservative postmodernist film, a drooling homage by a director who sees little difference between . . . a director who undoubtedly made bad films and one with talent who was ruined by the system in Hollywood" (SCREEN-L messages #24 and #33, Week 1, March 1996).

Williams might seem to be overreacting, if only Alexander and Karaszewski had not said essentially the same thing. "By the end of the film," Alexander says in the commentary track of the 2004 DVD, "you should be totally rooting for Ed not to have his exterior shots match. Tim [Burton] compared Ed's work a bit to folk art. It's primitivism. Nobody is saying it's necessarily good, but isn't it just as valid as somebody with the talent of Van Gogh?" Alexander and Karaszewski are being deliberately audacious here. On the other hand, once the image forms of Kirk Douglas playing Ed Wood, desperately pleading with prospective backers to finance his movies, not only is the target of parody obvious, but it also becomes clear that a way to revise the biopic genre is to rethink its criteria. In late consumer society, celebrity and consumerism have confused cultural values in terms of what figures the culture mythologizes and why. For instance, Oliver Stone, in justification of *W.,* said, "[George W.] Bush may turn out to be the worst president in history . . . but that doesn't mean he isn't a great story" (Svetkey 25). Meanwhile, the culture does still seem to reserve the mantle of greatness for a few indisputably superior athletes (Tiger Woods, Michael Phelps, Le Bron James) and performers (Luciano Pavarotti, Daniel Day-Lewis).

The idea that biopics must be about people deemed important in high or middle culture appears ripe for postmodernist revision, with not all postmodernist biopics being about the likes of Glenn Gould. Biopics are about transcendence, and in the world of media cults, losers in life can sometimes be household names in death, just as Rembrandt and Van Gogh died penniless (as did Ed Wood). Now some people argue, perhaps not entirely seriously, that Ed Wood's films were not really the world's worst ever. "Unfairly tarred as the 'worst director of all time,'" wrote Andrew Hultkrans, Wood made films that "float to the top of the slag heap of '50s horror/sci-fi/ exploitation because of their unmistakable passion and honest idiot glee" (Hultkrans). "The world is a big place," concedes Kathi Maio. "But even if you assume the worst films of this planet come from the U.S., Mr. Wood's strange little B-movies can't even come close to being the worst, because, in their own inept and bizarre way, they come from the heart" (74). Ed Wood is in a camp pantheon of directors, despite, or because of, the fact that he would not even qualify in the "first circle" of Andrew Sarris's criteria for auteurs. Sarris, who does not mention Wood in *The American Cinema,* his 1968 book cataloging scores of directors by their value as auteurs, decreed that "if a director has no technical competence, no elementary flair for the cinema, he is automatically cast out from the pantheon of directors. A great director has to be at least a good director" ("Notes" 562). Critics like Tony Williams, however, who hold with the quaint idea that the study of art and culture should keep to a set of standards, find in films like *Ed Wood* a postmodernist threat. Scott Alexander's use of the supremely relative term "valid," which derives from the Latin *valere,* meaning to be strong or to have worth, becomes a sliding scale on which anything can qualify and nothing can necessarily be *valued* over anything else, making a biopic subject analogous to Kane's warehouse, where "Everything goes—the junk as well as the art." *Plan 9 from Outer Space* didn't premiere at the Pantages any more than Edward D. Wood Jr. and Orson Welles met one another (as they do in the film). Indeed, writes William D. Routt, Wood's movies were "made-for-TV, direct-to-video, before such forms were invented." However, Alexander and Karaszewski demonstrate that failure has its own myths too; the disastrous Edsel is much better remembered than any successful car sold in the single year of its production, 1958.

In framing *Ed Wood* as if it were a studio-era idol of production story, with a hero who is driven to convince an out-of-touch world of his dream, Alexander and Karaszewski make an absurdist film in which insanity takes the place of what is commonsense reality in most biopics. Ed remains on one hand the serenely confident biopic man of vision and on the other a Travis Bickle whose weapon is his incompetence. "What's great with these anti–great man biopics," said Scott Alexander, "is they're full of conflict. And as a screenwriter, you want to have as much conflict with your lead character as possible. The conflict is that these characters are wrong. They're wrong throughout the entire movie, but they've got a burning will to prove themselves right. And so they're in conflict with all the rational people in society. Who's going to pick a fight with Gandhi? He's right." Larry Karaszewski replies, "It isn't so much that, because there were lots of people who picked fights with Gandhi." "All right, bad example," concludes Alexander (*Ed Wood* DVD).

This exchange underlines just what a reversal the anti–Great Man biopic is; it reverses the classical idol-of-production biopic in the first films in the cycle, and the idol-of-consumption warts-and-all variant in some of the later films, such as *Auto Focus* and *American Splendor*. Mike Clark of *USA Today* dryly marveled as he included *Ed Wood* on his ten-best list for 1994, "When it comes to Hollywood biopics, it figures that Charlie Chaplin would get a stinker [1992's *Chaplin*, directed by Richard Attenborough] and Edward D. Wood would get a great one" (05D).

At times, the film's Ed Wood blurts out assertions such as "Filmmaking is not about the tiny details. It's about the big picture," which are just as wrong as they can be, as Burton's own direction demonstrates in the very movie we are watching. As we've seen, the idol of production must prove his idea correct over a solid wall of opposition from the establishment. When Ed shows *Glen or Glenda* to an executive at Warner Bros., who laughs through the screening, figuring he's been the victim of a practical joke, the film reverses, say, the plot in which the medical establishment scoffs at Louis Pasteur and forbids him from publicizing his views. After the executive says that Ed's movie was the worst he'd ever seen, Ed replies, "Well, my next one will be better," like an upbeat salesman. Ed is not only wrong, but as Burton explains, "there's such a delusional quality to [making movies]. You understand that when you make a film because you get very passionate about it, very excited about it. And you think you're making the best movie in the world; you get into that weird energy. And you can see how [Wood] deluded himself in his writings and his letters and all. And I find that quite beautiful and realistic somehow" (*Ed Wood* DVD).

Along similar lines, Alexander and Karaszewski find a subversive truth in the ideological structure of the Hollywood biopic, to which their subjects are perversely suited. "All these guys are just great Americana stories," said Alexander. "As Americans, we are a country of people who can pull ourselves up by our bootstraps. You can start off poor and become rich, and whatever you want to make of your life, you can do it in this place. That's what these movies are about. They're just about guys who did it in really freaky ways" (*Ed Wood* DVD).

Accordingly, Fredric Jameson in his much-cited definitions of parody and pastiche asserted that pastiche operates in the absence of "that still latent feeling that there exists something *normal* compared to which what is being parodied is rather comic" (114). A rejoinder to Jameson long has been that parody does reduce norms themselves to ridicule, especially gender roles and other manifestations of social hierarchies. In regard to the biopic, there certainly is "something *normal* compared to which what is being parodied is rather comic," and that is the common-sense conception of accuracy, factuality, and reality, which is behind most critical objections to the biopic. It takes a parody like *Ed Wood* to point out a certain embrace of the biopic genre as a mythological form, one whose enduring conventions stand out when the meanings are turned around. In the postmodern age art passes through an ironic period before it can be taken seriously again. It has to disclaim its seriousness, paradoxically, before it can reclaim it. A title card in the epilogue of *Ed Wood* tells us, "Ed was voted 'Worst Director of All Time,' bringing him worldwide acclaim and a new generation of fans." Certainly it is an askew value system that refers to "worst director" status as "acclaim" and names those who call him that "fans." But in the mixed-up world of celebrity and popular memory, criminals and failures can become immortals and people who were successful in their day often are forgotten over time.

Wood and *Plan 9 from Outer Space* were unearthed in the 1980 book

The Golden Turkey Awards by Michael and Harry Medved, and they are still talked about today. Meanwhile, even most movie buffs probably can't name the director of the 1956 Academy Award winner for Best Picture, *Around the World in 80 Days*. (It was Michael Anderson.) Michael Medved, later known as a right-wing film reviewer, would probably worry, along with the nervous academic critics of postmodernism, about "the assault on standards" (the title of a later Medved book) represented by Wood and his merry band of cross-dressers, giant Swedish wrestlers, would-be transsexuals, and phony clairvoyants. Linda Hutcheon, in an article written four years before *Ed Wood* was made, defines "postmodern parodic film" as showing "both a respectful awareness of cultural continuity and a need to adapt to changing formal demands and social conditions through an ironic challenging of the authority of that same continuity." Inside the commercial system, filmmakers can realize "the possibilities of the positive oppositional and contestatory nature of parody" (25).

How is Ed like the classical biopic subject? He is unflappable and determined. Ed has a vision he tries to make others understand. He has something he wants to say to the world. Wood is rebuffed, discouraged. Ed is unique; through his charisma and drive, he gets others to see his uniqueness. Ed overcomes obstacles and achieves his vision. He has a sidekick/mentor (Bela Lugosi), finds a life partner (Kathy), has an eleventh-hour inspiration (meeting Orson Welles), tells off the unbelievers (the Baptists who finance the initially titled "Graverobbers from Outer Space"!), and leaves to the world his transcendent creation.

To understand the full extent of the parodic reversal, compare the final scenes of *The Story of Louis Pasteur* and *Ed Wood*. Both feature the subjects arriving at a gathering at which they are the guests of honor. Each arrives with his wife or girlfriend on his arm; Pasteur expects pillory and finds himself applauded by some of the people who were once his opponents-turned-converts in the course of the film. Wood draws wild applause as the director of *Plan 9*. Both scenes have obvious elements of dramatic invention. For instance, Pasteur, who in the film arrives at the French Academy of Medicine having been told his theories will be attacked by the evening's speaker, surely received an invitation to the ceremony and knew in advance he would be honored.

The Pantages premiere of *Plan 9* would never have occurred except in Ed Wood's wildest dreams—and that is where it does take place. In granting him the vindication scene that most Great Man films throughout the

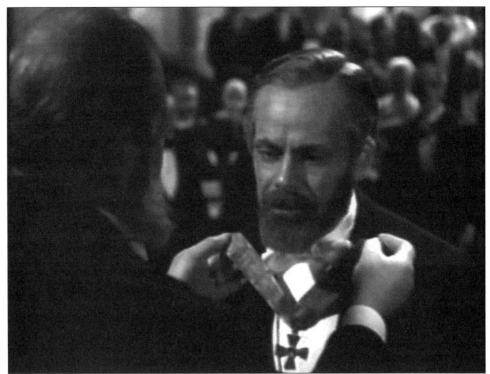

20. The classic vindication of the biopic subject in *The Story of Louis Pasteur* (William Dieterle, Warner Bros., 1936): Pasteur (Paul Muni) is honored by the French Academy of Medicine, with many of his former adversaries in attendance. Digital frame enlargement.

21. The fantasy vindication of Ed Wood (Johnny Depp) at the *Plan 9 from Outer Space* premiere that never happened (Tim Burton, Touchstone Pictures, 1994). Pasteur's vindication probably didn't happen the way the film dramatizes it either. Digital frame enlargement.

decades have afforded their subjects, unless the point of the film is to cast doubt on their accomplishments, *Ed Wood* plays as if the conventions of the genre really should work for the "worst director." The audience that applauds as he enters, the master of ceremonies, an important figure in the subject's life (in this case Criswell, the cheerfully sham clairvoyant), the gracious acceptance speech—all of these notes are sounded. But there are just as many cues that this entire scene is a dream sequence, as surreal as anything Luis Buñuel ever filmed. The opening shot of a searchlight, with the theater marquee reflected in it, suggests that we are through the looking glass. There is an absence of crowds, of cars lined up, of police lines, of an entry canopy, of any of the usual trappings of a premiere. Ed and Kathy pull up in their jalopy and are able to park right in front, as rain begins to pour. A full house has somehow materialized and is seated inside. The crowd is still there as the couple leaves for the desert to get married, like any number of outlaw couples in westerns from *Stagecoach* onward. This sequence is only slightly less stylized a Happy Ending than the sunny conclusion that Robert Altman much more sardonically stapled onto *The Player* (1992).

To Rosenbaum, the idea that the scene is imaginary "would never occur to most viewers" ("Allusion" 175). It might occur to them, however, if the biopic stopped being thought of as strictly factual, and became more commonly understood as a genre with recognizable conventions and the license to invent creatively, while adhering to the fundamental truth of the actuality. If I can casually refer to Ed and Kathy's romantic getaway to a Valhalla "over the border"—a syntactic application of conventions of the western to the semantics of the biopic—why shouldn't one refer to the vindication ending of biopics, to name one of numerous conventions, in just as recognizable a sense? Or does that admit too readily for comfort that there exist generic conventions in narratives based on actuality?

The very fact of *Ed Wood*'s production as a class-A Hollywood film (albeit in black and white with a budget of $18 million; Burton's previous movie, *Batman Returns* [1992], cost roughly three times that much [Corliss]) eclipses the reality that Ed Wood's life in 1956 and thereafter was very sad. The film's story, which begins soon after Wood's arrival in Hollywood in 1946, ends with his "career peak," the release of *Plan 9 from Outer Space*. Like many biopics, *Ed Wood* finds its story in the most intense, dramatic part of the subject's life; even *Nixon*, which spans a period of about fifty years, omits the final twenty years of the president's life. *Ed Wood*'s "happy ending" recuperates for the 1990s Wood's collection of misfits and losers. When Ed, in close-up, whispers in dazed inspiration as he watches his *magnum opus,* "This is the one. This is the one I'll be remembered for," the irony is delicious because Wood is right, just probably not in the way he imagines. Perhaps no director talks this way about one of his films, and the very statement represents a projection of fan enthusiasm onto the subject himself.

This parody of auteurism may capsulize the Ed Wood cult, a camp concept of greatness that honors passion over accomplishment. Burton could have made a debunking, downward-trajectory film that showed Wood to be a desperate sub–Poverty Row hustler and his friends and co-workers pitiable hangers-on. Such a portrait, however, would probably be no closer to the "facts" than the ironically sunny view created by Burton, which captures the truth of how many people feel about Wood in retrospect. The film romanticizes the friendship of faded star Lugosi and aspiring filmmaker Wood, which is touching on the merits. The movie, furthermore, cannot be said to falsify Wood; he *is* portrayed as an inept filmmaker.

There is a difference between parodying a genre and using parody to expose the ideological limitations of that genre. Ed Wood would never "deserve" a biopic except in a form that is being parodied, in which his triumphs, nonexistent in life, play as surreal. Biopics, and historical films in general, cannot help but be about past events and people as they are remembered and construed in the present. Burton's films, moreover, going back to *Pee Wee's Big Adventure* (1985) and especially *Edward Scissorhands* (1990), his first film with Johnny Depp, vindicate the losers and misfits of the world against the emptiness and fleeting success of the "overdogs." Thus, when Bela Lugosi Jr., in the 1996 documentary *The Haunted World of Ed Wood,* points out that while many directors with successful Hollywood careers are forgotten now, Ed Wood is practically a household name, the vindication of the losers is complete.

A film with fine production values, high-grade acting, and the imprimatur of a corporation, in this case, Disney, whose adult Touchstone subsidiary produced and distributed *Ed Wood,* inhabits a different universe from the tawdry world of an Ed Wood. To linger over Rudolph Grey's book, or to watch *Flying Saucers over Hollywood* (1992, Mark Patrick Carducci), the documentary filmed as an apparent adjunct to it, is to be plunged into a world of poverty, alcoholism, desperation, and failure. If there is a dark underbelly of Hollywood, Edward D. Wood Jr., whose career lasted from 1946, when he was a twenty-two-year-old Marine Corps veteran of World War II, to his death in 1978, embodied it. Gregory Wolcott, who acted in *Plan 9 from Outer*

Space, and had a lengthy Hollywood career in films and television, told Grey, "Ed's films are another category. Three rungs below B movies—dingy, third-rate fringe type films" (77). About Grey's book itself, Scott Alexander said, "It's a collection of conflicting anecdotes. A lot of the people in the book are heavy drinkers and have very clouded memories. The guy who did the book let them all talk and babble about their memories of Ed Wood and none of the stories add up. All of the guys contradict the guy in the chapter before him and the chapter after him" (Simkins). Thus Tim Burton and the screenwriters make cohesion from these contradictory stories. Vampira tells the one about the angry, unruly preview audience (107–109). Kathy Wood provides the story in which Ed drives to the premiere of *Plan 9* during a downpour in a convertible whose top won't go up (84). Ed describes Bela Lugosi's street corner performance of the speech from *Bride of the Monster* (70).

The film integrates these incidents into the narrative, playing them as comic, romantic, and poignant, respectively. The movie grants Lugosi vindication throughout; where Lugosi is concerned, the film plays as an ironic and realistic valedictory. Lugosi is not just a victim of Hollywood; he is given dialogue throughout in which he rues decisions he made, turning down the role of Frankenstein because "it would be degrading for a big star like me," and instead allowing himself to be typecast. Except for *Auto Focus,* which studies Bob Crane's unconscious self-destruction with a coldly objective eye, and *Man on the Moon,* which puts us in the point of view of a bemused audience at an Andy Kaufman performance, the films of this type see their subjects from the protagonists' point of view, which helps account for the movies' upside-down worldview.

The screenwriters point out that Wood's reputation, from the Medveds' book, had been as somebody to make fun of, with Wood himself as much the object of ridicule as his films. Grey's book, on the other hand, portrayed Wood and his companions as pitiable. "What if you treated Ed Wood sympathetically," the writers asked, "because nobody had done this. He was just famous for being terrible" (Simkins). Friends and writing partners since soon after meeting as film students at USC, Alexander and Karaszewski became known professionally for the critically panned but popular comedy *Problem Child* (1990) and its 1991 sequel—the genre of "stupid comedy," for lack of a better term. Burton also related how his own films *Pee Wee's Big Adventure* and *Beetlejuice* (1988) had received "some of the worst reviews I had ever seen" (*Ed Wood* DVD), although they did have their defenders. Thus here were people not from the prestige-film, Oscar-season side of Hollywood filmmaking but—Burton especially—from the commercial end of post-1976 blockbuster Hollywood. Here was the director of *Batman* (1989) and *Batman Returns* making a film that would reconfigure the biopic by celebrating the cinematically pitied and ridiculed. At this point, therefore, the biopic turns from its traditional role as a genre that carries its subject into cultural mythology (as *Thirty Two Short Films,* for all its investigations of Glenn Gould, nonetheless does) or even that psychologically and critically investigates a nevertheless important subject (*Lawrence, Nixon*). It becomes a genre that reverses its own premises by questioning even what sorts of people biopics can be about.

Tim Burton's direction and Johnny Depp's acting both do much to pioneer, as it were, the aesthetic of the anti–Great Man film. Depp plays Ed in a broadly comic style, but with the obsessed, visionary fervor projected by classical biopic stars such as Muni and Ameche; Depp said that his Ed comprised equal parts President Ronald Reagan, "American Top 40" radio host and *Scooby-Doo* voice actor Casey Kasem, and the Tin Man in *The Wizard of Oz* (*Ed Wood* DVD). Furthermore, Burton reportedly whispered, "Andy Hardy, Andy Hardy" to Depp between takes (Maio). The real Ed Wood was an alcoholic throughout his adult life, but the film goes for the absurdism of the boy-next-door—Mickey Rooney as Young Tom Edison making grade-Z schlock as if it's *Citizen Kane.* (The film does hint at Ed's deteriorating future—and liver—showing him at a bar drinking cheap whiskey; in fact, in the film's most delicious joke, at the same cheap bar, he meets Welles, played by Vincent D'Onofrio in another embodied performance.)

Ed is so upbeat his face is usually tilted up. The signature Depp/Wood gesture—a gape-mouthed, awe-struck shake of the head as he gazes at the marvels being performed before his camera—grows out of what the film depicts as Ed's unrequited love of the movies. What should be clear from Depp's long list of influences is that they all come from movies and showbiz. Depp's Ed is another self-made man, an invention of his own mind. How can anyone so determined, aggressive, likeable, and, apparently, so gee-whiz *nice* become immortal as the poster boy for failure? In the most profound of the film's reversals, *Ed Wood* turns Ed's badness into enigmatic transcendence, just as the talent of the classic biopic subject is a mystery, a wonder. The spectator watching *Ray,* for example, is meant to marvel at how much talent and skill could emerge from this blind youngster. The spectator of *Ed Wood* wonders how a man with such passion and drive could turn out such bad pictures, and furthermore how he could seem so perfectly satisfied with them.

22. The ever-hopeful Ed Wood lines up a deal, while Dolores Fuller (Sarah Jessica Parker) watches. Orson Welles appears to be looking on too. Digital frame enlargement.

What the protagonist of what I'll call the Biopic of Someone Undeserving (BOSUD) shares with the subject of what Alexander and Karaszewski might call "*non*-anti-Great Man films" is belief. *Ed Wood* wouldn't work if Ed didn't believe. He is first seen at "Press Night" of his play, *The Casual Company*, at a dingy stage theater in downtown Los Angeles; no press are there, just a driving rain and leaky roof. Ed sees none of the negative; he stands in the wings, excitedly mouthing the emotional dialogue of his play as if he has it all inside him. Indeed, Wood's drama plays better on Depp's face than it does on the stage. Of the three basic types of biopic performance in the post-classical era—fully embodied impersonation, stylized suggestion, and the star performance—Depp's portrayal of Ed Wood is a stylization. Wood himself is not a personality whose face and voice are well known; thus an embodied performance is not necessary or even possible. Wood is a remote figure to us now. As we'll see with female subjects, the matinee-idol good looks of the actual Ed Wood (as shown in Grey's book) by themselves might have made a film about him a suitable vehicle for a conventional leading man (imagine Robert Taylor or Roger Moore as Ed Wood). However, the fact that the subject is Edward D. Wood Jr. merely adds to his incongruities. If the film were made in, say, 2004 instead of 1994, one could see it attracting actors like Brad Pitt and George Clooney, who take every opportunity to efface or mock their glamour-boy appearances.

Depp beat them to it, however, as a male heartthrob who made it his project as an actor to play against his looks. Depp/Wood's lacquered pompadour, his snappy wardrobe, and confident, unflappable demeanor make him an attractive figure. What he does—what he produces—becomes increasingly unattractive. It's who he is who is attractive, and this might be the greatest reversal of all. It goes back to *Citizen Kane*. "It's not enough to say what a man did. You've got to tell us who he was."

Perhaps this is, as critics such as Rosenbaum, J. Hoberman, and William D. Routt charged, putting a happy Disney face on sad, sordid actuality, a positive spin on the hollow motto, "It doesn't matter what I say; it's how I say it." For example, in one scene, after admitting that his televised predictions are "horseshit; I made it up," Criswell lectures Ed that "we're in showbiz. It's all about razzle-dazzle—appearances. If you look good and you talk well, people will swallow anything." Ed's thoughtful look in reaction to Criswell's lines is followed by a cut to a backers' party to raise money for the next movie, where we see that Ed has grown a stylish mustache. It's a small touch, but it shows Ed doing everything he can to put himself over. Filmmaking may not be about the tiny details, but image-making is. Ed actually thinks his movies are good, so he sees nothing wrong with promoting them with all the ballyhoo he thinks they deserve. Alexander and Karaszewski, who initiated the project, then found that Tim Burton was interested, decided to "reward Ed Wood because he tried. Maybe the movies weren't good, but he got them made. He had a lot of friends and he gave them all a purpose, and they had dreams of being put on screen and he put them on screen. And they had a good time" (Simkins). This, therefore, starts to rework the axiom "It doesn't matter *what* I say, but *how* I say it" into "It doesn't matter *what* I say, but *that* I say it." "The movie's getting made," Ed says at one point; "that's all that matters." The irony is that Burton, Alexander, and Karaszewski make a very good movie, one that helps reinvent the entire genre, by rethinking the kind of person the biopic can be about.

Burton and Depp pull off a remarkable bit of alchemy. While Burton is known for creating fanciful worlds, from Gotham City to the suburban wonderland of *Edward Scissorhands* (1990) and the nineteenth-century London of *Sweeney Todd* (2007), *Ed Wood* is set on the nondescript streets of Poverty Row Hollywood and the lower-middle-class tract house neighborhoods of mid-1950s L.A. The underside of Hollywood where *Nightmare of Ecstasy* takes place is as much a state of mind as it is an actual place. It was the refusal of Columbia Pictures to make the film in black and white that caused Burton to move the project to Touchstone, a subsidiary of Disney. By filming in black and white, Burton provides Ed with drab but sun-washed streets

on which to ply his trade. Burton and his cinematographer Stefan Czapsky
work in a realist style in which Ed's blond wigs and angora sweaters seem
as unremarkable to us as they do to him and his fiery paper-plate flying
saucer special effects might almost get by (as *Plan 9*'s almost work, after you
have been dazed by Wood's unbelievable diatribes of passionate, incoherent
dialogue). Color would have been alien to Wood's cheapjack brand of filmmaking. The combination of realism and subjective conviction provides the
BOSUD with a naturalistic underpinning that makes the events seem plausible and gives even a fantasmagoria introduced by Criswell as he emerges
from a coffin the sense of a fantasy world on the cheap, determinedly conjured up amid grimy actuality.

Depp finds the perfect style for a postmodern pastiche of the biopic,
referring to the fervor and conviction of the classical protagonist, playing
in a style that recalls farce, except that *Ed Wood* is not a farce, and none
of the other actors are performing in a farcical style. Meanwhile, Burton
takes the opposite approach, with a restrained, observational naturalism that
set the aesthetic for the subgenre. One sequence that I will analyze twice,
once from the standpoint of Depp's acting and once in terms of the direction, illustrates this point. Eddie and his cast are in their second go-round at
the Brown Derby, where they hold a backers' party to try to scare up money
for their horror movie, after the funds they thought they had the first time
dried up. A standard establishing shot of the outside of the restaurant is followed by a shot of Lugosi in close-up and profile dryly quipping, "Well, here
we go again." Wood's makeshift banner announces the fund-raiser and the
scene of quiet desperation going on behind Bela. In the polished elocution
of Criswell, Ed proudly proclaims, "Bela Lugosi will portray Doctor Eric Vor-
noff," as if announcing the new season of the Royal Shakespeare Company.
One skeptical fat cat, worried about Lugosi's age, motions offscreen and asks,
"What role does Vampira play?" We already know Vampira (Lisa Marie) as
the L.A. television personality who, dressed in Charles Addams-ish garb,
interrupts late-night horror movies with lame wisecracks. Caught off-guard,
Wood asks, "Vampira? Why do you ask?" "She's standing right over there,"
says the would-be donor. A cut to an archway indicating another party room
in the restaurant shows the unmistakable actress with long stringy blonde
hair talking to people in the other party. Wood, temporizing, says, "Well . . .
she plays . . . Excuse me one minute."

At this he darts out of the shot. In the initial long shot of the archway,
Ed scampers toward Vampira. Literally invading her space, he introduces

himself and gives his spiel, offering her a role in his movie, if that would please the backers. As Vampira doesn't understand this strange intruder, Ed explains, "We started shooting but after three days [of a five-day schedule!] we got shut down. Now we're having a backers' party to raise some more money." Vampira, eventually seeing through him, rebuffs Ed, telling him she has "real offers from real studios." Vampira starts to leave to eat dinner, but Ed, realizing she might be his best chance at a meal ticket, isn't giving up. Imploring now, he falls to his knees in the classic position of either a dog begging or a suitor proposing marriage. "Miss Vampira," he says, arms outstretched. "Please." The maître d' calls her; she and her party leave as he remains, kneeling.

Depp plays the scene, as he plays the entire film, in a Brechtian style in which Ed's attitudes, decisions, thought processes, and emotions are *shown,* rather than embodied as a naturalistic performance would do. Depp often telegraphs his actions before he makes them; this makes his performance, visually, an outright pantomime. Earlier in the scene, while thinking about how he will answer the backer's question, he knits his eyebrows and purses his lips (making a mockery of his dashing new mustache). Now arching his eyebrows and raising an index finger, he improvises, "She plays . . ." Shown from behind, with the camera in the place of the backers, Ed runs bow-legged, looking like Oswald the Rabbit, an early Disney cartoon bunny. Reaching Vampira, he gives his customary upbeat pitch. When that meets with incomprehension—"Do you want my autograph," she asks—Ed, brought up short once again, lowers his chin, raises his eyebrows, and, in a surprised tone, replies, "Uh. No," his voice rising on that second syllable. One hallmark of Depp's performance here is that he always makes the surprising choice in terms of timing and vocal variety. As Ed is confronted with a situation, rather than just react, Depp keeps us waiting a few beats to see *how* he will react. Next, after looking all around at the people with her, he leans forward from her point of view, again in advance of his line and in a confidential pose that might signal conspiracy or seduction. Ed lowers his voice and says, "I think my film is perfect for you." "You want me to show it on my TV program," she asks. "Well, I have nothing to do with that. You'll have to call the station manager." At this, he physically turns her around to face him, saying, with his back to us, but without losing his pleasant composure, "No, *no.* I don't want you to show the movie. I want you to be *in* it."

Ed begins to level with Vampira about the straits he is in, concluding desperately, "I thought you might just like to come over and say 'howdy,' to some of the backers," giving a smile and wave of the hand, a ludicrous idea given that waving and saying "howdy" is the last thing it is possible to imagine the morose Vampira doing. Turning her around yet again, Ed resorts to the feeblest of pleas, still with an optimistic smile—a mask that hides a mounting desperation. "One second. Please. There's a really nice dentist from Oxnard." It is the most devastating of put-downs from Vampira—"I don't need to blow some dentist for a part"—that causes Ed first to flail his arms and then finally to sink to one knee, a gesture that Vampira and her party utterly ignore.

Depp's acting in this scene epitomizes his performance throughout the film. Like the subjects of many classical biopics, Ed essentially doesn't change; he is a force that brings change. His sunny, salesman-like determination and refusal to take no for an answer are played for their absurdity, but without overdrawing the character or stretching him into caricature. Alexander and Karaszewski's parody of the Great Man film depends more on Depp than on any other element besides their own writing. The supporting characters, in effect, live the life that Ed has created for them, as in many "straight" biopics. With the exception of George "The Animal" Steele, a wrestler recruited to play Wood's wrestler-actor Tor Johnson, comic actors such as Bill Murray, Sarah Jessica Parker, and Jeffrey Jones play in a style of comic naturalism. They are bookended by Depp's Wood, who lives to convince the world to buy his vision of reality, parodying the classical biopic subject who cannot be satisfied with the world as it is, and by Martin Landau, who plays the only character in the film (besides Welles) who is well known. Thus Landau gives a fully embodied, transformative impersonation. In most of his scenes with Landau, who achieves the kind of transformation that wins Oscars, as his performance did, Wood/Depp recedes into a quieter mode, happy to give pride of place to his hero Bela, just as Depp must have known the film would belong to Landau, a veteran actor and teacher of acting enjoying his career peak.

Burton directs Alexander and Karaszewski's script in a restrained, realistic style that manages to tell the story from Ed Wood's point of view and to depict him as he looks to the rest of Hollywood, often at once. The scene at the Brown Derby, again, is a good example. The scene begins with Lugosi alone, looking weary and uncomfortable, introducing the backers' scene and setting the tone for its grim futility. As he sips a drink and grimaces (cheap liquor, no doubt), Ed's voice is heard on the sound track, as if there's no doubt who dominates this ritual of begging. The scene, however, slips more and more out of Ed's control. There are three basic camera setups in the first half of the scene, all of them mostly static. The first is a group shot with an elderly potential backer in the foreground, over the shoulder (played by Gregory Wolcott, the male lead in *Plan 9 from Outer Space,* an actor with a long Hollywood career who was in the choir of the Baptist Church that bankrolled *Plan 9* and did the film for nothing as a favor to the pastor) (*Ed Wood* DVD). In the middleground is the "lovely ingénue, Loretta King," played by Juliet Landau, daughter of Martin, a nepotistic coup worthy of Wood. Ed/Depp is toward the background, hardly dominant in the shot. When the backer starts to express doubts, Burton cuts to a shot of the threesome from a reverse angle that puts Ed in the foreground on the far right and the backer on the left in back; but as the skeptical moneyman, his questions take the initiative away from Ed and put Ed less in the forefront than on the spot.

It is when Ed dashes to the end of the restaurant where Vampira has been spotted that Ed's position turns visually frantic. The end of the sequence is particularly telling. Ed is on bended knee beseeching Vampira as she walks away, ending Ed's audience with her and, it would seem, the scene. Burton, however, continues to hold the shot with Ed still on his knees. Ed appears too humiliated to get up, but also like an actor playing a big scene, he has worked himself up into such an emotional state that he may not yet be ready to break the moment. A return shot to the backers, in which one says, "I'm getting a bad feeling about this. Let's get out of here," is followed by a long shot covering the actual distance between the backers and the place where Ed has been left, a tiny figure, still kneeling, lowering his arms as if he has finally forced himself to give up. He looks back in the direction of his own party, as another attempt to gather funds to make his movie has ended in abasement and failure. His diminishment in the final shot shows us how small he must feel, but also demonstrates how low he will stoop in his determination to make a picture, as well as what an insignificant figure he appears to anybody outside his small circle of friends.

Burton often reflects Ed Wood's desire to transform reality into magic, leading to scenes that display a double consciousness. In an early scene set at Lugosi's house on Halloween, Bela's disappearance behind a flimsy curtain to shoot up with morphine (Ed doesn't yet know of Bela's addiction and neither, exactly, do we) plays in Czapsky's beautiful black-and-white cinematography as the actor's transformation into his most famous character. Count Dracula emerges from behind the drapes with perfect timing, going to meet some terrified children on trick-or-treat night. Burton recalls both 1950s realism and the look of the early 1930s Universal horror films.

Burton's distanced style set the table for directors such as Milos Forman and Paul Schrader, who customarily work in an objective and dispassionate mode. Where Burton left himself open for accusations of falsifying actuality, in *Man on the Moon* Forman photographs the life of Andy Kaufman whose art was devoted to the confusion of what's real and what's an act. Kaufman's performance art was almost a theater of cruelty, which made him a kindred spirit with Forman, whose work had long flirted with adapting the surrealist playfulness of his Czechoslovakian films, *Lásky jedné plavovlásky* (*Loves of a Blonde,* 1965) and *Horí, má panenko* (*The Fireman's Ball,* 1967), to commercial Hollywood films (*One Flew Over the Cuckoo's Nest* [1975], *Amadeus* [1984]). In *Man on the Moon* Forman's unobtrusive realist style is perfect for the is-it-real-or-is-it-part-of-the-act comedy of Andy Kaufman (Jim Carrey), in which Kaufman's odd mixture of childish behavior (he often made Howdy Doody and children's artifacts from the 1950s, like box phonographs and the theme music from *Lassie,* part of his act) and bullying hostility— the wrestling with women, his on-air disruption of scripted skits—seriously dented his popularity and rendered him a hard act for his manager to book. Forman views Kaufman from the outside. We never know his motivation or what's really in front of us, so that Kaufman even seems to appear, via videotape, at his own funeral. Many who knew him suspected that he must have faked his death; like Elvis, whom Kaufman imitated onstage, he was always expected, by his cultish fans, to show up.

Forman stages the various Kaufman events that Alexander and Karaszewski collected and detailed for their script and photographs them with an outsider's eye. For instance, when George Shapiro (Danny DeVito) goes to a supper club to get his first glimpse of Tony Clifton, Kaufman's confounding alter ego, an untalented and obnoxious would-be lounge singer, Forman films the scene with the camera a fly on the wall. Even the frequent reaction shots to Shapiro are taken from an eight-foot distance. The effect is that Kaufman's bizarre antics are all taking place in actuality (with Carrey doing a more than convincing transformation of a fellow comic) and we are observers left to make up our minds of what we think of him. Even the epilogue, when he (or Tony Clifton) appears to show up at his own memorial tribute at the Comedy Store, is shown as ambiguous reality. Forman concludes nothing for us. Kaufman, said Forman, was loved by comedians "because

every comedian feels he's a failure. And Andy was the first comic who con-
quered this fear of failure, by including failure in his act. So if people either
applauded or booed, it was a success. The failure worked" (Alexander and
Karaszewski *Man* 197).

Like many artists whose parody becomes a form of its own after a while,
Alexander and Karaszewski have gone from being pranksters playing tricks
on tradition to upholders of their own new convention. By the time of *Man
on the Moon*, the pair seems as serious about valorizing their subject as any
other biopic creators, just as Strachey's later biographies lost the satirical
tone of *Eminent Victorians*. In Alexander and Karaszewski's case, some of
this may be due to a difference in subject. It's easier to put over Andy Kaufman as a legitimate avant-garde artist—and do it with a straight face—than
to render Ed Wood an auteur or Larry Flynt a First Amendment crusader.

When Alexander and Karaszewski, as producers, supervise another
screenwriter, Michael Gerbosi of *Auto Focus*—who ends up channeling
them—the new writer produces a portrait that is both funny and horrifying.
Bob Crane is portrayed as a sunny master of upbeat denial, fiddling happily
while his life burns all around him. The filmmakers create the kind of relentless downward trajectory that perhaps the likes of Wood, Flynt, and Crane
actually called for. The reduction of the Great White Man to such cheerfully
decadent bottom dwellers as these seems to ratify the devolution of the idol
of consumption, as Michael Rogin refined Leo Lowenthal's concept. If these
men are the chosen, the figures produced by cultural demand, then more is
being satirized than just the biopic genre. Not surprisingly, the most conservative movie in this cycle was its only real box office hit, Steven Spielberg's
Catch Me If You Can. In the typically Spielbergian resolution of the story
of teenage international forger George Abagnale (Leonardo DiCaprio), the
FBI agent (Tom Hanks) who chases Abagnale for years ultimately becomes
the father figure Spielberg's young protagonists are usually in search of. In
a not so different vein, Ed Wood's slow but early death by alcoholism at age
fifty-four is mentioned in the epilogue but cut from the story. More emphati-
cally, the tragic implications of Larry Flynt's tawdry destiny—the death of his
wife from AIDS, his own life as a paraplegic—are airbrushed away. There is
no ironic triumph (unless one counts Flynt's bizarre vindication at the U.S.
Supreme Court), just a sense of awful but absurd waste.

Bob Crane is the only one of these subjects to die violently. His 1979
murder has never been solved. In *Auto Focus*, as directed by Schrader, Crane
is so spiritually dead by the end of his life that his murder is seen as de-

liverance, albeit one whose significance Crane, always the superficial light comedian, cannot begin to fathom. His post-mortem voiceover ends with the words "Men need to have fun," delivered in the cheerful singsong actor Greg Kinnear maintains throughout. Crane recalls the protagonists of Schrader's sometime collaborator Martin Scorsese, especially Henry Hill in *Goodfellas,* a film that Schrader did not write. These guys are blind to the moral lessons with which their lives are rife. Even Alexander and Karaszewski failed to see any significance at first in the apparently pointless life and death of the *Hogan's Heroes* sitcom star/porno auto-videographer/unsolved murder victim. Their initial advice to Gerbosi about how to write the story of Bob Crane was "Don't do it" (*Auto Focus* DVD). However, Schrader, as he did most famously with Jake LaMotta in the script of *Raging Bull,* can sniff out the spiritual tragedy in any story about human failings, no matter how trivial. The fall of Bob Crane from such grace as he knows coincides with Crane's rise in show business.

Forman tried to pitch Larry Flynt as an outrageously unlikely and inadvertent champion of First Amendment rights, and Schrader directed the kooky, bizarre, and pathetically sordid sex antics of Crane as the stern moral tale of an unconscious, unflappable "normal guy" whose lapse into insanity is apparent to everyone but him. The key to most of the Alexander-Karaszewskian films is a sunny Americanism wrapped up in the weird and the marginal. Andy Kaufman attains the American Dream by challenging the audience with postmodern humor, comedy that really isn't funny; Ed Wood is a World War II veteran who wore women's angora sweaters under his uniform in battle. Bob Crane is a middle-brow early-sixties entertainer who dresses in the casual cardigans made popular on television by Perry Como and Andy Williams, and who reminds his agent that he was supposed to be the next Jack Lemmon.

Mary Harron's *The Notorious Bettie Page,* which I discuss in Book Two, might be seen, more than a dozen years after the BOSUD subgenre began, as an answer to *The People vs. Larry Flynt.* Bettie Page's life is in the absurdist realm of the strange-but-true, believe-it-or-not tale in which apparently level-headed people do off-the-wall things routinely, as if they're selling insurance or painting the Mona Lisa—the Ed Wood common person as weirdo (and back again) syndrome. While the *Flynt* film ignored "the First Amendment debate over pornography" that "has been polarized by the argument that it oppresses women" (Bernstein H36), *The Notorious Bettie Page* sees a side of porn that is expressive and freeing for women. Nina Bernstein in the *New*

York Times called *Larry Flynt* a movie "that likes to have its kitsch and tweak it too" (H36), and the same charge—which might be synonymous with Tony Williams's "conservative postmodernism"—can be applied to all the films in this cycle. The exceptions might be *Auto Focus* (Paul Schrader sees only dark self-delusion in Alexander and Karaszewski's "freaky" heroes) and *The Notorious Bettie Page* (which sees a not unambiguous feminine *jouissance* that if nothing else certainly queers the feminist debate over pornography as it retakes the female image from the male gaze). While Ed Wood cannot see past his delusions, and Bob Crane doesn't recognize that he long since crossed the lines between "fun," obsession, and destructive addiction, Bettie Page in Harron's film can hang up her spiked heels and turn literally to devotion. Thus in a film made by women, Bettie does the sensible thing, if not in life, then at least in myth.

8

Spike Lee's *Malcolm X*

Appropriation or Assimilation?

In rhythm and trajectory [contemporary] bio pics [*sic*] . . . reprised the bio pics of Hollywood's classical era. In Lee's *Malcolm X* . . . the life of the black nationalist ideologue [is] presented in the same cadenced narrative—the progression from humble roots through coming of age, self-knowledge, assumption of the mantle of leadership, death in the cause of the group's redemption, and, finally, admission into the hagiography of leaders who revealed the common humanity of their people—that moviegoers in Hollywood's classical era viewed in *Abraham Lincoln* (1930), *Juarez* (1939), and *Pride of the Marines* (1945).

—THOMAS CRIPPS, *HOLLYWOOD'S HIGH NOON*

The Black community does not need myths; it desperately requires practical solutions to its pressing problems.

—MANNING MARABLE, "MALCOLM X"

Can Hollywood cinema be appropriated? Can a minority filmmaker gain the resources—the genres and production values—of mainstream cinema and use them to tell a story and create an experience from a specifically minority point of view? Is a would-be appropriator bound to be assimilated into the conventions? Or is the assimilation actually part of the appropriation, a bending of the majority, mainstream form to the purposes of a minority?

In other words, can the classical, celebratory biopic be used against itself? Can it mythologize radical, revolutionary minority figures? Perhaps above

all, should it? In African American communities, in particular, appropriation has usually been thought of as a one-way street, with white majority culture appropriating everything from musical forms like gospel music, blues,
and jazz; to narrative and literary tropes like the trickster; to the African
American face and body themselves (blackface minstrelsy). Film may be the
only field in which some black appropriation of the medium itself and of
larger Hollywood and world cinema forms has been noted. Thus Manthia
Diawara has written about "noirs by noirs," the African American cycle of
film noir; black westerns have been acknowledged as an appropriation—
indeed a reappropriation, since the large-scale migration of former slaves
to the Western territories following the Civil War was forgotten once the
myth of the west began to be etched in literature and movies. There have
been very few African American biopics; those that were made prior to Lee's
film were white-controlled exploitation films of either low budget (*The Jackie
Robinson Story* [1950], *The Joe Louis Story* [1953]) or high budget (*Lady Sings
the Blues* [1972]), prompting Thomas Doherty to call the biopic "the motion
picture equivalent of an all-white neighborhood" (37).

Neither Spike Lee's *Malcolm X* (1992) nor any other biopic by a black
filmmaker, American or not, has been recognized as appropriating the
form. Amiri Baraka, Lee's severest critic (which is saying something), found
"much progressive . . . Pro-Black Self-Determination" in a blaxploitation-
era reappropriation of the western, such as the little-known and underrated
Buck and the Preacher (Sidney Poitier, 1972) (32). Meanwhile, the only appropriation associated with *Malcolm X* has been cited by critics who think they
see it stealing off in the other direction. Brian Norman cites Lee's career as
an example of the way "Hollywood siphons off creativity by appropriating
the work of independent filmmakers" (107). Jonathan Rosenbaum declares
that "Malcolm X himself has gone off into some next chapter, now written
by Warner Communications. If Spike Lee, who signs the text, thinks that either he or Malcolm wrote it, he has rocks in his head; radical sound bites or
not, most of the heart and guts of this movie was written by Hollywood studios years before he was born" ("Hollywood Radical" 153). In other words,
both subject and filmmaker have been sold out to the hoary conventions of a
genre and indeed of a general means of production that have been discredited (perhaps by the selfsame critics).

Contrary to my discussions of the deconstruction, fragmentalism, and
parody of the Great (white) Man, I am echoing here a debate that has gone
on in literary criticism since the 1980s: Once minorities at long last gain

notice and thus access to a discourse or art form, the white establishment declares the discourse over and done with and not worth owning, or, in the case of the biopic, never worthwhile at all. Elizabeth Fox-Genovese eloquently wrote,

> The death of the subject and of the author may accurately reflect the perceived crisis of western culture and the bottomless anxieties of its most privileged subjects—the white male authors who had presumed to define it. Those subjects and those authors may, as it were, be dying. But it remains to be demonstrated that their deaths constitute the collective or generic death of the subject and the author. There remain plenty of subjects and authors who, never having had much opportunity to write in their names or the names of their kind, much less in the name of the culture as a whole, are eager to seize the abandoned podium. But the white male cultural elite has not, in fact, abandoned the podium. It has merely insisted that the podium cannot be claimed in the name of any particular personal experience. And it has been busily trying to convince the world that intellectual excellence requires depersonalization and abstraction. The virtuosity, born of centuries of privilege, with which these ghosts of authors make their case, demands that others, who have something else to say, meet the ghosts' standards of pyrotechnics. (162–163)

Thus near the time that other filmmakers were approaching the genre with *Kane*-like interrogation, postmodernist fragmentalism, feminist revisionism, or parody, Spike Lee gave the revolutionary Black Nationalist Malcolm X the heroic classical treatment. This bewildered some and outraged others, with both groups confused as to why the director of a Brechtian hip-hop agitprop masterwork like *Do the Right Thing* (1989) would make a film about the Nation of Islam (NOI) minister and Black Nationalist leader Malcolm X (1925–1965) in such an apparently conventional form. More has been written about *Malcolm X* than about probably any other biopic, with nearly every aspect of the film—its quality as a literary adaptation, its treatment of women, its place within the Hollywood cinema, its depiction of Black Muslimism and Black Nationalism, its significance for its subject's legacy, its address to its audience, its marketing and promotion—contested or defended repeatedly over the years since its release.

Lee, therefore, is in the unusual position of performing an appropriation that might look like assimilation. The first time an African American filmmaker lays hands on the levers of big-time Hollywood epic biopic filmmaking, it is to limn the life of the Black Muslim separatist spokesman of a radical-racial sect, a figure to whom many lay claim but whom no one sees as a character for the masses. This irony and contradiction caused audiences, and especially critics, to give the distinct impression that they had not all seen the same film. The attributes pointed to by the film's proponents are often the same ones cited by its sharpest critics. "Never before in American cinema," declared Michael Eric Dyson, "has an alternative black spirituality been so intelligently presented. One montage of Malcolm's rhetorical ripostes and verbal volleys extends, incredibly, for several minutes. And throughout Lee's treatment of Malcolm's Nation of Islam stage, his words, thought, and ideas and those of the Nation are vigorously presented. This is no small accomplishment in our anti-intellectual environment, which punishes the constituency that has made Malcolm its hero: black teens and young adults" (139). Thomas Doherty, however, complains that "a major portion of the film's running time" is given over to verbatim recitations of speeches, press conferences, and letters.

> Again and again, images of the archival Malcolm X are restaged, gesture for gesture, note for note as if the director feels his biopic will be the only record of the man to pass down to future generations, and that, in the fullness of time, scholarly completion will be more salient than judicious cutting. Sometimes splicing together color and black and white footage of precisely the same scene, Lee shifts back and forth from dramatic to docudramatic styles for visual variety, but no matter how dynamic the performance and the crowd enthusiasm, the ritual reenactments still play like hectoring from the screen. (Doherty *Malcolm X* 44)

Since the late 1960s, producer Marvin Worth (1925–1998) owned the rights to *The Autobiography of Malcolm X*, first at Columbia and then at Warner Bros. James Baldwin was originally engaged as writer and given a collaborator, Arnold Perl. After it became clear the film would not be made, Baldwin extricated himself from the project and published his script as *One Day When I Was Lost* in 1972. For their part, Worth and Perl made a documentary from the material, *Malcolm X* (1972). Still pursuing the idea of a

Malcolm X biopic, Worth put a succession of prominent writers to work on scripts over the next two decades, including Calder Willingham, David Mamet, David Bradley, and Charles Fuller. With a script by Fuller, Norman Jewison as director, and Denzel Washington as star—the team that made *A Soldier's Story* (1984)—the movie was announced for production in 1990.

Jewison's race-relations films, such as *In the Heat of the Night* (1967), typify how "so often, we have stories about . . . Black people . . . [that] end up being about the white people," as Lee put it ("By Any Means" DVD). Lee told reporters that he felt the Malcolm X story should have a black director. Worth set up a meeting between Lee and Jewison, who, as Lee recounted it, "very graciously bowed out when I had a talk with him to explain how maybe he wasn't the best person qualified to do Malcolm" (Als 40). For Lee, his production of *Malcolm X* was not an appropriation, but a *re-appropriation,* a taking back of black stories from "outsiders," who, as James O. Young writes, "have not lived as insiders and cannot have all the knowledge insiders have." Thus, "if outsiders' representations are based on imperfect knowledge of a culture, the representations are bound to be, at best, flawed because incomplete. At worst, they will be misleading distortions" (56).

No sooner had Lee achieved his initial re-appropriation, however, than he himself was accused of being an outsider—and in the blustery language of poet-playwright-activist Amiri Baraka. Seizing upon a copy of the fourth draft script before the film even went into production, Baraka wrote:

> Spike's films reveal him as the apologist for [the] sector of the Black petty bourgeoisie that holds Black life as a caricature. . . . Black struggle is mainly *commercial,* economic as a pay raise. "The Civil Rights Movement" is passé, hypocrisy or delusion. It has *been* over! (Remember that, and you can make some money!) African Kings and Queens can be put to work for Budweiser. Martin Luther King for McDonald's and Malcolm X for Warner Brothers. ABC makes millions from our *Roots.* ("Malcolm" 21)

Note that criticism of historical films comes down, as it usually does, to money, with Spike Lee implicitly assimilated into the corporation of Warner Bros. (even though he denounced it as "the Plantation"). Warners, which released *I Am a Fugitive from a Chain Gang, A Face in the Crowd, Bonnie and Clyde, The Learning Tree, A Clockwork Orange, Mean Streets, Bad-*

lands, Dog Day Afternoon, Full Metal Jacket, and other films not precisely affirmative of middle-class values and standards, becomes equated with McDonald's, purveyors of trans fat and bad cholesterol. Baraka also referred to "the syndrome Lenin spoke about that once opponents of the bourgeoisie are dead, the rules transform these class enemies into ciphers or agreeable sycophants of Imperialism . . . who are now 'rehabilitated' all the way into being represented as the very opposite ideologically of who they actually were in life" ("Malcolm" 18). Some of Baraka's charges were echoed by critics of the movie following its release. Armond White declared that "the figure of the slain Black politician [was Malcolm X a politician?] has been thoroughly domesticated. This may be part of a natural cultural process at work despite daily promulgated racism—yesterday's headache becomes today's pillow just as yesterday's tragedy becomes today's big-budget Hollywood extravaganza." As a result, according to White, "*sellout* is too common a word for an outrage of this shame and magnitude" (574).

Was Lee victimized by the very expectations he had done so much to create? In a story now almost as well known as that of Malcolm X, Warner Bros. sent Spike Lee into production with an $18 million budget, which in 1992 was the ceiling for a black film to which a studio expects to draw black audiences but not to cross over to a wider public. Lee sold foreign rights, which added another seven or eight million to the budget, but he "said from the beginning the film would cost about $33 million" (Lee 32). In the 2005 DVD documentary, Lucy Fisher, a production vice president at Warners at the time of *Malcolm X,* said that "while Spike wanted [the film] to be a studio version of a Spike Lee movie, the studio hoped that it would be a Spike Lee version of Malcolm X," a misunderstanding of almost farcical proportions. ("By Any Means"). Meanwhile, Lee and his cinematographer Ernest Dickerson had their sights set on *Lawrence of Arabia,* no less. "We saw the restored version," Dickerson said. "The close-ups were so sharp, so immediate. We wanted to shoot *Malcolm X* in the same way" (qtd. in Jackson 122). So the impasse was set. Lee decided to "go forward knowing we are going to come up short in the end. But we will have the film in the can. Maybe we can try and get some outside investors to come in later" (Lee 32). This gambit climaxed after a year of media stories about the Completion Bond Company (a movie budget insurance firm that takes over from the studio when a film goes over budget and a studio declines to provide more cash) firing the editors and leaving Lee to fend for the film in postproduction. At a press conference on 19 May 1992, Malcolm X's birthday, Lee announced that the film would be finished thanks to financial gifts from high-profile African Americans (among them Bill Cosby, Janet Jackson, Michael Jordan, and Oprah Winfrey). Moreover, Lee said publicly that children should miss school in order to turn out for the film's opening day, 18 November, a Wednesday, which was chosen to calm the fears of big-city exhibitors that there would be riots if the movie opened on a Friday. After such a furor and publicity buildup, the perceived conventionality of the actual film confused and disappointed some critics, who, as reviewers often will, reviewed their expectations rather than the film itself.

In a scene much remarked upon, by Lee no less than by others, a gang of Klansmen, having threatened Malcolm Little's mother, rides off into a giant horizon-level moon. The shot audaciously condenses the climax of *The Birth of a Nation* (1915) with the innocent, magical ride of Elliott and the extraterrestrial in Steven Spielberg's *E.T.* (1982). Lee may be showboating, as has been alleged. That is by no means all he is doing, however. The image is an announcement from a filmmaker who is appropriating for black filmmakers and audiences the epic tradition established in American (and probably world) cinema by D. W. Griffith's Civil War saga. As the image comes in the first fifteen minutes of the film, it can be seen as Lee putting his signature to the work as it begins. Lee also stakes his claim to the contemporary blockbuster cinema epitomized by Spielberg. One can accept and appreciate this while rejecting Lee's far-fetched comparisons of Simi Valley, the site of the trial of the Los Angeles policemen seen around the world on video beating a black man named Rodney King, to "one of those suburban lily white Steven Spielberg communities if there ever was one" (Lee 160).

Thus the confusion for many of Lee's critics: Lee publicly battles the Hollywood studios, calls Warner Bros. "the plantation," and takes swipes at successful white filmmakers like Spielberg. Yet his film pays homage to David Lean (as do many of Spielberg's films) and uses the syntax and vocabulary of the classical Hollywood biopic. Can one honor a tradition and criticize the institutions that produce it? For Lee, for those who study his films, and for those who want to understand the biopic as a genre, I believe the answer is yes. Lee should be considered a cinematic integrationist. As an African American public figure, he has partaken of both the quotations with which he ends *Do the Right Thing*: the King statement on nonviolence and the Malcolm X declaration that violence can be "intelligent." Similarly, as a filmmaker he has often juxtaposed the bold politico-aesthetic gestures of Eisenstein, Godard, and Brecht with the classical pictorialism and linear storytelling of Lean, Ford, and Kurosawa. Combine this with the flair for publicity and topicality of David O. Selznick, Stanley Kramer, and Otto Preminger and you get a filmmaker with something to confound everybody. Lee makes his way by sticking his finger in the eye of Hollywood. At the same time, he expertly works from and respects many of its traditions, but also appropriates them for the purposes of an African American commercial moviemaker and auteur.

Lee is a kind of cinematic pamphleteer; there is a rhetoric in Lee that wants to exceed the narrative and address the audience directly. He sometimes risks having his films look and sound like commercials, with bright colors, snappy slogans, and catchy jingles. Lee flummoxed some of his critics and some of his supporters in *Malcolm X,* however, by stifling his tendencies toward ad art, slogans, and agit-prop and making what, for the bulk of its 202-minute running time, seems a conventional, classical biopic. In so doing, Lee virtually invented a new tradition, emulated since, of films that reappropriate the classical biopic form, free of irony, parody, or deconstruction, employing it to tell the stories of figures who were by definition outside the mainstream culture in their time. The crossover that Lee's film represents was widely debated and, indeed, misunderstood when the film appeared. The infamous X ballcaps and T-shirts, while they might have helped build interest and defray some of the film's costs, gave to African American critics in particular ammunition to attack Lee for commodifying Malcolm and cheapening his legacy.

On the other hand, Lee knows he must sell his film because he can't count on the white film company to do it. In his tie-in book, Lee wrote:

> I realized that being a Black filmmaker, I'm never going to have the same amount of money spent to market my films as I would if I was a white filmmaker with the same number of notches on his gun, the same amount of success. . . . When I was in film school, I would see these guys who had spent four or five years, and sometimes even longer, trying to raise money for their films. And these were often good films. . . . If anything, we'd end up seeing them at a screening at a museum, or at a university, or during Black History Month, and that's all. But I knew I didn't want hundreds of people to see my films. I want millions of people to see my films. . . . It comes down to marketing in the end, and my activity comes from knowing that nobody is going to spend $20 million advertising and promoting my films. (22)

Still, one wonders how much more favorable the reception to *Malcolm X* might have been had Lee refrained from emblazoning fashion merchandise with the anti-name of the Black Nationalist leader. A counterargument, however, is that with the ball caps and T-shirts, Lee had created too much awareness of the film for the studio to try to bury it or to cut it down to a more "commercial" length. The director was going to make sure that the film got promoted; by doing it himself Lee would become his own one-man "enterprise zone." His antics may have burned his bridges with one studio and foreclosed the financing of future biopics of African Americans. As of this writing, more than fifteen years later, Lee has yet to produce another large-scale biopic. Despite abortive projects about Jackie Robinson and James Brown, moreover, the only major biopic of an African American figure in the years since 1992 has been *Ray,* by a white director, Taylor Hackford, and an African American screenwriter, James L. White. As for *Malcolm X,* Lee got a $35 million, three-hour-twenty-two-minute film made and distributed exactly the way he wanted. However, as the first African American director to harness the Hollywood vehicle of dreams in the auteurist era (or ever), there is little doubt that Lee has sometimes overplayed his hand, on and off the screen.

The Autobiography of Malcolm X breaks into three sections—Malcolm Little's early life and especially his days as Detroit Red, a young thief and hustler on the streets of Harlem and Boston; his years in Charlestown Prison in Massachusetts; and his life after becoming Minister Malcolm X. During Malcolm's years in prison, he was reformed and converted to Islam by his brothers Reginald and Philbert and sister Hilda. He was paroled and brought to Detroit, where he began his ministry at the service of the Honorable Elijah Muhammad of the Nation of Islam, a sect founded in 1931 by W. D. Fard (who is not mentioned in the film, but whose framed portrait in the Messenger's office is seen in several shots) and Elijah Muhammad. It preached that

> no heaven was in the sky . . . and no hell was in the ground. Instead, both heaven and hell were conditions in which people lived right here on this planet Earth. Mr. Fard taught that the Negro in America had been for four hundred years in hell, and he, Mr. Fard, had come to return them to where heaven for them was—back home, among their own kind. Master Fard taught that as hell was on earth, also on earth was the devil—the white race which was bred from black Original

Man six thousand years before. . . . The black people, God's children, were Gods themselves, Master Fard taught. And he taught that among them was one, also a human being like the others, who was the God of Gods . . . supreme in being and power—and His proper name was Al-lah. (Malcolm X and Haley 238–239)

As adapted to Lee's film, each of the three sections has its own style and feeling, distinct from those of the book. It is not so much that Lee has ex-cised the more controversial aspects of Malcolm's life, doctrine, and oratory and kept the more palatable ones. It is rather that Lee has made Malcolm somewhat less a religious leader and more of a Black Nationalist political figure, less the proselytizer of a private sect and more a public personage and a role model. The particular theological underpinnings of Malcolm's discourse are made secondary to his general critique of race in America. To Lee, this is what gives Malcolm his lasting transcendence. One can say, however, that Malcolm began to become a myth right after his death with the eulogy given in Harlem by Ossie Davis, not a Black Muslim. His myth-ification was solidified by the posthumous publication of the autobiography later in 1965, and indeed had begun as soon as Malcolm left the Nation of Islam eleven months before his death.

Amiri Baraka pointed out more than a year before the film opened, "De-troit Red holds center stage in Spike's screenplay. Even the character Shorty appears more than Malcolm's father or mother. So Spike sees the Detroit Red years as 'real time' while the early years are just disparate flashes of memory. This is because, to Spike, Detroit Red is the *real* Malcolm, and flashbacks are all that is required of the formative years" ("Malcolm" 19).

Forgiving Baraka's foolhardiness in assessing a screenplay draft before shooting begins (as we know, Lee overshadowed the opening of his histori-cal drama with the "burning X" prologue, which is not even in the version of the script Lee published in 1992), his point is worth considering. The classical biopic begins just before the time when the subject goes into the world and begins to do the thing that will make him or her known or signifi-cant. The "Roxbury 1942" opening serves to introduce us to the "original" Malcolm, the Malcolm who will be remade several times in his short life. Malcolm X's story is a quest, with teenage hoodlum Detroit Red the object lesson, the unknowing product of a white society that deliberately wastes black youth.

Malcolm's saga is a journey in several stages: (1) On the streets: sin, ignorance, and unknowing victimization; (2) In prison: religious awakening, education, submission, devotion; (3) After prison: triumph, work; the devotee makes himself useful to his master and his God; (4) After years as Minister Malcolm X, a national figure, he is dissociated from the Nation of Islam and his mentor, Elijah Muhammad; he experiences betrayal, disillusionment, and confusion; (5) On his own: He makes new explorations and discoveries, and continued but abortive transformations; he joins with world Islam and renounces the much narrower and racist Nation of Islam. All of this happens under the watchful eyes of the world media, of the FBI and the CIA, and his former comrades and now his bitter foes at the Nation of Islam. (6) Finally, after his assassination, he achieves transcendence; his legacy is lasting though uncertain.

Therefore, Detroit Red provides the starting point as well as a reference point. Detroit Red is part of the myth; Alex Haley wrote that while taking notes on Malcolm X's press conference after his return from Mecca in 1964, "I was thinking, some of the time, that if a pebble were dropped from the window behind Malcolm X, it would have struck on a sidewalk eight floors below where years before he had skulked, selling dope" (Malcolm X and Haley 475). It was acknowledged by the time the film was made that the misadventures of Detroit Red were probably exaggerated, so as to magnify Malcolm's conversion to the Nation of Islam. "Malcolm was not the big-time hustler he was made out to be by Alex Haley's book," Malcolm's brother Bob told Lee. "He hustled, but everybody hustled one way or another because it was about trying to survive. I think the book was heavily dramatized" (Lee 45).

Malcolm was originally meant to play the role of John the Baptist within the theology of the NOI, the mortal who speaks in advance of the prophet (known in the NOI—as Elijah Muhammad was—as the Messenger). Unlike T. E. Lawrence, Malcolm X never appears to start feeling that *he* is the prophet, so sincere and disciplined is Malcolm in his role as loyal foot soldier, spokesman, and advance man. Lawrence-type presumption is what he is eventually accused of, however. Once the Messenger disavows him, Malcolm, with all his fame, searches for more profound meaning in Islam, race, and blackness in America. Paradoxically, all this is what makes him too saintly, too selfless perhaps, to be believed as a film protagonist. No one, moreover, who commissions a writer to help craft his autobiography can be totally uninterested in mythification, and Malcolm apparently saw himself in mythic terms, or at least Alex Haley did as he wrote the book; one of its chapters is even entitled "Icarus." The story of Malcolm X and Elijah Mu-hammad is the myth of the protégé who exceeds his mentor; while there is untold drama in this relationship, actuality will probably not permit its full exegesis to be realized now, or ever.

The film has its own myth of origin, as Baldwin wrote: "Having fallen into the trap of accepting 'technical' assistance, I would not, at the cutting point, be able to reject it; and the script would then be cut according to the 'action' line, and in the interest of 'entertainment' values. How I got myself out of this fix doesn't concern us here—I simply walked out, taking my origi-nal script with me" (*Devil* 99). Baldwin's published screenplay begins with Malcolm X on his way to the Audubon Ballroom in Harlem on the last day of his life. What ensues is no ordinary flashback but a roundup of his many identities; "I have had so many names," he repeatedly intones in voiceover, as a montage of his identities appears: "Malcolm Little," "Malcolm X," "Satan," "Detroit Red," "Omowale" (the African name for "He who has returned"), and his Muslim name acquired in Mecca, "El-Haji Malik El-Shabazz" (*One Day* 6–8).

Compare this with the opening of Spike Lee's film. Over the "blue sky" Warner Bros. shield, followed by a fade to the opening titles over a black background, a young minister at a Nation of Islam assembly offers a prayer and introduces Minister Malcolm X. A clash of cymbals and a sounding trumpet accompanies a shock cut to a screen-filling American flag, recalling the opening of *Patton*. A rich, booming baritone voice, recognizably Denzel Washington's, immediately declares, "Brothers and sisters, I'm here to tell you that I charge the white man. I charge the white man with being the greatest murderer on earth. I charge the white man with being the greatest kidnapper on earth. There is no place in this world that that man can go and say that he created peace and harmony." On the last phrase, the film cuts to a tape seen around the world, the video of policemen beating Rodney King in March 1991. On the lines, "He didn't say, black man, black woman, come on over and help me build America. He said, 'Nigger, get down in the bottom of that boat and I'm takin' you over there,'" the flag bursts into flames that burn down to reveal an X underlying the American flag. The speech ends on the words, "We don't see any American dream. We've experienced the American nightmare."

The two openings display differing approaches to the biopic. Baldwin's features the time-worn flashback structure, but in a variation that antici-pates the multifaced Bob Dylan that Todd Haynes presents at the beginning of *I'm Not There*. Jonathan Rosenbaum likened Baldwin's opening scene to the work of Alain Resnais in its shifting, amorphous, and fluid sense of memory ("Hollywood Radical" 150). Baldwin's structure is rhetorical, setting out a range of possibilities and using his screenplay to illustrate each one in turn, with the narrative becoming more linear and sequential as each of the identities is revealed and elaborated upon. As Brian Norman points out in an article on Baldwin's screenplay, "Malcolm's story disrupts distinct stages of Black history; rather, Malcolm is a historical participant whose conflicting naming ceremonies navigate America's racial struggles" (105). Lee's opening makes a statement of immediacy. *Do the Right Thing* opened with "the Negro National Anthem," "Lift Up Your Voice and Sing," played by solo saxophone over the studio logo (Universal), before a shock cut to Public Enemy's "Fight the Power" and to a young Rosie Perez, aggressive yet fetishized, dancing feverishly in the credit sequence in a series of stylized shots. Similarly, the sound in *Malcolm X* begins with tradition, decorum, and ceremony, before Lee launches a powerful cinematic montage. This opening sequence presents The Essential Malcolm X, both out of time—in a kind of transcendent, eternal space—and of the spectator's own time.

The burning of the American flag—a provocation at any time—and the X revealed underneath suggest two things. First is the blot of slavery and racial hatred that underlies American culture. Malcolm explained many times that the X signified the refusal of African Americans to bear surnames given to slaves by their masters, and to replace them with anonymity. What name more befits an invisible man than "Mister X"? Thus the X of Lee's credit sequence reveals repressed racism but also anger and activism, both of which the "colorblind" culture of the post–civil rights era, which acts as though all racial issues have been settled, prefers to forget. Lee showed himself to be an Eisensteinian dialectician in *Do the Right Thing*, colliding violence with nonviolence, intelligence and activism with ignorance and apathy, responsibility with neglect, and ethnocentrism with multiculturalism. Here he associates through juxtaposition the Rodney King tape, the verdict that exonerated the cops, the burning of South Central L.A. that followed, and the X embedded in American culture. The second thing the sequence establishes is immediate relevance of Malcolm X for the present. This brings a more conventional dimension in that it introduces us to the subject as he was best known and stresses his importance; however, what is emphasized is not just the subject's transcendence of all time, but also the subject's relevance for our time. The agit-prop confrontationalism of the sequence is not really leavened by the nod to biopic convention. Baldwin works, therefore, in the manner of *Citizen Kane* and anticipates postmodernist biopics that begin with the whole myth of the subject and break it down over the length of the film. Lee's sequence, by contrast, takes the form of agit-prop crossed with music video. It interjects, outside the space and time of the film, a currency and immediacy that announces unmistakably that Malcolm X is for our time.

Notwithstanding two brief mentions, some critics take Lee's omission from his film of the Nation of Islam tenet that whites are devils as evidence of whitewash. When Lee goes directly to some of Malcolm X's most fiery rhetoric, however, illustrated and reinforced by the fresh evidence of the Rodney King video, it is hard to accuse the film of backing off from the anger and immediacy of Malcolm X's message. Some of the deleted scenes that Lee included in the 2005 "Special Edition" DVD reveal the extent to which he had refrained from creating a "crossover Malcolm" (though he was accused of this anyway). In a scene that would have come after Malcolm checks into the New York Hilton on his last night on earth, a young woman approaches him and asks, as a student had years before, what a good white person could do; Malcolm's reply then was "nothing." Lee's Malcolm para- phrases the *Autobiography,* where Malcolm explains what he *does* tell "well- meaning white people" (in 1965): "Where the really sincere white people have got to do their 'proving' of themselves is not among the black *victims,* but out on the battle lines of where America's racism really *is*—and that's in their own home communities" (432–433). Lee told Greg Crowdus and Dan Georgakas just after the film's release that he didn't use the scene because "the acting just didn't work," evidence for which is nowhere in the scene itself.

This deleted scene accompanies another one in which Dr. Mahmoud Shawarbi, the Muslim scholar who authorized Malcolm's hajj, presses upon him the moral need to return to America and undo the hate he has sown; his dialogue is not from the book, but conveys a general sense that sectarian hatred is against Muslim principles. The scene also would have been the film's only mention of Malcolm's post-Mecca trips to African countries, in- cluding Ghana and Nigeria, another omission for which Lee took criticism. Lee's excision of both scenes demonstrates the difficult position he was in. If he emphasized too much Malcolm's moderation of his NOI teachings and his adoption of orthodox Muslim principles as a black leader, Lee could be accused of pitching too obviously to the crossover audience, giving Malcolm nearly a climactic reconciliation with whites (as well as counteracting Lee's everywhere implicit desire not to provoke the present-day NOI). Excluding such moments, however, does make the film appear to flatten the nuances of Malcolm X's evolution. In a sense, to return to the eternal Liberty Valance metaphor for cinema (and perhaps for popular culture), Lee chooses to print the legend, leaving the "actual" Malcolm X always a work in progress, afloat in his own unrealized possibilities. "I am Malcolm X!" shout the children of Harlem, and then Soweto, at the end of Lee's film. But Malcolm X, like many biopic subjects, exits life and the film an enigma, a signifier of growth, strength, responsibility, and change. And manhood. "Our shining black manhood," as Lee brought Ossie Davis back to repeat from his long-ago eulogy.

Where this leaves women is a real issue. The omission from the film of Ella Little Collins, Malcolm's half-sister with whom he lived after his release from prison and who played a pivotal role in his conversion to the Nation of Islam, is for many critics a structuring absence. Critics assume she was "erased," as bell hooks put it, but was that erasure out of Spike Lee's control, like the absence of a credit for James Baldwin (d. 1988), whose name was removed from the credits at the request of his estate (Rosenbaum 147)? Ella, along with Malcolm's brothers Reginald and Philbert and his sister Hilda, are missing from Baldwin's published script, in which there is a single line that refers to Ella—"I may never be able to pay my sister back," Malcolm says before leaving for Mecca (Baldwin *One Day* 234). Baldwin, in *The Devil Finds Work,* wrote that "my producer had been advised, in an inter-office memo which I, quite unscrupulously, intercepted, that the writer (me) should be advised that the tragedy of Malcolm's life was that he had been mistreated, early, by some whites, and betrayed (later) by *many* blacks: emphasis in the original. The writer was also to avoid suggesting that Malcolm's trip to Mecca could have had any political implications, or repercussions" (96).

It is plain from Baldwin's published script that he disregarded these dictated musts-to-avoid. He came up, however, with avoidances and compromises of his own, including the creation of an invented character who himself would have many names (Luther in Baldwin's script, Bembry in Lee's published draft, Baines in the film), who substitutes first for Malcolm's brothers Philbert and Reginald and finally for Elijah Muhammad, who is not a character in Baldwin's script. Indeed, one wonders what pressures Baldwin was feeling besides the predictable ones from the studio. As usual, Spike Lee takes the blame. Did Lee, in picking his fights twenty years later, restore as much as he could of the truth of Malcolm X's *story*, while accepting some of the same types of omissions and displacements that were forced on Baldwin?

Unlike most commentators on the film, I find in Lee's movie an objectivity that is one of the film's saving graces. Lee, who had to staff a second unit to film in Mecca because non-Muslims are not permitted there, keeps himself at something of a distance from the material (Crowdus and Georgakas). I never feel that Malcolm's point of view is necessarily Lee's; this is significant because we see that Malcolm's recurring self-reinventions and evolution come out of his constant tendency to create his own reality, or to allow it to be created by others. Not until his break with the Nation of Islam, when, as he says publicly, his statements can be taken as his and not the Nation's, does Malcolm come into his own. It is this change that allows Lee, like Alex Haley before him, to present Malcolm as a more generalized black leader, and not as just the highly articulate and provocative voice of a specific and marginal sect. Indeed, the 1972 film by Worth and Perl, which Thomas Doherty called "the documentary precursor" of the Worth-Baldwin-Perl project that culminated with Lee, stresses Malcolm's status as Black Nationalist leader, downplaying his twelve-year devotion to and identification with the Nation of Islam almost to the point of nonexistence (33). This echoes the much-reported problem with the "third act" of Baldwin's screenplay, which stemmed from the writer's "big problems," in Lee's words, with the deterioration of the Malcolm X–Elijah Muhammad relationship (Lee 25). Because of the numerous contentious interests that Lee had to mediate—from the Nation of Islam, whose leader, Louis Farrakhan (Louis X in Malcolm's day), implicitly threatened Lee, to Malcolm's wife, Betty Shabazz, to sideline noise from the likes of Baraka, to the suits at Warners and the Completion Bond Company, to the black audience whom Lee knew he could not let down—the director stands outside the material, giving all these differing interests equal time, as it were.

Betty Shabazz functions the way female leads in Hollywood films often do—as a reality check on the male hero. Shabazz plays the woman-as-outsider who sees clearly what her man is entangled in. Because she depends upon him, moreover, she is more vulnerable and has more at stake. He may tell her not to raise her voice in "his" home, but she must get this "true believer" to see reason. "Are you blind?" she asks him. Betty is not the nagging wife described by bell hooks in what is decidedly not one of that estimable critic's finer moments. (Her analysis, which also claims that Detroit Red's white girlfriend, Sophia, is in "nearly half the film," when actually she enters fourteen minutes in and exits, except for two quick insert shots, at the one-hour mark, pays so little attention to what's actually on the screen that one wonders if she saw the film or just read the early draft script that Amiri Baraka had been waving around.)

Malcolm's often fraught relationship with his wife, who "was alternately supportive and sternly self-willed (she left Malcolm after the birth of each of their first three children)" (Dyson 141), is smoothed over here, though through a layer of tension that does not always appear to be motivated. The actress Angela Bassett tries to suggest what the script does not supply, hinting at the complex of love, resistance, understanding, and cold realism of an intelligent woman living within the rigidly misogynist and hypocritical culture of Black Muslimism. More important, Betty succeeds in removing the scales from the eyes of Malcolm the disciple. Unlike in the *Autobiography*, there is direct causality from Betty's entreaties to Malcolm's pursuance of the truth. After his argument, if that's what it is, with Betty, Malcolm takes what amounts to his first step independent of the Messenger; he interviews the young women Elijah Muhammad impregnated and finds out for himself the extent of his master's betrayal of him.

Moreover, just before this sequence comes the much-commented upon shot that shows a large temple meeting with the women partitioned between a metal mesh partial screen in a seating section over which hangs a banner with the words "We must protect our most valuable property: our women."

23. The fraught but loving relationship between Malcolm X (Denzel Washington) and his wife, Betty Shabazz (Angela Bassett), in *Malcolm X* (Spike Lee, Warner Bros., 1992). Digital frame enlargement.

Lee films Malcolm speaking before a huge congregation, in a setup that recalls the political rally in *Citizen Kane,* except that Malcolm is orating before a giant portrait of the Honorable Elijah Muhammad, not of himself. The scene, like the one in *Kane,* portends the protagonist's downfall; Kane self-destructs but Malcolm is betrayed. Even more subtly (and necessarily so), when Lee shows Malcolm being cheered by banner-wearing Nation of Islam members, he uses reaction shots of the crowd the way Leni Riefenstahl did in *The Triumph of the Will;* this is slyly appropriate given that these scenes precede and foreshadow the betrayal to come and intimate the lockstep devotion to which the Black Muslim legions are indoctrinated.

One senses that Lee has more to say about the Nation of Islam, which he believes assassinated Malcolm X, than his film could possibly show outright. (Perhaps Lee once again had *Lawrence of Arabia* in mind, specifically the one moment in that film when women are shown, sequestered in the shadows of Auda abu Tayi's camp.) That Baines is shown looking uncomfortable on the speaker's platform, applauding Malcolm only reluctantly, is significant here too. By this time Baines has become Lee's all-purpose scapegoat, a composite like Brighton or Ali in *Lawrence* who, in this case, turns from mentor to nemesis as the narrative demands. It all leads up to the sense of a totalitarianism that will expel Malcolm because of envy, against which Malcolm frequently warns in the *Autobiography.* The content of Malcolm's speech, about a "powder keg in the house" that is about to explode, ironically is shown to refer to him and his position in the "house" of the Nation. The house that will explode, as it turns out, is Malcolm's own.

"I could conceive death," said Malcolm; "I couldn't conceive betrayal" (352). In Nation of Islam theology, Elijah Muhammad is the Christ, seated on the right hand of God the Father, with Malcolm in the place of John the Baptist or Saint Paul, he who bears witness. In the end, therefore, Elijah Muhammad is both more and less than a man. That Mr. Muhammad chose to cut off his right-hand man suggests that he did not believe these claims himself. How total a charlatan Elijah Muhammad was is a question taken up by no one—not by Malcolm, not the film, nor even by the "debunker" Bruce Perry, the publication of whose biography of Malcolm in 1991, on the eve of the film's production, threw still more controversy on a project not exactly lacking it. The story of Malcolm X and Elijah Muhammad seems the tragedy of the protégé who outstrips his mentor; Malcolm apparently actually was the pure vessel that the Messenger spoke about but failed to be. Malcolm adhered to all the sect's precepts while The Messenger did not. The

24. Between the eyes. Malcolm himself is unwittingly inside the powder keg about to explode, as he describes it at Nation of Islam rallies. Digital frame enlargement.

film, however, omits the facets of Black Muslim doctrine that might make Malcolm appear deluded or fanatical. Among these are the fact that Malcolm was prepared to teach Elijah Muhammad's adultery as the fulfillment of prophecy, after the Messenger told Malcolm, "I'm David. . . . When you read about how David took another man's wife, I'm that David. . . . You read about Lot, who went and laid up with his own daughters. I have to fulfill all of those things" (Malcolm X and Haley 345).

Had some of this been included, either the whole tenor of the enterprise would have had to become more circumspect and multi-perspectived, pulling it away from the *Autobiography of Malcolm X,* or such moments would have provoked unintentional laughter (as would the Nation's preposterous formulas, as patiently explained in the *Autobiography,* about how the devil came to earth as the white man). "Spike Lee's film," writes Nell Irvin Painter, "reveals why so many black Americans were drawn to the Nation of Islam through Malcolm X's preaching of black beauty and power; but by deleting the inane portions of the creed, it eliminates the mystery of why so intelligent a person as Malcolm X would stay twelve years in such a narrow-minded movement" (436). Dyson, moreover, finds fault with "Lee's portrayal of Malcolm toward the end as harried but hushed, a man of saintly moral attainment. Lee's intention to portray Malcolm as having it all together on the inside while his world crumbles around him not only is romantic, but does a disservice finally to the greater truth that Malcolm continued to work even in the midst of the palpable premonition of his quickly approaching death" (140).

Pardon me for not only failing to see the difference between the two states Dyson describes, but for thinking that there wasn't much else Lee could have done. Yes, he could have perhaps forgone the trip to Mandela's present-day South Africa in order to represent instead countries such as Ghana, Nigeria, and Lebanon that Malcolm visited in 1964, and thus show "the greater truth that Malcolm continued to work." Doing this, however, would sacrifice the director's attempt to balance historical complexity and authenticity with the film's rhetorical address to its audience in its own time. Nonetheless, the structure of the film does seem something of a miscalculation, which is why the middle section—from Malcolm's release from prison and his elevation as a minister through to his fall from grace and his trip to Mecca—is easily the strongest. Perhaps an already very long film could not have negotiated the intrigue involving the Molotov cocktail of forces that were conspiring to stop Malcolm as well as the changes in philosophy and the alliances Malcolm was trying to forge in his last eleven months.

In addition, because there had not been major films by black filmmakers about African American historical figures, the time was surely not right for a truly critical study of that figure's rise and fall (and rise), especially when so many of the basic facts of his life have been in dispute. Pinned between the rock of the Nation of Islam and the family of Malcolm X and the hard place of the movie studio, Lee already was forced to be less than frank about the pressures on Malcolm (but far more so than Baldwin's original script, which delved into world politics but fudged completely on Malcolm's personal and institutional relationships). Overall, however, Lee's purpose was to present Malcolm X to a new and unsettled generation and to celebrate his brilliance, resilience, self-reliance, courage, gifts for personal responsibility, self-reliance, and self-reinvention.

No purpose would be served in bringing the little-understood story of Malcolm X to the screen in 1992, after twenty years in Hollywood "project development hell," in order to debunk Malcolm's own story about his father's life and death; to meditate on Malcolm's betrayal amid the narrow sectarianism of the Nation of Islam; to open up the mystery as to who fire-bombed Malcolm's house, the Nation of Islam or Malcolm himself; to pick apart his apparently complicated marriage; to focus on Malcolm's late realization that "I was a zombie then—like all [Black] Muslims—I was hypnotized . . . I guess a man's entitled to make a fool of himself if he's willing to pay the cost. It cost me twelve years" (Malcolm X and Haley 493); and to ask what, if anything, he accomplished. Such a study would be dramatic and interesting. However, it would not only dwell heavily on the downward trajectory, but it might just appear aimless and even in a way racist if its only point seemed to be the failure of Black Nationalism, if Malcolm's distraught line to Alex Haley, which he does say in the film to Betty—"We had the *best* organization the Black man has ever known. *Niggers* ruined it"—somehow ended up as the film's point (472). Lee needed an affirmative film and this meant translating *The Autobiography of Malcolm X* to film by appropriating the form of the classical celebratory biopic, not in a deconstructive spirit to be sure, but in a spirit of updating and expansion. Malcolm X scholar Manning Marable wrote:

> Lee has rendered the life of an American original in terms that are both poignant and insightful. . . . In taking the risk of defining and interpreting a figure entwined in racial and cultural controversy, he has sent us back into our own memories, or to books or documentaries, in search of the truth for ourselves. And he has done more than that. He has set the nation talking about a figure whose life deserves to be discussed, whose achievements deserve critical scrutiny, and whose career merits the widest possible exposure. Many great films have achieved considerably less than that. (143–144)

In a real sense *Malcolm X* is an appropriation in two ways, or better, it is a reappropriation from white-centered cinema of a black story, and it is an appropriation of a Hollywood genre and production values in order to tell that black story. In the end, however, many critics could not get past the fact that *Malcolm X* was made for a major Hollywood studio, even if the director deliberately defied the studio on the inadequate glass-ceiling-for-black-films budget and embarked on a chicken run with Warner Bros., with the Completion Bond Company poised between them (although Lee maintained that he was the one caught in the middle). Jonathan Rosenbaum, Armond White, and other critics appear to want Spike Lee and other black directors to have the purity to ignore the studios, leaving mass audiences and event films to white filmmakers and in this case leaving us, probably, with Norman Jewison's version and to wonder what *Malcolm X* would be like with black filmmakers to conjure with it.

Moreover, scholar Brian Norman in 2005 writes that Lee's movie "imagines Malcolm X's project completed simply because it is the subject of a major Hollywood film. . . . Lee explicitly casts his film as the end point of Malcolm X's challenge to a racist America: 'We had to fight tooth and nail, fight like hell to get what we wanted on the screen.' . . . Thus, at the moment Malcolm X adorns the silver screen, the projects of Civil Rights and Black Nationalism enter the past tense" (107). This is absurd on its face. In highlighting Nelson Mandela, recently released from prison and working to build a government, Spike Lee alights on a current example of how the project of equal rights and human rights continues. Lee's early career and his films from 1986 to 1992 seem to address, validly or not, a vacuum in the dialogue on civil rights and Black Nationalist issues. In making *Malcolm X*, Lee unquestionably believed that he had built his own film oeuvre to a certain endpoint, if you will, but not that he had brought to closure all African American liberation projects in the United States! If Lee is guilty of anything, it might be his implication that it takes his films to reignite debates that had become dormant. Implicit as well is the idea that if his Malcolm X movie is a conventional biopic, then Malcolm, and by implication African American culture in general, has earned a place in the traditional pantheon of American myth. In these ways, the film is an appropriation, and a significant statement in the history of minorities and mainstream film.

9

Raoul Peck's *Lumumba*

Drama, Documentary, and Postcolonial Appropriation

Obscure politicians not news. Send more about cannibals.
  —Telegram in 1960 from Scripps-Howard newspapers rejecting an
  interview with Patrice Lumumba by reporter D'Lynn Waldron

They say the son of Tolenga is dead. But they cannot show the body.
  —*Lumumba: Death of a Prophet*

The two-month prime ministry of Patrice Lumumba in the newly independent Congo in 1960 has been chronicled, discussed, covered up, storied, debated, repressed, researched, and mythologized within the Congo, but much more especially outside it, since the thirty-five-year-old politician's assassination in January 1961.

Lumumba's fate is much too complex to be attributed to any one cause, be it treacherous Belgian colonials, contentious Congolese factions, the haste and unpreparedness with which independence came to the former Belgian Congo, the Cold War, the UN, the CIA, or Lumumba's own inexperience and poor judgment. Each of these played its part. Alive, Lumumba was the only political candidate who in 1960 stood for national unity and the first elected prime minister in a country with neither a democratic tradition nor a unitary, non-tribalist identity (Johnson "Heart" 3). "The dead Lumumba," Jean-Paul Sartre wrote in 1963, "ceased to be a person and became Africa in its entirety. . . . He was not, nor could he be, the hero of pan-Africanism: he was its martyr" (Sartre 200). Writing more critically some forty years later, Congolese historian Didier Gondola observed that "a prophet . . . is profitable only when dead and made to speak by ventriloquist scholars, artists, or politicians . . . a figure that owes his mystique to the fact that he means different things to different people, that he has become an idea" (3).

Among the "ventriloquists" is Raoul Peck, a Haitian-born writer-director who spent part of his childhood in the Congo, where his parents went to work for the new government in 1962, when Raoul was eight, and stayed for twenty-five years. Peck presents himself as an artist so haunted by the smothered potential of Lumumba and the quick demise of Congolese freedom that he made two films about the prime minister less than a decade apart. *Lumumba: la morte du prophète* (*Lumumba: Death of a Prophet,* 1992), a sixty-nine-minute documentary, is speculative and exploratory; it reopens a conversation that had been quashed. In this film, Peck wants to get at truth, long since annihilated; to do so, he must reanimate the myth in order to discover the man and the movement that he, almost solely, represented. At the same time that we want "to know who Lumumba is," writes Manthia Diawara,

> we want to know who Raoul Peck is, what his class position is, and why he is making this documentary on Lumumba. . . . We see Peck's class position from the home movies of his childhood. He grew up privileged in a country where the majority was exploited and kept illiterate and where Lumumba was killed for trying to bring a revolution. . . . Making a film on Lumumba is therefore a process of self-examination for Peck. Even though we learn about Mobutu's betrayal of Lumumba and Belgian racism toward the people of Congo, what concerns us most in the film is how Peck feels about Lumumba. (195)

Lumumba (2000), a feature-length biopic, wants to bring back the man in the full verisimilitude of dramatic cinema. Both films want to stir in the spectator a sense of loss, waste, and outrage. "Thirty lost years," intones the 1992 film's voiceover narrator (Peck himself). "One day we will have to start again at zero." The story of Lumumba calls for approaches that can sort out leadership qualities from personal flaws and voices of self-interest and bias from authentic voices. Simply put, the documentary asks its questions and the biopic later tries to answer them. But every director who makes a documentary about a biographical subject does not go back and make drama out of that same subject. Werner Herzog followed up his documentary *Little Dieter Needs to Fly* (1997), about a German-born American air force pilot, Dieter Dengler, who escaped from a prison camp in Laos in the early days of the Vietnam War, with a biopic, *Rescue Dawn* (2006), made after Dengler's death. But the practice is still unusual. Other directors known for crossing from one form to the other, including Luis Buñuel, Barbet Schroeder, Agnès Varda, and Spike Lee, have apparently not felt the urge—or had the opportunity—to dramatize one of their nonfiction topics.

The question then for Peck is: why is drama necessary? To answer this, we should consider the aims and accomplishments of *Lumumba: Death of a Prophet* to examine what took place during the eight-year interval between the two films that made an answer in drama seem necessary, and finally how Peck in both films weaves a coherent authorial vision through variations on a theme in different media. It does seem certain that the second film would not exist without the first. The myriad uncertainties of the interrogative, deconstructive documentary seem cleared up somewhat by the more definite diegesis of fiction moviemaking, while the documentary makes the drama appear less of a settled view of history—the only version of Lumumba's life there could be—and more of a continuing and contentious dialectic. Peck still conveys his ambivalent position as insider and outsider: even though Peck is a black man with experience in the Congo, the Congo itself still has no voice of its own, and it had one only briefly, for a couple of months in 1960. Peck made his biopic in the shadow of Ludo DeWitte's book *The Assassination of Lumumba*, published in Dutch in 1999 and in English two years later. This Lumumba revisionism forced an investigative report by the Belgian government, released in 2001, which admitted extensive Belgian responsibility in the Lumumba overthrow and murder ("Parliamentary Committee"). This development was followed in 2002 by the opening of classified U.S. documents that revealed the extent of American involvement in the case, long alleged by many—including Malcolm X, who mentioned Lumumba in his infamous "chickens come home to roost" comments following the assassination of John F. Kennedy (Weissman).

No more personal films could be found than Peck's Lumumba movies. The questions they pose, writes Jessica Powers, are "Why was Lumumba killed? And more to the point, why does Peck obsess over this particular question?" A theme of this book is that particular artists—writers and directors—are interested in particular biographical subjects at certain times. Their reasons often have little or nothing to do with the desire of the studio-era producer or the TV network executive, to capitalize on public interest in an individual, or to find a good role for a star (which, of course, still happens, though not as often). They also often go beyond or may seem counter to a subject's commercial appeal in the contemporary era. The two films are in the end similar in their aims and in the personal voice permeating them. In form, however, they couldn't be more different.

Part detective story, part journey into memory, part poetic meditation, and part wake-up call, *Lumumba: Death of a Prophet* documents a series of shadows, a clandestine truth—the long tragedy of Congo, unending to this day. Peck's camera disturbs the hiding place and all the places that profit from keeping the truth hidden. Mostly, Peck documents silence, signified by scenes of a wintry Brussels, and broken by unwelcome intrusions from the past. Peck's primary method is to interrogate old photographs and to deconstruct historical documents, including films. He follows "Lumumba Arrested," a newsreel from December 1960, with a shot of commuters bustling through a Brussels subway station. In voiceover he tells us that British Movietone News charged $3,000 a minute for use of the newsreel and that the average laborer in the Congo makes $150 a year. The effect is to deconstruct the unquestioned function, the presumed objectivity, that such footage usually serves within a documentary. It is also to make a correlation between the worth that corporations attach to their properties—the very kind of worth that Lumumba's presence as leader threatened—and the absolute lack of value of unskilled African labor and of Africans in general. Similarly, a shot of supporters welcoming Lumumba as he arrives for the Brussels Roundtable on Independence in 1960 is instantly undermined by the voiceover: "Lumumba's future assassins are among those who embrace him upon his return. But that is another story." The commentary reminds us that Lumumba himself misinterpreted many a gesture and image in the heady days leading up to 30 June 1960, and that misinterpretation was more or less the order of the day.

Peck's 1992 Lumumba film works similarly to Alain Resnais's *Nuit et brouillard* (*Night and Fog,* 1955), one of the first films to break the postwar silence surrounding the Holocaust. Resnais juxtaposed new color film of the abandoned, overgrown yards at Auschwitz ten years after the end of the war with confiscated German footage of the death camps that was startling because most of it had not been seen before publicly. Peck similarly attempts to intervene in the placid Belgian society of the early nineties in order to restart discussion on Lumumba. The film documents silence because it tries to find a voice for those who have no voice. Cutting from grainy newsreel footage of Lumumba showered with flowers in a parade to an anonymous woman on a Brussels train as it pulls away in a shower, Peck in voiceover intones, "A prophet foretells the future, but the future died with the prophet." Belgium in winter might seem self-indulgently irrelevant to a film about a black Congolese leader, but the Congo in perpetual spiritual and political winter is the subject here. Even blustery bleakness and melancholy are luxuries for affluent Belgians. The topic is supposed to be the third world, but the first world occupies the screen, a visual displacement signifying a displaced leader and misplaced independence. "The gap opened up between the images and the narration," writes Elizabeth Swanson Goldberg, "holds the suggestion of complicity, of collective responsibility. . . . Patrice Lumumba died so that the lifestyle of these Europeans—and that of their North American and elite African partners—could continue, uninterrupted, fueled by the neocolonial relations that Joseph Mobutu would secure over the thirty years of his dictatorship" (258).

The victimhood pressed by analysis such as Goldberg's is problematized by revisionist historian Gondola, who debunks the myth of the prophet from a Congolese point of view. Unlike martyred prophets of the Americas, notably Martin Luther King Jr. and Che Guevara, "Lumumba is not noted for great achievements, nor for liberating his people, or even mobilizing them around lofty ideas." Gondola places the sainted Lumumba in the more controversial posterity of Malcolm X; with the difference that guilt was ascertained in the Lumumba killing, albeit after four decades. Both men were in part victims of the intense suspicions of the Cold War American government; their ideas made them dangerous, not their actions. For Gondola, however, "Lumumba stands out for the blunders that led to his downfall." These included the Independence Day speech, full of unnecessary rhetoric that panicked the Belgians and inflamed the already mutinous black soldiers of the Force Publique, whose instantaneous revolt Lumumba was unable to control. The 30 June speech also allowed his opponents to begin to call him "Satan" (as Malcolm X also was called, in prison), "terrorist," and "communist."

Also among fatal missteps, for Gondola, were Lumumba's "reckless" decision to launch a military campaign against the secessionary states of Katanga and Kasai, as well as his "botched escape" from house arrest, when, instead of making for the relative safety of his home base in Stanleyville, he inadvertently allowed his pursuers to catch up to him by stopping to address supporters, although De Witte maintains that the stops were involuntary, attesting to his popularity (53). Finally and most fatally came his promotion of Joseph Mobutu, his ultimate betrayer, into the upper echelons of the Force Publique, against much advice. Goldberg maintains that a "rhetorical mix of character flaws and political faux pas that brewed the myth of Lumumba as communist/terrorist threat" is usually given as an excuse for his murder (259). Gondola sees Lumumba as being more responsible for his fate, given the complex of interests that counted on his failure. Unlike many commentators, Gondola even faults Lumumba's aspirations to martyrdom. His "apocalyptic vision that only by sacrificing his life could he save Congo . . . from civil war and foreign control never came to pass" (2). D'Lynn Waldron sees him finally with two stark choices: "Had Lumumba been willing to compromise his ideals and his country, he could have been a dictator for decades and become the billionaire puppet of foreign economic interests, as Mobutu did. Instead Lumumba chose martyrdom." Lumumba's intimations of his destiny creep into his dialogue in Peck's biopic and are made explicit in the letter to his wife Pauline, portions of which open and close *Lumumba*, and which De Witte also quotes in its entirety in an epilogue (184–185).

Raoul Peck's aim in 1992, however, was to prick the memory and conscience of the world. After King Boudouin of Belgium and President Kasa Vubu give their speeches at the Independence Day ceremony, the narrator confides, "Someone prepares an unconventional speech. He is about to say things best unsaid." Whose point of view does this express? That of the Belgians? The Americans? Critics like Gondola who feel that Lumumba, like Nixon, gave his enemies a sword? Peck himself? History, knowing what disaster Lumumba's speech would spark? Peck cuts from Lumumba's words even before they become inflammatory, to a montage of latter-day interpretations that fall like dominoes back into the interests of neocolonialism. The discord of these voices, argues Goldberg, shows "historical narrative from 'official' public sources as contradictory, subjective to the point of bias, and designed to conceal more than they reveal" (263). She contrasts these with the stories from Peck's mother. The family, Peck tells us in the narration, went to Congo, as his father, an agronomist, responded to the need for educated, French-speaking black professionals to take the place of the Belgians who had left. Peck's mother became a secretary to the mayor of Leopoldville, now Kinshasa. Throughout *Death of a Prophet*, Peck scatters a series of stories that always begin with "My mother told me." This line is followed by a simple story which, altogether, writes Goldberg, provide "a stable, chronological narrative that highlights connections among historical events and steadfastly opposes brutality from any quarter. Employing the strategies of oral storytelling—the repetition, the ironic turns on language, the use of trope and metaphor—this thread of the film privileges a moral position delivered in an Afro-Caribbean narrative tradition representative of Peck's own heritage" (263–264). Peck also tells us, "My mother is no longer here to see these images." This places her stories among the film's many excavations of memory and time, and ranks the mother with Lumumba as a departed subject whose truth must rise from the dead to, as the narration says, "tickle the feet of the guilty."

The mother's tales impart to the film a childlike air, as Peck goes back over the stories from his childhood to understand their darker import, which is to say, their "real" meaning. One of his mother's tales concerns "the way the Belgians rule," which "is simple: Treat the Negroes well, but keep them stupid. But they rebel at this stupidity and become nationalists." To keep the Negroes "stupid" is to keep them childish; to uncover the "simple" truths of oppression and uprising behind childlike stories is to subvert the paternalistic "treatment" of the oppressor and throw him off his position of knowledge and into confusion. Peck frames the film around a poem by Henri Lopès entitled "Du côté du Katanga," in which a child addressing his mother corrects what "they tell you": "it was a giant, my mother, a giant who fell in the night. . . ." This poetic frame seems inspired by Wim Wenders's internationally popular West German film *Wings of Desire* (1988), made one year before the Berlin Wall fell. In it, Peter Handke's poem, "When the child was a child . . ." frames a postmodern pastiche combining the forms of fairy tales, history, documentary, and Hollywood fantasies like *It's a Wonderful Life* as a metaphor for the wish for a unified Germany. Wenders's children of Berlin, who can see the angels that hover above the city while none of the grown-ups can, are paralleled in the children who bridge Peck's two Lumumba films. In the first Peck shows a home movie of kids doing the twist in the front yard of their fashionable home: "Among them a future psychoanalyst, a truck driver, a lawyer, two businessmen, a film director, and a male nurse." This bemusing array of future occupations for a gaggle of kids goofing for a camera is disjunctive enough; our heads are continually snapped between guilt and innocence, childhood and experience.

The biopic parallels the childhood themes. In one key sequence Prime Minister Lumumba confronts Colonel Mobutu about atrocities in the counterattack on secessionist Katanga. After dismissing the man who will be his betrayer, he looks out the window and sees children in the yard playing ring-around-the-rosie. Lumumba then opens the door where photographers have been waiting for him. He sees his young daughter, Julianna, smoothly posing for photos that her father has been too occupied with crises to bother with, brilliantly striking every pose she's asked for. Is she a child who would not understand the poisonous politics and would dance to every tune the neocolonials call? Or does the child have an instinct for the images of politics that the father lacks? We're shown this scene, from Lumumba's point of view, but Peck does not cut back to the expected reaction shot. Instead he goes to a scene in which Lumumba curtly cuts off the American ambassador. This implies that Lumumba is too impulsive, speeding too wildly in the car going 200 miles per hour, in a Peck metaphor from *Death of a Prophet,* to have any recognition of his actions, let alone judgment. For the child, it's too soon for understanding; for the man, it's too late.

The eight-year interval between Peck's documentary and his biopic saw epochal events take place, both in the history and politics of the Congo and in the life and politics of Raoul Peck. The end of the Cold War meant that Mobutu's Western allies withdrew their support of his murderous, larcenous dictatorship, leading to his overthrow in 1996 by longtime opposition leader Laurent Kabila. The following year Mobutu, exiled to Morocco, died of cancer. Kabila himself was murdered on 16 January 2001—the eve of the fortieth anniversary of Lumumba's killing. Kabila's son, Joseph, became president. These last two events occurred between the Paris opening of *Lumumba* and its premieres in the United States.

The 1990s saw Raoul Peck return to Haiti to serve in the government of Prime Minister Rosny Smarth; he was guest-teaching at New York University when the position was offered to him. Peck served as Haitian minister of culture from April 1996 to October 1997; he resigned in protest of what he saw as an antidemocratic takeover by former president Jean-Bertrand Aristide. In the DVD liner notes Peck writes,

> I lived through eighteen months of harsh, ruthless political struggle, in a country that still hesitates between hegemonic populism and democracy, in the course of a history where "democracy" never managed to mean anything but an idea devoid of tradition. It was after this experience, as rewarding as it was tense, that I returned to my Lumumba project. As a way of using my own experience to sum up a political destiny distorted and compromised from the start. As a way of return-

ing to a territory whose contours I can now better make out. As a way of setting the record straight about a murder-sacrifice, forty years later. As a way of getting beyond my pain, my regrets, my rage.

Peck had made the documentary just before the fall of the Soviet Union. "The end of the cold war makes things clearer," he told the *New York Times* in 2001. "For me, the world is not divided; our histories are interwoven . . . the problems are still there and we can see they are not the result of the East-West conflict" (Riding). By the turn of the millennium, many were rethinking the division of the world into "thirds." "The three worlds theory," wrote Robert Stam, "not only flattens heterogeneities, masks contradictions, and elides differences, but also obscures similarities" (282). Certainly the story of postcolonial Congo involves the often secret intertwinings of American, European, and Congolese interests in ways that have become clear only after the end of the Cold War. Once historians had access to material that was unavailable even when Peck made his documentary, many missing pieces got filled in. "The Congo Crisis," wrote historian Jonathan J. Cole, was "an engineered conflict, perpetrated and perpetuated by Belgian, U.S. and U.N. forces" (27). "The madness," explained Robert Craig Johnson,

> sprang in large part from massive, clandestine intervention by the western powers. France, Britain, Belgium, and the United States would not let the Congolese decide their future for themselves because these nations feared that a rival—another western power or the USSR—would gain an undue say in the outcome and that foreign investors would lose money. But none of these countries thought that its motives and actions could stand much public scrutiny, either at home or abroad. They couldn't just send in the marines, as earlier governments had. From this sprang the . . . tools of secret, "low-intensity" wars throughout the remainder of the 20th century. (1)

Many American cities and some foreign countries did not see *Lumumba*, moreover, until after September 11, when it played somewhat differently. In early 2002 Ron Briley wrote,

> It is more important than ever for artists to explore the history of postcolonial Africa and Asia and bring this history to the attention of people around the world, especially the American populace. For it appears

that many Americans fail to comprehend or want to contemplate that American foreign policy of the Cold War era, which often placed the United States alongside anticommunist dictatorships . . . , has antagonized much of the world and contributed to 'blowback' terrorist actions directed at the United States. (38)

As we saw with *Malcolm X,* questions persist as to whether a subject who is not a First or Second World white male can appropriate the dominant discourse without being co-opted by it. *Lumumba* exemplifies the appropriation. It confronts accepted or forgotten truth, replaces it with a revisionist truth, and in the process makes the historical biography the vehicle of a director's personal expression. *Lumumba* was made for $4 million by a group of French, German, and Belgian companies. By the economies of the professional independent filmmaker, however, the film looks like it cost at least ten times more. Peck said he wanted the film "to look like Spielberg, only without Spielberg's budget" (Watson 231). Although Spike Lee treats Steven Spielberg as a negative force field, one senses that Peck would like *Lumumba* to have the impact of Spielberg's *Schindler's List, Amistad,* and *Saving Private Ryan,* films which, whatever their flaws, got many people thinking, talking, and reading about the historical events and personages the movies depict. The reality is, however, that *Lumumba* attracted a minor American distributor, Zeitgeist, and made a limited circuit in art houses, universities, African diaspora film series, and art museums before heading for DVD.

Peck talks about his biopic in terms of mainstream movies: "When I was twelve," he wrote in the *Lumumba* DVD notes, "I would have liked to see a film like this one, but none existed." If Peck is making a historical entertainment for the African Caribbean twelve-year-old in himself, then this is an acknowledgment of a desire to see black heroes, African men and women of destiny to match the white biographical subjects of Hollywood and European biopics. "It's refreshing to watch a film," wrote reviewer Dessin Howe, "that centers so squarely on African affairs, and saves all its dramatic high points for black actors." Furthermore, Peck, at least in promoting his film, calls it "an incredible thriller with all the characters of traditional crime fiction: bandits, thieves, genuine and phony policemen, spies, femmes fatales, adventurers, racist explorers, great intellectuals, journalists who stayed a week before going home to write a book." Surely Peck is not making a movie for twelve-year-olds, however. The film collides Lumumba's personal failings with the traditional tropes of the biopic. These include the man of foresight whose vision is not shared by others. He must either convince them of the rightness of his ideals or he loses or is martyred. But his loss does not necessarily make him less important; indeed, much of the point of the biopic is that the greatness of the subject transcends his or her physical existence.

Peck uses a nearly unheard-of tag, "Ceci est une histoire vraie"—"This is a true story"—whereas the norm for decades has been "based on a true story" or the slipperier "inspired by a true story." While Peck's assertion is bold, it is also immensely subtle. What is the truth of Lumumba's story? "My story is not a nice story," Peck's narration intones in the 1992 film, "but it is Patrice's story." Looking at the two films together, it is clear that Peck has replaced "his" wondering, questing voice, with his dramatized Patrice's own "answering" voice—a call and response across decades and across film modes. Is Peck's "fiction" actually any more fictional than his own wondering voice? At the end of the first film, Peck intones, "They say that Tolenga's son is dead. But they are unable to show the body." In the biopic the body is shown, reincorporated in flashback after it has been mutilated, destroyed, cut into pieces, annihilated, and concealed. Paradoxically, a re-creation in fiction becomes the definitive way to "set the record straight" cinematically. It is an interpretation, but as Peck's first Lumumba film demonstrates, so is documentary.

Many of the strategies of the first film adapt seamlessly to the second. In the documentary Peck audaciously describes the details of Lumumba's execution and dismemberment while his camera wends its way through an elite Brussels cocktail party. In the biopic there is also juxtaposition, this time starting in the title credits, between Belgian polite society and historical images of the brutal Belgian regime. These are crosscut with "present-day" color motion picture shots of those gathered to revere the majesty of the dictator, Mobutu. Peck overlays the "ambient" sound of glasses clinking and people chattering at a garden party with whispers, in African languages, ghosts from another time and place. Thus in a style of unobtrusive realism, Peck interweaves the themes of the first film, of glories of colonialism disrupted by the stifled voices of the colonized, but introduces a third factor, neocolonialism, in the person of Mobutu, who was necessarily offstage in the first film and now can be revealed as the "Africanist" dictator with whom the Western powers can feel "safe."

Peck reprises this juxtaposition at the end of the film as Patrice is driven in a demented motorcade to his backwoods execution in Katanga. Peck dissolves from a close-up of the badly beaten Patrice to a chorus chanting praise to the puppet Mobutu in Bantu, as a "native" dance troupe performs, whereas in Lumumba's time a Western Calypso-style pop group sang "Independence Cha-Cha," an ironic parallel Peck does not fail to make. We are back to the reception from the film's opening. An artless painted mural is revealed as the guests admire it. It shows Lumumba and Mobutu with identical facial features, and with the latter much larger and standing on the right. Peck's camera finds Mobutu at the Independence Day ceremony in 1966 where he declares Lumumba a national hero, with the straight face that his role requires. Peck holds a screen-filling shot of the crowd, staring back at the ruler with blank faces, then dissolves back to Lumumba's death march. Peck ties Lumumba's transcendent spirit to the tendency of the historical film in general, as Robert Rosenstone has defined it, to suggest that things are getting better. "Tell them I just came fifty years too soon," Patrice says in his letter. "Tell them that what we wanted for our country others didn't want. Tell them Congo has a bright future." As Lumumba, before the firing squad, falls against the bullet-riddled tree Peck had shown in the first film, he matches the shot to Mobutu standing at his throne. A slow zoom moves onto the faces of two defiant-looking teenagers, who could be Lumumba's own children, as they glare at Mobutu accusingly. They are the future of which Lumumba speaks in his letter. Will they ever have their day? Lumumba, it turns out, wrote a perfect eulogy, which we hear as the coda. "History will one day have its say. It won't be a history written in Brussels, Paris, or Washington. It will be the history of a new Africa."

Although "Patrice's story"—the story of his country, which continued to be a slaughterhouse well into the 2000s—is the bleakest imaginable, it is the rhetoric of the appropriation to go out on a positive note. In this way, Peck, no differently from the most experimental, agit-prop filmmaker, is hopeful that his film reaches an audience that can exit the theater and do something about the state of things. In a way, Peck appropriates not just the classical biopic or "Spielberg," that is, the kind of historical broad gestures for which Spielberg became known in the 1990s, but also Frank Capra's rhetoric. The symbolic martyrdom at the climax of *Mr. Smith Goes to Washington* is echoed in Peck's enactment of what is for him real martyrdom. Jeff Smith's gasped final line, "*Somebody* will listen to me," is here reprised by the courage and certitude of Lumumba.

The "truth" of Peck's biopic is in its speed. The period from May 1960, when Lumumba was whisked from a cell in Stanleyville, where he was held a political prisoner, to his meteoric rise, to his murder on 17 January 1961, is a nearly incomprehensible blur. Peck does not slow the events down to pretend otherwise. He also does not stop to probe the psychological effect on Lumumba himself of his brutal treatment by the Belgians virtually juxtaposed with his triumph in the national elections just a few weeks later. He makes no connections between the brutality Lumumba suffered—which must have bonded him all the more with his electorate—and his motivations for the infamous 30 June speech. Robert Craig Johnson writes, "'*Nous sommes plus vos singes,*' Lumumba thundered, 'We are not your monkeys anymore!' . . . Lumumba, elated by the electrifying effect of his words on the restive population, played to the crowds and at times even seemed to encourage attacks on Europeans and their property" (4). Johnson also writes, however, that "Lumumba enjoyed a wide following among the divided peoples of the Congo. He thus seemed well prepared for leadership and well qualified to unify the country" (4).

This contradiction between Johnson's first and second passages is typical of nearly all accounts of the Lumumba phenomenon. Lumumba was sometimes heedless but with cause. He could be an irresponsible demagogue at times, but if there was one person who could have united the tribal and regional factions of the Congo, it was he. Except that he didn't. Lumumba is the first great "might-have-been" of postcolonialism. Thus just as Spike Lee does not see his film in 1992 as the time and place for a thorough warts-and-all examination of Malcolm X, so Peck simply stages the pitiless fate of the Congo, seen in the utter extermination of Patrice Lumumba. Lumumba was gone as soon as he began to look like a danger to the West's hold on the copper, cobalt, uranium, and diamonds of the Katanga and Kasai states, and in a context in which possible opposition to capitalism (a belief that Lumumba probably did not actually hold) meant at least the openness to communism.

Peck puts weight, in both films, on Lumumba's inflammatory 30 June speech. It is not clear, however, that everything that befell Lumumba and the Congo would not have happened anyway, especially if one believes that the Belgians had determined to sabotage independence from the beginning. Even though Peck's biopic compresses the critical months from May 1960 to January 1961 into less than two hours, this feels like a "real-time" film. The events run past in a blur, as they did then. One of the several reasons that the brief prime ministry of Lumumba is one of those epochs that stands out from time, that always seems new, is that the events never made sense and took place in impulsive, hair-trigger ways. Jessica Powers's brilliant analysis

25. New president Joseph Kasa Vubu (Maka Kotto), left, and Prime Minister Patrice Lumumba (Eriq Ebouaney) pose for pictures as they announce their coalition government in *Lumumba* (Raoul Peck, Zeitgeist Films, 2000). Outgoing Belgian governor Walter J. Ganshof van der Meersch (André Debaar) pointedly inserts himself. Digital frame enlargement.

of one of Peck's personal vignettes in *Death of a Prophet* seems really apt here. She cites a moment that represents the first images Peck ever shot, when his father let him hold the camera at a bullfight in Spain. Years later, his daughter asked him how it felt watching the bull get killed; Peck tells his audience, "I didn't dare say my main problem was keeping the camera in focus." "On a metaphorical level," Powers argues,

> Lumumba is that bull, and he was being dragged to death. But what did these journalists and politicians, Belgians and Africans alike, "feel" as they watched it happen? Peck tries to determine the answer but it seems clear from their responses that all they felt at the time was an inability to keep focus, that they still have that trouble. Perhaps, he suggests, that is the reason for Lumumba's death. Nobody could see well enough to prevent it. Nobody could focus on Lumumba long enough to understand his true message, unity and peace. Instead they feared his words, then allowed him to be trampled by their own misunderstandings.

I wonder also if the scene does not illustrate our difficulty seeing past our immediate concerns to the large picture, especially when that picture features people of different colors, cultures, backgrounds, and grievances from our own. Moreover, Peck points out a syndrome of the postmodern age, when technology—keeping the camera in focus—often seems to outweigh whatever referent might be in front of the camera, when the way actuality is reproduced seems more vital than what is being reproduced. Ironically, Peck's biopic shows that while Lumumba's power of persuasion and modern media's ability to spread that persuasion gives him an advantage over the whips and clubs wielded by the brutal Belgians, it also makes him a danger to them.

Peck ends the scene before Independence Day ceremonies with one of Lumumba's more level-headed aides asking him, "Patrice, do you really want to say all that?" Then, finally, "Patrice, it's too dangerous." So Peck demonstrates that others in Lumumba's group were opposed to his giving the speech. But the film shows that it was popular, and yet somehow popularity didn't matter. In his Vietnam documentary *Hearts and Minds* (1974), Peter Davis makes the point that postwar America went from a "revolutionary nation to being a counterrevolutionary nation" in its foreign policy. Thus an American especially is apt to watch a film like *Lumumba* with confusion. This is the kind of story our own cinema practically conditions us to applaud; how shocking then to realize that we are villains in the very same type of story. The Independence Day speech montage shows white officers moving away from their radios as black officers, listening with great interest, take their places. Peck does show what Lumumba meant to black Congolese and why he could not be tolerated by the whites. Thus, even while cuing the triumphant music, Peck cuts right to the mutiny of the Force Publique and the images of Lumumba's independent Congo starting to unravel almost before he gets the words out of his mouth.

Peck writes Patrice's first-person narration in the biopic so similarly to his own voiceover in *Death of a Prophet* that, thinking about the two films, it's sometimes hard to remember who made which remarks in which film— Peck's documentary persona or his dramatic "Patrice." And yet the spectator accustomed to first-person voiceover in biopics may not realize how radical it is to put such a mainstream device literally in the mouth of a subject who was killed for what he said. Spike Lee punctuated *Malcolm X* with voiceover narration adapted from the autobiography; however, this was done in a sporadic way that never gave the sense that the story was being told from Malcolm's point of view throughout. Peck's Patrice, on the other hand, speaks noir-like from beyond the grave—"to tickle the feet of the guilty." This time, instead of being at a chilly remove from the perpetrators, we confront them as they do their dirty work—burning and cutting up the bodies of Lumumba

26. "He is about to say things best unsaid." Lumumba in short-lived triumph at the Congolese Independence Day ceremony in 1960. Digital frame enlargement.

27. No sooner are the words out of Lumumba's mouth than the *Force publique* mutinies and the new government starts to unravel. Digital frame enlargement.

and his ministers. The authority conferred by the voice makes their work, however hateful and destructive, seem temporary and ultimately futile. Thus the spectator always gets the sense that we're seeing a story no one wants told, from a voice that had been squelched but could not be destroyed.

"By killing me, they'd let history slip through their fingers. I'd given voice to a dream of freedom and brotherhood." "Liberté et fraternité" are the actual words, invoking the French Revolution as Lumumba did frequently in his rhetoric, however fatally undesirable if prophetic such implicit analogies to Robespierre and the Reign of Terror were to the end of colonialism in Africa. To the biopic's Lumumba, these were "Words they couldn't accept. Just words." And yet this was part of Lumumba's downfall, as the Raoul Peck who wove words so masterfully in the documentary must know: words are threats, especially to those who fear words so powerfully that they try to make sure their own signify as little as possible. Words, after all, were Malcolm X's sole weapons as well.

Much of what Peck said while the film was being produced and promoted was in the vein of appropriation, and of the appropriator who must stay true to the subject whose story he or she is telling. Peck said that he and his co-writer had to resist the temptation to inject a white protagonist into the film, as most commercial films about Africa have done, including *The Last King of Scotland, Catch a Fire,* and *Blood Diamond* (all 2006), knowing how much easier the film would have been to sell with one. Peck himself, in his HBO film *Sometimes in April* (2005), a fictionalization of the 1994 Rwandan slaughter, included the character of Prudence Bushnell, an actual personage who was deputy assistant secretary of state for African affairs at the time and one of the sole American voices calling for intervention when the Somalian massacre of American troops in 1993 was causing the country to shrink from further involvements in Africa. This is a case, however, where a white character was present in the story ready to be developed, and the fictional protagonists were black. Peck succeeded in attracting the seldom-seen Debra Winger to the role, which certainly enhanced its ability to draw financing as well as audiences.

This tendency of the biopic to celebrate the subject's lasting significance, however, brings back everything that is problematic about the Lumumba legacy. The hollowness of this optimism was later answered by Peck in *Sometimes in April,* which recounted the same episodes in Rwanda 1994 as Terry George's better-known *Hotel Rwanda* (2004). The film takes place on the massacre's tenth anniversary. This ascends to Peck's customary vantage point of questing, agonizing memory. *Sometimes in April* was attacked unfairly, I feel, by alternative filmmaker Jon Jost. Jost's point is that lushly produced films like *Sometimes in April* and *Lumumba* enable third-world tragedies to go on indefinitely by allowing their comfortable first-world audiences to suffer for a short while and then to go back home having sympathized with the plight of Africans; meanwhile nothing changes. Peck seems to counter such criticism when he says, as he did about the Lumumba biopic,

"Through the complexity of this story, my sincerest wish is that we will no longer be able to say 'We did not know.'"

Unquestionably, the "we" refers to the comfortable viewers of the first world, who have the luxury of entering a movie theater or renting a DVD or subscribing to HBO. Both of Peck's Lumumba films eliminate any means of saying "We did not know" and do this in two very different ways. Films may not be able to do much more than to change knowledge, which is to say that they change the way audiences think about history and about their roles in it. The documentary, as Diawara says, holds the spectator responsible for the conditions that allowed Lumumba's death (195). The biopic puts the spectator in the position of Patrice Lumumba, who, as he says in his narration, "wanted for our country things others didn't want." In both films it is the lost years, the lost ideals, and the lost lives that matter.

Finally, a word about Peck's allusion to writing a major white character into the Lumumba story. This idea always seemed preposterous, if financially sound given the international film market. But late in my research, I unexpectedly found just the right white protagonist for a *Lumumba* movie. And if ten movies come to be made about Lumumba, as well there could be given that there are almost as many sides to his story as to Nixon's, one of them might feature D'Lynn Waldron. A web site chronicles Dr. Waldron and her "life of high adventure, royal romance, and scientific discovery." As they emerge from the piecemeal linkages of a web site, Waldron's exploits are just unlikely enough for a corking good biopic. In 1957, as a twenty-year-old art student from Cleveland, Diane Lynn Waldron, an individualist who apostrophized her first and middle names, set out on a publicized trip around the world. She published her adventures, illustrated with stills. (Waldron, who later earned a Ph.D. and became a noted scientist and patron of the arts, is also an accomplished photographer.) Waldron appears to have been something of a Zelig during these years. According to her web site, Oscar Hammerstein II (who died of cancer in August 1960) had begun working on the script for a musical based on Waldron's book *Further Than at Home* (1959). Waldron herself was at the Twentieth Century Fox lot negotiating possible screen rights to her book, by chance on the very day in September 1959 when Nikita Khrushchev made his famous visit to the studio. In her travels Waldron met Prince Basundhara of Nepal, to whom she was briefly married. At the beginning of March 1960, she undertook a hitchhiking trip through Africa as a roving correspondent for Scripps-Howard newspapers in the United States. By the end of that month she had escaped arrest in

South Africa after learning through interviews that the price of mining gold was far less than what the Afrikaaners told the public (Waldron). The *Cleveland Press* chose to report that she was deported and to include nothing of the information that the anti-apartheid white South Africans who helped smuggle her out of the country hoped she would spread to the West. This was typical of the way reports out of Africa were laundered and distorted to reflect official American interests and preconceptions (see Cole 28–34). Waldron was to learn this lesson again in May, when she traveled up the Congo River to Stanleyville, where she became the first American correspondent to interview and photograph Patrice Lumumba.

If stories like those of Malcolm X and Patrice Lumumba are "wrong" for mainstream cinema, however, D'Lynn Waldron's tale is probably wrong too, and for many of the reasons her newspaper copy was, in effect, censored. Waldron's story of a strong, independent woman who spent her early years in Africa and went on to have an improbably successful life as a Ph.D. scientist is one that Hollywood would have no more use for than it would for Lumumba's. As we will see in Book Two, a story like hers would be as unintelligible to the biopic of her time as Lumumba was to the Western powers that destroyed him.

BOOK TWO

A WOMAN'S LIFE IS NEVER DONE:
FEMALE BIOPICS

10
Prologue

My life was never my own. It was charted before I was born
—LILLIAN ROTH, EPIGRAPH TITLE CARD FOR *I'LL CRY TOMORROW* (1955)

Biography requires a protagonist who has done something noteworthy in the public world. Women historically have not been encouraged to become the subjects of discourse, at least not of any discourse that is taken seriously by a patriarchal society. Women cannot be consistently posed as the objects of male looks and language and also be the subjects of their own stories. In ways that vary historically somewhat but not nearly to the extent seen in the Great Man films and bios of minority figures, biopics about female subjects catch women up in the contradictions between the public positions—positive or negative—they have achieved and the "unladylike" activities or ambitions that may have landed them there. Female biopics play on tensions between a woman's public achievements and women's traditional orientation to home, marriage, and motherhood. In consequence, female biopics often find suffering (and therefore) drama in a public woman's very inability to make her decisions and discover her own destiny.

Such critics as Carolyn Heilbrun and Linda Wagner-Martin explored the reasons why at all times many fewer biographies are written of women than of men, a disparity also found in film. To Wagner-Martin, "the writing of women's lives is problematic in part because few women have had the kind of success that attracts notice. Women's biography is most often based on private events because few women . . . live public lives" (7). Heilbrun said that when successful women write their autobiographies they almost always downplay their ambition and initiative, traits unbecoming to women in our culture. These drives are usually transferred to male associates, making success appear to be a gift a woman never wanted for herself, or a happenstance that she fell onto by near-accident (23–26).

The genre of woman's biography, in film and literature alike, is infamous for displacing public ambition and achievement onto male partners, managers, and/or husbands, for gravitating to public women who lost control of their private demons and were brought down, and for focusing on women more famous for suffering and victimization than for anything they accomplished or produced. Lytton Strachey's Florence Nightingale chapter in *Eminent Victorians* exemplifies the story of an ambitious woman of purpose who struggles against the hidebound patriarchal institutions whose idea of "reality" makes no allowance for a responsible woman. The gadfly obsessiveness and demonic fervor of the Stracheyan Nightingale are displaced in these films onto male subjects. It is precisely Strachey's point that not only was Nightingale a powerful woman whose force of will brought her into confrontation with formidable patriarchal institutions, but that posterity had cast her into the safe and unthreatening role of the nurturing, saintly nurse, a kind of national Blessed Mother.

This reassuring symbol of feminine virtues was actually a prickly protofeminist who made life uncomfortable for the masculine status quo. Strachey's rendering is a subversive recasting of the nineteenth century in the terms of the suffragist twentieth. Strachey thinks within a feminist framework when he writes that Nightingale "moved under the stress of an impetus which finds no place in the popular imagination" and that if "in the real Miss Nightingale there was more that was interesting than in the legendary one; there was also less that was agreeable" (101). That last word, coming from Strachey, seems typically loaded: "agreeable" to whom and with what? For biopics, alas, the ultimate irony is supplied not by Strachey but by the studios. Female subjects in biopics are either excruciatingly demure and deferential like MGM's Madame Curie, or sanctified like Warners' Nightingale, who, Frank Nugent lamented in a review of the gratingly titled *The White Angel* (1936), "walks, talks, and thinks like a historical character, . . . [as if] striving to live up to Longfellow's 'Lady with the Lamp'" (24), or else they are victims who pay the price for their ambitions, as occurs in countless films.

Strachey clearly sets out the expectations for young women. Equally clear though implicit is the ostracism that comes from defying convention.

Mrs. Nightingale, too, began to notice that there was something wrong. It was very odd; what could be the matter with dear Flo? Mr. Nightingale suggested that a husband might be advisable, but the curious thing was that she seemed to take no interest in husbands. And with her attractions, and her accomplishments, too! There was nothing in the world to prevent her from making a really brilliant match. But no! She would think of nothing but how to satisfy that singular craving of hers to be *doing* something. As if there was not plenty to do in any case, in the ordinary way, at home. There was the china to look after, and there was her father to be read to after dinner. (102)

Strachey satirizes the norm, and never more so than when he writes about a child's "healthy pleasure" in tearing the arms off dolls, as opposed to his subject's "morbid" desire to make the doll whole again. What indeed could there be for a young woman who "moved under the stress of an impetus which finds no place in the popular imagination" (101)? Strachey is laying out the pattern for feminist biopics, idol of production films that were never produced: the ambitious young woman who wants only to do good and goes up against patriarchal institutions at every stage. Here is the "conflict" about which Scott Alexander speaks. Instead of being "wrong" in the way that the half-baked heroes of the Biopics of Someone Undeserving are wrong, a heroine like Florence Nightingale is wrong because she is genuinely threatening—forcing the attention of Great Britain to the "wrongs" in army hospitals and bureaucracies and bringing change where before there was only apathy and inertia. As late as 2000 Steven Soderbergh and Julia Roberts may have made something close to a Stracheyan female biopic in *Erin Brockovich,* whose heroine may amount to an earthy, foul-mouthed Florence Nightingale for American democracy in an age of irony, one without the original's social graces and breeding.

The Lady with a Lamp (1951), a British film by the husband-and-wife director-actress team of Herbert Wilcox and Anna Neagle, who made films together from the early 1930s until 1959, was made for the British market in the transitional period immediately following World War II. Marcia Landy refers to the 1930s movies of the Neagle-Wilcox team, including two biopics celebrating the most eminent Victorian of all, the queen herself, as "films of empire" (*British Genres* 69). By 1951, however, Empire was coming apart; the British had left India and would soon relinquish colonized countries in Africa and the Caribbean. "Like other postwar films, with their ambivalent portrayals of women's status," says Landy, Wilcox's Florence Nightingale biopic "seems rife with compromises. Women in public life are portrayed as having to sacrifice their personal desires and their femininity in order to excel in the world of men" (*British Genres* 91).

The compromises to which Landy refers extend from Nightingale's own life of frustrations and accomplishments to the filmmaking, which seems constrained by the remnants of nineteenth-century rigidity and stupidity that persist into the mid-twentieth century. The frequent scenes of Gladstone's cabinet meetings, as they consider the chief army nurse's latest request for supplies or increased authority, are telling in this regard: a tableful of slumped, lazy, and uninterested men ignorantly pass judgment on matters that seem settled beyond question. Gladstone tends to be composed deep in the shot, making him seem weak and inconsequential. Neagle's unflappable performance style presents Nightingale as a woman surprised by nothing and ready to negotiate with everything with which the patriarchy can block her. The appearance of Queen Victoria, to whom Nightingale appeals as the enlightened figurehead of an ineffectual government, suggests that the wrong gender is in charge. The film itself is narrated by Sir Douglass Dawson (Cecil Trouncer) as he brings the Award of Merit in 1907 to an eighty-seven-year-old Nightingale, who becomes the first woman to receive it. The Lord's extreme condescension makes him not only an unreliable narrator, but the refusal of the then-bedridden Nightingale to see him seems her last revenge on a system that never gave her her proper measure of respect and understanding.

The "compromises" can also be felt as seething anger just under the surface. The film throughout seems fairly teeming with melodramatic outbursts that the filmmakers, the characters—everyone—seem to know better than to let loose with. This is Nightingale as Stracheyan stealth feminist; Wilcox's and Neagle's Nightingale was not going to give the British government the satisfaction of giving her a biopic vindication she knew that those bestowing it didn't believe in. Even with a subject as triumphant and influential as Nightingale (I speak as one who teaches film courses in the auditorium of a large nursing school with a bust of The Lady with the Lamp just outside the door), "the final image of the female" in the Wilcox film, writes Landy, "is one of isolation and entrapment in the home," even if the isolation seems willful, a statement in itself (*British Genres* 91). There's an angry, spirited biopic of Florence Nightingale still waiting to be made.

George Custen finds that female biopic subjects in the thirties were often queens, corresponding to the star status of the actresses who played them (Greta Garbo as Christina of Sweden, Marlene Dietrich as Catherine the Great, Bette Davis as Elizabeth I, Norma Shearer as Marie Antoinette) (102–104). These royal women were born to their greatness, thus the films avoid issues of ambition. The queen's power to command, however, is usually in conflict with women's emotional, romantic, dependent natures. Strachey's Nightingale is the Victorian woman of destiny. She is difficult; she takes on the system, makes great changes, and improves nursing and medicine for the future.

In contrast to Great Man films, however, female biopics overall found conflict and tragedy in a woman's success. A victim, whatever her profession, made a better subject than a survivor with a durable career and a non-traumatic personal life. Early deaths were preferable to long lives. Female biopics frequently depicted their subjects as certainly or possibly insane, made so by the cruelties of a victimizing world, or by the subject's insistence on having her own way in the world. These principles hardened into conventions. Films were made about Lillian Roth (Susan Hayward in *I'll Cry Tomorrow*), not Lillian Gish; Frances Farmer (Jessica Lange in *Frances*), not Katharine Hepburn; Dian Fossey (Sigourney Weaver in *Gorillas in the Mist*), not Margaret Mead; Billie Holiday (Diana Ross in *Lady Sings the Blues*), not Ella Fitzgerald. A late victimology-fetish female biopic, *Factory Girl* (2006), about Edie Sedgwick, the short-lived Andy Warhol "It Girl," looking for some justification for its production, ends with documentary interview sound bites accompanying the end credits. In one of them, a photographer named Nat Finkelstein says, "Who is Edie Sedgwick? Edie Sedgwick is a combination of all the tragic women who came before her." So of course there must be a movie about such an archetypal female! This convention, or principle, moreover, transcends national boundaries. In *Yuen Ling-yuk* (*Center Stage*, 1992), Hong Kong director Stanley Kwan's revisionist biopic of the early 1930s Chinese film star actress Ruan Ling-yu, who committed suicide at age twenty-five amid a marital scandal, Kwan interviews his cast members on camera. One of them, Han Chin, observes, "If Ruan Ling-yu hadn't killed herself, we wouldn't be filming her life story now." For *What's Love Got to Do with It?* (1993), about Tina Turner, who was known for an indomitable stage persona, Angela Bassett undertook weight training to attain the singer's tough appearance. The film itself, however, drags its protagonist through the usual circles of victimization hell. The newly minted post–*Malcolm X* convention of bringing footage of the real person onscreen at the end damages this film because we realize that we haven't seen how the put-upon character played by Bassett could have possibly turned into the badass icon introduced in the finale.

Mary Ann Doane finds that "the protagonist of a text of pathos is of a lower social status and, in some sense, a victim." Such a figure "lacks the social and moral elevation of the tragic hero" and is "nearly always passive in comparison." Therefore, "pathos is associated with 'lower' forms such as melodrama, forms historically associated with the feminine" (10). Doane makes generalizations here that should be interrogated, however. "The emotion of pathos is predictably excessive," she writes, but pathos itself is considered distinct from bathos, which is defined as excessive pathos. Moreover, Doane, like many latter-day scholars, considers melodrama in a strictly feminine context. Melodrama is a very broad class of drama; presumptively male genres like the western and the noir were also classified in their day as melodramas within the Hollywood system. However, as we saw in Book One, when the male biopic subjects who belong to the model of the late 1930s engage in melodramatic struggles with more powerful, established forces, they triumph. When they do fail, as does Woodrow Wilson in Zanuck's film, or when they face great sadness, as with Lincoln in Ford's movie, it is because they fall victim to dark forces outside their control. Later, however, the decline of a modern Great Man like Kane or Lawrence or Nixon plays as tragedy; these figures fall from great heights due to overreaching, but also from hubris, like a "Greek figure," in Oliver Stone's phrase.

In the 1950s female biography emphasized entertainers. Once the focus changed, so did the plot type, from one where the heroine must balance power with love—a way of dealing with the public-private dichotomy which is the key to biography in general—to one where a victimized subject battles the downward spiral that overtakes her. This tendency toward the downward trajectory in female subjects can be attributed to a number of causes—the decline of the importance of female audiences and female stars as the studio system crumbled; the rise of misogyny in Eurocentric postwar popular culture, keyed to the Cold War and the drive to keep women at home; and the influence of domestic melodrama and the "woman's film" on the biography. This was all an expression of an ideology that finds drama and what Robert Rosenstone summarizes as "truth" in the path of a female subject toward addiction and madness (*Visions* 75–76). The public world is not ready for or hospitable to women, such films assume. Suffering awaits women who try for public success. Any female biopic that wants to avoid the easy melodramatic victimization of the form must, as we'll see, approach the form with some kind of conscious strategy for countering this tendency.

The downward trajectory is the main narrative action of the two primary plot types of the postwar female biography: a two-act rise and fall structure exemplified by *Lady Sings the Blues* (1972), *Frances* (1982), *Dance with a Stranger* (1985), *Camille Claudel* (1989), and *Mrs. Parker and the Vicious Circle* (1994); and a three-act structure: rise, fall, and rehabilitation. Examples of the latter type are *I'll Cry Tomorrow*, in which the alcoholism of thirties Hollywood actress Lillian Roth is halted by a sympathetic Alcoholics Anonymous volunteer who appears to shape up as a romantic interest, and *Love Me or Leave Me*, in which Ruth Etting can escape her abusive marriage to a "bad man" only so long as there is a "good man" to catch her, in effect, after she flees.

A pertinent point of reference, though not a film I study at length, is *I'll Cry Tomorrow*, the biopic of early 1930s starlet Lillian Roth (1910–1980). Groomed by her mother for stardom, first on Broadway and then in films, Roth arrived in Hollywood at the dawn of the talkies and was cast in such films as *The Love Parade* (1929) and *Animal Crackers* (1930). Roth's natural shyness, however, along with the death of a beloved fiancé, led her to the bottle and a long, horrifying spiral. Entering Alcoholics Anonymous after years of addiction, Roth reformed and detailed her journey in a best-selling book in 1954. Hollywood lost no time in bidding for the screen rights, to be won by MGM, which cast Susan Hayward. *I'll Cry Tomorrow* ends up as a rehabilitation narrative of the sort later revived by *Ray* (2004). However, it is the wallowing in suffering, addiction, and degradation in the middle third of the film that is the most intense and powerful, and the suffering seems to be the point.

MGM, famously the most conservative of the studios, needs to recuperate authority and the family. Thus the mother is made somewhat sympathetic, but the filmmakers wait until nearly the end of the film to do this, after Lillian has toured the circles of Hell, with her mother to blame. The film shifts narrative registers nearly midway through, introducing Lillian's voiceover narration only at the point where she begins to become an alcoholic. So Lillian takes control of her story once she has declared her independence from her mother, only to screw up her life (as she tells it) without direct maternal help. The effect of this odd disembodied voice (Susan Hayward's), which comes from Roth's best-selling memoir, is to help kick the heroine down farther into her hellish descent. Because the voice is disconnected from the onscreen character, and especially because this voiceover Lillian does not introduce herself as the narrator of the story from the beginning, the voice actually becomes one more device to imprison Lillian inside her own degrading life.

I'll Cry Tomorrow is a warts-and-all biopic, a variant that began in the mid-1950s when the genre became more "adult," and when, as Custen found, films about entertainers far outnumbered other kinds of subjects. The warts-and-all film mined drama and conflict, playing on oppositions between public and private realms. Precisely, this type of biopic was heavy with story, usually emphasizing a central conflict or weakness. In *Love Me or Leave Me* (1955), the twenties singer Ruth Etting (Doris Day) is forced into a terrible marriage with a gangster who had given her some help at the start of her career; in *I'll Cry Tomorrow* Lillian turns to alcoholism as an escape from an abusive mother. America in the fifties, broadly speaking, was a progressive nation with an expanding economy. The country, however, bubbled with discord just below the surface—fears of communism and nuclear annihilation and still recent scars from the Great Depression and the terrors of World War II. American movies of the period are nearly obsessed with paranoid fantasies of a downward slide. In biopics this means melodramas with characters who lose it all, and of people with advantages who throw them all away. Warts-and-all also became favored by filmmakers sensitive to the criticisms of the genre's formulaic tendencies (which are usually summed up by another cliché, "rags to riches"). The warts-and-all variant was also well suited to the postwar preference for location shooting; it is a style, like film noir, that works best on actual streets. The physical realism suits the sense of emotional honesty that these films try to achieve. Thus the advertising tagline for *I'll Cry Tomorrow,* "This story was filmed on location—inside a woman's soul," perfectly sums up the subgenre.

Female biopics dramatize, with proper Aristotelian pity and terror, the process of a woman's degradation. This is what the downward trajectory essentially is. The dominant film institutions—and male directors—think they are being sympathetic to women by showing the process by which women are washed out as human beings, and wash themselves out. *I Want to Live!* (1958) shows how illuminating the results can be when male filmmakers truly imagine themselves in the position of the woman being held to the male legal standards of "reasonableness," as Drucilla Cornell discusses them, rather than take the patriarchal position in which the woman is irrational (19). It is this latter conditioning, ingrained in patriarchy, which conventionally had made real identification with a female impossible and has resulted in so many confused and deadening biopics about women.

Thus the downward trajectory, the drama in which the public woman can only be degraded and in which drama is perceived as possible only *in* degradation, grows "naturally" out of a structure in which women are seen as outside the norm. Public women, those who seek to go beyond their "place," start out with two strikes against them. When, in the world of film, the female star as institution was a norm, women as strong subjects were seen in some context of normality. When the stars played queens, born to their roles, they had two points in their favor; these mirrored the "two strikes" I mention above. Thus even in a studio-era film like *Madame Curie* (1943), whose script takes every opportunity to point out the freakishness of a brilliant scientist who is a woman, the female subject is normalized by the fact that Curie "is" Greer Garson, a "goddess" in the practical firmament of MGM in the forties. Bathed in three-point lighting, Garson can be anywhere the film says she is, and if the setting happens to be a laboratory or a Nobel Prize ceremony, the fact that Curie is Garson-at-Metro is all the spectator needs to be satisfied.

The norms of the studio system, in which viewing habits were thought to mirror the home, family, and habits of consumption as imagined in a film such as *Meet Me in St. Louis* (1944)—that is, female-determined—were gradually replaced after the war by an audience profile that tilted toward males and youth. The crisis periods of the Depression and the war were replaced by the postwar environment, which emphasized domestic "normality" and its pervasive misogyny. Woman, across all genres, becomes secondary, Other. When the genre is a biopic, the questions of a public woman become these: Why should she be there? What will she do, or what will be done to her, inevitably, to bring her heartbreak, failure, to *degrade* her, bit by bit?

In light of Cornell's legal critiques, it is interesting that not only does *I Want to Live!* deal with the female subject in a legal frame (perhaps literally), but a number of recent female biopics show women as outsiders to the law—*Dead Man Walking* (1995), *Erin Brockovich* (2000), *Boys Don't Cry* (1999). Even the rare female "biopic about someone who doesn't deserve one," *The Notorious Bettie Page* (2006), uses as its narrative frame a congressional investigation in which the subject is a key witness; like Mr. Smith in Capra's film, she is ultimately denied a voice in her own inquisition. In both *Erin* and *Bettie* the female protagonist feels free to show off her sexuality as part of her public persona but also as the person who "shines through." The difference is that in *Bettie,* made by women, the heroine's exhibitionism is one part of her; in fact, it's her living. It doesn't define who she is; indeed, when we first see her, she is demurely dressed in her Sunday best, covered from neck to knee and wearing delicate white gloves. Similarly, Erin Brockovich's sexual display, a habit of the actual subject, which happened to make her a provocative subject for a Hollywood movie, is not explained or given motivation. Female biographies are produced in a cultural framework that sees marriage, not public or artistic accomplishment, as a woman's ultimate fulfillment. The downward trajectory is nearly always motivated by a relationship with a man that failed either because the woman was preoccupied with her career or, more often, because the male was "the wrong kind of man," one interested in using a successful woman. Also common to these films is an extreme overdetermination of a peculiar feature that Custen finds in many biographies, the opposition of the subject's family (154–155). In *Frances* (1982) and *Camille Claudel* (France, 1989), as well as in *I'll Cry Tomorrow,* a chief villain is the mother, who projects her own frustrated ambition onto her daughter in ways that dramatize the monstrousness of female ambition, keeping the heroine sympathetic, as the film sees it, by rendering her "innocent" of a drive to exceed the ordinary expectations of women.

The patterns have been interrupted, as if by accident, by an occasional film such as *I Want to Live!* In this case male filmmakers anxious to make an anti–death penalty picture identified with the experiences of Barbara Graham, a convicted murderer executed, many felt unfairly, in California in 1955. *Star!* (1968), which like *I Want to Live!* was directed by Robert Wise, is an object lesson in what can happen when Hollywood slips and makes a biopic about an ambitious, successful woman with no particular need of a husband and no compensating "feminine" values. In general, however, these patterns can be broken only by deliberate efforts to rethink them and a definite desire to undo and rework them. The patterns can be undone in any number of ways, by means of parody and deconstruction, by combining them with other forms to create an ironic or critical perspective, by exceeding the patriarchal perspective through empathy with the female subject, by refusing to delve into the bathos of victimization, and by breaking past the limitations of the patriarchal form to find a genre that tells the woman's story in a female voice. In this way, as Carolyn Heilbrun writes, "the old story of woman's destiny, the old marriage plot, would give way to another story for women, a quest plot" (121). The trajectory of Book Two is to explore and analyze the films we find along the way to such plots.

11

Superstar: The Karen Carpenter Story

Toying with the Genre

Superstar: The Karen Carpenter Story (Todd Haynes, 1987) opens with a stark title card, white lettering on black: "February 4, 1983." A shot of a stereo receiver, the type of equipment that amplified Karen Carpenter's voice in millions of households, launches a handheld subjective camera movement, representing the point of view of Agnes, Karen Carpenter's mother, as she walks through Karen's apartment, calling for her daughter. The mother's voice becomes concerned and then frantic as she fails to find Karen in her bedroom. Finally, accompanied by synthesizer horror music, a cliché in films of the 1980s, she screams at finding her daughter unconscious. The shrieking sound track builds to a coda and then suddenly stops, as if switched off. The scene plays as a set of well-worn conventions, as if to say to the character, not "Don't open that door!" but "Well, what did you expect to find?"

The screen goes black, then fades in on a trucking shot of the sedate, well-tended homes and lawns on the street where the Carpenter family lived in Downey, California. Aurally, the female hysteria of the previous scene gives way to a silent pause, then to the kind of soporific male voice our culture has been trained to hear as calm and authoritative. "What happened?" drones the voice. This question, as Marcia Landy writes, "enlarges to focus on the 'crisis' of Karen's anorexic body" ("Storytelling" 10). A female biopic like *I'll Cry Tomorrow* finds through melodrama definite answers to "What happened?" In postmodern fashion, however, Haynes indicates that the question is the wrong one. Hollywood genres, or any mainstream cultural products, are not equipped to answer it. The question to ask is "What happens all the time?" in American culture. This question leads to an unconscious pattern of behavior and attitude. The anorexia-related death of a terrified young woman under the glare of a spotlight she did not choose would then seem a consequence of her environment and circumstances, not the aberration implied by "What happened?" "What happened," Haynes shows, cannot be answered so long as the culture fails to understand *what happens* to women (and men) through social conditioning. The "what happened?" is the film's Rosebud, Haynes being yet another director who structures a biography after *Citizen Kane; Velvet Goldmine* (1998), his disguised David Bowie bio-phantasmagoria, follows the *Kane* model even more closely and obviously. It is the question that cannot be answered, at least not in the narrow precincts of the biopic.

The assumption that a woman did not choose her path is a time-worn convention of woman's biography, going back to the lives of queens who wore their crowns unwillingly and with regret. Men who fail in the classical biopic are seen as intolerably victimized by unreasoning forces; women should not want something so non-nurturing, so unfeminine as worldly success. On the other hand, those who want it for them are less sinister and more sympathetic if they are men, no matter how flawed, such as Martin Snyder, Ruth Etting's gangster mentor in *Love Me or Leave Me,* Dolittle Lynn in *Coal Miner's Daughter* (1980), Louis McKay, the "good father" to the childish Billie Holiday in *Lady Sings the Blues* (1972), or Shirley Muldowney's son in *Heart Like a Wheel* (1983), than if they are women, especially mothers, as in *I'll Cry Tomorrow* or *Gypsy* (1962).

In his later films, from *Poison* (1991) to *Velvet Goldmine* and *Far from Heaven* (2002), Todd Haynes is concerned with reality as it is understood through film genres and other media. The 1971 Carpenters hit "Superstar," which, as in a Hollywood film, plays under the opening credits, after the "teaser" prologue, belongs as the title of Haynes's film. The song is the kind of pitiful, clinging plea to a rambling lover still often favored at that time by female singers: "Don't you remember you told me you loved me, baby? / You said you'd be coming back this way again, baby . . ."; Carly Simon's similarly themed but ultra-flip "You're So Vain" (1972) gave this song-type a well-warranted kiss-off. The Carpenters song's masochism fits the biopic genre nonetheless.

Haynes's film filters Karen Carpenter's tragedy through the genre of the melodramatic Hollywood female biopic and the medium of toys. Karen Carpenter died at thirty-two from effects of anorexia nervosa, from which she suffered for at least six years. Her celebrity death brought the first widespread public attention to the illness. Haynes's forty-three-minute "biopic" is "performed" by Barbie and Ken dolls. Haynes, bursting with ideas in his second film, made after completing his B.A. in semiotics from Brown University and M.F.A. from Bard College, places quotation marks around everything. He uses familiar motifs and contests them, placing these motifs in opposition to one another. For instance, the tag "A dramatization" is superfluous in a movie using dolls, especially when the film is pitched in the feverish *über*-melodramatic tone of downward trajectory. The poster to the film's message board on Internet Movie Database who burbled, "Barbie gives an Oscar-calibre performance!" facetiously caught the spirit of both Haynes's parody/pastiche and the idiom being referenced, one whose performers have often won or been nominated for Oscars.

Superstar is Brechtian biography, to a degree of which Charles Laughton could only have dreamed. Haynes disrupts his dramatic diegesis with an authoritative male announcer who sounds like he is on Quaaludes (a drug to which her brother Richard Carpenter was addicted). Later, a female lecturer expounds on the centrality of food in postwar America over a panning shot of a plentitudinous supermarket aisle. Over *this* are supertitles that discourse on anorexia nervosa, calling it "a fascism of the body." *Superstar* solves the problem in biography and historical film of how to venture out beyond the particular story and characters to address a larger condition— how to show "what happens." Haynes surrounds the genre of the female biopic with contrasting discourses to make a movie about anorexia and, beyond that, a film about the images that women are expected to conform to in modern consumer culture.

Superstar has been "banned" since 1989. The web site Time Out London, in placing it number one on an October 2007 list of the fifty greatest films—documentaries or dramatizations—about actual musicians, stated with marvelous tact that "the only way to see it now is by Googling it on the internet." The official cause of the film's illegality is that bane of many a student or independent filmmaker—the inability to obtain music copyright clearances, which can cost many thousands of dollars. Of course, artists can refuse to grant rights to a filmmaker for any reason, as Bowie did, greatly stymieing Haynes on *Velvet Goldmine* (Sullivan 61, 63).

Haynes breaks other copyright laws and risks libel as well, making

Superstar truly an outlaw film. There are close-ups of a brand name, Ex-Lax, shown in as villainous a light as it is possible to cast a laxative. Proper names, such as that of Tom Burris, to whom Karen was briefly married in the early 1980s, are used without clearance. Burris in fact did not clear his name to be used in the telefilm *The Karen Carpenter Story,* an "authorized" biopic that aired on CBS on New Year's night 1989. The practice of mingling documentary and staged scenes was still years from acceptability in 1987. Haynes pioneers the technique of interspersing (fake) documentary interviews into a biopic. Probably knowing the chagrin caused by Michelle Citron for using actresses as documentary subjects in *verité*-style interviews in *Daughter Rite* (1978), Haynes invites similar consternation. Clearly, the tagline "A dramatization" covers a multitude of "dramatic liberties," parodying the disclaimer while employing it. Haynes's film was made around the time when the Academy Award documentary committee reportedly switched off Errol Morris's *The Thin Blue Line* (1988) after the first thirty minutes because it included reenactments, which were then *verboten* in nonfiction films. It also was made well before Oliver Stone's *JFK* (1991), which, despite all the controversy it aroused, cleared the air for what Bill Nichols has called the "blurred boundaries" between documentary and dramatization—an important development in the history of the biopic. *Superstar* feels less experimental two decades later, not only because its director went on to become an acclaimed filmmaker, but also because much of its "audacity" became accepted artistic practice, as demonstrated by *Thirty Two Short Films About Glenn Gould* just six years later.

More than a matter of music rights, Haynes's "legal battle . . . with A&M Records and the Carpenter family" involves "the question of who was authorized to represent Karen's life and her voice" (Desjardins 24). Whose life is it anyway? The answer: not really Karen Carpenter's. She becomes lost in the squabble over ownership and authorship, which is precisely Haynes's point. Carpenter struggled in life to make her own decisions and to control what an overtitle in *Superstar* calls "the inner relationship with herself." This is the content, in different ways, of both Haynes's film and the TV movie. Karen's struggle is overshadowed, however, by the legal dispute over who has the right to represent her life: her family and the organizations of which she was a part and a product, or Todd Haynes, an outsider and artist, a consumer of her music and interpreter of her life and the meanings it might hold. In the terms of the legal system in which *Superstar* became mired, Haynes is both her investigator—a traditionally male role—and her advocate, a more empathetic, feminine position. Haynes's displacement of the real Karen onto a Barbie doll, a body too small, in a sense, has the effect of decentering the subject in the way advocated by the feminist film theory and avant-garde feminist filmmaking practice that were at the height of their influence in the 1980s when Haynes made his film.

Superstar, as Desjardins writes, is "one of the forerunners" of a 1990s subgenre of experimental star biographies, of which the best known are two by Mark Rappaport, *Rock Hudson's Home Movies* (1992) and *From the Journals of Jean Seberg* (1995) (27). These films, including *Superstar,* choose star subjects whose deaths revealed secret lives hidden from the public. Hudson and Carpenter died of diseases with profound social import. Seberg, an archetypal "victim of Hollywood," committed suicide. The films purport to speak for the subjects after death, to say what they could never have said within the cultural institutions that enabled and controlled them. These are far more radical and illicit than minority appropriations such as *Malcolm X* and *Milk* (2008), which were released by major studios or their indie subsidiaries, with all clearances and compromises duly made.

While appropriations seek to bring radical subjects to some kind of acceptance within cultural mythology, even while stretching the boundaries of what is "acceptable," Haynes hijacks a mainstream object and seeks to understand it in a radical context. It is hard not to conclude that the made-for-TV *Karen Carpenter Story* exploits Karen much more than Haynes's film, whose fault according to the copyright holders lies partly in its exposure and critique of such exploitations. On the other hand, *Superstar* itself becomes a melodramatic victim of "unfeeling" establishments, leading its spectators (those who manage to see it) to feel as deprived, put upon, and punished as the protagonist in a female biopic.

According to one description, Haynes "spent months making miniature dishes, chairs, costumes, Kleenex and Ex-Lax boxes, and Carpenters records to create the film's intricate, doll-size mise-en-scène" ("*Superstar*"). *Superstar* is a toy biopic. Just as the male entertainer biopic flashback formula was so elemental and familiar it could be parodied in a Bugs Bunny cartoon, *What's Up, Doc?* (1950), so the formula of the female musical biopic was so widely recognized that Haynes could stage it with toy actors. Toys replicate familiar objects from the culture as miniatures, as commodities and as artifacts. Toys have a taken-for-granted, objective quality; they represent *givens,* ideas that the culture accepts as facts without controversy. They are obvious, in the same way that Mary Ann Doane refers to Haynes's films as relying on the banal and obvious and then making from them something surprising and unexpected (13). Not counting characters from cartoons and other fictions, or fantastic figures such as dinosaurs, a toy is the pretend version of something real in the here and now. A toy model of the Volkswagen Beetle, for example, with doors that open, detailed interior and dashboard, and an engine under the hood, is experienced by a child as a copy of the original that you can hold in your hand; however, the toy is more special than the original for having been copied. Like a biopic, a toy version of an object from life is evidence that the object belongs to cultural mythology. Barbie and all her accoutrements, which chart changes in standards for young women since the doll's inception in 1959, are as emblematic of the restrictive values and ideals for women as the convention that film roles for women dry up after age forty and that female biopics dramatize, in effect, women who lived and lost.

A child designs his/her own scenario with the toy. The toy is objective, true to the object in life and verifying and magnifying the importance of that object. Each child is invited to bring his/her subjectivity to bear on the toy by playing with it, inventing situations and actions for it. Thus certain playthings become notorious in retrospect when adults realize the ideologies embedded in toys they played with in all innocence as children. White baby boomers who remember when the 64-box of Crayola crayons, circa 1960, included a Nordic tinge labeled "Flesh" realize that their innocent play was pervaded by ideological assumptions that were anything but innocuous, while children of color had to feel cast outside play, denied access even to their own imaginations. In the logic of a culture, therefore, in which little girls play with dolls that model the anatomically improbable, if not impossible, not only would a Barbie worry that she will get "too fat," but the children's plaything becomes the perfect vehicle to demonstrate the distorted body image of an anorexic.

Mary Desjardins finds rewards in comparing *Superstar* with the run-of-the-mill celebrity "disease of the week" TV movie, *The Karen Carpenter Story*. Both films put their heroine on the familiar downward trajectory and both take the "blame mother" approach. The starkest difference between the telefilm and Haynes's lies in the fact that the "body too much" contrast (see Introduction) between the sweet-faced actress Cynthia Gibb and Karen Carpenter, whom she plays, involves the usual evaluations: Does Gibb suggest Carpenter in any number of dimensions one could raise? Does she suggest the anguish that Carpenter must have been going through? Is there a concept to her portrayal, or is the performance little more than a physical impersonation? *Superstar,* on the other hand, substitutes a Barbie doll for Karen Carpenter and ignites an extensive discourse on female beauty standards, role models for young women, and postwar American consumerism's boundless capacity for getting inside the minds and imaginations of children from an early age. *Karen Carpenter is a Barbie doll,* the film asserts. Haynes's metaphor sounds like a smart-aleck way of "explaining" her anorexia—a sick joke similar to Haynes's naming the film's company "Iced Tea Productions," after the drink that, along with salad, is later shown to be the anorexic Karen's sole nourishment. However, the film far exceeds camp audacity and bad-taste devilry.

The authenticity of Karen Carpenter's voice and the Carpenters' music, an actress's plaintive portrayal of Karen on the sound track within a naturalistic mise-en-scène, and hand-held, documentary-style camera work all combine to present Karen's story as melodrama that obscures a cultural tragedy. In orchestrating the downward trajectory-victimization show business female biopic, replete with predatory producers, a controlling mother, betraying brother-mentor, and helplessly self-destructive protagonist, and then juxtaposing this with the "objective" authority of a sociological documentary, Haynes accomplishes several things: he shows how a celebrity like Karen Carpenter never stops entertaining us. Her great, sad life turns easily into melodrama, echoing the female biopic of the subject who never wanted her success, for whom the American Dream becomes an unmanageable dilemma. The dichotomy of the public and the private here is violated.

The telefilm, on the other hand, seeks to preserve what it construes as the essence of Karen's and the family's privacy. The film's producer claimed that "we're not really making a film about anorexia. It's about Karen Carpenter and her career of 20 years" (Desjardins 31). Desjardins characterizes the producer's claim as "a fictive construct that recognizes the version of Karen's life authorized by the Carpenter family, especially Richard Carpenter." In interviews, "Richard Carpenter expressed skepticism over the social and cultural causes of anorexia, claiming it was genetically determined and had little to do with family dynamics or show business" (38). Desjardins finds the family's interest in heading off connections between Karen's illness and external causes to be at odds with the "pedagogical or even therapeutic role" often played by made-for-television movies. Once Karen's illness is sealed off from external causes, the filmmakers can focus almost solely on her struggles. This strategy exposes a gaping contradiction, however, between the genre's demand for drama, which means a focus on Karen's troubles and unhappiness, and the desire to deny that those troubles were related to family, business, and cultural pressures. At the same time, Karen is portrayed as the irrational female, in a tizzy over senseless fears. Richard comes off as the virtuous visionary following his muse. Even his addiction to Quaaludes stems from his sleepless devotion to the band; he is shown drawing the inspiration for the group's records during some of his bouts with insomnia. What's more, his addiction is attributed to a suggestion from ever-blameable Mom, another risk-free target.

In time-honored female biopic tradition, the telefilm is as much about a man, Richard Carpenter, and the Carpenters as a musical group as it is about Karen. It seems exploitative of the network to name its film *The Karen Carpenter Story,* a title capitalizing on morbid curiosity that would not have been present without Karen's death. More rightly it should have been titled *The Carpenters.* Much attention is given to Richard's musical talent as the leader of the band; he has the dramatic "Eureka!" moments, such as getting the idea for the hit record "We've Only Just Begun" when he hears the tune on a commercial for a Los Angeles bank. The telefilm is half "man of vision" male biopic and half "stuff happens" female biopic. One of the ironies is that Haynes stirs up controversy by what he *doesn't* show about Richard. The telefilm spends nearly as much time on Richard's addiction to Quaaludes as it does on Karen's illness, minimizing the importance of Karen's fatal disorder (the word anorexia is not spoken until the last twenty minutes) by giving her brother's problems equal time. Haynes, on the other hand, doesn't mention Richard's troubles, only alluding to them in a scene in which Karen counters Richard's threat to tell their parents that her anorexia has relapsed: "You do and I'll tell them about your private life. . . . They're going to find out sooner or later. . . . What, do the Carpenters have something to hide?" After tantalizing the spectator with this hint of something hidden in Richard's "private life," Haynes drops it, not only committing the narrative sin of introducing a plot point and then failing to follow up on it, but potentially libeling Richard Carpenter by suggestion.

By sketching the outlines of the warts-and-all female entertainer biopic, Haynes broadens his subject beyond her own individuality, making her story more sociological. Doane writes that "Haynes's cinema demonstrates not so much that the image resides within a genre, but that the generic invades the image, reducing its singularity, making it available for recognition." She continues, "Perhaps Haynes's predilection for genre can be explained by an acknowledgment that a certain obviousness or banality is crucial to his project. The force of the image, its legibility, and even its radicality are dependent on its recognizability and its effect of immediacy" (12–13).

This sense of the tragic is intensified by Haynes's use of the Barbie metaphor for the image that Karen unconsciously wants to attain and the gap between the appearance of an actual Barbie and that of an anorexic woman (which Haynes shows by, among other things, cutting the doll's face to suggest wasting away and other kinds of female self-abuse). Who could be more of a mirror-stage ego ideal for girls than Barbie? Who could be more of an idol of consumption (in the innuendo of the word's once-common use as a synonym for tuberculosis)? Who could better exemplify the manipulation of female identity in the patriarchal symbolic order than Barbie? What could provide a better parody and pastiche in the postmodern sense of the film illusion of character than a film that, on one level, makes you believe that a Barbie doll is embodying Karen Carpenter dying of anorexia, in all its poignancy and pathos? What better metaphor could there be for the ways that female stars and ordinary women mirror each other?

Karen tells her mother, "In my work, you have to look good," modeling herself after a standard of female beauty that, as a celebrity, she also sets. Haynes thus suggests a kind of endless "mirror, mirror, on the wall" that renders women not only separate from themselves, but also separate from an image. This is the hall of mirrors in which the subjects of female biopics are trapped. In entertainer biopics, moreover, countless emotional scenes take place in front of the mirrors of dressing rooms, with the camera behind the shoulder of the protagonist as she faces her agonies. This mirroring is exemplified in a frequently cited shot in *Love Me or Leave Me*. Ruth Etting (Doris Day) fields a come-on from gangster Marty Snyder (James Cagney), with Day in the left of the CinemaScope frame and Cagney on the right. Meanwhile, Day's reflection in the mirror, centered in the shot, describes exactly the object, the product, that Marty sees in Ruth. By the end of the film, even after Ruth has left Marty, who had coerced her into marriage, raped her (or so the film strongly suggests; Day wrote in her memoirs that a rape scene was filmed), and shot the man she started seeing after she left Marty, the star nonetheless opens Marty's new nightclub for him. "Recessed in the diegesis," as Kaja Silverman put it, ensconced in a dollhouse of Marty's own making, Ruth is shown only in long shot (the film's trailer includes close-ups of Day in this sequence, which were not used in the film). Meanwhile, Marty literally gets the film's last word: "The girl can sing. About that,

I never was wrong." "The girl" may be able to leave him; but her male mentor still reserves the right to have discovered her and claim her as his product, "fulfilling a contractual obligation," as he tells the press.

Part of Haynes's audacity in *Superstar* is to turn a real-life tragedy—one that was emblematic of the experiences of thousands of anorexics and bulimics—into a panoply of self-conscious pop culture tropes, with Carpenter's death rendered all the more poignant for it. In *Superstar* as in the telefilm, a single trade paper review glibly referring to Karen as Richard's "chubby sister" sets off her weight-loss obsession. This taps into the theme of celebrity tragedy whereby an inexperienced young talent is exposed to the relentless scrutiny to which the famous are subjected, before she has built up the defenses to handle it. The theme of consumption opens the film; Karen's mother arrives to go shopping, saying, "It's nearly quarter after and Saks is jammed by 11; we'd better get going." This marks one of the "dramatic liberties" that Haynes takes, in the spirit of the genre. On the morning of her death, Karen had planned to go with her friend, Olivia Newton-John, to sign the final divorce decrees.

The film opens *in medias res,* as well as voyeuristically. The camera discovers Karen performing for herself, singing along with Dionne Warwick's recording of the Burt Bacharach–Hal David song, "I'll Never Fall in Love Again." Typically for a biopic, the opening condenses many narrative ideas. We are told later in a talking head interview insert—by Haynes, who plays a smug disc jockey—that the music of the Carpenters came "out of the Herb Alpert–Burt Bacharach sound of the sixties." We spy on Karen; we enter, Hitchcock-like, through a window. This inaugurates Haynes's appropriation of classical cinema in a movie "performed" by voice actors and twelve-inch models. A panning shot enters the living room as Richard and his mother discuss his new band, with the father sitting silently. "Mother, I can't sing," Richard protests, "and play keys, and lead a band." Mother, having a brainstorm, hears Karen and demands to know, "What's that? Is that Karen?" Then a close-up on her "Eureka!" moment: "It *is* Karen! Richard," she exclaims. "I think we just found you your singer." "And lost me my drummer," Richard replies.

Exaggerating the narrative strategies of the biopic, which must work as much authentic detail and incident as it can into the running time of a feature film, Haynes exposes a great deal of information in this opening, despite the near-absurdity that the family would not have known about Karen's singing talent before this, and the implausibility that such a fateful decision would be made so rapidly. More important, visually and in dialogue, the film embeds its female subject in the narrative and the mise-en-scène. This makes her an object in a story of which she is ostensibly the subject, a common fate of women in biopics. Karen is spied upon and talked about; life-changing decisions are made for her. Karen's preference is to be not a singer but a drummer, a percussively male occupation. When her exceptional singing style is singled out, it becomes a problem for her brother, not her. The female protagonist, whose concerns are not listened to, cannot work out her anxieties; she can only internalize them. In the manner of a pastiche, Haynes lines up at the outset elements so archetypal that they need no elaboration. These include the controlling mother and the ineffectual father. Richard occupies the mentor/sidekick role; with the repression implicit in the family dynamic, however, his unsuitability for that role is already foreshadowed.

Karen enters the scene only when she opens her door; this centers her in a classic deep-focus composition that establishes her as the object in a situation out of the very sort of family melodrama that the breezy, carefree Carpenters–Burt Bacharach & Hal David sound negates. Musically, Haynes appropriates the tradition of the musical melodrama established in *A Star Is Born* (1954) and its biopic equivalent, *Love Me or Leave Me,* whereby songs are chosen that comment on the action. Haynes twists this convention ironically; the irony comes from the songs themselves. In the Bacharach & David–Carpenters song-type, light, breezy melodies laugh off lyrics whose sardonic bitterness is itself leavened by cute rhyming patterns ("What do you get when you kiss a guy? / You get enough germs to catch pneumonia. / And when you do, he'll never phone ya. / I'll never fall in love agaaa-aaa-aaa-ain").

Haynes, in a whip pan, segues from Warwick's record of "I'll Never Fall in Love Again" to Karen and Richard's cover of the same song, as a radio is switched off. Haynes cuts from the "first great success" montage of the biopic genre, beginning here with the Carpenters recording "We've Only Just Begun" in the studio. Then on the line "Sharing horizons that are new to us," he cuts to Karen and Richard "going places" in their car and then arriving home where Mom and Dad display the sibling team's whole new wardrobe, befitting the success of these idols of consumption. The familiarity of these conventions allows Haynes to refer to them while also employing them faultlessly, and thus involving the spectator in the story, the quintessential postmodern hat trick.

While the mother in the telefilm (played by Louise Fletcher) is an infuriating passive-aggressive, the mother in *Superstar* is just aggressive, the archetypal stage mother who, in decreeing that her two children will not go the way of so many young victims of fame, ensures that that is exactly what they will do. Haynes knowingly reprises the "momist" monsters of fifties warts-and-all biopics like *I'll Cry Tomorrow* as well as the musical *Gypsy* (1962), melodramas to which, we know from *Far from Heaven* especially, Haynes has a special affinity. The hideous mother and pathetic daughter make the archetypal team, with the mother pushing the daughter to unstoppable self-destruction. The character of the mother who, out of her own unfulfilled ambition, turns her daughter into a little performing robot allows the genre to displace onto women the show business industry's manufacturing of star actresses and singers, making the heroine the victim of an other's unyielding ambition.

Haynes presents these tropes baldly, without character motivation. In *I'll Cry Tomorrow* Mrs. Roth explains late in the film why Lillian's stardom was so important to her, rendering her character, if not sympathetic, then at least understandable. The grotesque, burned-face mother in Haynes's film recalls the virtual prohibition on aging placed on female stars in America. The film itself perpetuates the image of the aging harridan or at least represents the dread of aging—that Karen can only grow into her mother, even though Karen seems to have more in common with the silent, recessive father, a marginal figure drawn by others. Richard seems to have taken after his mother, nagging and cajoling Karen that what is best for him is what is also best for the family. He also runs The Carpenters, as Mrs. Carpenter runs the home. Both of them run Karen, who is shown to have no say over her life.

A number of critics have discussed the way that Haynes in *Superstar* connects the Carpenters to larger political contexts. Mrs. Carpenter, like a good, uncritical member of the Silent Majority, is excited about the invitation to perform at the White House. Haynes ties the Carpenters to Nixon's strategy for showcasing clean-cut, non-drug-taking, unprotesting young people. Karen and Richard perform the most innocuous song in their repertoire, "Sing," a children's ditty first written for *Sesame Street*, which was not actually one of the songs on their White House program ("Carpenters—Now"). "A clean-cut brother-sister pop act from Orange County," writes Rick Perlstein, "cooed their way into prominence in 1971. 'The Carpenters are hardly what you'd call political,' the *Chicago Tribune* music critic wrote . . . , 'but friends of mine on the West Coast tell me their music is known in some circles out there as 'Nixon music'" (597). Haynes combines the song's solo piano part with old footage of Vice President Nixon playing the piano on *The Tonight Show*. This shows the president insinuating himself into their act, giving ideological significance to a segment of pop culture that resists a political reading. The actual concert took place during a state dinner for West German Chancellor Willy Brandt on 1 May 1973. The evening before in a televised address Nixon announced the resignations of his closest aides, Haldeman and Ehrlichman, and fired John Dean, who was cooperating with the Senate Select Committee on Watergate. Nixon told speechwriter Ray Price, "Maybe I should resign, Ray. If you think so, just put it in" (Reeves 602). Of course, *this* was not known on that night of 1 May, when Nixon basked in the sunlight of the Carpenters' celebrity for the entertainment of a foreign dignitary.

Thus the denial of the family and Richard Carpenter about Karen's illness seems aligned with Nixon's denials, which were building up into a prison-house of their own. Moreover, Downey, California, where the Carpenters lived, is a stone's throw from Nixon's hometown of Whittier and his birth-place in Yorba Linda, a relation probably not lost on the president. Karen and Richard must have also reminded Nixon of his dark-haired daughter Julie and her husband, David Eisenhower. The Carpenters do bear some resem-blance to this couple, who often seemed put on display as a kind of First Bar-bie and Ken. Thus when Nixon pronounces the well-scrubbed, soft-pop Car-penters as representing "all that is good about young America," the sense is palpable that Karen is being used as "a pawn in their game" (to quote a song by the subject of Haynes's *I'm Not There,* a tunesmith who surely would not have sung for Nixon, and was not invited to), being played for advantage in a larger discourse, a frequent fate of female biopic protagonists.

Karen is surrounded by predators. James Morrison finds that "the image of the exploring, grasping, feeling or groping hand appears recurrently" in Haynes's films. "In *Superstar* intercut close-ups of the reaching hand of a sleazy music producer suggest Karen's surrender to the grip of the corporate music industry" (141). This is an instance, however, like much in *Superstar,* where the texture and outside resonances of the scene outweigh what actu-ally happens in it. The time of day, as indicated by the scene's lighting, is best described as "quarter-to-noir." But the producer isn't necessarily "sleazy," unless one finds Herb Alpert, the co-founder of A&M Records (whose logo is displayed in the scene, another of the film's uncleared trademarks and one of the entities that pushed the film into illegality) and the best-selling leader of the Tijuana Brass, innately unsavory. Haynes's doesn't just "suggest Karen's surrender"; he intercuts a disembodied hand metonymically belonging to Alpert as it stretches out to seal the deal, with shots of Karen's terrified reaction. The sequence climaxes with archival footage from the Holocaust of an emaciated corpse being dumped into a pit. Even Oliver Stone might find this touch extreme; however, it fits Haynes's pastiche of the downward trajectory. Thematically and narratively, it inaugurates a sequence of events that will end up, as we already know from the flashback structure and our knowledge of how Carpenter died, with another emaciated body piled onto the pop culture landfill.

What makes the imagery even more devastating, however, and typical of Haynes's ideological strategy of connecting the particular malady of his biopic subject to ordinary American objective "normality," is that Herb Alpert is recalled as a benign figure. Along with Bacharach and Henry Mancini, Alpert was one of the few purveyors of popular middlebrow 1960s music to attain great success in the rock-dominated music scene, bringing the sounds of Mexican mariachi bands into American Top 40 pop. This belies the Anglo-centricity later associated with the Carpenters, even though no one associated with Alpert's band, the Tijuana Brass, was actually Latino. Alpert's sensibilities were closer to Wonder Bread than to tortillas, just as Karen suggests to Richard that the Carpenters are not all they appear to be.

Haynes melodramatically attributes Karen's death to an overdose of ipecac (the name itself evokes the gag reflex), although she actually died of heart failure, a cumulative effect of her anorexia. The TV movie, as serves *its* purposes, first stages a wrenching scene in which mother Agnes refuses a psychiatrist's entreaties to tell Karen she loves her. The telefilm ends with the mother at last uttering the three little words, bringing a smile to the daughter's face. A title then comes onscreen, telling us that Karen's death by cardiac arrest caused by the anorexia was already assured by this time; she was a walking time bomb. Thus the mother is off the hook, and the daughter is relieved of intentionality, as if the anorexia has become an agent of fate with a life of its own. Karen's treatment in New York is made to look like a last-ditch recovery attempt, brave but futile. If the telefilm, approved by Richard Carpenter and Agnes, who lived until 1996, has the kind of careful Hollywood ending that plays like an elaborate contract settlement (as it may have been), Haynes opts for sensationalism befitting not only the melodramatic tradition, but also the infotainment age of celebrity. Karen's death by overdose in Haynes's version is carried by the relentlessness of addiction and the inevitability of victimization and destruction. Her hospitalization in New York (she returned home two and a half months before her death) plays here as tragedy's last glimmer of hope, the grasping at straws before the subject's final and inevitable slide into the abyss.

The TV movie emphasizes domestic tranquility and the essential good-ness of the family, with the nonsensical insistence that they all lived hap-pily ever after (except for the inconvenient detail of Karen's death). Haynes, however, returns to the horror movie motifs of his film's opening. A camera moving through the apartment is now accompanied by Karen's voice. On the phone, she assures her doctor that she "hasn't had an Ex-Lax or even thought about it." Ipecac, an emetic to induce vomiting in cases of poisoning, is now her drug of choice. We hear a jumble of Carpenters songs, layered over each other. At the same time, a real pair of hands, doubling for Karen's, opens a drawer in an immaculate bathroom, takes two bottles of ipecac syrup, and, in camera movements representing the backward tilt of Karen's head, downs each of them. Synthesizers shriek; in almost subliminally quick cuts, a woman screams in stock footage, and a Holocaust body is dumped into a grave. Then, as at the beginning, blackout, silence, and that serenely in-scrutable pan past the neat row of houses in Downey. The film ends on two images—the establishing shot of the family home, which cannot be entered again, followed by a shot of Karen onstage, colored lights all around her, the archetypal image of enduring fame, glamour, the biopic's perpetual promise of transcendence. Except that here the music has stopped; Karen has been stopped. Is there any transcending the conditions that brought Karen to this end? Or is there only the end that ensures another beginning—not "what happened?" but "what happens?"

The biopic's promise of meaning and value that outlives the physical life is therefore brought up short. Could anything have averted Karen's death? Or does the ideology of beauty, happiness, consumerism, heterosexuality, and middle-class respectability ensure that a Karen Carpenter story will happen everlastingly? The ending subtly but firmly recalls *Citizen Kane*. It reverts to the exterior, the protective covering. There is no "No trespassing" sign onscreen, but Richard Carpenter provided that later, just as Hearst's minions tried to enshroud *Kane*. Even Todd Haynes, who made *Superstar* at the Wellesian dangerous age of twenty-six, would not have wished for so close a resemblance.

12

I Want to Live!

Criminal Woman, Male Discourses

I Want to Live! (1958), the personal project of veteran independent producer Walter Wanger, who hired Robert Wise to direct, illustrates the problems of telling lives of women in the genre of film biography. It also demonstrates a way that the genre can be approached, even in a presumptively sexist era. Not many biographies consciously depict the clash between a well-known woman and the culture's expectations of her, although they may well embody these. Fewer yet are critical of those expectations. In the interests of realism and of rhetoric against capital punishment, however, *I Want to Live!* takes the side of Barbara Graham (1924–1955), a convicted murderer executed in California. In sympathetically telling the story of a woman many felt was railroaded to the gas chamber, the film finds itself lined up against systems of discourse, in this case, media and the law, by which patriarchy speaks of and for women.

I Want to Live! is a product of the 1950s, when women's film biography had been greatly devalued in comparison to the previous two decades. Until recently, the 1950s have been remembered simplistically as "an affluent era of broad political consensus and cultural conformity," with little attention paid to the tensions and conflicts that marked the era, especially its gender politics (Medovoi 255). Jackie Byars, one of a number of critics who have reassessed the films of the decade, points out a latent conflict in them between dominant ideology and what Alison Jaggar terms "outlaw emotions . . . that are incompatible with dominant perceptions and values." To Jaggar, "people who experience conventionally unacceptable, or . . . 'outlaw' emotions often are subordinated individuals who pay a disproportionately high price for maintaining the status quo" (Byars "Prime" 200).

Certainly Barbara Graham paid with her life for "outlaw emotions" that she, caught in a cycle of crime since her youth, acted out in the most literal sense. The law and the media freely equated her illegal activities with her status as "an attractive, redhaired woman," a phrase almost always included in the lead paragraphs of newspaper stories about her. Graham's sexual promiscuity was conflated with her participation in criminal activities usually associated with men, such as robbery, forgery, and perjury (although her rap sheet also included arrests for prostitution). The combination made her easy to brand a brazen freak, an example to women who live beyond the boundaries that had been carefully set out in postwar popular culture.

Nonetheless, the film about her life throws into confusion the "good girl/ bad girl" dialectic that bedevils even the most circumspect studies of gender in fifties film. *I Want to Live!* declines to condemn its heroine or blame her demise on some fatal transgression. It also shows how Graham's faults and weaknesses were exploited by a nimble and powerful system of law and representation. As the film portrays it, this system itself transgressed the standards of humanism and fair play held dear by the liberal social problem genre to which the film also belongs.

Susan Hayward plays Graham as a brassy yet dignified woman intent on holding onto her individuality. The film shows how an actress's ingenuity can give a vibrant voice to a victimized character. What is equally intriguing is that the male producer, director, and screenwriters tell this woman's story not by investigating her, or coolly staging her downfall as spectacle, but by identifying with her, showing how her personal deceits and misrepresentations were matched and exploited by the larger deceptions of the law and the mass-audience misrepresentations of the print and electronic media.

The trajectory of victimization and suffering began to dominate women's biography after World War II, when female biopic monarchs became outnumbered by entertainers, especially singers, who lived hard lives. This shift in focus can be attributed to two large-scale phenomena. One was the distinct misogyny of much postwar popular culture, as the division between the man's world of work informed by his war experience and the woman's life as mother and "homemaker" in the newly developed suburbs drew the genders ever further apart. In an era rooted in fear of communism and atomic terror, "her" sometimes seemed one of the many "thems" being demonized. In both cases containment was deemed best. Historian Elaine Tyler May writes, "Hollywood's professed advocacy of gender equality [in the 1920s and 1930s] evaporated during the forties. . . . After the war, as subservient homemakers moved center stage, emancipated heroines gave way to predatory female villains" (67). The other was the collapse of the Hollywood studio system and the mass audience for movies. One of the consequences was a decline in the importance to the industry of female audiences and female stars. However, the biopic began a significant shift around the end of the fifties. While George Custen was correct that there were fewer biopics after 1960, the ones that were made, as we saw in Book One, were often more probing of their subjects, more interested in differing points of view, and more interested in demystification than were the biopics of earlier decades (Custen 102–107). *I Want to Live!* obtains most of its freshness from a tension between postwar-style realism and thirties-era female star glamour, and from contradictory pulls toward documentary and melodrama. Like *Citizen Kane,* the film tries, albeit not very hard, to leave doubts about its largely sympathetic heroine. As in *Kane,* there is skepticism toward the "official story," as given out by Kane's empire and the "News on the March" newsreel in Welles's film, and as produced by what *I Want to Live!* all but depicts as a potent conspiracy between the law and the press. Although I do not want to press the well-known point that director Robert Wise had been one of the two editors of *Citizen Kane, I Want to Live!* includes one out-and-out quotation from *Kane.* A shot of a newspaper composing room shows two alternate headlines being prepared to announce Graham's conviction or her acquittal, recalling the famous election-night scene following Kane's disastrous campaign for governor. But unlike *Citizen Kane's* strategy of turning its Great Man subject into object, *I Want to Live!* does exactly the opposite: it emphasizes the complex humanity of a woman whom the press caricatured in her own time.

Susan Hayward won an Academy Award for *I Want to Live!* on her fifth nomination in twelve years. Of those five nominated films, all were melodramas built around her, as opposed to adventure-romances such as *David and Bathsheba* (1951), *The Snows of Kilimanjaro* (1952), and *Demetrius and the Gladiators* (1954), which paired her with male stars. Of the Oscar-nominated films, the last three were biopics. Four, moreover, had first-person titles: *My Foolish Heart* (1949), *With a Song in My Heart* (1952), *I'll Cry Tomorrow,* and *I Want to Live!* While all these titles indicate a protagonist's ownership of her story, each one also includes a key word, such as "heart" or "cry," that suggests "feminine" emotionalism. These titles speak of self-pity or emotional, irrational choices ("My Foolish Heart"), or repression ("I'll Cry Tomorrow").

The pronoun "I" in a title often connotes a sincere testimonial, a personal confession; at the least it's a declaration of subjectivity, from *I Am a Fugitive from a Chain Gang* (1932) to *I'm Not There* (2007). Alone among the Hayward titles, *I Want to Live!* could easily adorn the story of a man, with its assertive, exclamatory demand. This speaker shouts her "want" simply and unmistakably, with no hint of self-pity or hesitation. There is no implied Freudian figure asking what this woman wants; her desire is unmysterious and basic. This is a story of a woman, Barbara Graham, who in a yellow journalism tradition had been a completely spoken subject. She had been named, defined, and determined by an interlocking system of law, language, imagery, and public opinion. Thus, the title introduces a tension that the film will develop between the heroine and the cultural and institutional systems that determined her fate.

Graham, a prostitute, robber's and gambler's shill, and convicted perjurer, was found guilty along with two men, Emmet Perkins and John Santo, of the fatal March 1953 pistolwhipping of Mabel Monahan, a sixty-one-year-old woman from Burbank, California. A fourth member of the gang, John True, turned state's evidence and testified against the trio. He claimed that Graham, whom the press dubbed "Bloody Babs," did the actual killing. The three were put to death at San Quentin prison in June 1955, following several stays of execution that the film faithfully recounts.

Many close observers of the case, led by Ed Montgomery, a Pulitzer Prize–winning reporter whose stories for the *San Francisco Examiner* largely formed the basis of the film, sharply questioned the guilty verdict. Graham's conviction was obtained partly on pre-*Miranda* police procedures that included entrapment. She was not read her rights, informed of the charge against her during interrogation, or allowed a phone call. The court-appointed defense was underfunded and inept; although investigators determined that Monahan's killer was right-handed, and True testified that Graham beat her repeatedly with her right hand, the defense failed to point out that Graham was left-handed, as those working on her appeal discovered too late. Many suspected that Perkins and Santo pinned the killing on Graham in the belief that the state would not execute a woman and would spare their lives along with hers. The letter from Graham to her appeal attorney Al Matthews,

28. The police interrogation of Barbara Graham (Susan Hayward) on the night of her arrest typifies the alignment of realism with melodrama in *I Want to Live!* (Robert Wise, United Artists, 1958). Digital frame enlargement.

from which the film's title comes, expressed what many involved in her final months saw as a maturation and spiritual conversion. She wrote to Matthews on 8 March 1955, "Do you believe there is any hope at all on the commutation, Al? I would appreciate your honest opinion, bad or good. Remember how I felt about one at the beginning? I have changed now. Life does seem very dear to me. I do want to live" (Graham).

I Want to Live! appears to adopt the rhetoric of the real Al Matthews, who was interviewed in a documentary-style promotional trailer for the movie. Matthews says of Graham's trial: "At all times, methods were used to invade her mind, to seduce her body, in effect, to wash her out as a human being" ("Special Trailer"). These were the sentiments of a defense attorney who sympathizes with his client in order to argue her case. Coincidentally or not, they also sound like a feminist attack on an institution, be it the law, the media, or the cinema, that stereotypes, objectifies, and dehumanizes women.

Matthews's next comment summed up the experience of Graham as a universal example: "I felt if they could do those things to Barbara Graham, and get away with it, they could do it to each one of us. I felt that justice was being abandoned" ("Special Trailer"). Thus identification with the "invasion" and "seduction" of Barbara Graham is taken out of the realm of gender and generalized to "each one of us." Nonetheless, the gender specificity was evidently taken as given, both by those involved in the case and by the filmmakers; in a March 1957 letter to Hayward early in the film's planning, Walter Wanger wrote, "The more I read, and the more I hear, the more certain I am that this will be the greatest film ever shot to end capital punishment and the public believing everything it reads about people apprehended by the law, especially women" (Wanger to Hayward).

The phenomenon of men in a presumptively sexist era identifying with a woman who was victimized through means that could be called spectacularly invasive, or invasively spectacular, stemmed from the film's producer. Walter Wanger was known in the thirties and forties for paying lip service to the power of film to effect progressive social change. He was also personally committed to the studio-era tradition of the charismatic female star; his films included *Queen Christina* with Garbo and *Joan of Arc* with Bergman. His career ended with the notoriously out-of-control production of *Cleopatra* (1963), a project Wanger initiated as a unit producer for an adrift post-Zanuck-era Twentieth Century Fox.

In a confluence of events almost too contradictory to conjure with, Wanger served four months in prison in 1952 following his "passion shooting" of a man he suspected of being his wife's lover. Although gender double standards abounded in the case, all of them redounding to Wanger's benefit, *I Want to Live!* resulted from Wanger's apparent identification with the ordeal Barbara Graham experienced as a woman in the hands of the legal system. Detractors were quick to accuse Wanger of an ulterior motive in making the film, due to a parallel he apparently found between his and Barbara Graham's run-ins with California law enforcement. In December 1951, upon finding that his wife of eleven years, the actress Joan Bennett, was having an affair with her agent Jennings Lang, Wanger trailed Bennett and Lang to a restaurant parking lot where he shot Lang, inflicting a minor wound to the arm. It mattered little that Wanger was apparently a compulsive philanderer who had been unfaithful to Bennett far more than she had been to him. In a classic case of double standards, Bennett's film career was destroyed by the publicity, while Wanger, after serving three months and nine days of a four-month jail sentence, was able to rebuild his career. Studio heads and fellow producers rallied to Wanger's support, in a show of concern not extended at the same time to those suspected of having communist affiliations. In fact, Wanger, who was involved in many leftist causes in the 1930s, ironically was let off the hook politically by the scandal over the shooting, which took place in the midst of the House Un-American Activities Committee's destructive second round of Hollywood hearings in 1951–52 (Bernstein *Wanger* 273–278).

A socially conscious filmmaker and president in the early 1940s of the Motion Picture Academy, Wanger had long made pronouncements on the cultural importance of film that were not often matched by the films he produced. However, on his release from jail in September 1952, he told the press that the prison system is "the nation's number one scandal. I want to do a film about it" (Bernstein *Wanger* 281). *Riot on Cell Block 11* (1954, directed by Don Siegel), a taut, earnest thriller made at the low-budget Monogram studio (renamed Allied Artists in 1952), fit the bill and helped rehabilitate Wanger's reputation. *I Want to Live!,* which received six Oscar nominations, capped his comeback and confirmed his return to class-A filmmaking.

As Richard Maltby and Ian Craven argue, Hollywood's need to satisfy a wide audience and to avoid criticism and reaction from governments and interest groups has caused it to avoid broad critiques of systemic social problems (361–362). Wanger and his collaborators, however, saw the need to distinguish their look at Barbara Graham from that of the media and law enforcement officials of her trial. One newspaper account of her execution, for example, read as follows: "Barbara achieved a strange beauty in her last moments. Her soft, brown hair was perfectly in place. Her face was an ivory cameo, lightened by the mask and her rouged, crimson lips. . . . She wore a beige wool suit with covered buttons, pumps, gold pendant earrings and an engagement ring and wedding band" (Cook 1).

In taking the point of view of the woman who was subjected to such scrutiny and to lurid, even morbid, fascination with her "femininity," the male filmmakers were forced to turn a jaundiced eye on the systems that objectified Barbara Graham. As an example of a mid-1950s social problem drama in Great Britain, Marcia Landy considers a Diana Dors vehicle *Yield to the Night* (1956), inspired by the sensational Ruth Ellis murder case in Britain. In that film the depiction of an ultra-feminine prisoner and her masculinized female captors adheres to gender typing (*Cinematic* 203–204). For Barbara Graham, however, it was such typing itself that helped condemn Barbara Graham, and the filmmakers critique it.

The topic of capital punishment confronts filmmakers with a rhetorical stance more radical than that of most social problems for the simple reason that to tackle the death penalty is to take on American law. Jackie Byars, echoing Michael Wood, argues that "all social problems are treated the same way in these films. . . . The problem can be named and social institutions are created to cope with it" (*All* 115). With the death penalty, however, the social institution itself is the problem. It is conventional wisdom that although Hollywood may single out corrupt or misguided *individuals* within a system, it leaves the system unscathed. *I Want to Live!* takes exactly the opposite tack: individuals within the system are at best kindly and well meaning and at worst nondescript functionaries "just doing their jobs." It is the *system* that defames, humiliates, and kills.

Furthermore, to attack capital punishment is to confront public attitudes that keep the practice going. This involves what Joseph L. Mankiewicz disdainfully called "making 'the public' the heavy": the filmmakers debated the extent to which the public's lurid fascination and desire for retribution would be confronted. Some forties "problem" films, particularly those against bigotry, such as *Gentleman's Agreement* (1947) and *Intruder in the Dust* (1949), did openly prod audiences to examine their own attitudes. Mankiewicz emphasized to Wanger, however, that "no film has ever succeeded in making 'the public' the heavy. Because 'the public' is the jury. And they won't return a verdict of guilty" (Mankiewicz 3–4).

Nonetheless, Graham's arrest is played as a kind of mass peep show, with dozens of onlookers, most of them male, hoping to get a glimpse of the notorious woman as she's clapped in irons. Her response is to come out into the street like a famous actress (Susan Hayward?) dramatically appearing onstage, clasping her baby's toy tiger (the "tiger lady") as if it were an Oscar. The headline in the next day's paper could as easily read, "Promising Newcomer Makes Strong Debut." Graham's behavior and Hayward's performance are responses to the excessive attention that Graham received as a woman. Putting on a red nightgown for her last night before execution, Graham says, "can't disappoint my public: 'Bloody Babs spent her last night decked out in pajamas of her favorite color, flaming scarlet.' That's what they call red when I wear it." The playing of the execution scene, with a horde of fifty onlookers, all of them middle-aged men, crowding into the room, surrounding the gas chamber, and staring through the windows like men attending a striptease, makes this point, as does Graham's final request for a mask: "I don't want to look at people. I don't want to see them staring at me."

This mode of critique led Wanger and Wise to adopt a "realistic" style by means of which people and places would be depicted in the realm of the semiotic "real," outside signification, however impossible that is to achieve. The review in *Variety* termed this approach, where the actors were concerned, "casting for character rather than for type" ("Powe"). Wanger termed the style "adult realism." He told Mankiewicz, whose production company Figaro produced the film, "It should be as far from the Hollywood pattern as possible . . . semi-documentary, episodic, realistic, emotional, powerful, no usual construction, no characters going all the way through, no expensive cast of names except Susan" (Wanger to Mankiewicz, 29 October). The independent casting director Lynn Stalmaster established his reputation for casting little-known actors from television and local theater from this film, one of the first to credit a casting director.

Almost any time a Hollywood production tries for realism, the results are likely to be tension between a deglamourized mise-en-scène and the artificiality of performance styles and narrative conventions. The film begins and ends with written statements by Ed Montgomery attesting to its "factual" nature (these briefly threaten to be the words of a man claiming ownership of the story). The prison sets were modeled closely after Graham's quarters at Corona Women's Prison and San Quentin. TV newsmen George Putnam and Bill Stout reenacted their roles as reporters on Graham's trial. The film was shot in a black-and-white gray scale with the effect of natural light rather than Hollywood three-point glamour lighting. Wanger, Wise, Hayward, and the screenwriters interviewed everyone connected with the case who would talk to them, from the priest who administered the last rites to Graham to the nurse who attended her during her last night at San Quentin. Most realistic of all are the film's last forty minutes, in which the preparations of the gas chamber for execution are simply and painstakingly detailed; this was Robert Wise's contribution near the end of pre-production, after he interviewed San Quentin personnel (Bernstein *Wanger* 332–333).

The earnest attempt to re-create the world Graham moved through "as it really was" yields some interesting results. Viewers today may be struck by the large number of women shown in workaday jobs—as prison orderlies, nurses, guards, and administrators, and even as reporters and undercover cops, with no attempt made to characterize these women in any particular way. Clearly this reflects the actual numbers of women in the workforce in the fifties, but it collides with the mistaken impression later, and to some extent then, that all women of the era were June Cleaver–like homemakers. It is also clear that although women populate the system, it is run by and for men, a point made obvious by the absence of women at Graham's execution, and by the fact that Graham regards men as her chief accusers and executioners (she addresses her sardonic post-sentencing remarks to "the gentlemen of the press").

The film's publicity materials took pains to point out that even Hayward's wardrobe and makeup were exactly in character for Graham as she actually was:

> Mrs. Graham's taste in clothes is also reflected in Susan Hayward's costumes. The four-time Oscar nominee long ago proved in "I'll Cry Tomorrow" and "Smash-Up" that she was not one of those misled stars who insist on perfect hairdos and beautiful clothes despite the contrary demands of a script. It should nonetheless be pointed out, for the benefit of those whose skepticism of Hollywood claims to accuracy is not easily allayed, that the handsome wardrobe and meticulous grooming displayed by Miss Hayward in the film only serve to heighten the fidelity of her portrayal. . . . Attorney Al Matthews recalls not-infrequent hour-long waits while his client prepared her make-up. (United Artists)

Of course, this might be exactly what makes the material a suitable star vehicle. Indeed, for all the film's elements of authenticity, which are considerable, the centerpiece remains what Mankiewicz said would be "a magnificent tour-de-force for a female star" (Mankiewicz to Wanger, 27 August). In Wanger's scheme of a realistic film outside signification, the only character who is plainly a sign is Graham herself, a star amid "real people." The film struggles to delineate her as a vital, complicated person chafing under the gender stereotypes that the culture, especially the press, has forced her into. Susan Hayward employs performance codes that collide not only with stereotypes of the dangerous, transgressive woman, but also with expectations of how a beaten, trampled-upon victim would act. Thus a spectator might see Graham, and the film about her, as somehow victorious over systems that aim to take away her dignity, "to wash her out as a human being." Thus Hayward's ferocious performance is the key to the film's indirect rhetorical thrust against the death penalty. Hayward, more than the male filmmakers, is Graham's speaking subject, the one who articulates her and gives her life.

In the studio system, which in various ways shaped Wanger, Hayward, Wise, and Mankiewicz, biopic subjects were shaped to fit star personae (Custen 45). Hayward's fitness for the genre typifies this tendency. "All of Hayward's impersonations," writes Custen, "were headstrong, colorful women, marked in some way by tragedy. And this was one of Hayward's characteristics—she suffered with sublime intensity—the biopic was a niche into which her talents could be fitted" (66). Hayward's ferocious and active demeanor in *I Want to Live!* is quite different from the demure and passive though tenacious women of *I'll Cry Tomorrow* and *With a Song in My Heart.*

Susan Hayward, born Edythe Marrenner in Brooklyn in 1917, began working as a New York advertising model just after graduating from high school, and also took acting classes. After Hayward and her modeling agency were featured in a 1937 *Saturday Evening Post* story entitled "A Day in the Life of a Model," Kay Brown of the New York office of Selznick International Pictures contacted her. She was interviewed by George Cukor, who arranged for a screen test in Hollywood. Although the test did not lead to a contract with Selznick, the young actress resolved to stay in Hollywood. Eventually she was signed to a six-month option at Warner Bros., where her name was changed. As a contract player at Paramount from 1938 to 1945, Hayward drew mostly thankless supporting roles and leads in undistinguished B-films. At the end of her contract, she was signed by Wanger's independent company and attained stardom playing strong-willed heroines in several western- and southern-themed outdoor melodramas, including *Canyon Passage* (1946), *Tap Roots* (1948), and *Tulsa* (1949). She earned her first Oscar nomination in one of Wanger's works of "adult realism," *Smash-Up: The Story of a Woman* (1947), in which she played an alcoholic. Wanger sold her contract to Twentieth Century Fox in 1949, where she continued to make large-scale films in which she played the love interest as well as grittier melodramas and biopics.

Throughout her run as a major star, from the mid-1940s to the early 1960s, Hayward was portrayed in publicity and in press reports as both a stunning and glamorous former model and a no-nonsense, hard-driving "girl from Brooklyn," as she characterized herself. Press stories, from early in her career until her death from cancer in 1975, recounted her progress from modeling in New York to her attainment of star status after years of hard work. Her *New York Times* obituary, by Lawrence Van Gelder, noted:

> To sketch her life in swift scenes would be to create a catalogue of events that seem like clichés culled from a thousand movies: the lucky break that started her modeling career; the director [George Cukor] who saw her picture in a magazine and offered her a screen test; a rejection for the role of Scarlett O'Hara in *Gone with the Wind;* hard times in Hollywood and a bicycle accident that cast her onto the lawn of an agent who

changed her name to Susan Hayward; the starlet routine with cheese-cake stills but no roles; the gutsy appeal to a convention of distributors that set her career rolling; stardom; Academy Award nominations; an Oscar; public triumph but personal tragedy—an unhappy marriage; a custody battle over twin sons; divorce; attempted suicide; a taste of scandal; a second, apparently happy marriage; her husband's death; and the final years, marred by illness. (30)

The two biopics, *I'll Cry Tomorrow,* which opened nationally in January 1956, and *I Want to Live!,* received as career peaks, appeared to emerge from highly publicized events in Hayward's life in the mid-1950s, namely her contentious 1954 divorce and custody proceedings against her first husband, Jess Barker, after nine years of marriage, and in April 1955 an unexplained suicide attempt. *I'll Cry Tomorrow* also seemed to come out of the cauldron of her tempestuous personal life; Hayward began work on the film three days after her release from the hospital following a near overdose (Linet 191). The film, about a Hollywood actress's descent into the depths of alcoholism, was based on the life of early 1930s film musical actress Lillian Roth, whose tell-all autobiography was optioned for filming soon after its publication. The public's knowledge of Hayward's overdose and hospitalization, which were page one news around the country, formed part of the background against which audiences saw the Roth biography. *I Want to Live!,* by contrast, was viewed against the calmer backdrop of Hayward's marriage to Eaton Chalkley, her residence outside Atlanta, and what some press reports took to be her semi-retirement (E. Johnson).

Thus her performance as Barbara Graham, the dignified petty criminal, is perfect for a star who, like many, embodied the glamorous and the ordinary. Some seven months after her death, a story on her fight with brain cancer began, "Susan Hayward's best movie, *I Want to Live!,* captured her fascinating emotional mix. She managed to be as formidable as she was sexy, as courageous as she was abused, and as cold-blooded as she was hot-tempered" (Greve 1E).

Hayward plays Graham in a regal, larger-than-life manner, as if Garbo's Queen Christina or Greer Garson's Madame Curie turned up as a petty crook in 1950s California. There is a lack of naturalism in Hayward's performance that, although it contrasts with the film's "realism," seems part of a careful strategy worked out with Wanger and Wise and prepared for in the

screenplay. Graham was conceived in the mold of the thirties biopic heroine, in order to capitalize on the incongruity that would result. This design
can be seen in a complaint Wanger made about an early draft of the script:

> The characterization of the girl is not Barbara Graham—definitely
> not the character that was sold to Susan Hayward through what she
> read and the people she talked to. Barbara Graham was not a hysteri-
> cal "thing," but a woman who could carry off, whether she was acting
> or not, a great scene, with dignity, much to the embarrassment of the
> people who thought they could break her down. Even the night she left
> Corona to be executed at San Quentin, she sat in the Cadillac as it drew
> her out of Corona with her head high, like Queen Elizabeth going to
> her coronation. (Wanger to Mankiewicz, 22 November)

Hayward plays Graham with self-conscious panache, making her not a
masochistic, passive object to whom things happen, but a humiliated figure who nevertheless plays the great lady with determination. This is what
makes the performance unusual and the film that features it not just another 1950s biopic about a victimized woman on a downward slide. As Graham, Hayward's movements look studied, deliberate, as if the character were
thinking out every move before she makes it. Is it Hayward or Graham who
physically mimes cool, frustration, defiance, hopelessness, or joy as if she
were modeling expressions and stances from the late-nineteenth-century
manuals for actors of François Delsarte? She does not hesitate to fling herself about at moments of despair. Graham/Hayward's eyes flare with defiance, especially toward the end of the film when Graham, ironically, appears
to inhabit a space all her own, the more her execution nears. Her eyes light
up brightly and coquettishly at those moments when Graham is lying to
herself, and they turn dead and steely when Graham is resigned or discouraged. Hayward's voice is a versatile instrument, feathery and kittenish at
times, gravelly, guttural, and brassy at others; as with the body and the face,
the impression is not just that the character is speaking but that the actress
is using her voice, choosing the right timbre, volume, and tone the way a
cinematographer chooses the lens and lights that he needs for a given shot.
All performers, of course, do this. The difference is that in keeping with the
so-called invisible style of classical cinema, the usual performance effaces
these codes by means of naturalism.

Hayward portrays these complications and this poignance by making an

29. Hayward as Graham, here in pathological liar mode: The epitome of the female biopic star performance, using every color in the emotional palette. Digital frame enlargement.

inspired choice, especially in a film that prides itself on realism: she fore-grounds the melodrama of the genre, which plays off against the surface realism of the social problem drama. These two genres are often aligned, however, in the class-conscious Manichean oppositions of rich and poor, good and evil, weak and strong, to which both forms gravitate. This alliance moves Landy to call the social problem drama "a conduit through which melodramatic affect flows" (*Cinematic* 195).

Melodrama, with its excessive significations of good and evil, would seem to be what moves the film away from the sort of even-handed treatment that would leave Graham's guilt or innocence undetermined, and tips it more toward an assumption of innocence. Christine Gledhill writes in her essay on the connections between melodramatic traditions, acting, and the insti-tution of movie stardom that "notoriously, the production of melodramatic identities involves excess of expression: hyperbolic emotions, high-flown sentiments, declamatory speech" (212). Peter Brooks in *The Melodramatic Imagination* writes that "melodramatic good and evil are highly personal-ized. . . . Most notably, evil is villainy; it is a swarthy, cape-enveloped man with a deep voice" (16). Gledhill elaborates, "Moral forces are expressions of personality, externalized in a character's physical being, in gesture, dress and above all in action" (210).

The changes Hayward rings on these principles, and the ambiguity of her performance, dwell in her playing of several moral forces in turn: she is at various times the heroine in distress (the beaten wife, harassed suspect, entrapped defendant, death-row convict "tortured" by endless stays of execution), the villain who ties her to the railroad tracks (the compulsive liar, the amoral person who won't take responsibility), and the hero who saves the day (the tough woman who won't let hostile men touch her, who won't break down during a police "third degree," who insists on her way in the most institutional circumstances, playing jazz and wearing negligees in prison, simply to keep her own identity). The performance denotes masculine traits as well as the expected feminine and thus does much to deflect "Babs" as the object of the gaze that she is constantly being made into.

The filmmakers set out to depict Graham as a person with many facets, almost in defiance of the virgin/whore types on which 1950s Hollywood sometimes traded. In an interview in which Wanger refused to rule on Graham's guilt or innocence, he enumerated a catalog of her contradictory and "fascinating" traits: "She was a bright girl, a stupid girl, a sexually attractive girl, a feminine girl. She had a wonderful heart. She was also a pathological liar. She had good taste in books and music. She was a good mother and, sometimes, not a good mother. She had a sense of humor that never left her to her dying moments" (Manners 11). The producer reels off a list of characterizations which individually may sound like sexist judgments, many of them typical of things said about Graham during her trial. Juxtaposed, however, they amount to a refusal to define her as any one thing, an allowance that she was a person and that people are complicated, rather than that women are incoherent. Wanger's own life and career, furthermore, were said to have been "full of contradictions" (Bernstein *Wanger* viii). The film's refusal to jump to conclusions about Graham, as the public did during her trial and as the culture does about women in general, may show again Wanger's unconscious tendency, if not eagerness, to identify with his wronged heroine. In any event, women in fifties culture rarely were permitted this range of contradictory traits.

The film softens Graham somewhat to ease sympathy for her, cutting the number of her children and eliminating her alleged drug abuse, while emphasizing the addiction of her last husband, Henry Graham. For the most part, however, the film confronts her amorality, especially in the opening sequences. We see that she habitually lies; while at a party with sailors in San Diego, she blithely tells a young man that she can't spend a weekend with him because her mother, who abandoned her when she was young, wants her to go with her on her yacht.

This sets up the following scene, in which she agrees to testify falsely in the trial of two friends indicted for armed robbery. She makes the decision with an imaginary roll of the dice, letting chance appear to choose her course. Then she returns to the party, dancing herself into a joyful frenzy; the spectator is invited to experience the *jouissance* that blinds Graham to her own denial of moral responsibility. To show that Graham herself chooses "the wrong fork in the road of life," as a TV journalist melodramatically puts it much later, the film offers for contrast her friend Pat ("Peg" in the film), who refuses to commit perjury for the unsavory characters Graham sees as "nice guys." Pat/Peg "cuts out," leaving the shady life, only to resurface much later after Graham's indictment for murder. By this time she has gone straight, gotten married, and had two children. Pat/Peg's presence in the film (the real woman was interviewed by Wanger and the screenwriters) suggests that Graham had choices that she did not take, and that some women know how to make them, by turning their backs on the life of crime and doing it on their own.

However, the film also shows that those choices were never clear to Graham. After all she announces later that she's leaving a life of crime to get married (not because crime is wrong, but because "it's not fun anymore"). She tells Perkins that she's quitting "the life" to become one of the housewives she sees in the supermarket, "a square." But the man she marries is a bartender she meets when he warns her that she's about to pass a bad check to a plainclothes cop. Her new husband helps her continue her life of crime, while his drug habit later guarantees that she will have to further it, throwing her back into the company of Emmet Perkins, for whom she earlier shilled and drove the getaway car.

The life of "squares," a world of love, family, work, citizenship, and, presumably, good men that women can count on, is one that Barbara vainly wants. (When Peg reintroduces herself to Barbara, she says proudly, "I'm a real square.") However, she neither swears off her criminal life of unreliable, exploitative men nor seems to know how. Furthermore, the film is confused about whether the men on the right side of the tracks are any better for women than criminals and junkies. From the beginning, Graham is shown with cheating men who have in their wallets photos of wives, kids, and houses with white picket fences. When a radio is turned on during

Graham's last night, a newsman announces the suspension of a male high school coach on a morals charge. The nurse who keeps a vigil with Graham the night before the execution says that she's serving her husband with divorce papers for desertion: "Separated, divorced—the way men are these days that's the only way you can live with 'em." Furthermore, the film depicts the bonds Graham forms with women from the "square" world, such as her friend Peg and the San Quentin nurse, who is also named Barbara.

Nonetheless, the film hangs much of its sympathy on Graham's respect and desire for love and family. Her opening scene establishes her in all her contradictions. After a slow crane up to a hotel window, there is a cut to the side of a bed in a dark room; the camera is just above the bed, facing the window. Suddenly, the figure of Graham/Hayward springs into the shot. Backlit, she lights a cigarette and, shaking herself with postcoital happiness, hands it to the unshown man next to her. Wearing a slip, she runs to the foot of the bed, draws up the covers, and playfully claws at the still unseen bedmate like a cat. Cut to the room slightly later, as Graham and her now visible lover are dressing. A cut to the hallway finds a hotel clerk pointing out the room to a vice cop. Back inside the room, Graham looks at the wallet of her companion and sees a snapshot of the man and his wife and two children shown outside a white frame house. The man takes the wallet from her and they embrace. Just then, the plainclothes officer comes in as the woman instinctively rushes into the bathroom and locks the door. The cop knocks on the bathroom door; Graham opens it, stands with authority, and asks unconvincingly, "What are you two gentlemen doing in my room?" The officer is about to charge the man with violating the Mann Act when Graham informs him that she brought the man to the room, as a prostitute would a customer. The man looks at her wonderingly, as the cop grabs her roughly to get her moving. "Get your paws off. I soil easy," she tells him, while taking the time to tie a scarf jauntily around her neck. As she leaves in the policeman's custody, she hands the wallet, open to the picture, to the man. "Don't lose this," she tells him, smiling. Realizing that she has turned herself in to keep him from scandal and probably save his marriage and good name, he says, "You know, life's a funny thing." Graham turns and asks, "Compared to what?"

This scene accomplishes several things that resonate through the film. First, Graham enters the frame; the camera does not seek her out as an object. This establishes her as an active presence in her own story. Next, she's not a hypocrite. The film suggests that her john is a supposedly solid citizen having a fling with a woman in a neighboring state (and the previous scene in a hip jazz club showed sugar daddies in late middle-age slumming with very young women). However, she is ready to take the consequences—"I've been there before. It's a misdemeanor, no federal rap"—but not before trying to lie her way out of it. Although the action of the scene has her submitting to authority, her surrender plays as a victory. Just as she enters the scene actively, claiming her sexual pleasure as her own—not as male desire projected onto her—so she refuses to be manhandled or rushed. She even sets the terms of her arrest. In losing, she appears to win, an impression maintained throughout the film and a total reversal of the convention of other female biopics in which success gives way to suffering.

However, her answer to the man's dime-store philosophizing—life is funny "compared to what?"—indicates that this is a person who improvises her way through life, in another parallel with jazz. She takes what comes, a trait that puts her in a position both active and passive. However, the film clearly expects her to have moral groundings and not simply to get those from men or from the cultural system. In the lengthy and powerful sequence depicting Graham's last night, when sympathy for her is at its height, she reverts to form and tells Nurse Barbara an outrageous lie about her "wonderful" husband Henry and how she selflessly left him, sacrificing her happiness in order to protect his position at "a very big bank." Not only does this story sound like the plot of the sort of woman's picture many critics might classify this film with, but it reminds the spectator that Graham is not an ordinary woman. There is still some doubt that died with her, not in relation to male standards but to other women, a point made as the scene ends on Nurse Barbara, who clearly stores the incident away mentally, not knowing what to make of it.

Whatever Barbara's responsibility for her fate, the law is continually shown as the force waiting to snatch her with its teeth when she falls, and to help her fall if that suits its purpose. This is seen, for instance, in Wise's clever match cut from the bongo drum at the San Diego party to a gavel stand on a judge's bench as Graham is sentenced for perjury. It is also shown very strongly in the sequence in which Graham is entrapped. In the film's sequence of events, Barbara is visited by Peg soon after the murder indictment. She laments her own failure to see where her life of crime could lead: "All the stuff I read, but I could never read the handwriting on the wall."

This is apparent self-knowledge, but it plays more like the habit of a compulsive liar who tells his/her listeners what they probably want to hear. It is soon belied when her court-appointed lawyer tells her that since she can't find her husband, who might corroborate her claim that she was with him the night of the Monahan murder, she has no chance of acquittal. Given what we know of her character, this almost guarantees that she'll do something desperate to get an alibi and then claim she had no choice. After talking to a fellow inmate who, it turns out, has made a bargain with police for a suspended sentence, Barbara makes the first step toward arranging the false alibi. As the scene ends, she walks past "the handwriting on the wall," in the form of a sign that warns, "Keep healthy. Stay clean." She doesn't learn from her earlier perjury conviction. Her amorality, clearly set out at the start, shows itself now. She even once again rolls the dice, after having compared herself to "the little ball bouncing around a roulette wheel, everyone betting on me to land where it's going to do them the most good—votes for the D.A., circulation for the newspapers, promotions for the cops."

However, it's the law that is stealthy, underhanded, coy, and ultimately inscrutable. The law's alliance with an inmate serving time for manslaughter, in order to provide the prosecution with an airtight case, resembles Barbara's shilling for criminals and resorting to dishonesty in her defense. The difference, as the film makes clear, is that the law has power, means, justification, and credibility—all of which are denied to the woman in the sight of the law.

If the law has the power to accuse and judge the woman, the media have the power to characterize and prejudge her. If Barbara fantasizes her life as if it's a Barbara Stanwyck woman's picture, the reporter Ed Montgomery, as portrayed at the beginning, has read too much hard-boiled detective fiction. Graham to him is a *femme fatale,* one of the "angel-pusses who'd shoot their grandmothers in the back and take bets on which way they'll fall." At the moment when Graham is being questioned without knowing the charge, Montgomery pronounces his verdict, based on the type: "It's Mrs. Graham's tough luck to be young, attractive, belligerent, immoral, and guilty as hell." His dubbing her "the tiger woman" is shown as infinitely ironic. The toy tiger that she carries becomes a complex symbol of her inner life. To her it is a reminder of the little boy she's left behind; to Montgomery and the press it represents female danger and depravity easily sold to a fearful public. Moreover, the film's failure to explain Montgomery's conversion from being convinced of her guilt to believing in her innocence serves to shift the focus away from Graham as a site of mystery and inconclusiveness. No doubt

30. The criminal as celebrity. Barbara makes the evening news in *I Want to Live!* Digital frame enlargement.

the filmmakers had to take the newspaperman's change of heart as a given, since he wasn't offering any explanations. The result is that Montgomery becomes an object of mystery. A letter from Graham read in voiceover expresses this: "I don't know what's making him change toward me in his old age, but he sure seems to have."

Moreover, Montgomery's conversion is not presented as a great gift for which the recipient should be grateful; instead, both protagonist and film seem to regard it as too little, too late. When the reporter tries to accompany some bad news about Graham's appeal with an apology to her for his reportage of her trial, she won't let him finish, turning her back with the line, "What a sendoff you're giving me. Everything but confetti." Up to the end, Graham takes the newsman's benevolence with a touch of cynicism. Told that he will be keeping an execution-eve vigil outside the cells of Perkins and Santo in the hope that one of them will make a statement clearing her, she snorts, "An *exclusive* statement, no doubt." The film's last scene, in which Matthews meets Montgomery outside San Quentin with a letter from Graham thanking him, has the effect of giving Graham/Hayward, in voiceover, what are literally the film's last words. This would seem an example of what Kaja Silverman, in *The Acoustic Mirror*, calls the "contained" written voiceover, the woman's voice that is at the man's beck and call and can as easily be discarded or silenced (if he chooses not to read it) as it can be activated. *I Want to Live!* uses the voiceover, however, to reinsert Graham pointedly into a space from which she has been forcibly removed. The effect is intensified when Montgomery turns down his hearing aid, tuning out the clamor of the traffic jam caused by the men who came to view her death, as they rush to get on with their busy, destructive lives. This effective muting of the scene indicates Montgomery's—and the film's—choice of Barbara's voice over that of the world that condemned her. Furthermore, after seeing Graham's visual image being claimed, defined, and misinterpreted, the audience hears her disembodied voice as the authority of her objective self, which cannot be misconstrued or taken away.

As the film demonstrates, Graham may not have been guilty of murder. "Bloody Babs," "the tiger lady," was referred to in newspaper accounts as simply "Barbara" and never without reference to her appearance and her sexuality (inseparable, in this case and at this time, from her gender). What she was guilty of beyond a reasonable doubt was a violation of the norms of femininity. What is equally profound is that male filmmakers have told her story not by investigating her but by identifying with her and by seeing the specific ways in which her femininity, made synonymous with her criminality, rendered her an object of invasion and dehumanization by the media and the law. This is done by means of cinematic codes and an aggressive star performance and is motivated by the desire to tip public opinion against capital punishment, and do it within the diegetic confines of Hollywood narrative film.

For all this *I Want to Live!* should not be regarded as an amazing anomaly. It should instead be seen as early evidence that with awareness and effort male filmmakers can tell a female protagonist's story without forcing it into the formulas of victimization and the downward trajectory. We shall see further examples, from several eras, of the biopic as female star vehicle, as well as the throes through which the genre goes—and through which it puts its female protagonists—before filmmakers attempt to rethink the genre, bypassing the formulas almost completely.

13

Barbra and Julie at the Dawning of the Age of Aquarius

The first time I saw *Funny Girl,* [it] just seemed to me, I must say, okay. . . . It's a very difficult film, I think, to describe because intellectually and from a paid critic's point of view, it is sort of old-fashioned, corny. . . . People seem to like it, but I wouldn't want to have to be a critic reviewing it.

—BARBRA STREISAND, CIRCA 1982

Barbra Streisand's defensiveness years later toward *Funny Girl* (1968) illustrates the tension even she felt between the new kind of smart female stardom she represented in the late sixties and the obsolescent vehicles that established it. The cinema of the epochal cultural year of 1968 gave rough treatment to anything that presented itself as an uncritical, unrevised, or non-ironic rendition of what had been accepted in the past. The term "anachronistic" no longer meant just out of place in historical time; it could also mean out of place in current time.

Two hard-ticket roadshow musicals that opened within a month of each other in the fall of 1968 were biopics of female stars of the theater and in Fanny Brice's case, radio. Brice and Gertrude Lawrence were figures from an age beyond the memories of the baby boomers and perhaps even of their parents. Although both were modern figures who had died early in the previous decade while in their fifties, Brice (1891–1951), the heroine of *Funny Girl,* and Lawrence (1898–1952), the subject of *Star!,* might as well have been from the previous century, so dead were their inhabited worlds of vaudeville, music halls, the Ziegfeld Follies, prewar Broadway and the West End, mass entertainment radio, and 78 rpm records. "Long past the time," wrote Custen, "when the studio mode of production was in good operating order Hollywood still produced major hits . . . that drew upon this 'old' culture. But, more often than not, the formulaic reflexivity of star biopics that characterized the postwar era failed to find a public" (29). That moviegoing public was increasingly made up of young people as the baby boomers came of age. The new trend was launched, ironically, by a biopic, *Bonnie and Clyde* (1967), which appeared when both of these 1968 musicals were in production. *Bonnie and Clyde* rediscovers the gangsters of the Depression era as populist romantics, beset by a class-driven ruthlessness and violence. *Bonnie and Clyde* reinterpreted a recent chapter in the American past as it might have been lived by everyday people, and as youthful sixties rebels might have wanted to imagine it.

On the other hand, everything about *Funny Girl* was obsolete, with one crucial exception: its star. *Star!*, meanwhile, unwittingly violated so many expectations of the audience and conventions of the female biopic as to be virtually indecipherable in its time. One of the most underappreciated and interesting Hollywood female biopics, *Star!* failed commercially and critically for, among other things, taking an indiscriminate and exhaustive look at its protagonist that is neither entirely damning nor entirely flattering. The films are musical biopics, although they approach that subgenre in idiosyncratic, off-angle ways. *Funny Girl* and *Star!* demonstrate elaborately why the female biopic and the female star as institution expired together at the end of the 1960s. They inaugurate a long deep blackout of the Hollywood female biopic and the institution of the female star of which it had been an important adjunct. The few female biopics that follow, such as *Lady Sings the Blues* (1972), plunge headlong into the spiral of masochism and the downward trajectory, places where the Barbra Streisand and Julie Andrews showcases have no desire or reason to be, even when convention dictates that they head there.

Star! and *Funny Girl* exist in order to glorify their female stars in, as it turned out, a last moment in limbo before the onset of male-skewing demographics, low-budget filmmaking, heightened realism, and New Hollywood's vehement reaction to feminism. As we will see, when female biopics did return to fairly frequent production in the 1980s, the nature of stardom and of the Hollywood cinema had changed, and not in ways that often redounded to the subjects' favor. *Star!* and *Funny Girl* deal with ambition, the dialectic of public and private, the meaning of celebrity, motherhood, the successful woman in the world, and the nature of stardom. These movies and their reception say much about why the female biopic became and in some ways remains an untenable form. *Funny Girl* attracted a large audience, but its success was attributed almost entirely to Streisand, without whom it too probably would have floundered as a relic of an outmoded genre. Streisand was acclaimed for what reviewers saw as a performance conveying truths about both Fanny Brice and herself.

Funny Girl

I don't know where Fanny ends and Barbra begins.
    —RAY STARK

Funny Girl is an adaptation of a Broadway book musical with a largely original score (lyrics by Bob Merrill, music by Jule Styne) and a heavily fictionalized account of Fanny Brice's rise and her relationship with her second husband, Nick Arnstein. *Funny Girl* was brought into being by movie producer Ray Stark, whose determination to make a film about his late mother-in-law Fanny Brice drove him through several writers and concepts in the late fifties until he found a script to his liking. It was "My Man," drafted in 1960 by Isobel Lennart, whose earlier credits included *Love Me or Leave Me*. After Stark interested Columbia Pictures, the project hit snags over casting. Wanting to get the project off the ground, Stark hired composer Jule Styne (*Bells Are Ringing, Gypsy*) and lyricist Bob Merrill to write a score for a Broadway musical, using Lennart's script as the show's book. Streisand, who had attracted attention on Broadway at the age of twenty in a featured role in *I Can Get It for You Wholesale* in 1962 and recorded three albums for Columbia Records, was cast as Fanny. The show shed an hour from its playing time in out-of-town tryouts; most of the cuts were from Lennart's book. When it opened on Broadway in February 1964, *Funny Girl* drew mixed reviews but raves for Streisand, who landed on the cover of *Time* in April; the original cast album quickly went Gold, all leading to 1,348 performances on Broadway and a successful run on the London West End, starring Streisand.

Funny Girl as play and film is just slightly less fanciful a treatment of actual people and events than *The Sound of Music,* which changed the marriage of Maria and Captain Von Trapp from 1927 to 1938, showed Von Trapp leaving his fortune behind in Austria when in fact he had lost it all in a Depression-era bank failure, had the family fleeing Austria in secret when they actually left uneventfully by train with no Nazis after them, and had the Von Trapps escaping from Salzberg into Switzerland over the Alps, a route that would have taken them into Germany! For these reasons, *The Sound of Music* fails to qualify under Rosenstone's generous criteria for historical truth and is too much a fairy tale for the most forgiving biopic standards.

Funny Girl at least begins with Fanny singing at Frank Keeney's theater in Brooklyn and debuting with the Ziegfeld Follies in 1910 and ends with Nick Arnstein's release from prison following their divorce in 1927, all of which have bases in actuality (Kenrick). In between, however, the show sanitizes Nick beyond recognition, a potentially crippling transformation. "The actual Nicky was considered unacceptable as a leading man," said the 10 April 1964 *Time* cover story. "He was a shiftless con man with a column of mercury for a spine, a criminal record, and a cavalier attitude toward Fanny's devotion and fidelity" ("The Girl"). Karen Swenson put it more gently in 1982: "Nicky Arnstein was a colorful character—perhaps too colorful. His elegance was something many admiring friends and acquaintances tried to emulate, but he could also be amazingly cool and indifferent to people he professed to love. Something closer to the 'true' Nicky Arnstein would have been an actor's dream (Jack Nicholson would probably play him today), but taking into consideration all the people who may have wanted his character cleaned up left Lennart with little more than a storybook prince" (35).

The Nick in Lennart's 1960 script, "My Man," is not the vague but high-class card sharp in the ruffled shirt who never dreams of crime until he's desperate. He is a jack-of-all-trades, a high-rolling Ralph Kramden looking for the big score that will make him rich. In every version Arnstein has a different failed scheme in the second act—in "My Man," instant coffee (in the 1910s; Arnstein, ever the loser, rejects the label "instant," deciding that "concentrated coffee" sounds better); in the '64 play, Florida land deals; in the '68 film, Oklahoma oil wells. Lennart's original script, however, although it first sketches out Fanny's road from Keeney's to Ziegfeld to love and troubled marriage with Nick, is more complex about real matters, such as how much things cost (Ziegfeld reveals that he's losing $2,000 a week even while playing to packed houses every night, foreshadowing his eventual bankruptcy—not depicted in *Funny Girl*). Despite its complexities and considerable humor (it is about a comedian, after all), the script reads like a fifties show business family melodrama, with strong elements of the *Love Me or Leave Me–A Star Is Born* formula, the latter of which *Funny Girl,* show and film, falls back upon increasingly.

Nick is the chief problem of the show and the film—a character so amorphous that for the film Stark cast the Egyptian Omar Sharif to play a New York Jewish street hustler simply because he would look good in a tuxedo (another plus, unappreciated at the time, was that Sharif, the future author of a syndicated newspaper column on bridge, knew his way around a deck of cards). At least the film—unlike *Star!,* one of whose problems was its casting of a succession of nondescript stiffs as Gertrude Lawrence's suitors— had a male lead who was unlike anyone else we see. Press coverage centered on the pairing of Jew and Arab in a love story, and when the 1967 Six Day War broke out just before production began, the panicky studio suggested dropping Sharif (Streisand and the director William Wyler threatened to quit if he were fired). The spectator never has a chance to think about the social disturbance that would have been created by such an intermarriage in the era when *Funny Girl* takes place. (Another Broadway hit of 1964, *Fiddler on the Roof,* also set circa 1910, takes this issue as one of its main dramatic conflicts, and seems much more conservative for it than *Funny Girl.*) That the intermarriage is not an issue is an index of the film's power, a magical but very timely sense that Streisand sweeps differences and conventions into insignificance, despite the fact that marrying outside the Jewish and Catholic faiths was not yet acceptable in most communities even in 1968; in real life Streisand had taken a nice Jewish boy, Elliott Gould, for her first husband.

An impression given by Lennart's first script is that it would have homogenized the Jewish identity of Fanny, her upbringing, her comedy, and her marriage to Nick, anglicizing an ethnic story as Old Hollywood invariably did. Tellingly, when the film version of *Funny Girl* was first being planned late in 1965, Columbia wanted Shirley MacLaine for the role, despite Streisand's four Gold Records and a highly rated, Emmy-winning TV special, *My Name Is Barbra,* all by the end of that year. Had Stark shot Lennart's script in 1961, when Streisand was still an unknown, the then-twenty-seven-year-old MacLaine, the star of *The Trouble with Harry* (1955), *Some Came Running* (1958), and *The Apartment* (1960), who was typed early on in waifish roles, might have handled Fanny's raw early years. But could she have been Fanny Borach from the Lower East Side, as well as Fanny Brice of the Follies, which in a very narrow but quite profound way Barbra Streisand was?

Streisand was promoted as an "original," which, a pre-release featurette helpfully explained, means "never having occurred or existed before." The authoritative narrator adds that "audiences feel, sense, know, that nothing like Barbra Streisand has ever occurred before" (*This Is Streisand*). Accordingly, *Funny Girl* had a persistently contemporary streak, despite a plot that might have been found in a two-reel melodrama from the early years of Brice's tenure with Ziegfeld. The fifties-sixties-style Broadway musical comedy score by Styne and Merrill is a fairly strong one of its genre, but most of the songs take the show out of period. Wyler adds more up-to-date cinematic techniques (freeze-frame, zoom lens, jump cuts, sun spots on the lens in outdoor shots) than one expects to see in a film of this type. The movie's makeup and hairstyles are pure 1960s. One critic noted that the Ziegfeld girls look like they stepped out of *Playboy;* however, Linda Mizejewski, in her book *Ziegfeld Girl,* points out that Ziegfeld established the standards of American femininity that Hugh Hefner would carry on in *Playboy*. What modernity *Funny Girl* really had was Barbra Streisand, and everything that her presence as a new movie star at the end of the 1960s was taken then to signify.

The press early on portrayed her as a rampaging egotist. Cast members claimed that she had ordered their scenes cut; she was said to have clashed with Wyler. The cutting of Nick's solos from the play was taken as evidence that Streisand could be the only star of this show. All of this was denied at the time and later by Wyler, Stark, and Streisand as well. In performance, the alleged ego in Streisand is undercut by self-effacing humor and demure behavior. *Funny Girl* vacillates between a Fanny who wants things done her way and a Fanny who is willing to give it all up for her child and "her man." She would not make up her mind ultimately but let men do it for her, except for those moments when she is suddenly defiant of Ziegfeld. Thus her decisions seem intuitive, almost accidental, and do not seem the products of consistent determination.

"I knew that I would do [Fanny] justice by being true to myself," Streisand told Swenson in 1982. "*Funny Girl* is about me. It just happened to Fanny Brice earlier" (35). In order to be true to herself, therefore, Fanny/Barbra has to lampoon the Ziegfeld Girl conventions by turning a Ziegfeld "beautiful bride" into a comic pregnant one. But why would Ziegfeld want to pretend that Brice was no different from his other girls? In *The Great Ziegfeld* (1936), a biopic made at MGM when Irving Thalberg (d. September 1936) was still influencing the studio's major pictures without ever taking a pro-

31. Director William Wyler leaves his star alone on the stage to sing "My Man" at the end of *Funny Girl* (Columbia, 1968), a composition more reminiscent of Streisand's television specials than of Fanny Brice and the Ziegfeld Follies. Digital frame enlargement.

ducer credit himself, Fanny Brice, age forty-four, plays a "body too much" to herself at nineteen. Ziegfeld takes the ruffles and frills off her costume, leaving a waifish and tattered black dress. Even in a movie so fanciful that Fanny sings "My Man" in 1910, ten years before it was written, Ziegfeld complains to his costumer, "I did not engage Miss Brice as a showgirl." She begins to sing "My Man" with tears in her eyes from being made to wear an old shawl and play a street urchin deglamorized by the glamorous Ziegfeld. The impresario, played by William Powell, points to the women in the rehearsal hall who listen, transfixed and moved. He's turned Brice into an identification figure. As Streisand in the last scene of *Funny Girl* comes out on stage in black and belts out "My Man," Wyler acts as Irving Thalberg's idea of Ziegfeld had.

Ziegfeld's teary-eyed female spectators were Wyler's interlocutors as well. "My Man" was written as "Mon Homme" in 1920 by Maurice Yvain for the Paris music halls, where it was sung and recorded by Jeanne Bourgeois, who went by the stage name Mistinguette. Translated for Brice in 1922, the torch song in waltz time became her signature number. Gone from *Funny Girl* is the lengthy prologue of "My Man," part of which includes the lines, "I don't know why I should. / He isn't good. / He isn't true. / He beats me too. / What can I do?" Even the 1936 film cuts away just before Brice gets to these lyrics, although Billie Holiday included them in her iconic 1950s renditions of the song. For the 1960s, the song becomes a swingy, brassy showstopper, traveling a route similar to that taken over the thirty years between Brecht and Weill's composition of "Mack the Knife" for *The Three Penny Opera* and Bobby Darin's top-forty rendition in 1959. Stark was unable to obtain the rights to use "My Man" in the Broadway *Funny Girl*. Between the play's production and that of the film, however, the song in its sixties incarnation did become identified with Streisand. She sang it on her first CBS special, *My Name Is Barbra,* in April 1965, with the music from this program released on the record album of the same title. On the black-and-white broadcast, Streisand sang "My Man" wearing a plain black dress and illuminated in front of a black background. The rendition of the first verse in both the '65 TV and the '68 film versions is different from the second. In *My Name Is Barbra* the singer eases into it lightly and intimately, in the style of a Vegas-type nightclub singer (which Streisand already had been). The prologue, used here as interlude but without the "He beats me too" bridge, segues powerfully into the repeat of the chorus, this time with an intense swing rhythm that is both soaring and hard-hitting.

The arrangement of the first stanza for the final scene of the film is halting and emotional. Singing almost a cappella, Streisand leads the viewer/listener to believe that she could break down on her next breath. The background is not completely black, but when we see the whole set the first time, it is lined with four vertical rows of red, white, and blue spotlights with gauzy film around them. We never see more than one of these rows again during the scene. Audiences watching the film in pan-and-scan TV and video prints, the only way it could be seen until the DVD era, probably did think the background was entirely black. None of the numerous *Funny Girl* scripts on file at UCLA, including Wyler's own, end with "My Man." According to a biography of Wyler, the director called everyone to the studio and recorded the song live, doing ten takes, with Omar Sharif standing behind the black curtains and talking to Streisand, at Wyler's instructions, "to help build up her sadness" (Herman 447). With the prologue/interlude entirely gone, Fanny/Streisand launches into the finale. Even though the film used different arrangers from the television special and the album, there is scarcely any difference between the film's rendition and her 1965 performances. By the end Streisand has taken over the film, Brice, the nothing male lead, everything. If audiences feel they are in the 1910s and 1920s with Fanny Brice during the film, they unquestionably leave in 1968 with Barbra Streisand.

What are the implications of this? For one thing, this Fanny Brice is genuinely New York Jewish, certainly more so than she would have been with other actresses who might have played the role, MacLaine for the film, and in the play, Anne Bancroft or Carol Burnett, both of whom turned it down. Streisand helps bring Hollywood out of the decades-old semitophobia that led Twentieth Century Fox to make *Rose of Washington Square* (1939), a thinly disguised film about Fanny Brice and Nick Arnstein (so thin that Brice sued, successfully), starring WASPs Alice Faye and Tyrone Power. "In her first screen appearance," wrote Kevin Thomas in a review of the restored film in 2001, "Streisand smashed the old restrictive Hollywood standards of physical perfection." In doing so, and doing so as Brice, Streisand paradoxically exorcised the demons of the previous three decades by conjuring up even older devils.

Streisand broke the long period of silence during which the Eastern European Jews and their descendents who ran Hollywood avidly assimilated, assiduously avoiding portrayals of Jews on the screen. "A Jew can't play a Jew," Samuel Goldwyn said. "It wouldn't look right on the screen" (qtd. in Rogin *Blackface* 154). Michael Rogin reported that "the only Jews in front of the camera at Harry Cohn's Columbia Pictures were said to be playing Indians," alluding to a long comic tradition of Jewish comedians in Indian garb, from Eddie Cantor in *Whoopee!* (1930) to Mel Brooks in *Blazing Saddles* (1974) (154). Cohn, who died in 1958, might well have spun in his grave at Streisand's "oy vey"-laden performance ten years later at his old studio. Eddie Cantor in *Whoopee!*, performing Jewish self-hatred for the entertainment of the masses, claimed his nose to be that of an Indian fire chief, positioning his profile beneath a Pueblo wall scaler and declaring, "Here's my hook and ladder." Streisand's nose, on the other hand, became what *Time* in 1964 called "a shrine" ("The Girl"). Similarly, Goldwyn, who lived until 1974, might have winced to see the debut guided by Wyler, his former leading director. In short, Streisand paraded Jewish identity before the cameras, as charisma, as sexuality, as glamorous-impersonates-the-ordinary stardom, and indeed nobody rained on it. She drew the sunshine to herself by exhuming old demeaning stereotypes, rereading them and making them work for her instead of against her. In effect, Streisand reappropriated as an asset an identity that was long considered a liability. As Brice explains to Ziegfeld after comically subverting his wedding production number by playing a pregnant bride,

FANNY: I couldn't do it straight, as if I thought I was [*pause*] one of those other girls, I mean, they woulda laughed at me.

ZIEGFELD: And they did.

FANNY: Yes, but, but it was my joke, you see. They laughed with me, not at me. Because I wanted them to laugh. But, uh, I mean, you know what I mean.

ZIEGFELD: No. Explain it to me.

While it is hard to imagine that The Great Ziegfeld could have been so dense, Mizejewski makes the point that the Jewish Brice and the African American Ziegfeld star Bert Williams were "situated in the ambiguous intersection of stardom and social contempt" (133). Brice biographer Barbara Grossman writes that "Brice did not conform to the prevailing notion of female beauty and, more specifically, to the Ziegfeldian definition of it" (qtd. in Mizejewski 29). *Funny Girl* makes this point obvious. "The pregnant bride routine depicted in *Funny Girl* never happened," writes John Kenrick. "If it had, Ziegfeld would have fired her on the spot, no matter what the audience thought of her," adding that "Fanny and Ziegfeld had few (if any) disputes and always treated each other with professional and personal respect" ("*Funny Girl*"). However, the show must invent conflict between Fanny and Ziegfeld's "Glorifying the American Girl" standards. To become a "new kind of star" in the sixties, Streisand has to turn the old style of self-hating Jewish comedy performed by Brice and Cantor against its sponsor Ziegfeld and the culture he entertained. Ziegfeld comes around because, as he tells her, "I love talent," as do the biopic and the musical. Fanny refuses to believe the production number's song, "His love makes her beautiful." After all, the theme of *Funny Girl*, as Pauline Kael wrote, is that "talent is beauty" ("Bravo!" 133). Fanny Brice, Mizejewski points out, "buckled under [in 1923] to cultural standards and had plastic surgery on her nose" (134). Streisand's "shrine," in contrast, remains inviolate well into her seventh decade (reportedly because she is concerned surgery would harm her singing voice).

Here as on many of its themes, however, the film vacillates, ultimately making *Funny Girl* a conservative text despite all its standards-smashing. The refusal of the Starks to represent the actual Nick Arnstein leaves the film a hackneyed tale of a husband unmanned by his wife's success; moreover, the film undermines its premise that Fanny's/Barbra's beauty dwells in her talent. In the penultimate scene, on the day Nick gets out of prison after eighteen months, Fanny waits for him to make the decision about whether

32. Fanny battles Flo Ziegfeld (Walter Pidgeon) as if Ziegfeld had hired her as a showgirl, not a comic. Digital frame enlargement.

or not to get back together with her. If Nick wants Fanny back, she tells Ziegfeld, she's prepared to give up the theater. So, because Nick understands Fanny better than she herself does, he will not ask her to do that. Nonetheless, the film asks its spectator to believe the same old silly lies about a successful woman's marriage naturally being more important to her than her career. Which takes us back to that ending in basic black on the nearly bare stage. Not only does that recall the '65 TV show where Streisand first sang "My Man," but Wyler had been preparing to direct *Patton* when script delays allowed him to pick up *Funny Girl*, whose first director, Sidney Lumet, had been let go by Stark. Francis Ford Coppola had already submitted his draft of *Patton*, which featured the famous opening with the general alone on a stage, backed by a huge American flag. (After finishing *Funny Girl*, Wyler gave up *Patton* for health reasons.) Both sequences find character in performance and provide unique moments (less so in musicals) where a character on a stage seems almost separate from the rest of the film. *Funny Girl*'s ending recalls the noble "This is Mrs. Norman Maine" endings of every version of *A Star Is Born*, a film that Streisand later felt compelled to remake. As Jule Styne pointed out, the ending of the Broadway *Funny Girl* was different:

> My only disappointment [with the film version] was that in the latter portion they destroyed Fanny's character. Fanny was a strong woman, nothing could defeat her. . . . In the movie version . . . they interpolated the song "My Man" for her to sing at the end, and that made her self-pitying and timid. . . . When Nicky left Fanny, she was about 35 years old; she wasn't a baby. In the play she became strong at that point. She

cried to herself for a moment, then got *mad* at herself for crying, and when they say 'On Stage' she says 'Nobody's gonna rain on my parade,' and even has the line 'I'll cry a little later,' so she *becomes* strong. (Swenson 45)

The new lines of the reprise of "Don't Rain on My Parade" were

> Hey Gorgeous. Here we go again.
> Well, here it goes, kid
> No looking back
> Set up your nose, kid
> Let's give 'em hell, Brice.
> I'll cry a little later.
> Well, Brice, that's life in the the-ay-ter . . . (Lennart *Funny Girl: A New Musical*)

When she sings "Nobody, but nobody is gonna rain on my parade" the second time, those "nobodies" include her ex-husband. The song does give the show the kind of uplift expected of Broadway musicals of the period, like the ragtag boys' band in *The Music Man,* which turns into a gleaming multitude worthy of John Philip Sousa at the final curtain, or the reunion of Fagin and the Artful Dodger in *Oliver!* as carefree, lovable rogues, an ending that must have left Dickens, if not spinning in his grave, then at least scratching his head. On the other hand, the film of *Funny Girl* goes out with the heartbreak and pain of a woman's picture and a female biopic. At least in the show, Fanny for the first time lives her life for herself instead of for men, addressing herself "Hey, Gorgeous," in a recurring line that had been first, "Hey, Mr. Keeney," then "Hey, Mr. Arnstein." This is a long way from the simpering that begins "My Man" in the film. When she does work her way up to strength, it's hard to know what it signifies except that she will go on holding the torch for Nick, although she's done wonderfully well without him during the time he spent in prison. Furthermore, the last scene's camp appeal surely arises from the disjunction between the significance of Streisand's pure star power and her larger-than-life suffering.

The character is left an incoherent figure, but the star who plays her emerges perfectly coherent. The film finally is about the arrival of Barbra Streisand, a new star reaching back before the Old Hollywood to an ethnic authenticity the culture had rendered in demeaning caricatures—including blackface, in which Brice was known to perform in the Follies. While Streisand re-creates Brice, she also leaves her behind, inadvertently making *Funny Girl* one biopic that moves its subject from out of the past and into the present and future. It does this only by virtue of the actress who plays her. However, by abandoning Fanny Brice, as it were, *Funny Girl* leaves a poor model and a lack of direction for any female biopics to come. Joseph Morgenstern in his 1968 *Newsweek* review called *Funny Girl* "a good old-fashioned show with a great new-fashioned star. But good old-fashioned shows have nowhere to go but down, even if they have Miss Streisand to rescue them from the more manifest ravages of time" ("Great Girl" 96). Streisand told Morgenstern the next year, "I have all these possibilities. I'm slightly dumb, I'm very smart. I'm many things. . . . I want to use them, want to express them. It's kind of funny, because I'm in these sort of big pictures and yet I'm an oddball. I mean, I'm not a Doris Day or a Julie Andrews" ("Superstar" 38).

Star!

The actress who *was* Julie Andrews found herself uncomfortably in the shadow of Barbra Streisand in the fall of 1968. Whereas *Funny Girl* has the narrative of a fairy tale, *Star!* shows Gertrude Lawrence putting in long years in the chorus and as an understudy, paying her dues in the ensemble cast of a revue before reaching stardom. Where Fanny oscillates between brash impetuousness and feminine passivity, *Star!*'s heroine bristles with ambi-tion. Lawrence's talent doesn't just erupt out of her; it has to be developed through experience and emulation. Nor is her ambition displaced onto a male character or anyone else. For *Funny Girl*'s framing device, Fanny Brice sits in the New Amsterdam Theater on the day of her husband's release from jail and thinks back. Gertrude Lawrence is in a screening room on a work-day before the evening's performance, watching a new documentary film about her life and deciding whether to grant its filmmaker the approval he needs to release it. It is rare in biopics of all eras for a woman to wield the kind of power and independence that Lawrence holds in this film.

The film producer depends upon her, saying, "I need your okay to show this picture," to which she quickly adds, "You need it to use that title song, too, darling." Shows get produced and songs written and performed on her say-so, and even her eventual husband Richard Aldrich at first needs her to

33. The look of a successful career woman. Gertrude Lawrence (Julie Andrews) screens a documentary of her life in *Star!* (Robert Wise, Twentieth Century Fox, 1968). Digital frame enlargement.

appear at his theater on Cape Cod. However, she also shows her reluctance to commit herself: "I won't be rushed into making decisions." This foreshadows the "saga" of "poor Jenny," in the film's climactic song, "who would make up her mind," always with comically disastrous results. Jerry Paul, the fictional filmmaker, sitting at her side in a screening room, tells her, "Don't be afraid to tell me what you really think." "Oh, ho, ho, darling," she replies, in a medium close-up, "I've never been afraid to tell a man that in all my life." Given the spectator's familiarity with the biopic flashback frame, in which the subject reviews life events from the past, it's clear from the outset that nothing has happened or will happen in what we see to punish her for her quite unheard-of transgression, one for which the film itself would be flogged for years to come.

Star!, directed by Robert Wise and written by William Fairchild, goes against the once and future pattern of female biopics in which the subjects are women who died young, or were victimized, or notorious in some way, rather than women who triumphed over obstacles and maintained long careers. Gertrude Lawrence is not the doll-like creation of a stage mother, nor of a Svengali-like visionary male. There is no downward trajectory. The only thing close to tragic about Lawrence is her premature death from liver cancer at age fifty-four, and the film ends twelve years before that. Even at the time of her death, she was starring in the original Broadway production of *The King and I.* In a rigidly class-bound society this actress from the lowest echelons found, in show business success and stardom, the best way to rise above it all. It may be clichéd to say, but she and Noel Coward became queen and king of their own proscenium principality. Lawrence conducted herself as a kind of mock-monarch, dressing in splendor and behaving with an air of noblesse oblige. Even at that, however, she preferred to spend as little time as possible in England; she lived in America from 1936 until the end of her life and married an American in 1940. Unlike American film stardom, which purports to be ordinary, there is nothing ordinary about Lawrence's stage stardom. Her appeal was that she was "of the people," but she held herself as if born, like royalty, to the lofty position that she occupied. Lawrence, wrote Pauline Kael in her review of *Star!*, "looked as if she didn't give a damn what anybody thought. . . . If she could barely carry a tune in her thin, careless voice, she made it seem as if carrying a tune were beneath her. She wasn't even pretty. And that's what was so triumphantly witty about her: she had made herself a leader of fashion and a beauty the way a great chef is supposed to be able to make a superb dinner—out of nothing" ("Cripes!" 163–164).

As if to demonstrate, a clip from a 1931 film revue shows Lawrence speaking to the camera for "the first talking picture I've made in England." Displaying national pride by stating that only a song by an Englishman would do for the occasion, Lawrence proclaims that "when I let it be known I was searching for songs by British composers, I received over two thousand manuscripts in one week. Not bad." Standing in front of a closed grand piano, with the gentleman whose song she deigns to sing serving as accompanist, she performs a lilting ditty called "You're My Decline and Fall." The British Empire was still secure at the time, and Lawrence shows herself to be quite a bulwark as well; though reed thin, she is at once regal and casual. A long, straight frock fairly hangs on her in the style of the day, offset by a necklace of what one can be sure are real pearls. The most remarkable feature of the clip is that Lawrence performs the entire thing, from introduction through the song itself, with her arms folded over her chest. Is this crossed-armed position the involuntary, defensive posture of a stage performer uncomfortable in front of a camera, a device Lawrence did view with some disdain? (Her performance in *Rembrandt,* one of her few movies, was one of that film's least pleasant features.) Whatever the reason for it, it seems certain that arms crossed is the position least conducive to singing. This presentation confirms Lawrence's reputation for "effortlessness," and for seeming not to give a damn. Not only does she not appear to be trying very hard, but given the difficulty of singing with arms pressed against one's lungs, she hardly seems to be breathing! She's in wonderful voice, however, and the contradictions of plain dress with pearls, and confidence with defensiveness, produce a sense of casualness and reality that is quite striking.

One wonders how the makers of *Star!* thought a woman who loves the spotlight, performing before an audience, and pursuing her career above all else would be perceived in a pre-feminist era. A heroine who deflates a little when she's not working, who tries to combine motherhood and career (but who also throws out a drunken first husband when he mistreats the baby), who does not give up all for love, who decides when and if she'll go to bed with the various men who wait at her beck and call, and who luxuriates in finery in the midst of the Great Depression—how would such a woman be seen by a culture that puts women into categories and expects them to be punished for unsanctioned behaviors?

Star! is a notorious flop, one title in the litany of big-budget failures blamed in standard film histories for the near-bankruptcy of most of the film companies at the end of the 1960s. The critical reception was venomous, with reviewers attacking what they saw as the unsuitability of the perky, musically prodigious Julie Andrews for the role of the glamorously nonchalant Lawrence. They assailed what they saw as the monotonous, stagebound quality of the production numbers. Most strikingly, they zeroed in on what they saw as a nastiness in the conception of Gertrude Lawrence bordering on character assassination. *Star!*'s script, said Stephen MacDonald in the *Wall Street Journal*, "makes Gertrude Lawrence out to be a haughty shrew, and Andrews's singing isn't enough to make her likeable. . . . When a woman is just being entertaining we can accept her easily; when she's a shrew we need to know more. We want to know why. This need for character analysis tends to work against the music." This was the same script that Lawrence's friend Noel Coward "thought . . . 'charming and delightful'" (Fairchild to Wise, 19 June). To Pauline Kael, "One gets the idea that [Wise and Fairchild] didn't really like Gertrude Lawrence very much, and that, rather than make the usual star-bio, they were trying for a dispassionate look at her." The character, wrote Kael, is "a woman without a trace of feminine softness or fluidity or grace [who] isn't meant to be lovable. They've made her a bitch all right, but they've failed to make her a star" ("Cripes!" 161–162). "Miss Lawrence is portrayed as a kind of monster," wrote Renata Adler, who was the *New York Times* critic for fourteen months in 1968–69, "with none of the crispness or glamour or wit that would give her ambition style" (36). The uncredited *Time* review saw malice crowned by ineptitude, resulting in the musical-as-wax-museum: "a hollow, frantic caricature—The Character Assassination of Gertrude Lawrence as Performed by the Inmates of Madame Tussaud's."

The reviews had difficulty seeing anything of Gertrude Lawrence beyond Julie Andrews's *Mary Poppins/Sound of Music* persona. Adler noted "some sort of clash between [Andrews's] special niceness and the attitude that the film has toward Lawrence." Comparing the singing styles of the two women, as most of the reviewers did, *Time* saw Lawrence as

> one of those rare anomalies, like Lotte Lenya or Marlene Dietrich, for whom pitch was not important. She could wander off key in every bar, yet the song's content remained pure and intense. Andrews is ten times the musician Lawrence was; her voice never varies a hemisemidemi-quaver from the written notes. In the exuberant comic numbers, person and impersonator coincide. But when Julie attempts a bittersweet ballad . . . the styles collide. Lawrence always suggested a melancholy sensuality; Andrews continually gives the feeling that beneath the lyrics, everything is supercalifragilisticexpialidocious.

Much of the harshness and seeming overkill of the New York reviews can be attributed to the intense animosity of the "film intelligentsia" toward *The Sound of Music* and its immense success. The (false) legend still persists that Kael was fired from *McCall's* for panning it. The blockbuster film version of Rodgers and Hammerstein's musical opened up an undeniable chasm between critics and public taste that has really never closed. Dwight Macdonald, never shy about wearing his snobbery on his sleeve, noting the movie's sixty-million-dollar gross its first year in release and its five Oscars, sniffed that "the puzzle is why it grossed only sixty million and didn't win all the Oscars" (41). (One interesting element of *The Sound of Music* reviews, especially initially when critics were reviewing the film itself rather than the phenomenon, is that Andrews was generally spared; she was singled out as the one element of the film that seemed honest to some kind of reality. An irony—indeed, mystery—is that Andrews less resembled Maria Von Trapp and had less in common with her in terms of life experience than she did Gertrude Lawrence, who trod some of the same boards in Great Britain as Andrews did, more than a generation earlier. Yet no one has ever questioned her rightness for *The Sound of Music*.)

In this atmosphere the reviewers of *Star!* appear to have been lying in wait for the fat target of Andrews-Wise-Twentieth Century Fox to present itself and in their own Broadway-sophisticate territory yet. In retrospect, perhaps the makers of *Star!* could have covered themselves with a framing story that flashed back from Lawrence's final Broadway show, Rodgers and Hammerstein's *The King and I*, one Gertrude Lawrence role no one would have trouble imagining Julie Andrews playing. (Lawrence also played Eliza Doolittle in a 1945 Broadway revival of *Pygmalion*, the role that shot Andrews to stardom eleven years later when she played it onstage in *My Fair Lady*, Alan Jay Lerner and Frederick Loewe's musicalization of the Shaw play.) But the makers of *Star!* were not playing defense, partly because they were actually more in agreement with the critics of *The Sound of Music* than anyone could have guessed. Wise seems to have approached *The Sound of Music* as just a job; he turned it down once and only took it, with some prodding from Richard and Darryl Zanuck, after a number of big-name directors said no and it became clear that his ongoing project for Fox, *The Sand Pebbles*, was going to be delayed at least a year. Andrews, who had parodied the stage version of *The Sound of Music* in a skit written by Mike Nichols in her 1962 TV special with Carol Burnett, *Julie and Carol at Carnegie Hall*, asked Wise at their first meeting after she had been cast, "So, what are you going to do to get the schmaltz out of this thing?"—to which he answered, "You and I are going to get along just fine" (*Sound* DVD).

Charles Champlin, the *Los Angeles Times* critic, was gentler on *Star!* than the New York reviewers, and more thoughtful about some of the film's problems of perception:

> Fairchild's screenplay is . . . just revealing enough to suggest that Miss Lawrence was a rather saltier character than the well worn rags to riches ingredients might suggest, romantically untidy and not always endearing. And Miss Andrews's screen persona is so indelibly upbeat that a more penetrating look at Miss Lawrence would have only been still more confusing. As it is, the star of *Star!* leaves us unsure whether she's a good girl pretending to be naughty or a naughty girl pretending to be better than she is. Empathy is the loser in either case. (F1–17)

At the box office, the film, whose makers clearly expected it to be a blockbuster, died swiftly. The film was recut by the studio and in August 1969 a two-hour version was released with a new title, *Those Were the Happy Times*, and a poster that made it look like a sequel to *The Sound of Music*; the cut version was broadcast on American television in the 1970s and 1980s, albeit under the original title.

In the 1980s and early 1990s the complete roadshow *Star!* enjoyed a comeback; it was screened in revival theaters, mostly in New York and Los Angeles, and was shown in its entirety on cable TV. Reportedly, some audiences "came to laugh at what they expected to be a 'bomb,' but wound up cheering for Julie's performance and the production values" ("Saga of *Star!*"). A twenty-fifth anniversary showing at the Directors Guild of America in November 1993 reassembled most of the film's collaborators, including Wise, Andrews, Richard Crenna, producer Saul Chaplin, choreographers Michael Kidd and Shelah Hackett, and costume designer Donald Brooks. They and others participated in the running commentary for an exhaustive "collector's edition" Fox Video laser disc offered in 1995 at the Gertrude Lawrence–bracket price of $69.95. The laser disc package was released intact on DVD in 2004 for $14.95, demonstrating how democratic the institution of the deluxe movie disc had become between the age of the boutique laser disc and that of the mass-market DVD. With the deaths of Chaplin and Crenna in 1997 and 2003, respectively, and the passing of Wise in 2005 and Kidd in 2007, the historical value of the package intensified. The special features, which drew on archival material from the Robert Wise collection at USC, ironically gave one of Hollywood's most famous flops a far more loving and elaborate treatment on home video than has been accorded many far more successful films. *Funny Girl* received nothing like it. This was surely owing to the fact that nearly all the major collaborators were still living, and that Wise, a former president of the Academy of Motion Picture Arts and Sciences and the Directors Guild, retained a good deal of clout in the Hollywood community right up until his death at age ninety-one.

While warts and all in approach, *Star!* opts for a form not limited to a single conception of its protagonist. In his treatment, screenwriter William Fairchild wrote that the film's

> truth hinges on the character of Gertie. She was generous, impulsive, extravagant, and maddening. . . . Seemingly always contradictory. She was supremely elegant and of the earth, earthy. She could behave with perfect dignity and decorum at one moment and call her dinner companion a bitch at the next. . . . The actress craved the excitement and security of audience affection. The woman craved the excitement and

security of men's affection. Security and excitement aren't usually bed-fellows and when they are they don't continue to be so for very long. Gertie always hoped they would be and this was one of her troubles. This was why she was so often in a muddle, or a state of indecision, or surprise, or indignation about something or other. But . . . she had joy—in herself, in her life, in people. . . . [Her] love was so obvious, so clear, so instantly recognizable as genuine that . . . it inspired love for her in everyone else, even those who for one reason or other really dis-approved of her. We should see the rest of the story in the light of this character—indeed the story should happen the way it does because of this character. (*Gertrude Lawrence Story*)

The filmmakers never set out to understand the character within rigid definitions and expectations. The idea of imposing a plot on the character seems not to have entered anyone's mind. Fairchild's treatment sounds a lot like Walter Wanger's list of contradictions by which a spectator of *I Want to Live!* would experience Barbara Graham, and is in line with the approach to biopics favored by his director. Robert Wise's work was often marked by a realism that verged on the Bazinian in its avoidance of "a priori" meanings. Wise wrote to Saul Chaplin that "Gertie's character . . . is the spine, the driv-ing force around which the whole thing must spring. This will, hopefully, keep us from a lot of the ordinary kind of routine plotting for this kind of story" (Wise).

Fairchild quoted Noel Coward telling him, "I've always been against a film on Gertie's life. There's no story—a poor girl who became a success—then just success, success, success" (Fairchild to Chaplin). The fear of "no story" in a biography of an exceptional person turns filmmakers toward what makes drama with gendered subjects. For men, as we have seen, the drama grows from the struggle for acceptance, for the scientific breakthrough, for the achievement of his dream. For women, drama comes from defeat and victimization of various sorts. An intriguing formulation was voiced by director Sidney Lumet: "In a well-written drama the story comes out of the characters, and in a well-written melodrama the characters come out of the story." Lumet warns actors in melodrama, "I may need to ask you for a climax here that you may not feel, because the nature of the plot demands it" (Lim 23).

Male and female biopics thus can be seen in stark contrast. Male biopics of most eras feel "dramatic," in Lumet's definition, as if the male subject is determining the course of the plot. This is true in celebratory biopics, warts-and-all films, critical biographies, and biopics of men who don't deserve them. Only in the deconstructive biopics (*Glenn Gould, Nixon*) does the alignment of the plot with the subject come into question. Female biopics are more often "melodramatic," with the nature of the story—the kinds of lives women are presumed to live—carrying the subject along through the plot, and overdetermining the character development. The plot comes out of the male biographical subject; the female subject emerges from the plot (and where women are concerned there is only a handful of plots). *Star!*, then, is one of the first female biopics since the heroic films of the 1930s and early 1940s (notably *Queen Christina, The Scarlet Empress, Madame Curie*) to attempt to be "dramatic," with the plot coming from the character rather than the character coming from some course that "was charted before I was born." Indeed, it appears on the evidence that the men behind the film leaned very heavily on the character of Gertrude Lawrence, trusting that a plot would emerge from her.

Wise's three major biopics, *Somebody Up There Likes Me* (1956), *I Want to Live!*, and *Star!*, depict characters struggling between their natural talents and inclinations and the need for social attachments and love. The personalities of Rocky Graziano, Barbara Graham, and Gertrude Lawrence are irrepressible; yet in order to live in the civilized world, these characters have to try to color inside the lines of civilization. They either learn the consequences of failing to balance their drives and emotions—Graziano's "hate," which he learns to make productive in the boxing ring rather than destructive outside it; Graham's desire for "kicks" and dislike of being square; Lawrence's "magic," her love of applause, of luxury and pampering, her disdain for ordinary domestic attachments and her tendency to act the prima donna—or, like Graham, they suffer for their failure. These are grown-up movies about living in the real world. They deal with the most modern of themes—the Freudian imperative to balance being true to oneself with the repression and responsibility that are necessary to avoid living like an animal—civilization and its discontents, in short.

This is what Wise means, therefore, when he says "we wanted to make [*Star!*] a realistic approach to theatre . . . and not just . . . show the glamorous side of Gertrude Lawrence's life" (*Silver "Star!"*). In the framing device of *Star!* Gertie watches a documentary of her public life with a fictional film-maker, who must receive her approval or else, she tells him laughingly, "I'll say your film's lousy and you'll die broke." This might have reflected Wise's own knowledge that without the approval of Noel Coward, who insisted on reading a completed script before allowing himself to be portrayed in *Star!*, his own film would likely have been sunk. Even with the film's luxuriant production values—furs, jewelry rented from Cartier's and reportedly worth three million dollars, 125 costumes for Andrews—Wise, the sensible Hoosier, doesn't lose sight of reality. The spectator might wonder how even an extremely successful stage star could afford such extravagance, until we learn that the actress, who spent herself into bankruptcy (on both sides of the Atlantic) at the height of her earning power—and during the depths of the Great Depression—actually could not.

Star! is a kind of super-hybrid, part pre-fifties-style entertainer biography, part roadshow superproduction, part realistic warts-and-all biopic. The film is in the style of films such as *Yankee Doodle Dandy* (1942) and *The Jolson Story* (1946), which celebrated the lives of popular performers. Such films proceed in a chronological line, punctuating the performer's progress with staged re-creations of their famous songs, with the numbers often representing dramatic heights as well as career peaks. Such films are indeed hybrids: take out the musical numbers and what's left is the chronicle of a life, without a specific plot or narrative arc. Remove the dramatic scenes and you have a revue, a musical tour of the person's life in songs. This style would have been a bit old-fashioned for 1968 if not for the use of the documentary, which runs throughout the film. Most commentators on the film, in its time and later, assumed that Wise was drawing on his background as the editor of *Citizen Kane*. While "Jerry Paul's" film in *Star!* does not parody a given style of filmmaking, as "News on the March" took off on "The March of Time," there is a distinction between the impersonal, public, "objective" voice of the documentary and Gertie's private memories and knowledge of events behind the scenes. The newsreel often tends to sentimentality; Gertie/Andrews first intervenes in the film, which then breaks out into widescreen and color, to hoot at a line about "the poignancy" of the reunion of sixteen-year-old Gertie and her ne'er-do-well vaudevillian father who abandoned the family years before.

Throughout *Star!*, Wise cuts from the documentary's superficial public pronouncements to the quite different reality. Early, on her first marriage to Jack Roper (John Collin), "all their friends were there to wish them luck and happiness. And why not? They were young and they were in love." This launches one of the film's most remarkable passages, one that shows how very different Gertie's priorities were from those expected of a young woman in patriarchy. Wise cuts from a "newsreel" shot, as if taken by a news photographer through the back window of a car, to the same shot in his widescreen color film. The car drives off and Gertie says, "Jack, I shouldn't have done it." Jack laughs her off and offers her a drink of cheap whiskey from a flask, to which she says, "It should have been champagne." "We can't afford it," he replies, then adds for emphasis, "*Mrs. Roper*." She starts, then brightens up, exclaiming "Garn," from one Cockney to another, reminding us that by marrying the stage manager, she has stayed within her class, although her aspirations are much higher.

Cut to Gertie in their apartment a few hours later popping open a bottle of champagne; when Jack remarks about her buying not just champagne but twelve bottles of it, she answers that "the man said it was cheaper than just getting one," showing already signs of extravagance and a willingness to fall under the blandishments of luxury merchants. After the excitement over the bubbly wears off, she says, "Oh, Jack, I wish I knew why I married you." "Give it a chance," he says, as we see him from a high angle, making him look both ominous and vulnerable. "There's a lot more to marriage, you know, than just saying 'I do.'" A discreet cut shows Gertie sitting up in bed after they have had sex. "So what else is there?" she asks. Jack, entering from the bathroom, answers, "Well, you know, children." "Children?" gasps Gertie, lurching forward in the shot.

A pregnant Gertie is then shown, engaged in a cricket match, of all things, with the male stagehands in the alley outside the stage door of André Charlot's theater. Gertie hears that the running order in the revue has been changed because the star has fallen ill; Jack rules out using Gertie, the general understudy, because of her "delicate condition." She'll have none of that, whooping for joy and rushing in. Her husband says, "You can't do it." "Oh, yes I can!" she practically roars back. The song is a comic one with a male tramp who presumes all the privileges of rank, blithely declining to stay in his place, just as Gertie refuses to remain in hers. Before the song, Gertie appears in the wings wearing a Chaplin-like tramp costume as two chorus girls, concerned for her pregnancy, try to comfort her; her response is "Ssshh. I have to remember those words." Focused on her song, she goes out onstage and perfectly performs "Burlington Bertie from Bow." Although in treating her later stage numbers the film will dispense with most reactions from people offstage, here Charlot the impresario is shown looking impressed and Jack can't but laugh at her antics. Just after the number, more women come up to her. "You all right, luv?" they ask. "Ohhh," she purrs

34. Young Gertie Lawrence (Julie Andrews), the understudy who goes on for the star, drinks in the applause for her comic tramp number. Digital frame enlargement.

lustily, leaning up against a flat and lunging toward the camera, "It was lovely." Realizing she must take her bows—and she in no way is going to miss that—she scurries back onstage, drinking in the applause, squeaking "Thank you" like a little girl, quite overcome. A cut to her husband backstage shows him looking dejected. There is no question of asking her to choose between the stage and him.

This sequence shows that Gertie Lawrence's love is the stage. She is married, as Coward later tells a prospective suitor, "to her career." Just as Bertie the comic tramp thumbs his nose at English class proprieties, Gertie gives the raspberries to the protocols of marriage and motherhood, from playing stagedoor cricket with the male stagehands to obliterating her pregnancy beneath male drag. Gertie's blasé post-coital response on her wedding night is rhymed with her nearly orgasmic reaction to being the star and drawing applause. The sequence ends on the rejected husband, who could be thinking Emily Kane's line, "Sometimes I think I'd prefer a rival of flesh and blood."

The spectator, along with the audience in the film, enjoys Andrews's/ Gertie's performance; this is a triumph, and a private, personal one. For the film soon tells us, the star returns, the marriage ends, Gertie goes back to the chorus, and her breakthrough to stardom comes gradually. Here, however, conventions of the biopic, where nothing can be allowed to interfere with the subject's progress toward her goal, intertwine with those of the musical, where the show is the most important thing. In a musical we can hardly disapprove of something that gives us pleasure. In *Funny Girl* the heroine suffers when the man she loves cannot handle marriage to a woman whose success only reminds him of his failure. *Star!* so fully justifies Gertie and her love of the limelight that we are as eager as she is for the no-account Jack, whom she leaves after he takes her baby Pamela on a pub crawl on the night of the Armistice, to hustle himself off the scene.

Thus the documentary, rather than setting up a deconstructive interrogation of illusion by reality, allows for the conventional distinction between public and private. However, since the documentary derives its tone from the pieties of showbiz media rhetoric, this amounts to much the same thing, as the newsreel displays the hokum that has been pawned off on the public and the widescreen film represents Gertie's knowledge of the real events, by means of classical Hollywood cinema's combination of objectivity and subjectivity. Fox had a newsreel division from the World War I era until the early 1960s, and many of Twentieth Century Fox's biopics and historical films, from *Wilson* to *Patton*, made use of Fox Movietone News excerpts for a film's authenticity and to sketch in historical background. In Wise's film, as in Welles's, the newsreel itself is mostly illusion, with Andrews, Daniel Massey (who plays Noel Coward), and others enacting public scenes on the black-and-white Academy ratio screen. The film concludes with Gertie, after seeing the documentary's wrap-up of her wedding to Aldrich, telling Paul that Coward's rhyming telegram on the occasion *was* true, as if acknowledging that the details in such films—or in biopics—seldom are. Then she says, "Don't change a thing. Keep it just the way it is." In foreground, to herself, she adds, "just the way it was." The newsreel, as if by itself, reverses to the point where the car bearing her and Aldrich on their wedding day leaves the scene, but we are inside with them. "I've been accused a few times of having stolen from *Citizen Kane*," Wise has said. "That really wasn't a conscious thieving at all" (Leemann 193). Better he should have been charged with taking from *The Man Who Shot Liberty Valance* (1962), as Gertie tells the filmmaker in effect to "print the legend," with her private memories remaining with her—and with us, who have looked in on them.

The newsreel-like documentary in *Star!* also allows Wise to underline the difference between a cinematic past and present. While Hollywood draws on conventions from deep in its history, it tries to efface them with the latest technology. Sequences and songs were designed, from the scripting stage, with this difference in mind. The climactic number, "The Saga of Jenny," taken from the final dream sequence of Kurt Weill and Ira Gershwin's *Lady in the Dark*, a 1940 musical about psychoanalysis, opens, as Saul Chaplin describes it, "in black and white and small screen and monaural sound, and all you're hearing is one speaker and a small screen. At one point, Julie slides down [a] rope and breaks through a papier-maché [hoop]. As she breaks through . . . , the screen goes wide and suddenly there are six stereo speakers blaring at you. I always find that very exciting" (*Star!* DVD). The excitement has a lot to do with technology. The roadshow spectaculars of the 1950s and 1960s, which made the fullest use of 70-millimeter film processes and six-channel stereo sound, were as much about the allure of an updated cinema of attractions as they were about the ostensible subject matter. The format sought out historical projects like *Lawrence of Arabia,* with epic visual and aural potential. Musicals, which flood the ears and eyes with non-narrative sound and spectacle, were a natural for the format as well. After roadshows sputtered out circa 1970, so did the musical. So as with the female biopic and the female star, here are two other cinematic institutions that crashed against the absolute and final end of the long-declining Old Hollywood.

Wise and Chaplin appear to have been blindsided by the reception of *Star!* Undoubtedly their idea of Julie Andrews was not the public's. Wise said that he realized on *The Sound of Music* that Andrews possessed "a greater range than had been called on for any film so far." "We decided," Chaplin added, "that we never wanted to stop working with her in life" ("Silver *Star!*"). It was decided that while Andrews would wear makeup and hairstyles to suggest Lawrence—a broadening of the nose, a lowering of the hairline, a strawberry blonde wig—"Julie would just do a version of Gertie," Wise said, "that would not conflict with her own musical qualities and talent." She would sing in her own highly bankable, familiar voice, as Doris Day had done in *Love Me or Leave Me,* as Sinatra had done in *The Joker Is Wild,* and as Streisand did in *Funny Girl.* "The conception from the beginning," said Wise, "was that she would try to get as many as possible of the characteristics Gertie had: her determination, her feistiness, her kind of humor, her kind of anger" (Leemann 193). Andrews was seen by most who worked with her as the ultimate trouper, immensely talented, with an apparently infinite capacity for the kind of hard work that stage stars need not hide but movie actors must. On the stage from childhood, Andrews's greatest talent was her sparkling singing voice, which possessed a nearly unheard of four-octave range, surely a voice for shattering glass (which Blake Edwards, Andrews's husband/director from 1969 on, predictably made into a running gag in their film *Victor Victoria* [1982]).

While Jane Feuer has talked about the way the film musical conveys a feeling of naturalness in the singing and dancing, Julie Andrews conveys the impression of great effort. It is not only as Maria in *The Sound of Music,* one of her best film roles, that has to do with effort—trying to be a governess to seven children, trying to become a nun—but in her best known stage role, Eliza in *My Fair Lady,* she also played the dutiful student, a woman who transforms herself before our eyes. Much later, in *Victor/Victoria,* the character labors to convince cabaret audiences that she is a man posing as a woman. It is as if Julie Andrews is credible onscreen when some kind of Herculean effort is required just to live. In *Star!* this idea of strenuous effort and perseverance collides, oddly enough, with biopic conventions that militate against showing work and process, the genre in which success inevitably follows innate talent, inspiration, and destiny. It also conflicts with shared memories of Gertrude Lawrence, the key to whose popularity being that anyone could imagine herself in her very regal place. While millions identified with Andrews as Maria, she herself seemed like Mary Poppins, "practically perfect in every way," a superhuman talent one admires with awe. So in terms of the real-life subject, Julie Andrews was a "body too much" indeed—paradoxically "too good" in all senses to play Gertrude Lawrence. In terms of reception, there were several levels of disconnects. In this performance, Andrews nearly cries out to the audience, "I'm human. I'm difficult; I have flaws." But nobody in 1968 wanted to know who Julie Andrews was. No one wanted to explore complex human adult behavior with Andrews, although she was able and willing to go there. Nor did anyone want to see her as sexual.

The willful, joyful woman and the buoyant empress of the theater add up to a sympathetic human without the film turning her into a Margo Channing–like horror, although most of the film's contemporary reviewers obviously thought otherwise. *Star!*'s chief problem, like that of *Darling Lili* (1970), the movie that completed the commercial annihilation of Julie Andrews begun by *Star!,* is that the filmmakers are behooved to make the sexually messy, adult life of its heroine into a family-friendly musical. *Funny Girl* had some of the same issues, but handled them more deftly; "You Are Woman, I Am Man" is a fairly racy number for a musical of its era, with sexual innuendoes worthy of Max Ophuls's *La Ronde* (1950) (which also has a scene depicting a seduction in a private dining room). With Bob Merrill's witty lyrics and Streisand's charm, it becomes a scene with a subtext that grown-ups can appreciate while sailing over the heads of children. For a woman who Noel Coward said was "promiscuous, but [was] never a tart and always had good taste" (Fairchild to Wise, 26 July), Lawrence's affairs are presented with a chastity that seems to have been read as coldness. Reviewers blamed this on Andrews, with Kael mercilessly calling her "the least sensual young actress ever to become a movie star" ("Cripes!" 161).

Not only did little thought appear to be given to the new departure for Andrews and for the roadshow-format musical that this project represented, but absolutely nothing was done in the publicity for the film to prepare critics and public for the "new," "more adult" Julie Andrews that this film would introduce. This was the filmmakers' biggest misstep, and it appears to have come from an honest blindness toward Andrews's public image, and a kind of hubris, however understandable, that anything *The Sound of Music* team did next would be embraced by audiences. Although the film was released ten days before the MPAA Ratings System took effect and was in release alongside films that were rated, there is no question that *Star!* was made for the family trade. Most of the theaters that played *The Sound of Music* in its hard-ticket first run, for engagements that averaged between eighteen months and two years, eagerly booked *Star!*

The producer, director, star, and studio of what was then the all-time box-office champion failed to understand how very different their new picture was. No one, including production head Richard Zanuck, whose studio had been saved after the *Cleopatra* fiasco by *The Sound of Music*, seemed to have an inkling that *Star!* might require special handling, that the press and public should be prepared for a more "adult," complex Julie Andrews, and that perhaps it should open ahead of *Funny Girl*'s late September premiere. In fact, getting wind of possible plans to release the film in the summer, which in that era was not the season when big pictures tended to open (and when *Star!* did open in Great Britain), Wise furiously insisted that the New York and Hollywood premieres be kept in late October. The film would then go into wide release at Christmas, the standard and, it was felt, desirable treatment of a big roadshow picture (Wise to Raphel). Wise came to rue his reaction, saying years later, "I often wonder what the reception would have been to *Star!* if it had not been preceded by the opening and running of *Funny Girl*" (Leemann 195). Ironically, had the filmmakers made any or all of these adjustments, they might have felt pressured to contort Lawrence's life into a melodramatic female biopic, as *Funny Girl* had done, instead of the "joyous production," in Andrews's words, of a warts-and-all narrative ("Silver Star!").

The film does boil down the memoirs of Lawrence's widower, Richard

Aldrich, to whom the actress was married for twelve years, so that it appears that what she needs finally is a strong man to keep her in line. The marriage is what settles down the tensions Fairchild detailed in his treatment, providing the narrative with its resolution. Thereafter, Lawrence's life becomes too normal to be dramatic. However, the marriage provides the filmmakers with a recuperation of which even they don't appear persuaded. What they do seem convinced of is the film's final line, heard in voiceover over a long shot of Richard and Gertie's car as it moves off after their wedding: "I may not be as clever as you, but I haven't been an actress for nothing. I know an awful lot more about life and men than most people, and I know the only things that matter are understanding and happiness and being absolutely genuine all the bloody time." As in *I Want to Live!,* Wise ends a biopic with his heroine in voiceover, giving her the last word as well as ownership over the image. However, to an audience at the time it might have seemed as if after three hours, the film was still groping for something to say.

A moment, enacted in the documentary, has Lawrence being confronted by a reporter who asks her, "Don't you think this sort of thing is a bit out of date? Surely taking busloads of people to Atlantic City belongs to the early twenties rather than the late thirties. . . . I'm referring to the year, Miss Lawrence, 1937. The world is a pretty serious place." This dialogue means to illustrate Lawrence's failure to acknowledge the Depression and the gathering war clouds. It also displays showbiz insularity and solipsism, however, as she shifts the reporter's references to current events back onto herself and her world of theater. Much more than the subject's blindness, however, it shows a matching failure of the filmmakers to see any anachronism in their own enterprise, to realize that the reporter's line might apply to their film. At no point during the film's long three years of preparation could it have been possible to see what a "serious place" the world would be in 1968.

There is an axiom that every bad movie contains a line that exposes its failings. I think that *Star!* is a very good movie with a few telling flaws, and even those faults are interesting. That it was received as a bad film in its own volatile time is due to the impression that it was a relic, that it was a poorly done musical (the impression that was corrected first and foremost in its later revivals), and that Lawrence was portrayed as an unlivable shrew. (From numerous classes and friends to whom I have shown the film since the release of the laser disc, the last charge meets with incredulity; reading from Kael usually produces a response like, "Did that critic see the same movie I saw?")

35. "Don't you think this sort of thing is a bit out of date?" an earnest reporter asks Gertie in the documentary-within-a-film in *Star!* Director Robert Wise was not prepared to have that very question leveled at his own movie. Digital frame enlargement.

Star!, therefore, is a deeply divided movie—outmoded in one sense, cinematically sophisticated though classical in others, and held together by a female protagonist for whom a pre-feminist culture was in no way ready. In most ways, Gertrude Lawrence is brasher than any Hollywood female biopic subject until Erin Brockovich more than three decades later. Could *Star!* have failed because no one in 1968 wanted to see an even-handed, nonjudgmental take on an independent, successful woman? The film does not go out of its way to make the character more likable than she was in life. What is telling is that a woman who insists on having her own way, who was capable of letting her stardom run away with her, something that is never shown in Hollywood films except as an all-defining flaw, was widely seen as "a shrew," "a monster," "a bitch." Julie Andrews, like Jenny of the song, *would* make up her mind and sweat through critical and professional hell for her transgression. Shifting demographics made the great female star and the biopic as her enduring vehicle the cinematic equivalent of a dead language. *Star!* and *Funny Girl* speak their last words.

14

Hacked

Gorillas in the Mist and Other Female Biopics of the 1980s

She is the secret heroine of Hollywood movies: the divine masochist, the superior woman battered by fate, society, ham-fisted men and her own acute facility for self-destruction. Serious actresses, itching to play something more demanding than bimbettes and stand-by wives, love divine masochist roles. They get to run through huge emotions, from innocence through every sordid experience, often embracing rarefied forms of madness and an early, spectacular death. Playing the suffering saint can make and shape an actress's career. . . . It can win fans, raves and Oscars.

    —RICHARD CORLISS, *TIME*, 1982

A professor of English literature used to scoff at students who disdained his specialty, the eighteenth century. "How can you dislike an entire century?" he'd ask. A hundred years of literary works probably can't be written off, no matter how uninteresting one finds them. If there is a decade that most film critics, scholars, and fans would just as soon forget, however, it is by consensus the 1980s; A. O. Scott of the *New York Times* casually called the 1980s "at the moment [2007] everybody's least favorite decade in the history of American cinema" ("Francis"). A confluence of factors made the 1980s the dreariest cinematic decade, including the end of the vogue for foreign films and the decline of homegrown film industries in many countries; the demise of the American modernism that made the period 1967–76 so vividly creative; the eclipse of such 1970s auteurs as Robert Altman, Hal Ashby, and Martin Scorsese; the discovery by Hollywood of the youth demographic and the special effects blockbuster; a reliance on "high concept" formulas across all genres; and the political conservatism of the Reagan era that seemed to freeze the zeitgeist in timidity (although the pall falling over cinematic creativity was apparent by 1978, well before Reagan's election). Most of all, the (semi-) independent cinema, that low-budget "shadow Hollywood" that arose in the 1990s out of its first stirrings in the late 1980s from directors such as Spike Lee, Steven Soderbergh, and Gus Van Sant, had not yet taken shape.

The 1980s saw a resurgence in female biopics. More biopics about women were made and/or released by the major studios than since the heyday of Susan Hayward. This level of output, in fact, has not been equaled since. Beginning with *Coal Miner's Daughter* (1980), the smash-hit Loretta Lynn biography that won an Academy Award for Sissy Spacek, the decade produced *Frances* (1982), about Frances Farmer, a Hollywood actress of the 1930s who spent much of her life in mental institutions; *Heart Like a Wheel* (1983), about National Hot Rod Association (NHRA) driver Shirley Muldowney; *Cross Creek* (1983), about novelist Marjorie Kinnon Rawlings; *Star 80* (1983), about Playboy Playmate Dorothy Stratten, who was murdered by her boyfriend-manager, Paul Snider; *Silkwood* (1983), about a nuclear power plant employee and activist who died in a suspicious car crash on her way to a meeting with a *New York Times* reporter about shady practices at her work; *Sweet Dreams* (1985), an informal follow-up to *Coal Miner's Daughter*, about Patsy Cline; *Out of Africa* (1985), about author Isak Dinesen; *Marie* (1985), about a state official who blew the whistle on political corruption in Tennessee; *A Cry in the Dark* (a.k.a. *Evil Angels*, 1988), about an Australian woman whose baby was taken by a dingo while the family was on a camping trip in 1980 but who herself was convicted of murdering the child, only to be exonerated a few years later; *A World Apart* (1988), about a white South African activist in the fight against apartheid in the early 1960s; and others.

One might wonder why, at a time when the Hollywood companies and the larger combines that owned them would have been happy to have all their films be teen comedies, outer space extravaganzas, and action blockbusters of the *Rambo* stripe, so many biopics about women would be made. First, as we have seen, the biopic genre stays alive because film industries never entirely stop chasing prestige. Second, the period produced a group of smart, ambitious, and extraordinarily gifted young actresses eager to play the complex characters the genre offers. They included Sissy Spacek, Jessica Lange, Meryl Streep, Mary Steenburgen, Diane Keaton, Susan Sarandon, and Sigourney Weaver. These women were not stars in the Old Hollywood sense; they eschewed the traditional glamour treatment and seldom turned up on annual lists of the top ten box-office attractions (neither of the only actresses who did, Barbra Streisand and Goldie Hawn, was suitable for biopics by this time). They were highly prestigious, however, and each had appeared in one or two hits that placed them atop the A-list. By early 1983, each of the above-named actresses, except Weaver and Sarandon, had an Oscar to her name, and Streep had two.

The biopics they made grew out of the "Hollywood feminist" cycle of the mid- and late 1970s, established by films such as *Alice Doesn't Live Here Anymore* (1974), *An Unmarried Woman* (1978), and *The China Syndrome* (1979). They were mostly formulaic, Oscar-aspiring prestige items. Many of them (*Silkwood, Marie*) were social problem dramas in the most conventional sense. A problem develops, a heroine steps forward; she marshals social institutions, such as the legal system in *Marie,* to solve the problem, or is stopped in the attempt, as in the case of Karen Silkwood. Some took place against the backdrop of racial prejudice and/or colonialism (*Cross Creek, Out of Africa, A World Apart*). All are safely set in the past, even though in some cases, as in *A World Apart,* which was produced in the midst of a worldwide outcry against apartheid in South Africa, the past spoke directly to the present.

Some of the films seemed to have no *raison d'être* except to immerse their heroines and audiences into rank victimization (*A Cry in the Dark* and, especially, *Frances,* the latter of which might remain the all-time prototype of the downward trajectory female victimization biopic; the Corliss quote at the start of the chapter refers to Lange's film and to Streep's *Sophie's Choice,* based on the William Styron novel). The sources of fascination in *Silkwood* and *Gorillas in the Mist* (1988) were the mysterious and unsolved deaths of their protagonists. The enigmatic circumstances and the lack of hard information, however, made the stories of Karen Silkwood and Dian Fossey difficult to tell, while at the same time ensuring an intense interest on the part of audiences and filmmakers. Two films probably would have been made about Fossey had not the government of Rwanda, where she lived, worked, and died, essentially compelled the competing projects to join forces in order for either film to come about (Lessem 479). *Silkwood,* directed by Mike Nichols from a script by Nora Ephron and Alice Arlen, is as close as a movie can get to being a film about nothing, and all the mannerisms in Meryl Streep's repertoire cannot lend it substance. One constantly feels that the filmmakers are running up against episodes they can't re-create, characters they can't represent, information they couldn't get access to, or could but cannot disclose. If *Silkwood* were a book, there would be periodic white spaces where paragraphs should be.

Most of these films feel safe, timid, and compromised, and nearly all run their heroines through the wringer. If they are reminiscent of another cycle in movie history, these would be the French films of the so-called *tradition de qualité* in the 1950s. Like them, these 1980s movies are carefully written, painstakingly directed and acted, but made in a uniformly artless and impersonal style that gives them an insular, almost self-loathing feeling, a sense of suffocation; the chill that went through artistic communities during the reactionary Reagan era is palpable in the films. Most meet Sidney Lumet's definition of melodrama: the characters come out of the story instead of vice versa. Furthermore, the fact that so many are about characters in prisons of their own or others' making makes them vaguely despairing works, although none of them works up enough conviction or passion for outright despair. Like the *tradition de qualité* films, most of these films emit a bizarrely self-satisfied odor: society is rotten and nothing can be done about that. Moreover, many use the synthesized music scores in vogue in the eighties, and these might date the films more than anything else.

It must be said that for audiences in Australia, *A Cry in the Dark,* known there as *Evil Angels* after a best-selling book on the case, engages in a troubling examination of conscience. Spurred by sensational media coverage, national suspicion that the mother, Lindy Chamberlain, was lying about her infant being taken from a camping tent by a wild dingo hardened into consensus that nearly sent an innocent woman to the death house. This makes the film a kind of Down Under *I Want to Live!,* but with a bitterly happy ending. The villains of the piece are the Australian public, making *Evil Angels* unique in this cycle in that it compels an audience to look at itself in an unflattering light. Outside Australia, however, the preening newscasters and snarling person-on-the-street interviewees simply appear to be the nasty antagonists that are standard for this cycle. If *Evil Angels* were strictly an Australian film, made in Australia with an Australian director, screenwriter, and crew, it would be a special case. All these conditions apply except that Meryl Streep plays Lindy Chamberlain; her involvement attracted American financing and distribution and made the film an international production. The director was Fred Schepisi, one of a number of filmmakers of the New Australian Cinema of the 1970s who "went Hollywood"; he previously worked with Streep on *Plenty* (1985). With Streep earning for the role her eighth Oscar nomination in eleven years, the film plays outside Australia with little point except to wallow in suffering and masochism.

The films all had clear-cut villains and heroes; once the heroine stood up, it was often up to men to defend or rescue them; *Frances* even invented a central male character out of whole cloth for the purpose (See Storhoff, Waites). Fred Thompson, the former Republican counsel on the Senate Watergate Committee and future U.S. senator, and who represented Marie Raggianti in her wrongful termination suit against the Democratic governor of Tennessee, began his acting career by portraying himself in *Marie* as a slow-talking Lincolnesque lawyer.

The films of this cycle that play the best, then and now, are the country music biopics *Coal Miner's Daughter* and *Sweet Dreams,* which depict a realistic give-and-take between a woman and her husband on the road to success, and do not simply cede ambition to the male character. The two films might seem at first glance to give undue weight to the male character. *Coal Miner's Daughter,* especially, makes Dolittle Lynn (Tommy Lee Jones) the center of attention and the driving force for the film's first hour. A closer look reveals this is mostly to dramatize the way Loretta moves out of his shadow and comes into her own in the second half. The film threatens to move into *Funny Girl* territory, with the husband sidelined and emasculated by his wife's success. But this turns out to be simply a phase through which the couple passes, and it's up to Dolittle to find his place in it. The relationship that emerges finally is one of mutual dependency, exasperation, and love.

Michael Apted, an Englishman, became in time a mainstream Hollywood director, and was elected president of the Directors Guild of America in 2003. *Coal Miner's Daughter* was his first American film. His background in documentary films (the *Seven Up* series [1963–2005]) and his relative lack of knowledge of country-western culture and the Appalachian coal mining way of life allowed him to present what he found in a realistic manner free of the media stereotypes with which the lives of "hillbillies" had been encrusted by the media. *Coal Miner's Daughter,* based on Loretta Lynn's bestselling autobiography (with George Vecsey, 1976), was a film in which the subject was heavily involved. Lynn herself picked Sissy Spacek after looking at photographs of actresses that Universal Studios showed her (Apted and Lynn). Like Robert Wise, Apted shaped his approach and style to the material; he cast non-actors from the film's various settings—Virginia, West Virginia, Kentucky, Nashville—and saturated the film in local color. With the point of view supplied by the living subject herself, Apted's realistic policy of imposing minimally on actual cultural milieus served *Coal Miner's Daughter* better than probably any other approach could have. But Apted's laissez-faire realism, applied to a subject matter that needed a controlling point of view about feminine ambition and power and postcolonial world politics, has unfortunate consequences, as we will see, in his Dian Fossey biopic, *Gorillas in the Mist* (1988).

Besides the two country music films, the most intriguing of the 1980s female biopics is *Heart Like a Wheel*, which takes place in a similar working-class milieu in the "real" (that is, not New York City or Los Angeles) America. In it, a woman battles successfully for contention in a male-dominated profession, the dangerous world of hot rod racing. Shirley Muldowney holds her own against sexism and an extremely low glass ceiling in a film that does seem to want to hold her up as a role model. *Heart Like a Wheel* (1983), directed by Jonathan Kaplan, was soft-pedaled by reviewers as a well-made minor film. Seeing it on its original release, I wanted to like it more than I actually did; twenty-five years later and steeped in biography, I reacted the same way. Unlike better-known Roger Corman alumni from Francis Ford Coppola to Martin Scorsese, under whom he studied at New York University, Kaplan has never managed to make movies that didn't feel like B-films, even despite directing Jodie Foster's first Academy Award–winning performance, in *The Accused* (1988). This is a pity because there are few male directors with a better instinct for female protagonists and an understanding of and willingness to air feminist points of view. The Muldowney biopic never really found an audience; drag racing probably does not appeal to audiences interested in a film about a strong heroine who excels in a male profession, and the film's feminism and its dim view of the sexism Muldowney encountered probably would not appeal to those interested in a film about racing.

Its release history is telling; first issued by Twentieth Century Fox as an exploitation movie in April 1983, it played to empty houses in the South and Midwest. The studio reopened *Heart Like a Wheel* as a prestige picture in the fall, starting with a showing at the New York Film Festival. Reviewers damned it with faint praise; Janet Maslin of the *New York Times* termed it "a very good small movie rather than a more broadly ambitious one" (C30). A reviewer for *Psychology of Women Quarterly* in 1987 called it "a sobering and graphic lesson (especially for young women contemplating NTOs [Non-Traditional Occupations]) and for any woman who wants to make it, or just be her own person in the patriarchy" (Marlowe 276). Such a recommendation, if that's what it is, seems to warn the reader of a film that will drag NTO-gravitators around the familiar track to perdition for female ambition. Pauline Kael nailed the virtues and limitations of the film, calling it "the type of B picture in which characters say flat, emotionally neutral things in situations that seem to call for hyperventilating excitement. That kind of affectlessness is sometimes praised as realism and as art. But there's also a cost that Kaplan and [screenwriter Ken] Friedman pay: the film's 'objective' surfaces don't yield much to us beyond the facts of the characters' lives. *Heart Like a Wheel* has a B-picture sensibility. That's what's good about it, and that's what makes it not good enough" ("Hair" 79).

Heart Like a Wheel came out at a time when feminist film scholars and practitioners alike had given up on the conventional mainstream film, thinking it incapable of producing films about women that do not reproduce a male gaze, that do not express a male desire. The film is labeled with a "feminine"-sounding title; "Heart Like a Bulldog" would have been better, remarked an NHRA member ("No. 5"). *Heart Like a Wheel* also steps on its own feminism by casting Bonnie Bedelia, who was a minor star compared to Streep, Spacek, or Lange and who projected nothing like their presence. As a result, Shirley still seems surrounded by a constellation of males, her first husband Jack (Leo Rossi), her feisty crew chief-lover-adversary Connie Kaletta (Beau Bridges), and her teenage son John (Anthony Edwards), and it is they who predominate in one's memory.

Gorillas in the Mist (1988) provides the best lesson in how biopics about women often undermine their own premises. The fact that it is a product of the 1980s does not mean that it can be consigned to the film culture of a dimly regarded decade and written off. Although the intervening years have not produced many female biopics as problematic as this one, the output of biographies of women has been sparse in general, while the number of male biopics surged, especially in the 2000s. *Gorillas in the Mist* is a biography of Dian Fossey, the American primatologist who for eighteen years studied and championed African mountain gorillas, one of the world's most endangered species. The fifty-one-year-old Fossey was found hacked to death in her Rwandan mountain compound in December 1985; her murder was never solved. The life and death of Fossey, who became world famous for her articles in *National Geographic,* excited intense interest from Hollywood moviemakers. The eventual film's consolidation of two competing Fossey projects could not reconcile what turned out to be incompatible points of view. One was Fossey's own 1983 book, *Gorillas in the Mist,* which was optioned during her lifetime by Universal. The other, owned by Warner Bros., was a profile for *Life* magazine by Harold T. P. Hayes; Hayes's work was expanded into a book published in 1990. Hayes looked critically though objectively at Fossey's obsession with the mountain gorillas, which came at the expense of the Batwa "poachers" whose living often depended upon the trapping and selling of wild animals in a desperately poor country that, like much of Africa, had only recently gained independence. Fossey inadvertently laid bare many of the issues dividing conservationism from humanitarian concerns. It was important to protect gorillas, but Fossey made an unfortunate spokesperson for her cause. Her essentially colonialist attitude toward the postcolonial governments of Congo, from which she was ejected, and eventually Rwanda, certainly contributed to her downfall. The seeds of her demise grew gradually over her protracted and in fact interrupted time in Africa.

Gorillas in the Mist, directed by Michael Apted, becomes bogged down in a morass of feminist and colonialist issues. These are thickened by the tendency of the female biopic to lead its protagonist through a downward spiral, and by the apparent decision of the filmmakers to make *Gorillas* into a *Born Free*-like inspirational saga. Anything that might offend the audience for such a film was softened and screened out. Add to this the ideological and postcolonial myopia of the Reagan-Thatcher 1980s, and the result is a film that uncritically shares Fossey's cavalier attitude toward her black African hosts while blaming her for her ambition.

The film makes Fossey's story into melodrama by rendering her relation to the gorillas as a love too pure to exist in the world. The small circular clearing in which she repeatedly encounters the gorillas is pictured as a kind of heaven, far from the cares of the world and humanity, where the heroine attains a state of grace. Indeed, the Warner Bros. Fossey project was entitled *Heaven and Earth.* As this grace is increasingly disrupted, however, and the heroine becomes increasingly disturbed, the film's point of view splits irreconcilably. Are we to share Fossey's outrage at the Rwandans, cheer her reprisals against their poaching, and endorse her campaign to preserve the gorillas in disregard of the human cost? Or are we to grow critical of her behavior, and even horrified by some of it? One 1988 reviewer, Hal Hinson of the *Washington Post,* pointed out that

the movie hints at [darker] aspects of her character but tries to soften them; it strives to make Fossey—and her rage—more palatable. Basi-

36. *Gorillas in the Mist* (Michael Apted, Universal-Warner Bros., 1988) plays the story of Dian Fossey and the gorillas as a melodrama of a love too pure to exist. Digital frame enlargement.

cally, the filmmakers can't deal with her craziness, so they justify it by showing her campaign against poachers, burning down their huts and threatening to hang a captured poacher. Granted, all this seems extreme, but given the provocations—they had slaughtered Digit, her favorite gorilla, cutting off his head and hands for trophies—it also seems understandable, and far from mad. Whipping the testicles of a captive with stinging nettles—as she is reported to have done—is mad and, by leaving out such details the filmmakers have done more than sanitize Fossey's life, they've deprived it of any meaning.

What is the point of the film if it becomes only the chronicle of a woman whose devotion to animals makes her utterly insensitive to all human considerations? Apted's film applauds Fossey's documentation of the mountain gorillas and the great worldwide publicity her work brought to the issue, while seeming to show her warts and all, despite an overall sanitizing of Fossey's life and its aftermaths. The six drafts of Anna Hamilton Phelan's script on file at UCLA, out of a total of fourteen, reveal a process of softening and simplification that robbed both subject and context of nuance, humanity, and even human logic. For example, as Dian's working relationship with Bob Campbell, the *National Geographic* photographer, develops into a romance, in the script drafts Dian tells Bob before they make love for the first time that she knows he is married because of the way he shook the rain off his boots and parka first before entering her cabin (Phelan, 6 April). This shows an unexpected bit of human perception from Dian and casts them both as adults making a conscious choice. In the film, however, she tells him she knows he's married *after* they make love. Perhaps Apted thought he was making her look less like a wanton adulteress this way, but the effect is to make her heedless or secretive or manipulative or simply nonsensical. This is typical of the film's choices.

In shaving off details that would show Fossey as a troubling but understandable human being, Apted seems to think he is making her admirable, while actually what he is making her into is a feminine stereotype: strange, irrational, and erratic. He doesn't want to show her making bad decisions, so he shows her making *no* decisions, not seeming to realize that this confirms her in more sexist stereotypes than if her attitudes had been shown more directly and objectively. She exercises self-control and deliberation only when she is with the gorillas, when, before she has won their trust, the slightest wrong move could get her killed. In this way she is the artist, the genius subject. But to play her brilliance with the gorillas against her stupidity and destructiveness in her personal encounters would have required a definite point of view, and that is what Apted and the producers shy away from.

While the filmmakers display their blind spot for gender, they also expose their own colonialist attitudes, which don't appear to differ from Fossey's. "Apted's lovely vistas in the African highlands," wrote Henry Sheehan, "were captured with great effort, but the film's mindset is firmly planted in Apted's mid-Atlantic consciousness. The same voice that ignores the bitter legacy of centuries of European and Arab colonization and exploitation as it intones clichés about the failure of post-colonial Africa, that avers that black Africans are never so well off as when white men are making decisions for them, can be heard muttering in the undertones of *Gorillas in the Mist,* asserting that once again the white man must take up his burden." If the film's gender politics take *Gorillas in the Mist* the way of many female biopics, its cavalier attitude toward African cultures, replicating Fossey's own, underlines not only her undoing but a mentality in which gorillas outweigh African people in importance. This is where the film, by adopting Fossey's own attitudes, loses all distance from her and becomes entangled in confusion that enfolds even the film's production. A 1988 featurette included on the DVD shows Apted leading a long line of black Rwandan porters up the muddy, rocky mountain to the gorillas, no differently than Fossey did. In one of the film's most embarrassing moments, the black African porters who have toted goods for Bob Campbell, including a steel bathtub containing a gift puppy, on the three-hour trek up the mountain, stand around in the background while the white couple bills and coos and Dian's unattached loyal black sidekick Sembegare, who is Christian and speaks French-accented English, looks on approvingly. The moment reminded me of the way British films of the Raj era depicted the "natives" of India or of the plantation slaves who fill in the background as Scarlett and Rhett's romance blows hot and cold in *Gone with the Wind*.

In Phelan's earlier drafts, Mukara, a Rwandan official to whom Fossey complains after five gorillas are killed in an attempt to capture one for a zoo, tells her: "Rwanda is the second poorest country in the world. It is about the size of your state of Maryland with a *people population* of 4.7 million. Ninety-five percent of those barely manage to survive. Nine hundred thousand francs provides *people* with food, clothing, shoes, medicine. Do you want to compare statistics or priorities, Miss Fossey?" The script draft concludes that "her tunnel vision prevents her from really hearing him" (Phelan, 6 April).

Despite the attempts of the early scripts to create a point of view larger than Dian's "tunnel vision," the movie, wrote David Denby, "is entirely incurious about the native cultures Fossey is busting into and attempting to instruct." As an example of this incuriosity, in the finished film only the last two sentences of Mukara's speech are spoken, leaving out his capsule explanation of the population and the extent of its poverty as well as his emphatic contrasts of the needs of gorillas to those of people. Apted's film, however, makes into mere dramatic conflict Phelan's initial attempts to explore Fossey's "tunnel vision," and the implications of that conflict are mostly omitted. An irony of this is that the facts and figures the screenwriter placed into the mouth of the African official come nearly verbatim, *sans* emphases, from Fossey's own book. She describes the desperate need of land in Rwanda for farming and livestock. This need, in her logic, leads to "encroachment" of the population onto the natural habitat of the gorillas (Fossey 19–20). Thus Fossey in her writing shows an awareness of the human needs but then characteristically turns that knowledge back onto what it means for the gorillas.

One senses that Fossey would have preferred that the mountain gorillas be native to the Swiss Alps, to some affluent Western European milieu where postcolonial poverty and gross societal instability would not be issues. Her indifference to the culture of which she made herself a dedicated enemy showed that the social milieu was of no importance to her. One account after another attributes most of Fossey's difficulties to her refusal to learn or give a damn about the culture, politics, and people of the African countries who played host to her gorilla studies. "Fossey saw the Africans surrounding and encroaching onto the park only as despoilers, as enemies of her beloved gorillas. . . . Feeling as she did, she made no attempt to interact with the locals, or to see their problems, or to try to find possible solutions. She only wanted to frighten them to keep them out" (Hayes 274). The film takes no point of view on this, and indeed seems to share Fossey's indifference at best and disdain at worst. Fossey's story raises issues about the costs of protecting endangered species. The concluding valorization, conventional for the genre, proclaims in a title card, "When Dian Fossey arrived in Africa, the mountain gorilla was doomed to extinction. The result of her life's work was a significant decrease in poaching and the survival of the species." This title is superimposed over shots of her grave. The original competing Warners script by Tab Murphy began with the funeral, atop Mount Kirisimbi; Phelan's revised drafts, after the productions merged, incorporated this opening. One wishes that the film had opened with this title and then told the story of what Fossey did to achieve her result, with the spectator left to weigh the moralities of her actions.

In writing both on Fossey and on the film, it has been almost de rigueur to refer to her and the gorillas in terms of romantic love. The title of Hayes's article and book was "The Dark Romance of Dian Fossey." In promoting

37. *Gorillas* does not seem disturbed by images such as this one, portraying Dian's mock-hanging of a poacher. Digital frame enlargement.

his 2007 biopic *Amazing Grace,* Michael Apted said, "I need a love story. Whatever the film, I don't know how to tell the story unless there's something emotional happening at the center of it all. It doesn't have to be boy-girl, it could be any combination, [such as] girl/mountain gorilla (*Gorillas in the Mist*)" (Apted). Marsha Kinder wrote in 1989 that what Fossey "finds there in the mist and seeks to preserve is the prototype of the patriarchal family, which can be found even among our primate relatives" (10). With this concept, all who threaten the lovers are villains. These include African governments, European zoo dealers, and impoverished African people who poach on wildlife preserves for their livelihoods. It also holds Fossey's gorilla romance up against her human romance with Bob Campbell, an affair to which she is first irresistibly drawn and then finally rejects.

As Kevin Hagopian points out, the foundation of the biopic of the late 1930s and early 1940s is melodrama. In his formulation the biopic subject is an ordinary person up against powerful established institutions that are destined either to change or give way to the new truth the protagonist represents. This was a potent myth for the New Deal era when audiences needed hope that the Great Depression could be overcome, but to apply it to a world as complex as postcolonial Africa is profoundly problematic. Dian Fossey's life, with its lack of resolution, the love-her or hate-her responses from most who knew her, and her lingering legend, would seem to call for a multi-faceted, questioning approach: the *Citizen Kane* paradigm once again. Consider the perspectives on Dian Fossey catalogued by *New York Times* book reviewer Michiko Kakutani:

> To conservationists she could be seen as an icon of commitment, someone who put her own life on the line to help save an endangered species. To African nationalists, she could be seen as a symbol of American arrogance, a foreigner who had the nerve to tell them how to live and what to value. To feminists, she could be seen as a symbol of pluckiness and courage, someone who eschewed convention and braved enormous physical hardships to accomplish her own objectives. To moralists, she could be seen as a lesson in the dangers of excess, a monomaniac, who ended up paying for her obsession with her own life. (C23)

Rather than sort through all these different Fosseys, as a *Kane*-type investigation might, the film lodges itself between that carryover from the studio era—the celebratory biopic with a melodramatic base—and the third variant, the warts-and-all film, which, as in the two Robert Wise films, is more of an exposé than the celebratory biopic and less the probing of an enigma than the *Kane* model. At the least, Fossey's life probably called for a *Lawrence of Arabia*–like exploration of an extraordinary leader whose love of the Other and belief in herself as savior causes her to overreach. In working for a third-world constituency—for Lawrence, an Arab unity still defined by Europeans; for Fossey, the conservation of the mountain gorillas—the subject displays the worst kinds of first-world arrogance. If it sounds like I'm equating the Muslim tribes of Lawrence's day with gorillas, I'm not. My point is that the film's Lawrence forgets that he and those he leads are being used by European interests, as Fossey forgets that humans matter as much as gorillas.

The filmmakers who made *Gorillas* never chose among the three biopic modes, celebration, multi-perspectival investigation, and warts-and-all; thus the film is both all of them and none of them. What also happens is that gender outweighs all else; Dian Fossey is finally no more or less than a woman who did not know her place. The shotgun marriage of contentious producers and competing points of view out of which *Gorillas in the Mist* was produced resulted in a film without much affection for its subject—exactly the charge contemporary critics made of *Star!* The Dian Fossey forged by the melodrama is in over her head from beginning to end, a woman set up for failure and destruction.

Sigourney Weaver, as the six-foot-one Fossey, wearing Levis and shot from low angles, bestrides the landscape as decisively as John Wayne ever did. Fossey's actions themselves, however, are seen as consistently wrong, driven by emotion rather than by vision or goals. Weaver's own tall stature had been fetishized by *Alien* (1979) and especially its sequel, James Cameron's *Aliens* (1986), which not only made her a star but turned her into an action hero, with at least some of the outlandishness that the term implies. An action hero is not exactly what Dian Fossey was, despite her adventurous life. *Gorillas's* insistence on seeing Weaver/Fossey from larger-than-life mythic angles creates a dissonance with the observational approach. Apted is not able to help Weaver get the rhetoric of James Cameron completely out of her performance. The "heroic" signification succeeds only in making Dian Fossey a callous pretender and *Gorillas in the Mist* a cautionary tale about a woman who overreaches. Mamas, don't let your daughters grow up to be scientists. As we will see, a feminist biopic would show a woman's own responses, wants, motivations, strengths, drawbacks, even fatal flaws, but from a point of view sympathetic to her. Fossey's/Weaver's commanding presence and heroic stature are constantly played off against her femininity until finally they defeat it, leaving her bereft of any grace, decency, or humanity—except where the gorillas are concerned.

According to Harold Hayes's account, Dian Fossey had a loveless childhood and did not consider herself attractive. Much of what she did was motivated by a strong self-dislike that manifested itself in self-destructive behaviors. She grew up in a time when her height made her feel self-conscious and freakish. By the end of her life, she had emphysema from years of smoking, was malnourished, and sometimes went days without bathing. In terms of gender, Fossey's life as fodder for narrative sets one snare after another. On one hand, her life is full of masculine goals, risks, and adventure. On the other, it is easy to conclude that she became a kind of surrogate wife to Digit, the male gorilla whose death she mourned—the film suggests as much—and a mother to the younger gorillas and to the group as a whole. Obviously, any direction one turns, Fossey's life potentially presents stereotypes that would challenge the most ideologically clear-headed filmmakers, which these, in this era, were not.

In falling back upon, to paraphrase Hagopian, the trope of the common woman as uncommon woman, the film mixes in from its bag of American archetypes the girl next door. Fossey appears to have no special experience, skills, or talents that qualify her for a technical position under difficult conditions and in an alien climate and culture. Nothing but her glowering determination overcomes Louis Leakey's initial resistance (according to the film) and puts her on her way to Africa. It is also not clear what her tenacity and combativeness grow out of, except a generic mother instinct as well as Weaver's star persona. Just as Ripley in *Aliens* stood up to the mother of all monsters who threatened a child in her care, Weaver's Fossey becomes an enraged maternal figure. In the film's most celebrated scene, she breaks into the truck of a zoo broker who has paid poachers to abduct a baby gorilla and stalks the man through a fashionable restaurant, cradling the infant in her arms.

The insistence on recasting as romantic love Fossey's devotion to the mountain gorillas, a species with special meaning for human evolution, suggests that a woman's passion for a cause or principle must always be seen as a replacement for "normal" heterosexual love. In a male biopic such passion would be presented as the subject's vision of a world in which the mountain gorillas are preserved and valued for what they can teach us about ourselves. Whatever else the subject's flaws might be, this vision and the talent to pursue it and to persuade others of it would be the salient element.

Indeed, the vision is Leakey's, not Fossey's. "I want to know who I am," he pronounces in the film's first scene in rich British-accented tones, "and what it was that made me that way." Fossey desperately longs to be an agent of Leakey's vision, appropriating it until the time when she discovers the gorillas and converts the vision into a passion of her own. In actuality this was by design. Leakey reportedly preferred untrained women for primate studies; he considered them, according to Hayes, "more patient, more sensitive to mother-infant relations, and less likely to arouse aggression in males" (117). Phelan's earliest script opened with Leakey visiting Fossey at the Louisville clinic where she works as an occupational therapist, a career the film changes to "physical therapist," apparently out of concern that someone in the audience might not know what an occupational therapist is. The smallest omission, however, contributes to the watering down of Dian and the loss of her character's specificity; an occupational therapist, after all, works with "digits." Leakey looks approvingly at Fossey's legs (Phelan, 29 September). See, the film would have said to its spectator, he's a regular guy.

Apted's direction spares us Leakey's leer but still expresses it in his letters, as we hear in voiceover the Great Man's paternalistic disapproval of Fossey's spending the *National Geographic*'s money on feminine accoutrements such as hair dryers and nail polish, as well as indulgences like cigarettes and candy bars that make her seem something of a slob. There is a tendency to see Fossey in essentialist ways. Dian says that she batted her eyelashes for four hours in order to get her Rwandan work permit renewed and talks about "putting on the sexiest dress I can find" and going home to win back her fiancé; none of this has a basis in Fossey's own writing or in the available sources about her. The film's sexism and masculinism, like its colonialist attitudes, seem default positions in the absence of a coherent point of view and a controlling vision.

The actual opening of the film is not in any of the script drafts and appears to have been written and staged late in the process as panicked filmmakers realized they didn't have an opening scene for their movie. It takes place at a lecture hall in Louisville where Leakey is speaking. Fossey is introduced as pushy, selfish, flaky, disorganized, naïve, abrasive, impatient, and oblivious to others. This is the character the filmmakers thought they needed to establish? The actual Dian Fossey would not have arrived late for an event as important as an appearance by her hero and prospective mentor in the city where she was living; she would not have needed to borrow a pen from the person sitting next to her in order to take notes. But then Fossey herself had been to Africa before she ever met Leakey; she contacted the scientist by letter and he met her for breakfast during his 1966 visit to Louisville. Leakey was impressed that as a tourist, Fossey managed to see the reclusive mountain gorillas and take pictures of them. He discussed the possibility of sending her to the Congo to do a census of the mountain gorillas and then strung her along for months. In the meantime she quit the job she had held for eleven years and even underwent an appendectomy on Leakey's advice. The film's opening, however, in which Fossey is shoved aside by audience members and photographers following Leakey's lecture, doesn't establish much of anything and doesn't give Sigourney Weaver any character to play except a rude and self-centered woman. Even the archetypal biopic protagonist of vision and drive gets obscured.

If the vision belongs to Leakey, then the persuasion is Bob Campbell's. Fossey, thinking of the protection of her gorillas, reflexively refuses to allow Campbell to photograph them. He cleverly tells her not to blame the locals for trapping gorillas.

CAMPBELL: If you want to blame anyone, blame the doctor in Miami. He's the one that hires the bloke that hires the Batwa. The Batwa get to feed their kids, the middle-man gets a silk shirt, and the doctor gets a gorilla-hand ashtray for his coffee table, and a great big gorilla head for his wall.
FOSSEY: Well, I can't get to the damn doctor in Miami.
CAMPBELL: You ever been to a doctor's office that didn't have a copy of *National Geographic*?
[Long, thoughtful reaction shots of Fossey follow.]
CAMPBELL: Eh, have ya?

Once Campbell convinces Fossey of the power of photographs and the magazine to persuade, he becomes the spectator's eyes, even in a scene as powerful as the one in which we first see Digit approach Fossey and take her hand. These moments are made all the more riveting because, Apted always maintained, they were actual interactions between Sigourney Weaver and some of the same mountain gorillas who had known Fossey. The skillful editing of these sequences, however, makes it hard to know how total the interaction was. The director, moreover, cannot trust us to see how extraordinary her interactions with the gorillas are without inserting tight close-ups of Campbell's amazed reaction, as if a male look were needed to ratify the power of Fossey's work. All of Dian's accomplishments, including her contacts with the gorillas, happen through sheer intuition and instinct. At anything regarding deduction or calculation, she's a disaster.

As their affair develops, Campbell divorces his wife and proposes marriage to Fossey, offering a compromise of six months on the mountain and six months elsewhere. The actual Campbell did nothing of the sort. He remained married during and after his affair with Fossey and the pair never considered marriage. The film also omits mentioning the two abortions Fossey had during her affair with Campbell, even though they reportedly had lasting effects on her. The arrangement with Campbell that Fossey rejects is a fictional construction, entirely typical of the "Hollywood feminism" of the 1970s and 1980s, in which the heroine is presented with an ideal mate, supportive and virile. When she rejects him, she comes off looking more irrational than independent. Once Campbell is gone, expelled by Fossey from her story, she is on her own, which is not portrayed as a good thing. Even during his initial temporary absence from her, we see her first really disturbing action, as she takes prisoner a small boy from a poaching party and terrifies him by dressing as a red witch.

This is followed by one of the most heroic scenes, with the zoo broker, a composite white villain invented so that Fossey wouldn't appear to be on a racist vendetta against the Batwa. Stacking the deck further, this character is named Van Vecten, linguistic dynamite for the late 1980s when Dutch names in an African context carried intensely negative connotations of apartheid and the Afrikaaners in South Africa. In an acting tour de force, Weaver/Fossey storms through a crowded restaurant for Europeans with the baby gorilla she has re-abducted from Van Vecten's car. So the film goes back and forth between disturbing though sanitized behavior and heroic gestures (although they too, as we have seen, are also sanitized).

The film leaves out the most explosive and contested episode in the Fossey story, a possible rape at the hands of soldiers during the evacuations of foreigners ordered by Congolese dictator Joseph Mobutu during Fossey's first year in the Congo in 1967. Fossey's book does not mention rape or detail her two-week detention. "It was only after a 'visit' to the army camp," she wrote, "that I realized on reading a military cable, that I was earmarked for the general. With chances for my release lessening . . . I decided to escape," which she did by promising the soldiers money she told them was being kept across the border in Uganda (15). Hayes interviewed a number of people to whom Fossey had told varying stories about her ordeal over the years; some of these people said that she also talked about it with Leakey (who died in 1972). Hayes concludes that "whatever it was that did happen to her, she carried away from Rumangabo her own private horror" (164).

Three of Phelan's drafts include a lengthy rape scene, followed by an escape with the partly fictional, partly real Sembegare. The finished film omits the entire detention episode, and shows a none-the-worse-for-wear Fossey arriving across the border at the home of her friend, Rosamund ("Roz") Carr, an American woman who lived for over fifty years in Rwanda. Clearly the filmmakers, careening between portraits of Fossey as a crazed zealot—a madwoman in an open-air attic—and paeans to her as the savior of mountain gorillas, decided they wanted no part of the spectacle of a white woman at the hands of black Africans. Furthermore, less was known in 1988 than is known now about the brutality of Mobutu's regime in the country he renamed Zaire (see chapter 9's discussion of *Lumumba*). It would have been going too far, moreover, for the film to imply that the rape was behind Fossey's subsequent war on black poachers. However, the evident hesitation over the sequence shows the quandary in which these white first-world filmmakers found themselves in the face of the material, and explains why so much of the film seems limp and evasive and why the movie often invents drama that is less lurid than much of what actually happened.

The other major sequence eventually dropped from Phelan's draft scripts showed Fossey's hiatus in the United States between 1979 and 1983. It occurred after the American Embassy in Rwanda and Jimmy Carter's State Department intervened to get Fossey out of Rwanda because of the provocation and problems her continuing presence posed to the locals and the Rwandan government. It was during this period, spent in Maine and in Ithaca, New York, where she taught at Cornell, that Fossey wrote *Gorillas in the Mist*. The book was published in 1983, the year she received permission to return to Rwanda. Dramatically, the sequence could have served the purpose of the fourth-act pause in tragedy before the point of no return, the moment when the protagonist has one last chance to have the recognition that would turn her away from the precipice. The entire film makes Fossey out to be a recluse atop her mountain, when in fact she had frequent absences; besides the years in America, these included periodic trips to England, where she earned a Ph.D. from Cambridge. It also makes the death of Digit and Fossey's subsequent blowups appear climactic, when in fact those occurred in 1978, before her forced departure.

Because the American sojourn or any mention of it is left out, Campbell's departure (in 1972) seems to motivate everything about Fossey's downfall. It also increases the idea of self-imprisonment, as if she has been a hermit on her mountain for decades. Toward the end of the film, Apted's establishing shots of the outside of Dian's cabin become as ominous as Kubrick's shots of the hotel in *The Shining*. Her war on the locals appears to grow out of her lack of a man, especially since the film plays up her outrage at finding two of her students in bed together amid the mock-lynching and burning of huts that follows the murder of Digit. Her fury at the Rwandans, her disdain for her students, her love for the gorillas, and her loneliness get whipped up into an unpalatable brew of hysteria and psychosexual confusion.

Dian Fossey and the Hollywood film that tramples on her point of view as a subject while still reproducing her hostility toward Africans are symptoms of a deeper indifference. Two crowning ironies, seen from a later vantage point, present themselves. One is a sentence from Don Lessem's 1988 production story, which I found myself wanting to recast: "[Universal producer] Arnold Glimcher was about to leave his hotel in Kigali to go up to Fossey's camp at Kirasote to discuss the film with her, when he received word of her death" (417). Now the emphasis would be different: "When Arnold Glimcher received word of Fossey's death, he was about to leave his hotel in Kigali, the *Mille de Collines:* Hotel Rwanda." While the 2004 film of that title is one of very few American or British films on Africa to feature a black hero, *Gorillas in the Mist,* in order to focus on its white protagonist, commits the same error as Fossey, who chased out all of black Africa and opted to see her gorillas in the mist of colonialism.

Another irony involves Roz Carr, the American woman who lived in Rwanda from 1949 to the end of her life and who was Dian Fossey's best friend in Africa; she is played in the film by Julie Harris as what Marsha Kinder in 1989 called "a white goddess." According to Hayes, Carr saw Fossey off the mountain, in Kigali, where the primatologist was at her most social and on her best behavior. Long after Fossey's death, during the 1994 Rwandan massacres, Carr was forcibly evacuated by United Nations forces but returned as soon as she was allowed, setting up the Imbabazi orphanage for children left parentless by the devastation, then relocating it in 1997 when the original location was deemed too dangerous. She continued to help run the orphanage until her death from natural causes in 2006 at the age of ninety-four. She was a woman who clearly learned to love the country and its people. When can we expect the biopic about her?

Gorillas in the Mist also demonstrates that a female biopic will fall back into a stew of unquestioned preconceived notions of the dominant ideology, unless it has a controlling directorial vision to steer it to a deliberately different point of view. It is telling that in separate new documentary shorts on the 2003 *Coal Miner's Daughter* DVD, Michael Apted interviews Tommy Lee Jones and Loretta Lynn, having traveled on tour with Lynn in the late 1970s as he prepared to direct the film. It is unusual to see a director playing the role of disinterested interviewer of the co-star and the biographical subject of his own film. Moreover, in the running audio feature commentary, by Apted and Sissy Spacek, the director tends to interview his star as they watch their twenty-three-year-old film together. It is also surprising how much Apted seems not to have known about key aspects of Spacek's preparations. Overall he evinces a narrow and studio-era-like conception of what a director does. Contrast this with Spike Lee's comments in various sources on Denzel Washington's work for *Malcolm X* or Scorsese's remarks about De Niro's preparations to play Jake LaMotta in *Raging Bull*. However much the famously meticulous Washington and De Niro prepared on their own, their directors were aware of and oversaw every step, each knowing how he wanted the actor's work to contribute to the director's vision. One gets the sense that Michael Apted sees himself as an outside observer, a documentarist inclined to craft a film out of found material. This is not necessarily what all documentarists do, and since the list is long of undoubted auteurs who shift between documentaries and dramatic films (including Lee, Scorsese, Raoul Peck, Werner Herzog, and Charles Burnett), we cannot conclude that documentarists view themselves as disinterested servants of found material, just as one would never accuse committed nonfiction filmmakers of working without a point of view. It is very clear that the vision in *Coal Miner's Daughter* was compellingly provided by the film's subject, Loretta Lynn, and the filmmakers happily fell in behind it.

Because Lynn's lyrics have been widely credited with a feminism that comes from Lynn herself, *Coal Miner's Daughter* feels progressive and honest. Those qualities are what Apted found and duly transferred to the screen. *Gorillas,* by contrast, finds Apted outside his strengths. There is no Dian Fossey he can interview and observe, no cultural environment he can absorb and reproduce, except for one where he, like his subject, is an outsider. Apted assembles what his collaborators bring him, without much vision of his own, except to put "reality" on the screen. Because "reality" is ideologically determined, Apted's biopics can come out a mess of rancid ideologies, from the default colonialism and sexism of *Gorillas* to the undiluted middle-aged male fantasy of *Amazing Grace* (2007), in which the disillusioned and disheartened hero, early-nineteenth-century British abolitionist William Wilberforce, is returned to the passion of his principles by the love of an idealistic younger woman (who happens to be drop-dead gorgeous).

Gorillas in the Mist comprehensively demonstrates the patriarchal gaze that takes over the female biopic. Dian Fossey herself was a bewildering conglomeration of good intentions, dazzling achievements, appalling attitudes, and repellent behavior. By omitting her detention in Congo, her abortions, and her most outrageous actions against the poachers, the film scours out the most unpleasant facets of Fossey. But do the unfolding drama and the resulting portrait tell truths about Dian Fossey? *Gorillas in the Mist,* in attempting to make her, in some ways, better than she was, ends up making her worse. Made near the end of the 1980s female biopic cycle, it manages to summarize everything problematic and reactionary about the Hollywood female biopic at large: to start with, the choice of a subject who became a "tragic figure"; the failure to think out the protagonist in all her facets; the tendency of male points of view to take over; the lack of an attempt to understand the subject's point of view; the avoidance of ideological issues at the heart of the material; and an approach to the material that sensationalizes and softens it at the same time.

Madness, hysteria, sexual dependency, the male gaze, and a patriarchal authorship: that is the classical female biopic. When I show classes a succession of these films, including *I'll Cry Tomorrow, Love Me or Leave Me, Lady Sings the Blues, Frances,* and/or *Gorillas in the Mist* (and one could throw in more recent entries such as *Veronica Guerin* [2003], *Domino* [2005], and *Factory Girl* [2006]), the response, especially from women, is "Enough! No more! Make it stop!" Is there a way to tell the lives of women while critiquing, revising, and redirecting all these conventional tendencies? Is there indeed a way to make it stop? That is the main question surrounding the female biopic. There *are* films that suggest that the answer is, perhaps, yes.

15

An Angel at My Table

Re-Framing the Female Biography

I can't say that Janet's hair looks that odd to me, but then, nothing much looks odd to me.
—JANE CAMPION ON THE BUSHY RED HAIR OF HER PROTAGONIST, JANET FRAME

In discussing the "body too much" in the female biopic, a thorny but inescapable issue is beauty. Each of the subjects covered in this section is played by an actress no older than forty who embodies cultural standards of beauty. In some cases such as Julie Andrews for Gertrude Lawrence and Sigourney Weaver for Dian Fossey, the actress is more conventionally "beautiful" than the subject. Fossey joked with Arnold Glimcher in 1985 that she wanted to be played as a youth by Brooke Shields and as an older woman by Elizabeth Taylor (Lessem 416). Since she was reportedly unhappy about her appearance, the casting of Weaver relieves the film of exploring an unpleasant issue that it would just as soon ignore. Sissy Spacek, who is hardly an orthodox leading lady, proved perfect casting for the diminutive Loretta Lynn, a star in a field that places a premium on more "common" appearances, albeit with rhinestone embellishments. Two subjects who never set out to be public performers, Barbara Graham, the criminal on death row, and Erin Brockovich, the legal investigator, were "glamour pusses" in actuality. They were conveniently suited to Hollywood's demands for flamboyant roles as well as glamour for its actresses. Youth and beauty are not limitations that weigh heavily on the subjects of male biopics. Thus not only does the biopic run up against the culture's limitations on female ambition and accomplishment; it also exposes cinema's requirements of youth and beauty in its leading ladies.

An Angel at My Table (1991) was the second feature-length film and the first and thus far the only biopic directed by New Zealand–born, Australia-based Jane Campion. Previously, Campion had been known mainly for *Sweetie* (1988), which, as *American Film* magazine pointed out, elicited comparisons with the films of David Lynch (Drucker 52). *An Angel at My Table* was received by American reviewers as proof that Campion could work in a more conventional form, earning her credentials as a "real" director, at least as far as the press in this country was concerned. Much less conventional, however, are the ways *An Angel at My Table* acts out and then reverses and undoes the female biopic as I have discussed it.

The three-volume autobiography published by New Zealand poet and novelist Janet Frame (1924–2004) as *To the Is-land* (1982), *An Angel at My Table* (1984), and *The Envoy from Mirror City* (1985) presented Campion and her screenwriter, Laura Jones, with Carolyn Heilbrun's ideal of the quest narrative. The quest, however, does not really make itself felt until Part Three, after the traditional predestination and downward trajectory have been exhausted. The film would seem a prototypical warts-and-all biopic, except that the intimacy established with Janet from toddlerhood to early middle age means that we see her personality develop along with her talents. We feel we understand not only her feeling, but also the meanings and assumptions placed on her by her culture. This makes *An Angel at My Table* extraordinary as a biopic, a watershed in the telling of women's lives on film. To hear Campion and Jones tell it, much of this effect was accidental; Campion has made it clear for years that she considers *Angel* uncinematic.

Like Frame's memoirs, the film depicts the first forty years of the novelist's life. Frame was born and raised in rural New Zealand. Her father worked on the railroad; her mother ran the home. Frame developed as a poet and novelist, but in this place and time smart girls went into teaching, a profession for which her shy, unprepossessing nature left her unsuited; more to the point, Frame was not interested in teaching. Her great talent as a writer was ultimately her strength, but it also subjected her early on to nearly tragic misunderstandings and misinterpretations. The film's feeling of terror stems from the routine process by which someone who is a bit different is picked out of society and committed to a mental hospital. Frame portrayed a culture with little understanding of anyone who is "different," especially a woman. A situation that would seem to call for high melodrama is treated in a hyper-realist style whose effect is often surreal if not absurd. In Campion's film, moreover, Janet is more of a character, in a way similar to Tim Burton's treatment of Ed Wood and his friends. With three actresses— child, adolescent, and adult—wearing in turn the same curly red wig throughout, the film portrays Janet's "difference" as a badge of honor. The final acceptance by others of her difference is her validation, her triumph, rather than success, which the film, like Janet, views as a weird curiosity.

Frame's other strength was her family, one that endured great sadness: the epilepsy of Janet's only brother, George, and the drowning deaths of her older sister, Myrtle, and years later of her next youngest sister, Isabel, both as teenagers. A suicide attempt that Janet wrote about in a class assignment at Dunedin Training College prompted school authorities to recommend her to a hospital psychiatric ward; eventually she was committed to a mental institution. Frame continued to write poems and short stories amidst her eight-year hospitalization, during which time she underwent over two hundred applications of electric shock treatment. Shortly before a lobotomy was scheduled to be performed on her, she won the Hubert Church Award, a major literary prize, for her collection of short stories, *The Lagoon,* and was released from the sanitarium. After this sudden reprieve, she found supportive friends and mentors, received government literary grants, wrote and published novels, and lived for several years in Europe, where her diagnosis of schizophrenia was found to have been false. She finally returned home to New Zealand where, as the film implies, she lived the rest of her life as a productive and celebrated author.

The autobiography and the film are concerned with the painfully withdrawn Frame's quiet fight for her identity both as a writer and as a woman comfortable in her own skin. What Heilbrun writes in her book on woman's biography applies strongly to Frame: "The woman who writes herself a life beyond convention, or the woman whose biographer perceives her as living beyond conventional expectations, has usually early recognized in herself a special gift without name or definition. Its most characteristic indication is the dissatisfaction it causes her to feel with appropriate gender assignments" (96). Frame's story is an extreme example of how someone who deviates from the expectations for woman can be judged—and she will be judged in some way—as mad. Campion said, "The circumstances of her life were so difficult and so painful and her shyness so acute that a lot of her symptoms . . . for example, her suicide attempt, presented like she really did have some serious mental disorder" (*Angel*).

Campion made *An Angel at My Table* as a three-part television miniseries in a joint venture between networks in New Zealand and Australia. Only after the producers, over Campion's objections, assembled the three installments into a 158-minute feature and entered the film in the Venice and Sydney Film Festivals, where it won prizes and attracted distributors, was the director convinced that the series could work as a feature film. It was released theatrically in Europe and America to great acclaim and financial success, earning back more than twice what it cost to produce (McHugh 66). Danny Peary in his 1992 book *Alternate Oscars* named it the best picture of 1991 over more heavily promoted films such as *Thelma and Louise, The Silence of the Lambs,* and *JFK* (304–306). Ironically, therefore, the most important female biopic to the date of this writing was not designed as a feature film at all. "Had [Campion] known *Angel* would wind up in theaters, she would have found a more cinematic style for it" (Taubin 62). "I might have thought of dealing with a smaller time frame," said screenwriter Laura Jones. "And one wouldn't normally have such discursive storytelling in a feature film. But it worked, which made me rethink what *does* work" (Cantwell 44). It appears from the film that *something* was seriously rethought. Could it be that the mini-series format deprived Campion and Jones of the usual need to compress, to open the story as the young adult is about to go out into the world? Thus might the discursiveness allow the character of Janet Frame a chance to stumble gradually onto her own discourse?

In the film as feature, the volumes of Frame's memoir present themselves as three "acts." Three actresses, Alexia Keogh, Karen Fergusson, and Kerry Fox, play Janet as little girl, teenager, and adult, respectively. The linear birth-to-maturity structure gives an intimacy and completeness to this woman's story that the classic biopic which begins just before the subject's breakthrough to success often does not. We see Janet's artistry as it stands out from her rural working-class life of hard work and relative poverty, but we also see how it grows out of it. On one hand, Janet, with her brilliance as a writer and difference from the crowd as a person, is allowed to be what Campion saw when she read the book: "not the tale of a mad writer, but of an ordinary person with a great gift for detail and frankness" (Drucker 53). On the other hand, Janet does not come off as the generic "common woman as uncommon woman." The point of the film is that Janet is not the "com-

mon" young woman, who is brought up to look glamorous but to play a secondary role in life. This contradiction is condensed nicely in key scenes of
Janet's adolescence and young adulthood. By making it clear that Janet is the
exception to the rule, the rule ends up receiving a lot of the film's attention
and scrutiny. The implications are dreary if not dire for all those "common"
women who did not publish books and win awards. Frame scornfully wrote
of a friend at the Seacliff mental institution "who unfortunately had not won
a prize, whose name did not appear in the newspaper, [who] had her leuco-
tomy and was returned to the hospital" (223).

The first thing that distinguishes *An Angel at My Table* from most biopics
is that it does not have what Custen sees as the genre's usual beginning
in medias res, the opening that puts the subject at the point where he or
she starts to belong to the public. Custen points out that Hollywood biopics
played up the American myth of self-invention, which might be one reason
why film biographies are so often thought of as dropping out social, political, historical, and even familial contexts (149). With a female subject, the *in
medias res* opening means something else again; rather than self-invention,
a female biopic often opens at the moment where the opinions of others
toward the female subject are first formed. *Frances* (1982), about the 1930s
Hollywood actress Frances Farmer, who was diagnosed as insane and lobot-
omized, begins with sixteen-year-old Frances causing a furor in her home
state of Washington when she wins a contest with an essay questioning the
concept of God in organized religions. *Camille Claudel* (1989) opens with
the young sculptress stealing clay in the night as her family looks for her.
Even a line of soldiers she passes look at her suspiciously. In the films we
have looked at, the *in medias res* opening means that the film begins as the
female subject begins to be judged and sized up from outside. The opening-
credit sequence of *Lady Sings the Blues* (1972) shows a drugged-up Billie
Holiday being booked and thrown into jail; this action is shown in black-and-
white still photographs that recall *I Want to Live!,* accompanied by booming
Dragnet-style music. *I Want to Live!* displays Barbara Graham's erratic characteristics in the scene in the hotel room, Karen Carpenter's mother and
brother make her decisions for her in a prototypical biopic scene, Fanny
Brice's looks are appraised as all wrong for stardom, and Dian Fossey comes
off as disheveled and disagreeable as she fights for the chance to go to Africa. Only Gertrude Lawrence has possession of her own life in the opening
framing device of her biopic, and, as we've seen, *Star!* paid a high price for
flouting the conventions.

It's possible, God forgive me, to imagine reconceptualizing *An Angel at My Table* into a "cinematic" version that would open near the end of Part One, forty-five minutes into the film as we have it, with the newly introduced eighteen-year-old Janet agonizing over what clothes to take with her to college, hovering in the corner at parties, and covering her mouth so that others won't see her decayed teeth. In this rendition, strategically intercut flashbacks could cover the significance of Janet's childhood writing book, the death of her sister Myrtle, her humiliation before the class, and other events of her childhood. Another option might be to open the film near the end of Part Two, with Janet released from Seacliff; as she walks past the Seacliff sign, Janet could turn and look at it, cueing a flashback to the first time she saw the sign as a little girl, which would take the story up to the point of that opening; then the last third of the film would concern her new beginning.

The problem with the first approach is that Janet's point of view would never get a chance to be established. The film would begin with her worrying about the way the world sees her; shifting that perspective would be difficult if not impossible, as would putting the proper amount of emphasis on her writing. The second option, while better establishing Janet's own point of view, still emphasizes how she looks to others, as well as makes her gifts and creativity secondary to her problems and traumas; in short, the downward trajectory would be the film's point, the customary trap of the female biopic. Campion's film as we have it gives us the sense that we are living Frame's life with her, good and bad taken together, with no selection. Of course, this effect does result from selections, successful ones. Frame's three books are works of memory and literature; when Kerry Fox asked Frame how she felt about the film being made about her, the novelist replied, "The film isn't about my life; it's based on a book I wrote about my life" (*Angel*). Of course, compressions and selections had to be made in adapting a 435-page memoir into a film running over two and a half hours, with characters dropped and incidents omitted. And there's no telling what alterations Frame made to her own story. Nonetheless, it is very hard to make an *in medias res* biopic of the sort I have described without the agency seeming to come from the narration rather than the character. Indeed, Campion, who has always maintained that *Angel* fails to measure up to her own ideals for cinema, has said that all she did was put the spectators in the presence of Janet Frame, in effect, and then got out of the way. "I guess I'm kind of a film snob," she said, "and even though I think the Janet Frame story . . . is very touching

38. A "Jane Campion moment": Adolescent Janet Frame (Karen Fergusson, right) meets her girlhood friend Poppy (Caroline Somerville), who recites English class poetry before returning to the "commercial" track in high school; Janet takes the poetic road less traveled, in *An Angel at My Table* (Jane Campion, Fine Line Features, 1991). Digital frame enlargement.

and very affecting, to me it's still like a TV series and I like film that's a little more risk-taking or bold. . . . The heart of what's brilliant about the . . . story is just how incredibly vulnerable the Janet Frame character is, and it's really all to do with Janet Frame's writing in the first place. . . . We really just took everything away to let Janet just be there with the audience. I think it just connects with people's own vulnerability" (*Angel*).

Campion's objections notwithstanding, "reviewers noted the Campion touch, finding [*Angel*] 'instantly recognizable' as her work" (McHugh 66). Stuart Dryburgh, the film's cinematographer, cites certain shots as "very Jane Campion moments. . . . One girl [is] sitting on a sofa telling a very serious story and next to her is somebody standing on their head for no apparent reason except that it seems perfectly logical from the point of view of childhood. It creates a lovely sense of off-balance" (*Angel*). In another "Jane Campion moment . . . two people [are] talking across the frame. In the background somebody's doing something incomprehensible with a horse" (*Angel*).

The advantage of the discursive format is that it allows Janet's story to develop in a linear, lifelike way, without a plot having been imposed on it and without conflict having been contrived. Campion sees the development of Frame's life in three aspects: coming to treasure books, to develop her imagination, and to practice her skills as a writer; developing a severe sense of shame and thus of shyness; as well as a profound identification with the land and sky of New Zealand. These three aspects hardly relate to each other in a causal way. In terms of biopic convention Janet's writing talent, the inner voice that sings quietly and insistently, proves her salvation, and her nationalistic joy comes to be treasured by her fellow New Zealanders. Campion's presentation of it all, however, in a matter-of-fact way, lends an absurdity to Frame's story, a combination Patricia Mellencamp called "strange and familiar" (175).

We watch Janet groping, finding her path, embracing the things she loves, and wriggling her way around the things she doesn't. Biopics about women rarely allow the subject simply to feel her way through to her own subjectivity. Exceptions, such as *Erin Brockovich* and *Coal Miner's Daughter,* have been about living subjects with whom the films' male directors spent a great deal of time in the pre-production period; thus those movies can be said to have internalized their subjects' points of view. Both of them include a recuperative escape hatch, however; *Coal Miner's Daughter* in the partnership with Loretta Lynn's husband, who supplies the drive and ambition early on, *Erin Brockovich* in the subject's angry, aggressive, goal-oriented (read: "masculine") behavior. Male biopics seldom allow lifelike discovery for their subjects, either. The *Citizen Kane* model works its way through to a spectator-centered understanding of the character. Warts-and-all often deals with the more character-centered realization of a definite recognition or rehabilitation, such as Joe E. Lewis in *The Joker Is Wild* (unconvincingly) deciding to stop drinking, or Ray Charles in *Ray* kicking his drug addiction.

Kathleen McHugh argues that Campion becomes a conduit for Frame's viewpoint, and that Frame is a vehicle for the director; Campion admits as much, averring that some of the early vignettes come from her own childhood. Mellencamp proclaims that *Angel* "stars the point of view of women" (175). *An Angel at My Table,* like most female biopics from the fifties and after, draws on warts-and-all and appears to take after the male apotheosis of the subgenre, *Raging Bull* (1980); judging, moreover, from Campion's conversion of Harvey Keitel, who appeared in five Martin Scorsese films, into the unlikeliest of romantic leads in *The Piano* (1993) and *Holy Smoke* (1999), Campion has a strong affinity for Scorsese's films. *Angel* can be seen as a kind of feminine *Raging Bull.* The boxer Jake LaMotta's "talents"—his hand-in-boxing-glove violent aggression and his ability to endure punishment—are opposite sides of a masculine (and Catholic) pathology. Even though Scorsese depicts LaMotta's Italian-Catholic Bronx background in nearly ethnographic detail, LaMotta's rage, like the "talent" of the classical biopic subject, comes from somewhere deep within him; Scorsese aligns the "God-given" talent of the classical biopic subject with the Paschal Mystery at the heart of Catholicism. It is, however, defined by the streets and by Italian American expectations of masculinity.

Similarly, in *Angel* Campion's own talent for ethnographic observation (the first of her two bachelor's degrees was in anthropology) mingles with her gravitation toward the eccentric. The classical biopic's "natural" flair is here present in Frame's distinctive writing talent. Janet is shown finding and developing her inner voice from an early age. Even though she is uncomfortable with herself in her skin, in her body, her writing talent is her certainty and her spine. As a grade-schooler, Janet writes a line for a school poetry assignment that includes the line "evening shadows touch the sky." Her older sister Myrtle insists that she "rub out 'touch' and put 'tint,'" that "evening shadows 'tint' the sky" "sounds more poetic." Janet avers, "But I like 'touch'" and keeps it in, showing the rightness and sureness of her artistic decisions in the face of stereotyped preconceptions of what poetry should be. If only Janet could carry her determined disregard of literary conventions into other areas of life, just as if Jake could only confine his rage to the boxing arena. Moreover, just as LaMotta's orientation is the Bronx street, Janet Frame is grounded in the sky and the ground of New Zealand. Scorsese filters LaMotta's experience through the black and white of noir, of documentaries (like Kubrick's *Day of the Fight* [1950]), and of Italian Neorealism and fifties Hollywood realism (like Wise's two 1950s biopics). Campion films Frame's story in the stark color and light of New Zealand, especially in Part One, covering Frame's childhood. This gives way to the darker, more muted tones of Parts Two and Three, reflecting Frame's psychological and emotional experiences.

An Angel at My Table is a downward trajectory female biopic that takes its heroine down to the bottom and then rewinds and reconfigures itself, creating an alternative, parallel life for its heroine. Sue Gillet discusses the false impression, literally, given by Janet's gaze at the mirror, that what the mirror shows her is what she should be and that this is a feminine ritual. This disregards the male self-fashioning done in mirrors in Scorsese's films. These include the "You talkin' to me?" scene in *Taxi Driver;* the Brando "I coulda been a contender" monologue delivered in *Raging Bull* by a now fat, middle-aged Jake LaMotta who has torn down his life and can now only build up something redemptive; the Howard Hughes of *The Aviator* looking at himself in the mirror, trying to turn a phrase he can't stop saying, "the way of the future," into the hopeful motto of a visionary entrepreneur. The way of his future, however, is delusion and madness. Along the lines of what Jacques Lacan called "the misrecognition of a misrecognition," Scorsese's characters see what they want to see in mirrors. As an informal, low-key rehabilitation film, *Angel* weans Janet from mirrors and other signifiers that give her a false identity, helping her find her identity in New Zealand (this ends up being something of a patriotic film) and on the page.

McHugh cites Frame's statement that the autobiographies expressed "the desire to make myself a first person. For many years I was a third person—as children are" (65). Furthermore, this third person is discussed by teachers, doctors, and the seemingly socially and sexually secure people she meets after her release from Seabrook. Even her acclaim and success are attributed to a third person, the topic of newspaper reporters and awards committees. McHugh sees Frame's journey from being defined by others to discovering and living her own identity as paralleled by Campion's development as a major filmmaker. "Though born thirty years apart," she writes, "and into very different class backgrounds, Campion and Frame nevertheless shared New Zealand childhoods steeped in the arts, emphasized from a nationalist perspective. [Frame's] autobiographies, their setting, time, and subject, bridged Campion's own creative development and that of her parents" (66).

The class differences that McHugh mentions in passing, however, are key to how Campion is able to see through herself but also past herself, becoming Janet's subjectivity, as it were. Class differences account for much of Janet's awkwardness. Campion emphasizes this, opening the story proper with Janet in grade school stealing money from her dad's pockets in order to buy her classmates chewing gum, and showing Janet and her sisters in torn clothing. These children grow up in a culture where violent discipline is taken for granted; Janet's father, who clearly loves her and her sisters, goes after teenage Myrtle with a strap when he learns she's been engaging in sex play; Janet's friend Poppy shows her the welts on her legs from "where my dad whups me with his machine belt." This would constitute child abuse now, but in that time and place it did not. Moreover, her family has the working class's faith in authority figures; Janet's mother agrees to a lobotomy for her daughter because the encyclopedia says there is no cure for her mental illness and the doctors said that "it's for the best." This does not make Mrs. Frame a villain; far from it. Rather, all the characters do what they are bound to do given their social definitions. As a psychologist, Mr. Forrest sees a responsibility to try to get Janet help when she writes a course essay confessing her suicide attempt. To him, she is a troubled student crying for help; to her, she is an artist expressing herself. Later, when she refuses to leave the hospital with her mother after her first discharge, the guileless Janet doesn't realize that she's giving the authorities no choice but to interpret her behavior as disturbed and commit her to Seacliff.

An Angel at My Table provides a new take on not just the female biopic, but the biopic in general. Janet is different from the others, like all biopic subjects, but as a woman she is made to feel that "different" won't do at all, and she gives in to the pressure to conform, as nearly anyone in that culture at that time would have. Janet as a nationalist heroine, however, comes from the land and happily returns to it at the end. In keeping with the director's identification with the heroine, Frame is enshrined in myth more by Campion than by an implied culture. Moreover, while Janet is victimized, this is not a film that finds villains or holds individuals to account. In a sense nothing happens to Janet, except life and becoming. Watching *An Angel at My Table* makes one wonder why more biopics can't be about somebody simply becoming herself, realizing her identity, and finding a way to live.

Unlike other female biopics, with their objectifying openings, *An Angel at My Table* begins at the start of life, as we see in a series of blackouts, baby Janet lying on the grass, her mom encouraging her to walk, her mom's feet seen from the baby's point of view, and the baby's first steps through the tall green grass from about the hips down; we see what baby Janet could see and experience. From these first moments, the film engages in a dialectic between the social conventions women are made to measure up to and by which they are judged and interpreted, and a young woman's quest for her own voice. Janet Frame's memoirs provide a painful template for the destruction of patriarchally produced female subjectivity and a woman's rebuilding of identity out of her own imaginary. Frame does this out of her love of language, which was thought by feminists to be determined by patriarchal traditions; Campion does it with cinema, which similarly had been thought to be locked into a male gaze.

Cut from baby Janet to a shot in depth of eight-year-old Janet (Alexia Keogh) walking toward us up a long dirt road. As she draws closer, a craning camera lowers to meet her. She stops in her tracks as a child might before an adult. She faces the camera as the adult Janet in voiceover intones, "This is the story of my childhood. In August 1924 I was born Janet Patterson Frame. My twin, who was never named, died two weeks later." While the adult Janet talks, the child looks around; there are cuts to extreme close-ups of her little fingers clutching her velour dress. These peculiar cutaways immediately establish two things: the self-consciousness that will haunt Janet well into adulthood and the need for private space, which the film will consistently grant her. Young Janet then suddenly turns and runs down the road away from us, and into her life. Her story begins and we follow.

This sets out another aspect of the narrative; *An Angel at My Table,* unusually for a female biopic, is a road film, a journey, what Heilbrun calls "the quest." The film lays out the quest visually in the metaphor of the road. When each actress playing Janet is introduced, she is associated with a means of transportation: the child with the road and, soon after, a train (at first connected with Janet's father), and the adolescent with a bicycle. The adult is first introduced walking along railroad tracks at a crossroads, and will later be associated with cars, ocean liners, and rickety flatbed trucks. A pompous London publisher will tell her, ludicrously, to arrive at their meetings in a Rolls-Royce, the ultimate status symbol. While the film negotiates the public/private dichotomy of the biography in visual terms of open and closed-in spaces, respectively, the means of transportation predestine Janet, only to suspend and then reverse the destination later on.

Campion sets out the predestination motif, central to the biopic genre, from the beginning. Following an establishing shot of the train, the father, at work, comes into the compartment where his sleeping family is traveling. The train soon passes through Seacliff, home of the psychiatric hospital where Janet will spend many years. In close-up from outside the train window Janet looks. A sign moves into view. "Sea-cliff," pronounces Janet's brother, George (or Bruddie). "That's where all the loonies go." In a cruel irony Bruddie's classmates at school will mock the epileptic Bruddie as "loony." Janet's mother, attempting to block her view, holds up two hands. Characteristic of Janet's tendency to look past barriers, she turns the mother's hands into a frame ("Janet's Frame") through which Campion's camera looks, from the little girl's viewpoint, like a director using her hands to set up a shot. Through this "viewfinder," Janet sees a tortuously deformed man, without control of his face or body. This man, whose deformity becomes pure image, the sort that an impressionable child remembers, is shown more closely than Janet would actually see him. This shot will in retrospect appear a mirroring, as Janet becomes destined to see herself as that deformed person, even while hoping in mirrors to see a loved, glamorized self. In a rereading of the genre, Janet indeed has a destiny, and it is to be a great writer. Her writing

39. Young adult Janet (Kerry Fox) agonizes over her move to college, as her sister Isabel (Samantha Townsley) looks on. Digital frame enlargement.

talent, however, must outlast any number of false or stereotypical destinies held out to women in general and to her in particular—to be a teacher, to be a schizophrenic, to subject herself to the ministrations of those who would treat such an incurable "deterioration of the mind."

At the end of Part One, as Janet leaves to go to college, she burns the writing book her father had bought her as a child "to write more of your poems in." She waves to her family from inside the train, as we see them in the same position from which Janet saw the deformed man; her twelve-year-old sister June, who will be her main familial support in the future, runs along with the train until she can keep up no longer. In Part Two, when Janet is driven by car to the Seacliff hospital, she is shown in a three-shot in between two distracted girls. Not knowing where she is going, she looks out a side window to see the sign "Seacliff" whizzing by. This sequence deftly visualizes Frame's description in the memoir: "The six weeks I spent at Seacliff hospital [before being committed indefinitely] in a world I'd never known among people whose existences I never thought possible, became for me a concentrated course in the horrors of insanity and the dwelling-place of those judged insane, separating me for ever from the former acceptable realities and assurances of everyday life" (193).

Finally, in a sequence of events too bizarre to be fictional, Janet's lobotomy is called off after she wins a national literary prize and she is sent home. Campion shows Janet through a car's rear window as she walks past the "Seacliff" sign. After telling the driver, "Seacliff station," she looks out the

40. A confluence of events too bizarre to be fictional. Janet (Kerry Fox) signs copies of her first book while institutionalized, awaiting a lobotomy. Digital frame enlargement.

back window at the sign while the sign grows smaller in the distance. The return to Seacliff station, and home, completes her false destiny, unexpectedly closing a chapter that Janet feared would be never-ending. Thus, in a sense, Campion makes Frame's story into a film with a *Psycho*-like narrative; everywhere Janet thought she was going, and every place narratively where we thought the film was going, is suddenly suspended. The film at this point has an hour left to run. And yet, with convention as our guide, we may wonder where it can take us from here.

Campion depicts Janet's quest as inadvertent but crucial because the road that Janet is on is one seldom taken by women in films. When Janet in voiceover tells us of her literary grant to travel overseas in order to broaden her experience, she adds, "I knew if I stayed [in New Zealand], there'd be no second chance for my survival." What Janet looks for is what she never expects to find: a way of living as herself in the world. Mobility is denied to women, who are expected to stay in their appointed places as housewives, mothers, teachers, nurses, secretaries. The scene in which the seventeen-year-old Janet meets her girlhood friend Poppy along a back road is among a plethora of moments demonstrating Janet's alienation from her intended fate as a female. Poppy tells Janet that she's taking "Commercial," a high school track that trains girls for clerical jobs; Poppy says how much she hates doing "grammar logs," while grammar—language—is Janet's life. Janet realizes that she has nothing to say to this young woman who, when they were children, once lent her "special books" and shared her imagination with her. I'm reminded of what the artist Al Hirschfeld says in *The Line King* (1996), a documentary made when he was ninety-three and still working: "All kids draw. I just never stopped." What Janet does is seen as kid's stuff, something to grow out of, except that she doesn't. In accepting that childlike creativity and honesty are to be her life's work, Janet finally matures. This gradual, nearly imperceptible progression probably could not have been achieved by a more pointed, selective cinematic biopic, although I refuse to believe that somebody cannot make a fully feminist biopic in that format someday.

As we've seen, when female subjects bow to cultural pressure and listen to others, the results are disastrous (as in *Superstar, I'll Cry Tomorrow,* and *I Want to Live!*), and when they listen to themselves, they are read as "bitchy," either by the film itself (*Gorillas in the Mist*) or by critics and audiences (*Star!*). This is the Catch-22 of the genre and of women in the culture. *Angel* follows Janet down this familiar slope. Teaching is one profession, besides nursing and secretarial work, that was approved for educated women. When she studies to be a teacher, the intense discomfort she displays seems to have as much to do with her disappointment in herself for denying her own ambition as with shyness. Even after she changes her major to concentrate on writing, the seeds of her downfall are sown, and in its familiar mechanical way, the process of victimization takes over. What Janet fails at first to listen to, however, is herself. Like other female biopic subjects, she does what others expect her to do. She backpedals from her adolescent vow to herself, "I've made up my mind not to be a teacher; I'm going to be a poet." In a single forward tracking shot, Campion shows teenage Janet from behind, in her nightgown, reading and writing by candlelight so as not to disturb her sleeping sisters, while making to herself a youthful promise that she will not keep. A rhyming scene late in Part Three shows Janet in a London rooming house, again in a tracking shot from behind, writing by lamplight as a cacophony of bawling babies and blaring TVs (the year would be circa 1956) disturbs her concentration. Putting a record of the Beethoven violin concerto on the phonograph, Janet (with the help of some adroit sound mixing) tunes out the world, intent on her inner voice as it sings to her typewriter. It's significant, too, that in this scene Janet has blocked out most of a vanity mirror with reference books and other writing paraphernalia. This scene follows the moment of epiphany in which a therapist whom she sees after learning the truth about her corrected diagnosis not only suggests writing a book about her experience at Seacliff, but gives her the liberating advice, "If anybody tells you to get out and mix and you don't want to, don't."

However, unlike *I'll Cry Tomorrow* or *Superstar,* where the mother is all to blame, or *Lady Sings the Blues,* a blaxploitation-era crossover film in which whites, along with Billie Holiday's own weak (feminine) will, are the causes of all of her troubles, *Angel* presents Janet's problems as stemming from the culture; her obstacles are systems, not groups or individuals. In her quest Janet moves by means that are out of her control and ends up making them her own. Thus, Campion's camera dwells on the back of a truck with no shock absorbers carrying Janet and her suitcase to her Spanish *pension;* it lingers on the expanse of water accumulating behind Janet as an ocean liner takes her to a new world, however seasick she might get. Transportation provides Janet with her opportunities. It also allows her to transcend presumed limitations of gender, class, and nationality. By the end, when male newspaper reporters cross the meadows and, with difficulty, trudge up the hills we have seen her climb throughout her life, she has reached a peak where people whose unapproachability has made her so terribly uncomfortable must forge paths to approach *her.* This may be the ultimate vindication of the famous, validated in male biopics: people reach out to you; you no longer have to strive to reach them. So many female biopics show just the opposite; the subject never stops reaching, as with Fanny Brice yearning for "My Man," unless death has relieved her of the struggle, as *I Want to Live!* bitterly acknowledges.

Thus it is a bit bewildering to hear Campion call Frame's third book, *The Envoy from Mirror City,* "a very long 'what happens afterwards.' Things are happening, but they're never as dramatic as what happened to her in her twenties when she had a nervous breakdown" (*Angel*). Alas, this goes straight to what usually undermines the female biopic, the tendency to see living, discovery, and realization as anticlimactic and undramatic. Since female biopics rarely concern epic struggles with monopolies, seceding states, medical establishments, or the British Empire in wartime (*Erin Brockovich,* we'll see, is an exception), filmmakers look for drama in trauma, suffering, and victimization—the old trap. So it is ironic to see Campion saved from the conventions by the formats of Frame's memoirs and the TV miniseries. The "very long what happens afterwards" provides the two-act downward trajectory narrative with a totally new third act that takes the heroine in a direction that patriarchy would not know about. I, a male critic, do not pretend to lecture Jane Campion on what is feminist in her own film, but her re-marks show how awkwardly the telling of women's lives fits with narrative's need for drama and conflict. We'll see this quandary further in *Marie Antoinette* and *The Notorious Bettie Page,* both by women directors who avoided the traditional snares of the genre and were charged with making films in which "nothing happens."

Angel ends in 1964 in a camping trailer (or caravan, in New Zealand par-lance), kept on blocks in the suburban backyard of Janet's sister June. Her prepubescent niece, playing Chubby Checker's "The Twist" on the radio, practices the dance while Janet is in the trailer, which she has set up as a writing studio, complete with portable typewriter. In four shots, the se-quence plays out. In the first, Janet's niece is shown, outside a door, twisting to the music; she reaches into the trailer, turns up the radio unbearably loud, and bounds into the camper, still twisting. Her mother appears at the win-dow telling her daughter it's time for bed. Janet, who has been there unseen, moves into the shot. The scene is richly ironic, for it brings an unremarkable but hard-fought end to Janet's quest for a Room of One's Own, a place away from all other "womanly" responsibilities and definitions, where a woman can create, alone with her ideas. Janet, in finding comfort within herself and a loving though transitory life (her sister asks her if she wants coffee, as one would inquire of a guest), is in that place, and it is mobile. With a girl's bike, reminiscent of Janet's adolescence, propped up against the trailer, she moves outside and, sure that the lights are off inside and no one's looking, she gently twists, trying out this new fad in an ever-young spirit of cautious experimentation. As the craning camera follows her back into the trailer, Janet returns to her writing; the music suddenly disappears as soon as the song and Janet's dance are over, making clear that the music is no longer actually on the radio but playing in her mind.

Campion then ends with two shot sequences that rhyme with the Seacliff station scene. In one, Janet types and Campion cuts to what she's writing. This is unremarkable until one realizes that what Janet sees when she looks now is no longer a fanciful or horrifying mirror image, and is no longer a deformed "loony." What looks back at her is her writing, her true reflection on the page. This then leads to the film's final shot, Janet through a rain-splashed window, looking with satisfaction at what she wrote but returning to add more to it. This juxtaposition of the creative with the ordinary and the experimental with the furtive sums up Janet's peace, one that is her own.

The capacity for constructing one's own world that is both part of and apart from ordinary physical surroundings is the very soul of subjectivity. Campion creates a mise-en-scène where these elements coexist. It may seem that Campion and her screenwriter overdraw from the Frame memoirs a powerful sense of shame in who she is; it is this shame that hangs over the narrative events leading to Janet's institutionalization. It stems from Janet's feeling of glaring difference from what girls are supposed to be. Early in the film, little Janet enters her first of many dark, enclosed places, the closet where her dad hangs his overalls. There she steals some change. In the next scene, wanting to be liked, the girl doles out chewing gum to the kids in her class. A tracking shot shows kids seated at their desks smacking on the gum. The scene ends with Janet standing at the front, her nose against the chalkboard; Campion dwells on this shot in order to create a separate place where Janet is made to go out of shame. Much of what the first half of the film conceives as Janet's privacy is made up of self-imposed hiding places, prisons to which she has sentenced herself. These include the grave markers at the cemetery where she goes to read and to hide the soiled makeshift sanitary napkins she's ashamed to turn in with her laundry at college; the room at her aunt's house where she hides candy wrappers; the kitchen where she stuffs her mouth with scraps of meat left on plates, after telling her aunt she is a vegetarian to justify paying her less board; and her mouth itself, a pit of decayed teeth she is terrified to have the world see.

The early schoolroom scene rhymes with the student-teaching classroom that she flees just as she is about to teach a class before the superintendent. The camera concentrates on the space between Janet and the chalkboard as she turns to write something and instead stares at the chalk. The close-up of a piece of chalk, from Janet's point of view, is reminiscent of films in which everyday blank objects, like the glass of Alka-Seltzer in *Taxi Driver*, become profound signifiers of a disturbed mind. In addition, the shot of Janet guiltily facing the board reminds us that this twenty-one-year-old would-be poet trying to force herself to become a teacher is the same person as the little girl who was made a spectacle of, having been caught in a lie (and one of the children shown in close-ups staring at Janet is Alexia Keogh, minus the red wig she wore as the youngest Janet in that earlier scene at the blackboard).

It is significant, however, that Campion moves from the first schoolroom scene to one in which little Janet is in bed with her three sisters, who make a game out of turning in unison. This young woman who compared herself negatively to other girls has with her sisters a bond that forms the core of her being and is crucial, the film shows, in her development as an artist and as a person. That development stems from this artist's imaginative escape from reality into an alternate reality. The film avoids the traditional identification of the artist with what Catherine Soussloff refers to as the absolute. Campion could be said to achieve Soussloff's aim to "release the artist from this state of pure being between the knower and the known. . . . So that his [*sic*] social relations with culture can be detected and interpreted" (5). The great novelist here does not spring full-blown onto the world, gifted with perception and expression exceeding those of all other mortals.

If "the private" divides sharply between a life of the mind, heart, and imagination and a place to hide from physical awareness of body and inadequacy that brings shame, the public is an open arena where Janet feels exposed and is reminded of her shortcomings, of the feeling of being "different," and of her enclosure by mass emotion. She especially finds alien and threatening the popular emotions surrounding World War II, which ended less than three weeks before her twenty-first birthday. The "public," therefore, is where impressions are formed and conclusions jumped to. Between these two geographic realms—privacy as a place where shame requires Janet to hide and the public as the place she flees because the risk of exposure, disapproval, and misinterpretation is so great, there is travel, which is the unifier, the leveler. Travel proceeds to a destination but it is impartial. It can lead to the asylum and just as easily leave it in the distance. It can deliver one to death, as does the train taking Isabel to the beach where she drowns, or it can speed past boundaries and open up new possibilities.

The film is devoid of that staple of female biography, the male authority figure or driving force, the man who approves of her work and impresses upon her how great she is, as if Janet Frame needs to be told she can write. I feel that this is why the film treats Frank Sargeson so gingerly. Georgia Brown in *The Village Voice* complained that "Sargeson, the older New Zealand writer who takes Frame in and builds her confidence, becomes a jealous buffoon" (58). Sargeson, according to Campion and Dryburgh, however, was a great eccentric figure in New Zealand in the 1950s and had won the Hubert Church Award just before Frame did; he had no reason to be jealous (*Angel*). Campion adroitly avoids the moment where Sargeson, a sympathetic figure who helps to save Janet, might appear to speak for the film as male authority, passing judgment on the worth of Janet Frame. Other male authority figures are treated as parts of the system Janet spends years to overcome. John Forrest, the young university instructor who is responsible for Janet's initial hospitalization, romanticizes her illness: "I look at you, I see Van Gogh, Hugo Wolf. Lots of great artists have suffered from schizophrenia." For all the damage he did in getting Janet committed, however, he also apparently brought Janet's work to the attention of a press, resulting in the publication of *The Lagoon* during her hospitalization. Much later, her London publisher gives her best sellers to read so she can "study the form," recalling Myrtle's insistence that "tint" makes better poetry than "touch."

I do not see any of these figures as caricatures. Rather they are portrayed with a realistic even-handedness that reveals them to be part of a system that makes brutal judgments and molds people according to its values. Janet's success, quiet but real, is in resisting and outlasting all who have judged her and have tried to remake her by their norms. When Janet succeeds, furthermore, the judgments stay utterly offscreen or are handled with humor and irony. An acceptance letter arrives for her first novel, *Owls Do Cry,* and we don't hear what it says. The sanitorium head finds out about her writing award by seeing an item about it in a newspaper. Janet reads a rave *Times of London* review of *Faces in the Water* in the anonymity of a train station ladies' room. Reporters who wish to begin the job of mythologizing Frame in New Zealand after her return in 1963 have to climb an incredibly steep hill—it was actually a former volcano, according to Campion (*Angel*). Furthermore, class is behind much of Janet's early success. The father buys little Janet her first writing tablet because her teacher has praised her poetry. The parents are proud because a local literary society has given Janet a prize and opened up the library to her free of charge.

Janet has so many supports and comforts taken away from her that she is like Freud's "oceanic" person or Lacan's *"homme-lette,"* swimming like an amoeba in a frightened, unformed state. Like the classic biopic subject, Janet is led by her inner engine, that is, her great writing talent, into parts of the world and spheres of society for which she has no preparation, given her class, nationality, and her background as a diagnosed mental patient. Here is a shy, insecure young person from a working-class, provincial background, willing herself into places where socially she feels she does not belong, while in her mind and soul she is sure that they are where she does belong. Indeed, she may belong there more than some of the people who are already there; Janet, so socially inept, finds herself afraid to speak at parties where she's the only one who has actually published books, while the "in crowd" talks about the great books they'll publish someday.

Going off into unknown territory feels terribly dangerous to Janet but she has to take the risk. *Angel* takes the artist-film clichés I have discussed in the Great Man section and makes a spectator feel the risks and terrors of following the "no choice but to do it" impulse. Janet, without doing so deliberately, marches to her own drummer from the beginning. She is both immobilizingly timid and inspirationally courageous. She can stand in her father's shoes—certainly far from the predestination of a woman in patriarchy. The talent—her writer's voice—is what leads her out into the world in spite of every obstacle. Her writing is her spine, and it launches her out into prominence while all the pretty, sexual, loved people are sitting around talking about writing books and fantasizing about getting published by Faber & Faber. (In more vengeful hands, come to think of it, *An Angel at My Table* could have played like The Nixon Story.) What Janet has at her core is the land; she's joined to the land and sky of New Zealand. She and Campion create the land and sky as a kind of birthright, to be expressed through Janet's writing.

An Angel at My Table shows how a straight-ahead biopic can nonetheless be that most radical thing, a film that works against the conventions of patriarchal form and rewrites women's stories. It does this not by viewing the woman from the vantage point of the environment through which she moves, but by honestly examining that environment and establishing a subject position from which to critique it as the subject would. In telling the story of Janet Frame, whose life was far from easy, Jane Campion makes directing a feminist biopic look easy, even though it is also anything but. Does the compressed form of the theatrical film militate against the free and unforced expression of a woman's point of view? *An Angel at My Table* raises the question. To date no film has satisfactorily answered it.

16

Erin Brockovich

Hollywood Feminist Revisionism, after a Fashion

In life, as in fiction, women who speak out usually end up punished or dead. I'm lucky to escape with my pension and a year of leave.

 —Carolyn Heilbrun, upon resigning in protest from the faculty of Columbia University in 1992

Well-behaved women seldom make history.

 —Laurel Thatcher Ulrich

Erin Brockovich premiered soon after the turn of the millennium, in March 2000. A torn-from-the-headlines biopic about a contemporary subject, the film tells the kind of unlikely real-life story no fiction writer could invent. In 1991 Erin Brockovich, a thirty-one-year-old, twice-divorced single mother of three landed a job as a file clerk at the Los Angeles law firm of Masry & Vititoe, which had represented her in a lawsuit following an auto accident. While filing a case concerning the purchase by Pacific Gas & Electric (PG&E) of a residence in Hinkley, California, Brockovich noticed that there were medical records and blood samples included with the real estate files. She asked Ed Masry if she could investigate. Her interviews with one family whose members had developed cancer and other illnesses from Chromium 6, a harmful chemical from the PG&E power plant, led to discoveries that the water in Hinkley and neighboring communities had apparently been poisoned, knowingly and for many years, by the giant utility. Brockovich, through countless individual interviews with the people of Hinkley and research at county water boards and at UCLA, helped guide 634 plaintiffs through a class action suit brought by Masry and his partners. After four years in arbitration, the case was settled in 1996 for $333 million, the largest lawsuit in U.S. history.

Even before the settlement was reached, film rights to Brockovich's story were optioned by Jersey Films, Danny De Vito's production company with partners Stacey Sher and Michael Shamberg. The latter's spouse, Carla Santos Shamberg, was a patient of a chiropractor who also treated Brockovich for her injuries. The doctor told Santos Shamberg (obviously in the years before HIPAA rules governing medical privacy took effect) about this amazing patient and pitched her own prospective script to the producer's wife, lending truth to the impression that in L.A. everyone's writing a screenplay. Santos Shamberg's immediate reaction was that "this [would make] a great movie. And it's a great role model for women. She [Erin Brockovich] came to my house for the first interview . . . it was her birthday so I have to give her that. She had on black spiked heels, long tanned legs . . . black leather miniskirt and a black leather vest. That was it . . . And I looked at her, and one would think from the first impression if you don't go any farther that this girl's really 'out there.' But she sat down and this girl is so smart that I thought, this is a great girl. She's like a superhero" (*Erin*). Carla Santos Shamberg's initial impression sounds like that of some of Brockovich's co-workers, except that they failed to find her heroic. What they did find was an office dress code, from which they proceeded to measure the length of her skirts in the belief that they were shorter than what is allowed (*Erin*). This kind of humiliating detail, though comic, does not make it into the film.

The film is about the reaction of others to Erin, stemming from the filmmakers' own responses to a woman who was still only in her thirties when the film was made. She lived across town from them, where she was (and still is) continuing the work depicted in their film. The filmmakers had the unusual advantage of making a film about a female subject who was both larger than life and almost completely unknown. The film is built on the dualism between Erin's feisty demeanor around lawyers and co-workers at the office and the victims in Hinkley, whom she befriends and around whom she is warm and deferential. This is part of the multi-perspectival view built into the film by Susanna Grant's script, Steven Soderbergh's smart direction, and Julia Roberts's high-voltage performance, which recalls Oscar-winning turns like Susan Hayward's and Sissy Spacek's. The film's muted version of the biopic subject's closing tribute is an unsought and unexpected $2 million bonus check (even the size of the bonus is played down; it was actually $2.5 million), ranking Erin with other biopic subjects who were not out for their own personal gain or ambition. Thus in a big-studio Hollywood film the system rewards those who do the right thing. Because this is the kind of honor and reward so often denied to female biopic subjects, however, the film feels progressive in its sexual politics (and even here there are reservations), while it operates like a traditional social problem drama in which social institutions can be counted on to correct the excesses of American capitalism.

As we have seen, given the difficulty in the female biopic of the protagonist's ownership of her own body, image, subjectivity, and destiny, it follows that in order to secure those properties a subject has to wrest them away from the larger culture by force. This in turn may be why much of *Erin Brockovich* plays for comedy actions that are conventionally melodramatic. A biopic in which a woman takes over her own subjectivity overturns expectations, inverts norms, and is therefore funny. Like *An Angel at My Table* and other revisionist female biopics such as *The Notorious Bettie Page* and *Marie Antoinette*, *Erin Brockovich* employs transgressive humor, stranger-than-fiction plot twists, and believe-it-or-not turns of events. These films turn the excessive sufferings and outrageous reversals of fortune on the genre itself. In the resulting confusion, the subject is then able to slip unnoticed out a side door, as it were, as if walking away from a car wreck unscathed. While the other aforementioned films posit the traditional demure or naïve subject overtaken by circumstances and consequences, *Erin Brockovich* starts with a more conscious and experienced subject who takes what she thinks is hers. Unlike in many female biopics, however, the subject is not punished or victimized for her transgression, but celebrated for it.

The film's Erin takes a liminal role as she becomes important to the PG&E case. *Erin Brockovich* risks pushing its heroine's drive and her obsession with the case into *Gorillas in the Mist* territory, where a woman's rationality and judgment become clouded by passion for a cause. By her "stick-to-it-ive-ness" (in the real Erin Brockovich's motivational-speaker-ese, on display at brockovich.com), the film's Erin possesses the overriding virtue of being proved unequivocally right. *Erin Brockovich* as a female biopic is an exception that proves the rule. Steven Soderbergh's film sidesteps the built-in snares, whereby ambition is unseemly for women, devotion comes out of an excess of emotion, and dedication to a cause invites victimization, illness, and death—seemingly out of nothing more than what Alfred Hitchcock often called the desire to avoid clichés. Soderbergh avoided big courtroom sequences and what he called "the raised-fist scene" for the same reason. There is also cliché-avoidance in a lengthy passage Soderbergh cut from the beginning of the third act in which Erin, as she actually did, first develops nose bleeds and then contracts spinal meningitis, for which she is hospitalized (Grant revised draft 89–93). All of this was shot and is included among deleted scenes on DVD. Soderbergh in his voiceover commentary says,

> I didn't want people to think that this was going to turn into one of those movies where the protagonist gets terminally ill. . . . It was a tough call because Erin really did get sick and was hospitalized for a while. . . . One thing I miss, though, about these scenes at the hospital: it's really the only time in the movie when the two key men in her life . . . George and Ed, call Erin to task for her inability not to be so confrontational, and they both suggest that this is not always the best thing to do. And I thought this was an important point for somebody in the movie to bring up. . . . Cutting out the illness subplot . . . had an unexpected result. . . . And at the end of the town meeting, as Erin is walking out, she turns to Ed and says 'You did good.' And you feel like they've made up, and that she has—I don't know if 'forgiven' is the right word—but their relationship is back on course. (*Erin Brockovich* DVD)

The result of these cuts is that Erin exercises a freer, more active agency, less dependent upon what men think of her. She appears neither to be melodramatically victimized nor to need men to keep her in line. In the real world Erin's combative behavior probably *would* call for some scolding. As a character in a movie, however, Erin is an appealing identification figure who determines her own course. Since no one can challenge her, Erin/Roberts does dominate easily. Other characters exist, Roger Ebert complained, "only to react to her" ("Julia" 112). In writing Carla Santos Shamberg's "superhero," Grant in her script and Richard LaGravenese in his second-draft revisions took the character in the direction of warts-and-all realism. That approach, as we have seen, can lead to indiscriminate sprawl. The final cut, however, pulls the film back toward the initial concept.

Erin Brockovich is not a victim; she is unclassifiable. Like profanity that when spouted so much sheds its shock value and meaning, Erin's much-discussed exhibitionism loses its meaning as sexual objectification and becomes its opposite—the signifier of an individuality so fierce as to become aggressive. The conflict of the film is really not the discovered fact that PG&E poisoned the groundwater and lied about it. Hitchcock would have tagged that the MacGuffin, and Soderbergh in postmodern fashion treats corporate malfeasance as a given. On the other side, among the "ordinary people," somebody will call it out. Power is essentially corrupt, but people are basically good. This is the engine driving Soderbergh's film. "In truth," writes Brockovich, "it was my identification with the victims—the unglamorous, hard-working, dirt-on-their-hands, clothes-on-the-line, early-to-bed and early-to-rise folks—that helped me understand why in my own life for such a long time it had been so difficult to ever get anyone to listen to me *about anything*" (*Take It* 25). This explains the two sides of herself that she shows to the two sides in the case. She is feisty and manipulative with her boss, Ed Masry, contentious and hostile with his staff, and taunting and contemptuous toward other lawyers. With the victims of the water contamination, however, she is polite, warm, and gentle. She listens, and she knows what questions to ask and, later, how to tell these people the facts about what is happening to them.

The real conflict is between Erin and those who would cast her aside. Thus this is not a conventional social problem drama in which we are to be shocked that a powerful utility for decades knowingly dumped carcinogens into the groundwater around its plant and lied about it, outrageous though that is. Erin is ready to believe the worst of those with power and money, and has a working-class suspicion of those with more education than she. Erin, however, through her commitment to the case, exceeds the widespread assumption of the working class (and often the middle class as well) that a job is just a job, a way of paying the bills and providing for your family, not a calling to a higher purpose. In finding a cause to believe in, and to rally others to, Erin transcends the expectations of her class.

Erin Brockovich herself denies that she is "trash from the wrong side of the tracks. I come from quite an educated family. My dad is an industrial engineer and my mom is an English major specializing in journalism" (brockovich.com). The fact that she needs to defend herself, a couple of years after the release of the film, demonstrates the cultural slippage between "working class" and "low-class trash." It also shows how *Erin Brockovich* takes the class conflicts inherent in Brockovich's story, the points where class becomes conflated with gender, and heightens them. The first page of the second-draft screenplay and the final shooting script introduces the heroine as follows: "ERIN BROCKOVICH. How to describe her? A beauty queen would come to mind—which, in fact, she was. Tall in a mini skirt, legs crossed, tight top, beautiful—but clearly from a social class and geographic orientation whose standards for displaying beauty are not based on subtlety" (Grant *Screenplay* 1). The convoluted tact of that last clause gets the point across gingerly. Erin's version of class, which enables her to bond with the ordinary people of Hinkley, is not reflected in the women she meets there. They wear modest blouses, skirts, slacks, and dresses that could have come off the rack at J. C. Penney. Furthermore, Brockovich's "geographic orientation"—Wichita, Kansas—is not exactly known for va-va-voom fashions. Those are more likely to be tolerated in the city to which Brockovich moved, Los Angeles. It may be more correct to say that Brockovich is in a class by herself, in the tradition of most biopic subjects.

There is plenty of evidence that the film somewhat exaggerates Brockovich's actual class consciousness. Erin asks Ed why he cannot "afford to waste all the time in the world," as PG&E can. To her, an attorney with what's probably a low-six-figure yearly income is in the same bracket with a multi-billion-dollar corporation. When Ed tells Erin that the case is eating up his savings and forcing him to take out a second mortgage on his house, her response is "So?" Her blithe lack of concern seems a bit childish: Daddy will come up with the money somehow, and besides anybody who owns a house, as Erin does not, has to have it made, right?

On the other hand, Ed's personal concerns seem petty to Erin compared to the suffering of the families, and in seeming to make light of Masry's very real struggles and legitimate hesitations, Erin's "So what?" attitude can be read variously: as callousness, or as Erin's being so far off Ed's wavelength as to be practically in a parallel universe, or as Erin's playing the stalwart "stick-to-it-ive-ness" of the conventional *male* biopic subject (as well as of Brockovich herself).

Erin's appearance, mindset, and behavior fairly shout "working class." Abandoned by two husbands, left with three children, catastrophic injuries, and no job, Erin is at the bottom of the socioeconomic ladder as the story begins, victimized on all sides in the *female* biopic tradition. Like Barbara Graham, she is dealt a bad hand by life. Like Graham and Dian Fossey, she is undermined further by her own personality flaws. Her short skirts, low-cut, form-fitting tops, and stiletto heels, along with her potty mouth and brash manner, alienate the workaday world where she spends half her time.

Erin invites facile sexual stereotyping; "you look like someone who has a lot of fun," the film's Ed Masry stammers in trying to explain why he fired her after she didn't come into the office for several days, not understanding that she was beginning her field work. Erin's devastating comeback, "So by that standard, I should assume you never get laid," deconstructs everything his middle-class propriety represses. The film straddles the fence. Is Erin a product of "a class . . . whose standards . . . are not based on subtlety"? Or is she a biopic subject who just is the way she is, fired into indelible life by her own individuality?

Soderbergh puts us on Erin's side throughout. The defendant's attorney in the auto accident suit casts doubt on Erin's claim that "a doctor in a Jaguar" ran a red light and slammed into her car. However, by first showing in an objective camera setup Erin's '83 Sentra hit by a car running a red light at full speed, Soderbergh leaves no doubt that she is stating the truth, however much she is disbelieved. Although there must have been a police report corroborating her version of events, the film omits it, melodramatically making it her word against that of more powerful lawyers and doctors. Amid her conflict with Theresa, the buttoned-up attorney at the firm with which Masry partners on the case, Ed tells Erin, "Just because she dresses like a lawyer doesn't mean she didn't work her ass off in law school and shit positions to earn her way." Erin, not getting the point, can only say, "Well, excuse me for not going to law school," sounding like innumerable male working-class heroes of the Dirty Harry variety. Again, however, Soderbergh keeps us on Erin's side, playing Theresa as a caricature, a nineteenth-century spinster type, her hair pulled back in a severe bun. Thus any chance for a balanced character study of the *I Want to Live!/Star!* type is obliterated. It is not that the film's Erin doesn't have rough edges; it's that they become virtues of the forceful charisma of Erin/Julia. (And if anyone doubts the degree to which the star and biographical subject both intersect and separate, the real Brockovich appears in a cameo as a waitress with the nametag of "Julia.") The film does not make Erin a monster out of unfocused warts-and-all "objectivity." Here at least is a point of view.

Erin's flaws and quirks are in the *male* biopic tradition, as elements that make her special, even endearing. The film does flirt with simplistic role reversal, in the manner of a 1970s "Hollywood feminism" entry like *Norma Rae* (1979). George (Aaron Eckhart), her biker babysitter-boyfriend, suggests that she quit her job; "people do it every day," he says. We know, however, that Erin has no ordinary job; she has found important, life-sustaining

41. Erin (Julia Roberts) peers across the desert at the benign-looking factory in the distance, like the male subject of vision who sees what others disregard, in *Erin Brockovich* (Steven Soderbergh, Universal-Columbia, 2000). Digital frame enlargement.

work. People are counting on her. Erin does not play by the rules, any more than, say, T. E. Lawrence or General Patton. Her fresh perspective has not only enabled her to ask questions about the PG&E case that no one else thought to ask; it has made her genuinely concerned for the people made sick by the utility's policies and outraged by its practices. "Like many modern cinematic histories from Hollywood," observes Robert Brent Toplin, "Steven Soderbergh's film celebrates the superior virtues of the common person" (33). In short, the film harks back to Hagopian's common person as uncommon person.

A passage on the second page of the first draft of the script provides a hint of the direction in which the film would go:

A PARKING TICKET flaps under the wiper of an old Hyundai.
ERIN
Fuck.
Even when she talks dirty, there's a heartland goodness to her voice. Like
    Kansas corn fields swaying in the breeze. (Grant first draft script 2)

This line explains perfectly why the filmmakers went first to Julia Roberts rather than to a brassy sex symbol like Sharon Stone, who might have seemed a closer match to Erin Brockovich physically. It is easy to imagine

Stone in Erin's belligerent scenes, but not as the patient, empathetic woman who listened for hours and years to the victims of chromium poisoning in Hinkley. Roberts had never played an actual person in a biopic before, if one discounts her miscast role as the love interest in *Michael Collins* (1996). Nor had Steven Soderbergh directed a biopic or historical film. But a likable if not beloved actress was needed to depict Brockovich's two sides, her lack of patience for institutional protocols and office *politesse,* her anger toward power structures, and her ease and lack of pretense that enabled the citizens of Hinkley to open up to her. The real Ed Masry, who perhaps doesn't see many movies, told an interviewer, "When I heard Julia Roberts was gonna play Erin, I thought 'This movie is going to be a disaster.' I couldn't imagine Julia Roberts saying 'blow job' and 'f—k.' She's like the Virgin Mary!" (Giles 58). Masry may not have known that Roberts shot to stardom as the prostitute Vivian in *Pretty Woman* (1990), what writer Stephen Schiff called "one of a long line of virgin prostitutes in Hollywood films" ("The Star").

For a few years in the late 1990s and early 2000s, Julia Roberts was the type of star whose smile and charisma break all boundaries. There had not been a female star like Roberts for decades. "In the age of rampant auteurism and CGI FX," wrote Thomas Doherty, "she is a timely reminder of the absolute magnetism certain humans exert from the motion picture screen. Blessed with the elusive 'gene for the screen' as . . . Robert Wise dubbed it, she nourishes audiences by animated visage and magnetic personality alone. . . . How far back must one reach for an actress this illustrious and beloved? Mary Pickford? In the post-classical era, only Barbra Streisand challenges her preeminence, and Streisand's fan base comprises a niche market compared to Roberts's all embracing multitudes" (40).

Roberts's popular persona as a rom-com *farceur,* though with a film reel's worth of mostly failed dramatic roles during the 1990s, finds her signature role as Erin. Roberts is just "off" enough from the real-life Brockovich to make the character mostly likable instead of mostly abrasive, and for the character's foul-mouthed ripostes to sound shocking and unexpected but also funny, like one's friend/sister/girlfriend dressed in trampy outfits for a costume party. The movie's famed cleavage, itself a creation of costume design and plain old "acting," seems almost a put-on and a bit of an embarrassment. One wants to look away, but since the nexus of movie star attraction is the face, especially the eyes, this only intensifies the performance. Roberts has said that she doesn't do nudity because "I just don't feel that my algebra teacher should ever know what my butt looks like" ("Julia Roberts"). And yet in *Erin Brockovich* the algebra teacher is confronted with B-cups that runneth over, even if they are what a shop in Beverly Hills later advertised them to be—the products of a gel-filled pushup bra.

Erin Brockovich is about female bodies and what they mean, much as Julia Roberts's career had been explicitly about the use of the female body, separate from the actress and her talent and personality before the camera. In the wake of the success of *Pretty Woman,* a model named Shelley Michelle disclosed that she was the body double for Roberts, not only in certain key scenes of that film but also Photoshopped with the actress's face on the poster (and there was some degree of gender parity; Richard Gere, graying in life and in the film, was given a computer-enabled dye job for the poster). In a meditation on the body double and the stand-in, Ann Chisholm analyzes the opening scenes of *Pretty Woman,* in which Vivian (Roberts) dresses to go out on the street. Several shots show Vivian's (actually the body double Michelle's) buttocks, legs, and back before we even see the first shot of Julia Roberts's face or a full shot of Roberts in costume as Vivian. "The hyperbolic femininity instantiated by the double's body . . . signals the distance between the performance of the prostitute and the woman. The body of the double, in other words, is the body that first constitutes the gap between the hooker and the heart of gold" (144–145). This restates a description of one of Greta Garbo's doubles: "She has everything that Garbo has except whatever it is that Garbo has. . . . She had everything that Garbo had except the mysterious ingredient that made Greta Garbo" (Chisholm 128). "Thus," writes Hilary Radner, "the composite body that represents the fetish body emblematizes not only its status as fantasy but the self-conscious status of that fantasy for the film viewer, in which the image both simultaneously offers the fantasy and signals its impossibility. Even Julia Roberts is not in and of herself adequate to her own image, which must be created through an excess of bodies. She needs help. Claims one of her doubles: 'Julia was grateful to have someone else make her look good'" (73–74).

Here then is new meaning for the "body too much." The cleavage and the imaginative outfits that showcase it (a number of reviews cited the creative contribution of the costume designer, Jeffrey Kurland) are the most "actorish" gestures ever made by Roberts, an actress mostly known for "playing herself." It is in the category with the false noses and accents assayed by chameleon-like character actors from Laurence Olivier and Charles Laughton to Meryl Streep, Geoffrey Rush, and Cate Blanchett. What's more, by the end of the 1990s, her first complete decade as a major star, Roberts had taken the issues of nudity and the body double into her own hands, making much in her interviews and publicity later in the decade of her refusal to appear nude in her films. *Notting Hill* (1999), in which she plays a movie star much like herself, is a virtual metatext on her stardom. At one point, Anna Scott (Roberts) quotes from her contract the clause concerning nudity and the use of body doubles that one senses is probably from Roberts's actual contracts. A nude body double even passes totally out of focus in front of the camera. In these playful but somehow also deadly serious ways, Roberts turns around the discourse about needing to be "completed" by body doubles and takes control of it.

Furthermore, in playing Erin Brockovich, Roberts embodies a woman who publicly muses about the relation of her body to herself, which is the question over what the body double lacks ("the mysterious ingredient that makes Julia Roberts") and the physical perfection that Roberts supposedly lacks. Brockovich confesses that during her failing second marriage, she had breast implants in order, she says, "to boost my confidence." Later, she writes, "all men seemed to care about was my new, improved cup size. For the first time, this didn't seem like caring at all. Just the opposite, in fact. Ironically, by getting my implants, I had gained a new insight to my own, real worth, or at the time, the lack of it I was feeling" (*Take It* 50). The point for Brockovich is basically "Never judge a book by its cover." "What's inside of us," she writes, "is not as easily or instantly recognizable as what people see on the outside." Thus, she continues, "even after the case was settled, there were many people who naturally assumed . . . that it must have been my hot-cha clothes, big chest, and presumably loose high-heels that had led me to victory" (*Take It* 25).

Not to psychoanalyze Brockovich, but her own "hyperbolic femininity," to reiterate Chisholm, might seem a masquerade in Joan Riviere's original sense, an attempt to cover "masculine" behavior with an appearance that is definitively "feminine." When the film's actions took place (1991–96), however, fashionable femininity was being defined by a then-waning but still popular Victorian fashion and furnishings revival that highlighted lace, frills, and chintz. Brockovich's leather vests, micro-mini-skirts, and spiked heels ruptured this mood like a blast of heavy medal at a chamber music concert. It commanded attention, literally. Instead of an exhibitionism that makes the woman the passive object of the gaze, Brockovich's display puts the beholder, male or female, in an impossible place. One is forced to take note of her appearance, but is condemned if one reacts.

"This was the way I liked to dress," Brockovich writes by way of explanation in *Take It from Me: Life's a Struggle But You Can Win,* her 2002 "memoiriza-tion" of the movie. "It wasn't meant to impress or offend. It wasn't premedi-tated, and certainly it wasn't meant to anger anyone to the point of insult and ridicule. It was something I like to call 'individualism.' If I dressed a differ-ent way, would it make me any smarter?" (74). Of course, schools and busi-nesses have dress codes to guard against excesses of individualism; most re-sponsible parents would not let their teenage daughters go to school dressed like Erin Brockovich. Thus while the film enters Brockovich into myth, and indeed made her one of the best-known American environmental advocates, it is hard to see someone whose behavior is so flawed, if not inexplicable, as "a role model." (After writing this passage, however, I ran across David Edel-stein's original Slate.com review. Comparing the movie to TV's *Ally McBeal* and *Mary Tyler Moore,* Edelstein wrote, "Instead of a hapless woman whose lovable dithering inspires a mix of fatherly, brotherly, and lustful feelings in her male counterparts, why not make America's sweetheart a busting-out firebrand with a lively capacity for outrage and a filthy mouth? There's a role model for *my* daughter." Not having a daughter, I stand corrected.)

More than acting "provocative," as the errant teenager is warned not to be, Brockovich creates a real provocation, a challenge; she turns a "sign of the fetish" into her personal signature, "something I like to call 'individual-ism.'" In contrast, "PG&E's crime," Doherty writes, "is not a violation of civil law but a sin against nature, a rape of the land. Male, scientific rationality has poisoned the nurturing soil, defiling Mother Nature and deforming her off-spring. The tokens of Erin's fecundity ('They're called boobs, Ed') are the breast-plate of an avenging angel, the earthy mother come to banish the despoilers and nurse her children back to health" (41). Rather than signify fragility, debilitating passivity, and helpless exhibitionism, these "tokens of fecundity" denote power, activity, and efficacy. Erin's body is a weapon. It is wielded against those who might marginalize her for her lack of education in general and a law degree in particular. The former beauty queen chal-lenges the world to value her appearance without assuming that she has no brains. Finally, her look might be partly a defense against her learning disability: she is dyslexic, an important detail that the film—in every script draft—omits. In fact, what she calls her "weird combination of photographic memory and dyslexia" is the reason she didn't trust herself to write things down and so memorized files and client cases instead (*Take It* 76). In the film, her ability to reel off the phone numbers, diseases, and other personal circumstances of more than 600 clients comes off as just magical.

As one of the few commercially successful mainstream Hollywood post-1970 biopics to view a woman's leadership in the world as positive and unproblematic, it is no accident that *Erin Brockovich* brings back the female biopic-as-star vehicle, as almost none of the Streep, Spacek, and Lange vehicles of the 1980s did. Virtually every aspect of Julia Roberts's stardom trails her into the film (Giles 59). She brings the idiom of the romantic comedy, her signature genre, into the crusading social problem film, leaving both genres somewhat unrecognizable in the process. The director reportedly kept actress and subject from meeting until midway through filming, when Brockovich's cameo was shot (the real Ed Masry appears in the same scene). This is very unlike other films about living subjects, such as *Coal Miner's Daughter,* for which Spacek literally followed Loretta Lynn around, soaking up her speech patterns, singing style, and mannerisms on- and offstage, or *Raging Bull,* for which Jake LaMotta served as Robert De Niro's boxing trainer and sparring partner. Roberts's Erin can be called an imaginative creation, rather than an imitation, demonstrating the freedom that an actor has when she's playing a person not widely known. The film, as seen from the critical response—and the Academy Award that most assumed to be Roberts's as soon as the film opened, an entire year before the ceremony—is

42. *Erin Brockovich* brings back the female biopic as star vehicle, at least momentarily. With Albert Finney as Ed Masry. Digital frame enlargement.

"about" Julia Roberts's performance, much as *I Want to Live!* is "about" Susan Hayward, or *Funny Girl* is "about" Barbra Streisand.

After the film made Brockovich a celebrity, she began taking a strong public profile. In her appearances and lecture tours since the film, Brockovich, like Paul Rusesabagina, whom Don Cheadle played in *Hotel Rwanda* (2004), casts her film shadow into a parallel universe, less a "body too much" than a complementary body, the actuality on one hand, an artwork on the other. Rusesabagina, whom I heard lecture in November 2005, tells his story so compellingly that the film about him, even with Cheadle's excellent performance, fades. Introduced by Roberts and Cheadle, Brockovich and Rusesabagina take the biopic principle of transcendence a step farther, as they themselves transcend the dramatized images of them, an opportunity that, say, Dian Fossey or Karen Carpenter does not have.

Erin Brockovich, a story of the office "character," a kook, who sees what others don't and becomes a hero, probably is too outlandish not to be played as comedy. When the plot reaches its first turning point, as Erin asks a co-worker why medical records are in with real estate files, the woman snaps, "If you don't know how to do your job by now, I'm not about to do it for you." This sets up Erin as the biopic subject who sees what ordinary people don't, and begins to separate her from the working folk who see what they do at work as just a job. It's also a funny inversion, however, as the fuse that lights a $333 million lawsuit nearly gets thrown away like a wet match.

The filmmakers needed an actress who wouldn't make the character obnoxious, as the real Brockovich may well have been around the office, but also who wouldn't overwhelm the character with too much gravitas and earnestness, as a Meryl Streep or a Jodie Foster might have, and yet wouldn't play Erin as a Goldie Hawn–like flake. Roberts, with a gift for being natural and assertive in front of the camera, creates an Erin Brockovich who parallels the real person. The outrageous Brockovich, a woman who created her own reality, is presented by Roberts as a conscious acting stunt on one level, one that begins to give credence to John Waters's claim that "all stars are female [or male] impersonators," playing exaggerated, heightened versions of sexual identity ("The Star"). One can see the actress's exuberance in biting into such a juicy role, but her Erin is never less than authentic, and on one very important level Roberts was just trying to approximate the character from life. The left-handed actress also played the role right-handed, like the subject, a physical adjustment that received zero attention compared to other regions of the character's anatomy; nonetheless, Roberts's star power is

Erin's. The film, as some press reports noted, may be a rare example whereby the biographical subject is at least as magnetic and glamorous as the movie star playing her. The *Times of London* reported, "For once, Hollywood appears to have downplayed a character on the screen. . . . From the moment that the real Erin Brockovich appeared at the Los Angeles premiere, . . . it became clear that while the on-screen character was lifelike, the off-screen one was larger than life" ("Heroine's").

Similarly, the film downplays Julia Roberts's persona, while hitting almost every single one of its aspects. In an unpublished essay written a couple of years before *Erin Brockovich,* Debra White-Stanley defined the persona of Julia Roberts. White-Stanley found that Roberts often plays an "emotionally abused woman with outbursts of rage. The survivor of a difficult childhood, with a similarly difficult romantic history, she is often betrayed by her father, lover, husband. She doesn't take it 'lying down,' but . . . fights back." Her persona is that of "a working class woman with integrity and spunk. She is often a poor woman trying to work her way up in the world somehow . . . her films tend to portray her as a working person who attains the American Dream, and finds [it] lacking" (2–3). Moreover, *Erin* may be the apotheosis of this persona and also of Roberts's career as an actress. Roberts's "babe appeal," as White-Stanley defined it, which had matured from early films like *Pretty Woman* and *Mystic Pizza* (1988), is nearly caricatured in *Erin.* Her effervescence, likeability, and quite incredible smile make almost whatever Erin says and does more than acceptable. For the other aspects, however, Erin has survived not a difficult childhood, except for being considered "slow" due to her dyslexia—her parents were loving and supportive—but a tortuous adulthood, with two failed marriages by the time she was thirty, leaving her a single mother of three. The twin blows of undereducation and marital failure have left her hurt and angry at the world.

Stepmom (1998), the first of four Julia Roberts films (and box office smashes) within fifteen months, ending with *Erin Brockovich,* takes as its main issue whether Roberts's character is suitable for the mother role. *Erin* is the first film in which she plays a mother. Since the people of Hinkley appeared to regard PG&E, which employed much of the town, almost like a parent, Erin becomes the avenger of these "children" who have been poisoned and deceived by their guardian. Like the majority of characters played by stars in Hollywood films of all eras, Erin is fundamentally a good person who will do what's right and lead others to do the same. What gives the film its sense of realism more than anything is that, like the protagonists of other realistic works, Erin isn't "trying to work her way up in the world somehow," so much as she's trying to survive. Her reward is unsought; like the hero of the most old-fashioned, idealistic biopic imaginable, Erin dreams of justice. And her dream is ongoing, as the last shot shows Erin at the door of the next potential class-action client, continuing the fight. The ending is low-key for a biopic, with Erin's work just beginning.

In this social problem biopic comedy, what Bruce Robbins calls "the health visitor"—the archetypal representative of the welfare state who, like a social worker, intrudes on the private lives of individuals "for their own good"—and the upwardly mobile person who is helped up by the system are uncharacteristically the same person (187). This explains why Erin's charisma is important; the people of Hinkley like her while resisting what she represents. And what she represents are lawyers, which the working folk, like many in the audience, have difficulty separating from the corporation that inexplicably made them prey to disease and death. This explains the heroine's relationship to Ed Masry, a tired hack slouching toward retirement when Erin first meets him. What would conventionally be a mentorship develops instead through love/hate interplay. Erin, the researcher–social worker–saleswoman, must lead the senior partner into action; but because he's the one with the expertise and the law firm, nothing can happen without him. Plus, the collective—those 634 clients—need to be persuaded to take a chance on a procedure—binding arbitration—which sounds like the essence of bureaucratic red tape. All this while negotiating baby-sitting-by-biker and nose-holding cooperation with the snooty lawyers Kurt and Theresa. In a film that, Robbins writes, "does little to invite special critical attention" (187), the heroine comes out alive, well, and better off spiritually, mentally, emotionally, and materially, through her adventures in the public sphere. No small step for a woman in a man's genre.

17

Twenty-First-Century Women

I can understand Marc Pachter's disappointment when he failed to find the "real" Willa Cather living and breathing in the pages of my biography, regretfully observing that "Miss O'Brien has not delivered to us the presence of Willa Cather." But Ms. O'Brien, who was writing from a different set of assumptions about theory, gender, biography, and the self, never intended to deliver the real Willa Cather to the reader.

—SHARON O'BRIEN, "FEMINIST THEORY AND LITERARY BIOGRAPHY"

It's sometimes hard to separate this real person who actually doesn't have much of a voice and now give her this voice in the film.

—GRETCHEN MOL, ON BETTIE PAGE

As we look into the future at the beginning of the twenty-first century's second decade, the prospects for the female biopic are murky. The most bravura film of the 2000s was *La Môme* (American title: *La Vie en Rose*) (2007), a childhood-to-death biopic of the iconic French singer Edith Piaf. *La Môme*, directed by Olivier Dahan, is a French-made movie, of course. The film and the performance by thirty-one-year-old actress Marion Cotillard are tours-de-forces in such a familiar Hollywood mode that Cotillard won the Oscar for Best Actress, despite hers being only the third Oscar-winning non-English-language performance in the eighty years of the Academy Awards and the first in French. The life of Piaf is natural biopic material; had the film been made before the 1990s, the narrative would have slid straight into the downward slope with no way to turn back. With the maturity of the

348

genre, however, Dahan's film extricates triumph out of self-destruction; the film in the end is less about Piaf's own story than about the recent history of French popular culture. Since, in life, Piaf's rich, powerful voice over-came all the abuse and self-destructiveness the "little sparrow" could hurl at herself, Piaf's life lends itself to the neoclassical redemption paradigm epitomized by *Ray* and *Walk the Line*. For French audiences, *La Môme* is a luxuriant wallow in nostalgia for an iconic "Frenchness" that never quite existed. Outside France, Marion Cotillard's performance was singled out for the type of accomplished, fully embodied acting that such films require as a matter of course.

Meanwhile in the United States, the neoclassical biopic revival of the 2000s went on mostly with male subjects. The highly successful *Erin Brock-ovich* cued filmmakers to a new, positive tone in female biopics. Actresses won Oscars for playing strong women in support of male biopic subjects; these included Marcia Gay Harden as Lee Krasner Pollock in *Pollock* (2000), Jennifer Connelly for an all-American rendition of the Salvadoran Alicia Nash in *A Beautiful Mind* (2001), Cate Blanchett channeling Katharine Hep-burn in *The Aviator* (2004), and Reese Witherspoon assaying a level-headed June Carter to counter the erratic Johnny Cash in *Walk the Line* (2005). In 2006 two biopics of infamous women by female directors were released: *The Notorious Bettie Page* by Mary Harron and *Marie Antoinette* by Sofia Cop-pola. Starting with subjects defined by their images—Marie Antoinette, by repute the heartless, heedless queen who loved luxury so much she lost her head over it, and Bettie Page, the model with the sunny expression, even in bondage photos, whose photos from the 1950s remained curiosity items on the Internet fifty years later—these films quietly interrogate the female genre. Bettie Page (1923–2008) qualifies for the Biopic of Someone Unde-serving (BOSUD); Scott Alexander and Larry Karaszewski reveal that they considered writing a script on Page in the 1990s (Alexander and Karaszew-ski *Man* vii). Marie Antoinette, on the other hand, is the type of regal subject favored for the star movie queens of the 1930s and was the subject of an MGM biopic in 1938.

These movies reappropriate the male gaze directed at women. Each of the films posits an iconic female exhibitionist inside a very patriarchal or-der. These are women under glass, objects of a patriarchal gaze that vari-ously ogles them and indicts them. Both movies show the influence of Jane Campion, in that they adhere to an observational realism that stands back and does not intrude on the subject's privacy. While the portrait of Page that emerges is quietly heroic, Coppola's Marie lives an experimental life in the most regimented of circumstances. Both films explore, from a woman's point of view, what it feels like to be looked at, as an object, as a public fixture, and as a significant image. Each of these films wants to return to themselves women who have long belonged to the public.

Harron and Coppola clearly identify with their subjects; because of this, they approach them with respect, careful to find a way to enter their subjectivities without violating them. Thus both films examine the nature of female celebrity and subjectivity in the early twenty-first century. They also deal more consciously, deliberately, and from a feminist point of view with the female biopic. In doing so, they assiduously avoid melodrama, thus raising the question: Once one averts the melodramatic plot structure, the downward trajectory, the aesthetic of victimization, and the male gaze and outside scrutiny, what's left? The question itself is sexist. And yet these films might not feel to most spectators like full-blown biopics. Harron barely ekes ninety minutes out of the story of Bettie Page; Coppola's rendition of *Marie Antoinette* is some forty minutes shorter than the 1938 MGM version. Both films feel so fresh, however, because the filmmakers, working within the framework of the facts, leave the subjects alone, basically, with us, allowing them to discover themselves as we learn about them.

The Notorious Bettie Page: Free Will and God's Will

Mary Harron dares early in her film to use techniques inscribed with the male gaze. The opening sequences are worth looking at in detail. Harron opens her mostly black-and-white film in the mid-1950s with an undercover sting on a Times Square bookstore that sells bondage magazines from behind the counter. Cut to the convening of U.S. Senate subcommittee hearings held at the Federal Courthouse in New York and presided over by Senator Estes Kefauver (David Strathairn) of Tennessee. The hearings focused solely on the effects of "smut" on minors (Salisbury "Senators"). A Catholic priest with an Irish brogue warns that "Communism will never defeat America. . . . Something from within . . . will rot and corrupt it." A contemporary audience may well contemplate the corruption caused by the

43. Amid the slow camera movement up the young woman's body, the film's title appears, its "notorious" tag contradicting the demure appearance of the modest skirt and neatly folded, white-gloved hands (Mary Harron, HBO Films, 2006). Digital frame enlargement.

44. At the top of the camera movement is the sincere and apprehensive beauty of the woman (Gretchen Mol), who is instantly marked as a heroine in the Hollywood tradition. Digital frame enlargement.

priest sex abuse scandals that were occurring and being covered up even in the distant 1950s. Harron cuts to a shot of a woman's foot in black pumps, as the camera proceeds to perform the clichéd tilt up the woman's body, an overbearingly sexist device for introducing an attractive woman, treating her body as territory to be explored. Taking up from the line about "something rotten" within, Harron suggests that femininity is under investigation, and that American official culture and laws must restrain it. This is ground covered, as we've seen, in *I Want to Live!* Indeed, Kefauver's New York hearings took place the same week in early June 1955 that Barbara Graham was executed in California.

Harron's cinematic strategy is to start with the various patriarchal gazes and subjectivities that approach Bettie Page, appropriate those gazes, and return them to Bettie herself. The opening sequence insinuates that Bettie's femininity is officially seen as a threat that must be contained. The gaze implied in the tilt up her body evinces suspicion and investigation as much as it does lust. The tilt begins as the title *The Notorious Bettie Page* appears on the screen contradicted by the demure, decorous woman perched, with perfect posture and white gloves, on a bench in the courthouse foyer. The face at the top of the camera tilt is big-eyed and meltingly beautiful, with an innocent apprehensiveness that leaves no doubt that this is a heroine, in the Hollywood tradition of heroes and heroines as honest, determined, and sincere. There is also an authorial gaze here. The director said in a 2006 interview that "I wasn't interested in her being sexy. I was interested in what it was like to *be* that kind of girl. . . . What is it like to be the object of that much attention or that gaze?" The first several minutes of the film set out these questions and also establish a mystery of Page's life, without that mystery leading to wonderment at "Woman, the dark continent" or asking "What does woman want?" There is a touch of melodrama—the earnest protagonist outmatched by the stone walls and marble corridors of official authority. The spectator might think of Hitchcock's *Notorious* (1946), which also opened with a beautiful woman, under suspicion, waiting at a Federal courthouse.

According to one account, Page waited for sixteen hours before she was dismissed without being called to testify (Hancock 3). Harron punctuates Page's long wait with two flashback sequences. In the first, Bettie takes out a letter from her sister, triggering a flashback to "Nashville 1936." We see thirteen-year-old Bettie in church with her mother and sister. As she looks flirtingly at a boy from her pew, her mother smacks her hand. The preacher asks members of the congregation to come forward to give themselves to Christ. As he leads the people in a hymn, a close-up shows Bettie, clearly moved, singing along with the hymn. Later that day, Bettie and her sister suggestively pose in the front yard for a neighbor boy who takes their pictures with a box camera. As their father calls them into the house, he stops by the stairs. Sexual abuse is intimated when he mutters, slack-mouthed,

"Bettie, wanta see ya. Come on up." Having walked nearly up to the camera, she turns, her head bowed, and ruefully begins to climb the stairs, as seen from a discreet angle.

"In the style of a fifties movie," Harron says, "the worst things would happen off-camera" (*Notorious*). At this point, we see the adult Bettie's face, framed in the circular mirror of her compact. The young policeman at the courthouse, obviously taken with her, brings her coffee and a sandwich and asks if she has a boyfriend or husband to keep her company, obviously interested himself. She replies, no, she's not married and, yes, she'll be all right. As she stirs her drink, the camera looks into the cup, alluding to the long-take close-ups of the cup of coffee in Godard's *2 or 3 choses je sais d'elle* (1967) and the glass of Alka-Seltzer in *Taxi Driver* (1976). This leads to another flashback, back to 1942. Bettie is shown on another bench, this one in a park, reading a speech she is practicing for a debating tournament. Cut to Billy Neal and his friend who see her. A second shot of the two young men shows them in the foreground, talking about Bettie, while she is set deep in the background. This is another conventional male-oriented camera setup, with the female objectified in the shot. A flirtatious shot/reverse shot conversation follows, capped by a return to the master shot of the two men as they walk away, with Billy stating his will: "I'm gonna marry that girl." A return shot to Bettie, smitten, leads to a montage in which Billy does marry Bettie; he goes off to fight in World War II; he returns; and they live in a mill town. They fight, he hits her, and she leaves, as the Patsy Cline recording of the hymn "Life Is Like a Mountain Railway" is heard, providing Bettie with a little traveling music. After the breakup of her marriage, Bettie is alone in Nashville, working for a modeling agency, when she is approached by a young man who invites her to go dancing. In the car with this young man, Bettie realizes that she's being led into a gang rape. Bettie is shown running from this scene in some lonely place, at night. Cut to Patsy Cline and more traveling, this time to New York, where Bettie spends the next eight years and finds, in effect, her fortune.

In its first fifteen minutes *The Notorious Bettie Page* introduces Page as a bondage model who has become an "exhibit" in a U.S. Senate investigation, a young woman from a southern religious background who was abused by her father, was an honors student in high school, was in a bad early marriage, and had a terrible rape experience. All these things are presented less as events in a gathering drama—a cause-and-effect narrative—than as images in a collage. "Nothing makes sense," Harron noted in an interview, referring to the sunny, innocent expressions that shine out from gritty black-and-white photos of the model wearing high-heeled boots and leather corsets and wielding whips, "which is kind of Bettie herself. She doesn't add up as a person. The more you find out about her, every piece of the puzzle just makes it more mysterious" (Harron). Moreover, on the DVD Harron says that "we wanted to find a way to refer to trauma, to damaging things in her past without hammering it," and Gretchen Mol, the actress who plays Bettie, adds, "without making it the sum of who she is," showing, says Harron, "that these things happened but [they don't] define every aspect of her character, her life. Because otherwise the danger is that [the film would suggest] she was abused and therefore she became a pinup model and bondage queen as if it's a direct moral, *a tale of moral downfall*" (*Notorious*, emphasis added). And in her 2006 interview Harron remarked, "I think that if you have [had] those experiences, to be paid a lot of money just to dress up in costumes with a group of friends does not feel like victimization." Harron reiterated later in the DVD commentary that "[Bettie] never was a victim. She always held onto her space somehow." Aware of the generic trap, Harron states that one could say that "awful things happened to [Bettie] and isn't this all a tragic arc? But that doesn't feel like the truth of her story."

Harron's decision to allow strands of Page's life to stay unresolved gives the film a Brechtian quality of acting in episodes rather than in a unitary continuity that can be easily placed and defined. Indeed, Mol has stated that "not having all the answers is integral to being able to play her. Not knowing sometimes how [Bettie] gets from A to B to C" helped her "create the character" (*Notorious*). In a sense, then, Bettie just is. She is held together by the white gloves and the erect posture (early in the film Page is shown trying to perform the classic posture exercise of balancing a book on her head). Harron even said that she cast Mol because she could carry herself with the demure *politesse* of a woman of the 1940s or 1950s, which, again, harkens back to *I Want to Live!* Even "notorious," transgressive women of the time had a formality about them. Mol, in the modeling scenes, could strike the Bettie Page poses with their joy, fun, and spontaneity without slipping into parody or camp. In another hallmark of the BOSUD, the filmmakers re-create the cover of the April 1954 issue of *Nudists and Sunbathers* magazine (on color film yet) or little movies with titles like "Tease-o-Rama" and "Bettie's Clown Dance," as if they are staging the painting of the Sistine Chapel.

This is where, as we've seen, the BOSUDs demand to be seen with the same legitimacy as those on "deserving" subjects. Even *Kinsey* (2004), a film

with obvious parallels to this one, speaks the language of the late 1930s Warner Bros. scientist biopics, although in a context that would have been unheard of for those films. In Harron and co-writer Guinevere Turner's telling,
Bettie's actions make perfect sense to her. "God gave me the talent to pose
for pictures," Bettie says. "I don't know what God thinks of all this." She says
this in a scene with John Willie (Jared Harris), the borderline-sleazy fetish
photographer and cartoonist, with whom she strikes up the film's oddest
friendship. The model and the photographer are engaged in a photo shoot
in which Bettie wears a corset, is bound and gagged, and stands in a spread-
eagle position. The scene encapsulates the film's entire approach. Bettie and
John are in the same room, but they are scarcely having the same conversation. Bettie makes a confession to John as if he were God's representative
(and to Bettie, in a spiritual sense, perhaps everybody is God's representative), telling him that God will show her a sign as to what He thinks about
the posing she does. "If God is unhappy with what I'm doin,' He'll let me
know somehow."

Later in the film, at a party, Bettie is approached by one of her sadomas-
ochistic fans, who asks her to autograph some of her bondage photos. Her
boyfriend, Marvin, presented as an open-minded guy who genuinely cares
for Bettie, sees the bondage magazines for the first time and pronounces
them "disgusting." Bettie, escaping the party, goes out on the street and
stops at a travel agency window displaying her ultimate escape, Miami. From
this point, the film enters its final symmetry. Whereas it was Bettie who had
been approached by her first husband, Billy, by the man who entraps her
into rape, and by the photographer who helps her launch her modeling career, Bettie now does all the approaching and initiating. She comes up to an
attractive young man she sees reading on a bench in Miami, hands him a
camera, and asks him to take her photo; then she asks him out. As Armond,
who will become her second husband, takes her picture, we see through his
point of view as he takes an out-of-focus shot, indicating that for all its idyllic
romance, their relationship will not come into clear focus for either of them
before eventually fading out.

In Miami photo sessions, photographer Bunny Yeager (Sarah Paulson)
tells Bettie that she'll be posing for a new "very tasteful" magazine called
Playboy, which would like to know Bettie's age. Bunny is startled when Bettie tells her she's thirty-two: "No magazine wants a model who's older than
twenty-five." Her modeling colleague Maxie (Cara Seymour) tells Bettie her
own idea for getting out of modeling and setting up a photo studio. "You

can't be a model forever." The film now cuts back to its framing device, Bettie waiting outside the Senate subcommittee hearing. Irving Klaw (Chris Bauer), co-owner with his sister Paula (Lili Taylor) of the photo studio where Bettie models for the bondage photos as well as for more innocuous fare, testifies but takes the Fifth. Bettie then hears the testimony (all of which is taken from the films, transcripts, and press accounts of the hearing) of a man grieving the loss of his son, who died apparently in accidental auto-erotic asphyxiation.

This climax to which the film appears to be building, a confrontation with Senator Kefauver, in actuality did not take place. With no explanation, Page was dismissed without testifying. Thus Bettie is kept outside the law; by not being called to testify she loses the opportunity to speak for herself. The climactic courtroom-scene-that-wasn't may be the chief reason other filmmakers turned down Bettie Page as a biopic subject. Harron's film recalls again Sidney Lumet's axiom; in drama, as opposed to melodrama, the story comes out of the character. Rather than invent a highly charged scene, in which the two Tennesseeans would face each other—the ambitious liberal politician on a moral crusade and the Christian pin-up and bondage model—Harron lets the air go out of Bettie's modeling career, as it did in life. The film displaces the dramatic climax to New Year's Eve 1958–59, when Bettie, bored in her marriage to Armond, walks along a Florida beach, her feet in the water. Through the trees she sees a glowing neon cross; following it, she comes upon a new-fashioned church, enters it, and becomes born again. She presents herself to the preacher to be prayed for and is asked afterward how she felt; she replies that she felt "a liftin' up." This returns us to Bettie's original analogy of acting to being in church; "with all the singin' and preachin' and all, you get lifted up. Up out of yourself. You're taken to another place." In that earlier scene Marvin tells her that the bad luck that prevented her from becoming valedictorian of her high school class and winning the full scholarship to Vanderbilt that came with it was "maybe . . . fate telling you you were meant for something else." "Fate" leads Bettie to the modeling that brings her unlikely immortality, but that takes her ultimately back to God.

The types of inexplicable incongruities that Walter Wanger and Robert Wise had the sense of realism not to try to explain five decades earlier, Harron regards with a nostalgic wonderment. Harron has said that she wanted to make this a film about sex in the 1950s. Bettie is a pioneer in the corner of postwar consumerism having to do with sex; indeed, much of what the filmmakers learned about John Willie, the pornographer who shot many of

Page's bondage photos at Irving and Paula Klaw's studio, came from his correspondence with Alfred Kinsey, on file at the Kinsey Institute, as did Irving Klaw's letters to the sex researcher (*Notorious*). One wonders if, in a film full of fetish paraphernalia, Harron has fetishized the 1950s, by playing Bettie Page as if she were Doris Day—and not the dark Day of *Love Me or Leave Me* but the sunny girl-next-door Day of *On Moonlight Bay* (1951), or the Day of her black-and-white films, such as *Young Man with a Horn* or *Storm Warning* (both 1950). Another incongruity, which makes *The Notorious Bettie Page,* along with Harron's *I Shot Andy Warhol,* the only BOSUD as of this writing with a female subject, is that Mol plays Bettie Page with a sincerity and earnestness worthy of the heroine of a serious 1950s social problem drama.

This is important to the script as written, because Harron and Turner's Bettie Page could be called a Pin-Up and Bondage Queen with a Conscience. What makes a lot of the BOSUDs both absurd and moving, therefore, is that they mesh incongruous elements of the genre. Never has Michael Rogin's reformulation of the idol of consumption ever applied more closely or more ironically than to Bettie Page: "the chosen, not the chooser, the product, not the producer" (*Ronald Reagan* 8). The difference, typical of the BOSUD, is that she is chosen, in a trivial yet undeniable way, to be ahead of her time. In her time she is chosen, by her lights, to follow God, which is to reject the consumerism, however marginal, on which her former career was based. Herein dwells the contradiction that is this subgenre's bread and butter. Like John Ford's *Young Mr. Lincoln,* absurdly but earnestly, she looks for a divine sign. In this light, the film is a postmodern parody of the Alexander and Karaszewski variety. Harron and Mol's Bettie is so sincere, however, that even though she does exactly what she feels, she is never deluded like the male subjects of the BOSUD subgenre.

The filmmakers, most of whom are women, seem fascinated by Page as a woman who made her own way, even made most of the costumes she posed in, did what she wanted, enjoyed herself, and knew when to get out. Also, one of the things that truly did keep the Klaws on safe ground legally is that the bondage scenes never involved men and women, only women together. It apparently never occurred to anyone involved in making these photos that this could carry its own kind of eroticism not directed to males, but it obviously has occurred to these filmmakers; indeed, co-writer Turner, a dark-haired actress who might have played Bettie Page herself, has written, directed, and acted in a number of works of queer cinema, including the pioneering *Go Fish* (1994), for which she was co-writer and lead actress. The

45. Lost in the joy of modeling, Bettie cavorts for the movie camera while Paula and Irving Klaw (Lili Taylor, Chris Bauer) confer about their latest censorship troubles. Digital frame enlargement.

film feels like not only a feminist reappropriation of Bettie's joy in her own performing, but a queering of images ostensibly intended for a heterosexual male gaze. She doesn't belong to that, the film says, restoring Page to herself and to women.

Bettie is her own agent, makes her way from setbacks on her own, and has no need of a man to make decisions for her. Near the end, after the Kefauver hearings, she decides not to go away with her New York boyfriend, Marvin, who represents her failure to become an actress and her double life (as "respectable" girlfriend and "notorious" bondage queen). Instead she makes for her "heaven on earth," Miami Beach. Unlike the classic male subject, however, Bettie is not led by a vision, but she trusts her instincts and she trusts God, flatly telling a man who recognizes her at the end of the film that "God doesn't want me to pose anymore." Of Bettie's last scene, in which she preaches the Gospel to passersby in the park, Harron says, "We wanted to end on that moment where she had found her transcendence" (*Notorious*).

The Notorious Bettie Page is actually a wonderful example of artists who have transformed the point of view of their subject into their own. This spirit keeps the film's situations sometimes incongruous but never ridiculous; Bettie is a *hero,* a person of integrity no matter what happens to her. Indeed, Bettie is so good-hearted and enlightened as to be almost beyond belief. Bettie, walking along the beach at Coney Island in 1950, is asked if she is a model and if she would be willing to pose for photos by a man who identifies himself as Jerry Tibbs (Kevin Carroll), an off-duty policeman whose hobby is photography—and who happens to be African American. A crowd gathers and Tibbs advises Bettie that people are getting antsy at the sight of a black man photographing a white woman and that perhaps they should use his studio. Bettie lectures the crowd. "They're just prejudiced. I used to be when I was younger. But I grew up and I learned better." This is by all accounts an actual incident, which launched Page's modeling career in New York, more evidence that often there are events in actuality that fiction writers couldn't make up—because they fail to jibe with our accepted versions of history and of actuality.

Bettie's ambition to be an actress is never realized. In her acting classes with Herbert Berghof (Austin Pendleton) she becomes stiff and self-conscious. Harron contrasts Bettie's inability to relax and reveal truth in acting with her modeling, where she can be herself, free and creative. She finds the play, her inner child, in modeling, even when nude, which in the 1950s is the definitive illegality. She can't have fun with her acting, so she fails at it.

Taking the point of view of the insiders in this small "nudie photography" life of the 1950s, therefore, the filmmakers portray an upside-down world. Irving and Paula can't understand why they should be accused of indecency when the *New York Times* runs shots from productions of *The Taming of the Shrew* and *Kiss Me Kate* depicting spanking and whipping. Later generations of feminists would see the misogyny and exploitation in much mainstream imagery, making Irving Klaw, in the ironic manner of the BOSUD, a prophet. Bettie's "insider" world is freeing and empowering for her, with most of the important photographers, especially Paula Klaw and Bunny Yeager, being women. The "legitimate" world, on the other hand, offers mostly exploitation. A screen test with a Hollywood film company is a disaster; Bettie is given no direction by a curt and impatient director whose one instruction is a repeated "Look at me with your beautiful eyes," the last phrase snapping out like an insult. The producer, interested in a casting couch session, follows Bettie out of the test and all but propositions her. Just before Page makes her decision to leave New York for good, a casting director watches Bettie read, awkwardly, for a role in a play. Following his perfunctory "not bad at all," he says, "Thanks for coming in. It's quite a treat to meet 'the notorious Bettie Page.'" Bettie's "reputation," with everything that word still connoted in the 1950s, is thrown back at her the way Ransom Stoddard is reminded that he'll never escape his rep as "the man who shot Liberty Valance" in the last line of John Ford's elegiac western. Bettie skulks off the stage like an aging gunfighter at the end of the frontier, knowing there's no future in life as she has been living it.

The film never judges Bettie, although opportunities for judgment are everywhere. Her southern evangelical religion, such a ripe target of ridicule in the media, is played absolutely straight because it's meaningful to Bettie. One might also expect condemnations of pornography from a film made by feminists. These do not materialize (or when they do, they're from male members of the "straight" world like Marvin, or official moral watchdogs like Kefauver). The film takes the tack of feminists such as Linda Williams and Constance Penley who attempt to look at porn from the woman's side. Thus, Bettie receives what she takes as a series of signs from God. Marvin discovers the bondage magazines and the evidence of the "fan base" (represented in the film as furtive arrested adolescent males, although a "boyish" woman is among the members of the "camera club" who pay to take pictures of the pin-up models, whether there is film in the camera or not). She is apparently disturbed by the testimony she hears (through the doors) at the Kefauver hearings. She chooses eventually to turn her life over to God. There is a logic that we must go along with simply because it is Bettie's.

Bettie never has a recognition, as it were. She is made to see that the pictures she poses for might be harmful, because the society of her era says it is. When she moves from modeling to evangelizing, it makes sense to her within the worldview she has always had. Jake LaMotta doesn't clearly recognize that he is a brute, Ed Wood doesn't realize that he is not a director the equal of Orson Welles, and Bob Crane can't understand that his addiction to sex and videotape is about to kill him. Similarly, Bettie doesn't move beyond her worldview, in which posing and praying had also coexisted. But at least she is grounded by her faith, even as she is "lifted up." Thus her self-possession is genuine, whereas for the men of the BOSUD subgenre, it is only a part of their act.

In Harron's film the biopic validation is private. Paula, in the midst of burning negatives and films after the Klaw's photography business has been shut down, saves choice little bits from the bonfire. She holds up an 8-millimeter film reel. As we see it from her point of view, the film leaves its black-and-white milieu—a fifties urban movie universe that calls up films from *Marty* (1955) and *Killer's Kiss* (1955) to *Sweet Smell of Success* (1957) and even *I Want to Live!* It goes to color heaven, where the charming, happy Bettie dances and cavorts. It's a quiet transcendence in which the young model revels forever in her own *jouissance,* free from worries about what others may do with or make of her work.

Marie Antoinette: The Female Biopic Gets the Guillotine

Following the Columbia Lady logo and titles that seem to go more with another sequel to *Charlie's Angels* (2000) than to *Marie Antoinette* (2006), Marie herself looks out at us. Out of time but in her place, the queen of France, as embodied by Kirsten Dunst, reclines, dipping her finger into an exquisite cake at one end of the shot and receiving a pedicure at the other. She turns and looks directly out at us as if to say, What?

What? indeed. "Ah. This is the life!"? or "Look at what a decadent, callous ditz I am, too pampered and sugar-buzzed to know that my head will land in a wicker basket"? Or is she just saying, "This is my life . . ."? What *can* she say?

That's a question too. Sofia Coppola structures her historical biopic as a

46. The queen (Kirsten Dunst), in all her luxuriousness, confronts the spectator's gaze in the first shot of Sofia Coppola's *Marie Antoinette* (Columbia, 2006). Digital frame enlargement.

string of questions—Who am I now? What am I supposed to be? What if I can't produce an heir? What if my husband, born to be king, won't have sex with me? What if the people hate me, an extravagant foreign queen in the midst of a famine?

Kings may be born, but in the eighteenth century queens are both born and made. Thus Marie, while born to her position, also has to learn it; and she has to learn to rule, to occupy power in a new nationality and language. Marie has some answers too: I like to have fun; I like to order up new clothes and shoes, eat delicacies, drink champagne, and throw card parties. In the first half of the film, Coppola jolts the audience each time Marie so much as forms a declarative sentence. When, following her introduction to her morning ritual, in which the highest-ranking female courtier present has the honor to dress the Dauphine of France, Her Highness waits, naked and freezing, for the pecking order to sort itself out. To no one in particular, she reasonably comments, "This is ridiculous."

That statement appears as an earth-shaking affront to protocol, except that protocol is having none of it, continuing on its oblivious way. Marie is a little bird in the most grandiose and opulent cage. The bird speaks, but her voice is just a chirp in history's din. Marie's story is a pointed object lesson in what a target a woman can become when placed on too elevated a pedestal. While the person on the street can probably tell you that Marie Antoinette was the heartless queen who was beheaded for saying "Let them eat cake," Coppola, who wrote and directed, identifies Marie herself with cake. "She looks like a little piece of cake," gossips one courtier to another. Cake is an inessential but delectable commodity; it's the most decorative of food items. The adjectives applied to cake are also those sometimes applied to women: dainty, luscious, scrumptious.

Reviews of *Marie Antoinette* have emphasized the autobiographical nature of Sofia Coppola's foray into the historical biopic. This film, however, is no less autobiographical or, better still, personal than Coppola's earlier films, *The Virgin Suicides* (1999) and *Lost in Translation* (2003). Each of Coppola's films has been about young women, treated like little girls, who are enclosed in, look out of, and are looked in upon towers, structures built for them out of their social and cultural position, but also controlled to an extent by them. In short, patriarchy—with the large participation of a matriarchy of sorts too—may build the chamber, but the woman who dwells in it decorates it, inhabits it, makes it hers, even makes it *her*—an extension of herself. If she pays a price for the latter, this is not to say that she is victimized. She makes her choice in a situation that offers little choice. In two of the three films—the two that star Kristen Dunst—the heroine dies a death that is desired, caused, and lingered over by the larger world—or is it? These heroines are damned no matter what they do, but in their deaths, which always happen offscreen, they've found their own kind of redemption.

Marie Antoinette was featured by Hollywood in a 1938 MGM extravaganza, directed by W. S. Van Dyke, an attempt to make a lavish, sophisticated Irving Thalberg–style costume drama without Thalberg, who died in 1936, and with Thalberg's widow, Norma Shearer, still one of the greatest stars on Metro's lot. Based in this film on Stefan Zweig's 1932 Freudian biography of the ill-starred queen, the MGM film presents Shearer as a tragic figure, with 158 minutes' worth of opportunities to suffer radiantly. However, the Production Code–era film is unable to explore the failure of Louis Capei (Robert Morley)—eventually Louis XVI—and Marie to consummate their marriage for the first seven years. The movie plays up Marie's illicit relationship with Count Fersen of Sweden, played by young heartthrob Tyrone Power, but cannot truly deal with it either. Metro was reluctant in any event to cast many shadows on the virtue of one of its divas. These factors all doom the film to overproduced confusion. Shearer, at thirty-six, is a generation older than Marie, who was fourteen when she was sent to France to marry Louis. The actress lurches with the script from disillusionment, to wanton gaiety, to devoted wifedom, to wronged target of impoverished masses who look like figures in Pare Lorentz's Depression-era documentaries, to horrified and finally accepting victim of the guillotine. Much of this revolving-door characterization comes from the difficulties over the years separating out truth from myth in Marie Antoinette's life. A screenplay from most periods of film history would play like a debate among differing accounts of the Revolution.

Both films, of the 1930s and the 2000s, avoid portraying Marie as merely an unhappy wife in a dull marriage who finds excitement in the arms of a dashing soldier and diplomat—the MGM film, for reasons of the Code, the star system, and the aspirations of the prestige picture; Coppola's film because the truth is complicated and difficult to ascertain. Coppola finally grants the marriage of Louis and Marie some mystery, but also some kind of bond and accommodation. Marie Antoinette is a subject who seems camera-ready for all the conventions of the female biopic, from the apolitical, clueless woman who heedlessly spends the royalty into the ground, to the victim of court intrigue and national politics who helplessly finds herself in that always-irreversible downward spiral. Antonia Fraser, on whose 2001 biography, *Marie Antoinette: The Journey*, Coppola's film is based, writes that through "satire, libel, and rumour, Marie Antoinette had become dehumanized" (295). A conventional female biopic would drag the spectator through that process of dehumanization. A more thoughtfully sympathetic film would ask, who was this human being, and what was it like to be her? Thus Coppola looks out at the world from Marie's vantage point, rather than peer in on her through society's lens. She also creates Marie's ultra-isolated, ordered life at Versailles as an extreme version of the feminine domestic sphere.

Coppola's filmic influences here are readily apparent. They include the punk anachronisms of Alex Cox's colonialist biopic *Walker* (1987), Stanley Kubrick's meditation on the relation between eighteenth-century life and art in *Barry Lyndon* (1975), and Baz Luhrmann's use of contemporary music to make the past accessible in *Moulin Rouge!* (2001). The most salient influence, however, is a great anomaly of the studio era, *The Scarlet Empress* (1934), Josef von Sternberg's fantasm of Catherine the Great by way of Alice Through the Looking Glass, with the Archduke Peter by way of Harpo Marx, and the Mother Empress Catherine by way of Mae West and Marie Dressler. Sternberg's film seems a fabulous version of the comic trope, popular in the twenties and thirties, whereby the star comedian falls asleep and dreams he's a figure out of literature or history, from Buster Keaton's *Sherlock Jr.* (1924) to Eddie Cantor waking up in Ancient Rome in *Roman Scandals* (1933). The French Revolution musical that Cosmo Brown (Donald O'Connor) proposes in *Singin' in the Rain* (1952), "The Dancing Cavalier," features a "young hoofer in a Broadway show" who is backstage when a sandbag falls on his head, causing him to dream he's in Marie Antoinette's court. This old chestnut is also reconverted into a premise of Coppola's film.

Sternberg works his historical fantasy as his latest set of variations on the theme that was Marlene Dietrich. In his concept, an Austrian innocent is spirited away to a foreign country to marry an heir to the throne who has no interest in her. There she is subjected to the intrigues and dangers of a foreign court, until, changed by childbirth, she undergoes a metamorphosis (Sternberg suggests this literally through webs and wisps of gauze and other cocoonlike imagery) and emerges a strong queenly woman with her own commanding identity.

Sofia Coppola effects a similar narrative structure for *Marie Antoinette*. Coppola cuts down Fraser's biography, which receives a "based on" credit, to a bare-bones structure, beginning with the exchange of Marie from Austria to France. In what is referred to in film and book as "the handover," Marie is stripped naked and forced to give up even her little dog Mops by the Mistress of the Household, played by Judy Davis with oppressive obsequiousness. As with *The Scarlet Empress*, the first half of the story is marked by the innocent young Dauphine's realization that her marriage might never be consummated. While Archduke Peter has a mistress and is not interested in Catherine, young Louis, played by Jason Schwartzman, is not interested in sex for reasons that have no explanation in life or in film.

Coppola's film is a bold oil-and-water amalgam of realism and fantasy. It is a stark combination—anachronistic music and incongruous casting held up against rigorously realistic visual elements. Coppola shoots in the actual Versailles. The cinematography by Lance Acord favors natural light, candlelight, and a realistic look. The visual approach is objective, the narrative short on motivation and explanation. Kirsten Dunst told an interviewer that Coppola's film "looks like a girl fell asleep dreaming she was Marie Antoinette." While the film dwells visually in reality, with characters often remarking on the physical condition of themselves and others, the sound track and the casting seem wish fulfillments of the "girl who fell asleep." Former child actress Dunst was twenty-two when the film was made, but could look younger yet. She had never before had to appear to grow as old as thirty-four, Marie Antoinette's age at the royal family's flight from Versailles, which is when the film ends, four years before Marie was put to death. The film could rightly have been called "Marie Antoinette at Versailles," for her life there is Coppola's concern. Therefore, Marie continually looks like a young woman trying to grow into the role of queen, and succeeding after her own fashion; it is not her fault, as Coppola would have it, that the French monarchy became a hopelessly useless institution; nor that she became the scapegoat for its collapse.

The song "Natural's Not in It" by the Gang of Four, heard over the first shot, expounds upon "the problem of leisure; what do you do for pleasure?" Coppola adopts the *Moulin Rouge!* approach to film music, using familiar contemporary songs in order to make history "accessible" to today's young audiences. However, Coppola's film is much less rhetorical and more personal than Luhrmann's. It expresses the young queen's joy, her abandon, and her desire to indulge. The casting fills the French court with personages who might have been picked by a young indie-film fan in the mid-2000s: Marianne Faithfull as Maria Teresa, Shirley Henderson (*Topsy Turvy*) and

Molly Shannon as a pair of chatty duchesses, Rip Torn as the jowly old king, Steve Coogan as the Austrian ambassador. Coppola's authorial unconscious shows through in the casting of Jason Schwartzman as Louis (who wants to stage conjugal relations with one's own cousin, no matter how inbred royals may have been?), and in the use of fellow scions Tony Huston as Emperor Joseph of Austria, Asia Argento as Madame du Barry, and Natasha Fraser-Cavassoni, the daughter of Antonia Fraser and the author of a well-received 2003 biography of Sam Spiegel, no less, as an apparently fictional countess. The sound track frequently resembles that of an Altman film, with characters chattering about everyday things like how muddy the ground is or how tight their shoes are in the midst of "historical" events, undermining their supposed momentousness.

Marie's indistinct irresponsibility in the first half, which is matched by Louis's preference for hunting and locksmithing over his "responsibility" to produce an heir, is met in the second half by a sense of personal discovery. Marie starts to define herself, though remaining in a place where she is defined by others. Coppola sees Kirsten Dunst as a pretty *tabula rasa;* there is a tradition of directors who repeatedly worked with certain actors, treating them as blanks on which to project their own preoccupations. Examples are Sternberg/Dietrich, Antonioni/Vitti, and Leone/Eastwood. Coppola wants to assert the humanity—and a certain integrity and strength—inside Dunst's girl-woman prettiness-as-object. Dunst projects an inner sense of fun, matching the impression of the young Chateaubriand that here was a queen "delighted with life" (Fraser 281). The film is an impressionist painting of passive, clueless bewilderment, but also of innocent, impetuous pleasure. Marie's little enjoyments, accompanied by joyous girl group tunes like "I Want Candy," are not played according to melodramatic convention— that is, in a way that portends some disjunction that will violently break the mood.

Marie, like Sternberg's Catherine, has formed, following her metamorphosis, a certain strength of character, a resolve, and a sense of responsibility. Marie's trajectory is not downward; she can't help it if the ground shifts underneath her. This is surely a reason Coppola ends the film with Marie and Louis being led away from Versailles for the final time, rather than with scenes of prison, trials, and executions. Coppola doesn't want to dwell on the punishment of a woman she doesn't see even as a victim of circumstances. The film is not interested in political downfall, or any kind of decline. Antonia Fraser wrote at the end of her book:

Compared to [the] lurid picture of an evil, manipulative, foreign wife, the real substance of Marie Antoinette became as a mere shadow. Having looked without passion at the extraordinary journey that was her life, one is drawn to the conclusion that her weaknesses, although manifest, were of trivial worth in the balance of her misfortune. Ill-luck dogged her from her first moment in France, the unwanted and inadequate ambassadress from a great power, the rejected girl-wife, until the end, when she was the scapegoat for the monarchy's failure. (458)

Coppola wants to know what it is to *be* Marie Antoinette, cossetted by tradition and ritual. Much of the intrigue of the actual events is gone, as if surgically removed. Just as Coppola does not punish Marie, she also does not turn her into a melodramatic figure swept up by events. The MGM biopic seized upon opportunities for drama in such events as the Diamond Necklace Affair, a scandal in which scam artists took advantage of Marie's public reputation for extravagance. The 1938 film played as the villain and Marie's nemesis le duc d'Orléans, a courtier who turned radical and used his fortune to agitate against the monarchy. He was played by Joseph Schildkraut, an actor often cast as sneering scoundrels. Orléans is not in Coppola's film and neither is the necklace. As with Campion's and Harron's films, the conflict is not with any individual but with a system, a social structure and cultural climate.

As with *An Angel at My Table* and *The Notorious Bettie Page, Marie Antoinette,* above all else, avoids melodrama. Campion's and Harron's films are marked, as we have seen, by a matter-of-fact realism combined with a close identification with the protagonist. They are structured so as to underline the subject's heroism and to make her individual subjectivity will out against the sorts of forces that usually drag the female biopic subject down. Coppola has similar aims, although the structure of her film is looser and more eccentric. Indeed, its narrative may seem unbalanced and misshapen. In a 116-minute film (not counting end titles), Louis is crowned at the 67-minute mark; the consummation of the marriage—the plot's turning point—and the birth of the first child, Marie Thérèse—take place at 77 minutes; the affair with Count Fersen at 89 minutes; and the storming of the Bastille (offscreen) at 106 minutes. In short, Coppola is uninterested in the usual sense of proportion between historical time and film time. Out of Marie Antoinette's twenty-one years in Versailles, the first eight take two-thirds of the film. Very clearly what Coppola is concerned with are not events but Marie Antoinette's experience, as imagined artistically in a very personal way.

From black screen credits, we see Marie literally in the lap of luxury; she stops what she's doing and looks out at us, then returns to her luxuriating. The film returns to the black credits and comes out of them when curtains are drawn with a flourish. We see a girl, recognizably Kirsten Dunst, awaken, followed by a straight cut to the exterior of the Austrian palace. The girl, her blonde hair loose, is seen from behind in a flowing dressing gown, padding drowsily down the halls of the palace. Thus the blackness and the sudden waking give credence to the notion that this could be a "girl dreaming that she wakes up and she's Marie Antoinette."

Coppola takes the condescending notion that studio-era films presented a shopgirl's idea of history and appropriates it. In his treatise on the biopics of the 1930s, Kevin Hagopian refers to a lecture given by historian Charles Beard in 1934 in which he proposed the concept of presentism in the presentation of history. "History would be a chronicle of the past whose stance and purpose in the present would determine the way that past was narrated" (182). The "presentism" of *Marie Antoinette* lies in taking not the "eternal feminine" ideal in the fantasias created by transplanted Europeans in Hollywood such as Sternberg, Mamoulian, and Salka Viertel, but an early twenty-first-century notion of the "average girl"—or perhaps even the *Playboy* consumerist ideal of the "girl next door" as marketed not just to men but to women as a self-image. Coppola inserts this archetype into a place where her consumerist-fed longings coexist with a tough geopolitical environment, where public and private are actually confused with each other, as they are in monarchy. The archetype's goodness and acquired "coping skills" give her some chance at survival, at least for a while. Coppola, however, sidesteps the issue of class. The suffering of the starry queens of the studio-era films obscured the characters' class advantages, often because the characters fell from or gave up their positions (*Queen Christina, Mary of Scotland, Marie Antoinette*), were corrupt (*The Scarlet Empress*), or held their power at the expense of personal happiness (*The Private Lives of Elizabeth and Essex*). In Coppola's vision gender trumps class as well as politics.

Coppola posits her protagonist as a postmodernist stick figure, like the cut-out of the girl in a paper doll set before the clothes are put on. It is more complicated than this; I've written elsewhere about Kubrick's use of starring male lead types as the minimalist nub of what those types classically are made to represent (Bingham 253). As Tania Modleski refers to Judy in *Vertigo*, before she is remade by Scottie as "the original woman," so Coppola's young Antoine is "the original girl" before she is remade by the foreign power that will turn her into its queen (98). Her entrance to France takes place in an ornate tent situated on the country's border with Austria. "It is a custom that the bride retain nothing belonging to a foreign court," she is told. Ritualistically, she is born again and remade, emerging as the Dauphine of France. Marie, despite having visibly just come through a metamorphosis, appears indeed to have a stronger sense of protocol than the born-to-the-realm Dauphin of France. Louis Capei, as played by Schwartzman, seems a disappointment to Marie, who had spent much of her carriage trip to France toying with a cameo of Louis's painting, seemingly more out of boredom than anticipation. This isn't made clear, however, Coppola's style being much more realistically laissez-faire than Sternberg's Expressionism. Marie, Coppola never forgets, is not completely a naïve young thing; she was raised to make a foreign marriage, and is frequently reminded in letters from her mother how much more successful Antoine's sisters, married off to other heads of state, are at their marriages (that is, they are bearing heirs).

Marie Antoinette begins like a teen movie that turns into a coming-of-age story. On the trip to France, fourteen-year-old Princess Antoine of Austria gazes out the window, framed in a gilt window/cameo, reminiscent of images of the dreamer, such as Maya Deren in *Meshes of the Afternoon* (1943). Like a child, she asks, "Are we there yet?" As Sternberg did, Coppola consistently drops such anachronisms into the dialogue, not only as an absurdist jolt from the period setting, but as a reminder of how artificial are our "movie" ideas of how members of royalty spoke to one another almost 250 years ago, and how, as this director knows, authentic speech is likely to be "lost in translation." "She looks like a child," a gossip whispers. In Marie's impromptu tour of her quarters in Versailles, she peers in shyly, as a child would. Upon her arrival, Louis XV (Rip Torn), the "grandfather-king," played as a leering old goat, asks, "How's her bosom?" adding, "It's the first thing I look at." The question necessarily makes that part of Marie's anatomy the spectator's focal point, but given that it comes from a man who is at least old enough to be Marie's grandfather, we are apt to want to look away. Thus the satisfied look on the king's face after he greets Marie with a downward glance speaks not so much to a prurient interest but to Marie's purpose, which is to "produce an heir to our throne." The king's utterance of "*our* throne" instead of the more usual "*the* throne" bluntly states the expectation, making it sound parochial and emphasizing Marie's outsider position. After the cardinal blesses the bed and couple and the king pronounces "Good luck, and good work," the curtains around the bed are closed, ending the first chapter that had begun with Antoine's first awakening.

Thus *Marie Antoinette* lightly deflects the object of the gaze that the protagonists of female biopics constitute for onlookers. Coppola pinpoints early the public/private dichotomy at the heart of the biopic genre. The early scenes at Versailles underline the contrast between Marie's curious wonderment at the surroundings, as she looks about the palace and the grounds as a tourist would, and the court scenes in which she is the object of a curiosity far more cynical and shallow than her own. Most of the film is shot in the open form of realism, with the exception of montages showing Marie's consumption of pastries and champagne, as well as her enjoyment of female friendship, an aspect of Marie's life that the film goes out of its way to emphasize. Coppola's style of realism upends several of the conventions of the historical form, among them the expectation of literate and witty dialogue. The characters, contrary to film convention, are as banal and even as dull as their actual counterparts may well have been. The film is sometimes more in the style of Neorealist historical films, such as *The Gospel According to St. Matthew* (1964) and *The Rise of Louis XIV* (1966), closer to Rossellini than to Thalberg; it also shows the influence of Kubrick's *Barry Lyndon* (1975), set during the same period. Marie, an inveterate gambler, is just the sort of courtier who would have been bested at the card table and charmed, though probably not seduced, by Barry, the gentleman cardsharp.

The casting is the film's most eccentric element. Compared even to most other postmodern films, the characters in *Marie* seem much less embodied; Nicole Kidman, Ewan McGregor, and Jim Broadbent fill out their roles in *Moulin Rouge!* just as fully as the cast of any classical musical one could name, only with more self-consciousness. Coppola's casting, on the other hand, can best be called abstract, with the actors suggesting their roles rather than enacting them. The director has always tended toward off-casting, especially of her male characters. It's surprising to see the usually acerbic James Woods, for example, as the rather bumbling schoolteacher-father in *The Virgin Suicides*, and yet because Woods often projects a knife-like wit and potency, the goodhearted but deflated character he plays for Coppola feels poignantly ordinary and real. Similarly, in *Lost in Translation* Bill Murray seems a bit off from the action film star his character is supposed to have been. Coppola, who grew up around movie actors, creates a "body too much" phenomenon around a fictional character. Bill Murray is not Bruce Willis or Sylvester Stallone, and thus the character is both funnier and sadder than if Coppola had cast an actor who better fit the type. Here her casting exposes the essential silliness of casting contemporary American and British actors as foreign-language characters—the way Hollywood always has. Rip Torn looks no more ridiculous playing Louis XV than John Barrymore was in the 1938 film, less so, in fact. Barrymore's walk, especially, is so distinctive that when the king descends from his throne, he is distractingly John Barrymore, not the king of France.

Coppola's is an imagining, in terms of twenty-first-century American popular culture, of who in the current casting directories might resemble members of the Bourbon court. The director exposes the artificiality of casting actors who present an idea of history or a place called history. Coppola's approach is like *Marie Antoinette* as illustrated by Al Hirschfeld. It's not exactly Brechtian; Schwartzman does not remind me of every monarch I've ever read about. On the other hand, when Schwartzman in his flat Californian voice blandly speaks a line like "Very well. Send funds to America," the effect is distancing but also provocative. Americans, who often think of the French Revolution as taking place in concert with ours, are made to think about the contradictions of the failing monarchy in France losing popularity with its citizens for sinking money into the American Revolution.

It is up to Marie to make conversation with her husband, who remains aloof. When the court stops muttering about the infamous du Barry, the king's mistress, it turns to Marie. "I think she's delightful," says one. "She looks like a little piece of cake." The film loses little time in getting to the immediate conflict, what Marie's mother in a voiceover calls "your failure to inspire sexual passion in your husband." Coppola plays this "failure" as somewhat absurd, given the stolidity of the love object, Louis. It seems that Coppola directed Schwartzman to act dim, listless, and clueless in order to cast a contemporary gaze on royalty as dull (Louis's only interests in life appear to be hunting and making keys). Matters of state hang on the tiniest of social nuances, such as Dauphine Marie's behavior as she passes Madame du Barry in the hallways. The morning wake-up routine takes on the quality of repetition captured by Chantal Akerman in *Jeanne Dielman, 23 Quai du Commerce, 1080 Bruxelles* (1975), as any small deviation appears a rupture in an unchanging routine. (Perhaps, however, considering that Coppola had just previously worked with Murray, a better comparison is to *Groundhog Day* [1993].) While breakdowns in routine in Akerman's film lead to a violent revolt of a personal nature, in Coppola's they amount to small declarations of personality.

Marie finds that affairs of state and the everyday "girl stuff" of picking out shoes and clothes and listening to court gossip do not mix easily. In one scene she tries on outfits while Austrian Ambassador Mercy (Coogan) tries to get through to her about a crisis in which France and Austria find themselves on opposite sides of a power grab involving Poland. While she appears the "silly female"—telling Mercy she hadn't read the brief and asking if he likes a dress with or without ruffles on the sleeves—when he forces her to focus, she shows that she more than understands, intelligently asking, "Where will I be if there's a rupture between our two families? Am I to be Austrian or the Dauphine of France?" Marie often is amused by what goes on, as when a doctor trying to figure why Louis is not interested in sex asks him, "What do you have for breakfast?" Marie eventually seems to bear the burden of every mother-daughter conflict that ever was, as her mother writes, "Everything depends on the wife, if she is willing and sweet." Coppola juxtaposes the voiceover to a shot of Marie pressed against ornate wallpaper and sinking to the floor as she reads Maria Teresa's letter. Marie's travails are all the sadder given what we know historically of the ultimately moot issue of an heir. Again, however, the film observes Marie's small victories and does not dwell on her as a tragic heroine, deviating even from Fraser in this respect.

In yet another crossing of the biopic with a different genre, Coppola makes an unabashed "chick flick" out of the Marie Antoinette story. It is one, however, in which the protagonist, out of the patriarchal birdcage in

47. At Le Petit Trianon, her country hideaway, Marie finds privacy, away from the clamor of Versailles. Digital frame enlargement.

48. "Let them eat cake," burbles a garish-looking Marie in a tabloid-like shot that summarizes all the slander and gossip that increasingly composed the public image of Marie. Digital frame enlargement.

which she's been locked, finds her own way only to be defined and mocked every step of the way, finally fatally so. However, Coppola does not spend the film in foreboding of the royal couple's tragic destiny, but rather shows Marie coming into her own as best she can given her station. In Le Petit Trianon, the cottage which was the queen's own hideaway near Versailles, she could shuck off the jewelry, wear comfortable clothes, and find a chance to discover a self beyond the role she is required to play.

After the episode with Fersen, Coppola finally shows what has been going on beyond Marie. How can she, pampered as a royal, be expected to know what the real people experience? Starvation and uprising lurk away from Versailles, but they reach there eventually. This is indicated by sound over a long shot of the stately grounds of Versailles, pointing out just how isolated the king and queen are from the country. When she says, "Let them eat cake" (which she didn't actually say), she's in garish black-red lipstick, soaking in a bathtub, with bleached-blonde hair swept up in a Marilyn Monroe–like wave. Most significant, she's wearing the notorious Diamond Necklace (we see about the top half of it), which otherwise is not featured in the film. "I'm not going to acknowledge it," she says, referring to the nasty press reports about her, thereby committing what in contemporary American politics is known as the "swift boat" error, failing to answer political attacks until after they have sunken in with the public, and also sunken the public figure involved.

In the film's last half-hour Coppola moves in swift, condensed images:

a baby's cry over the bay of Versailles announces the birth of the Dauphin; a shot of an artist painting a portrait of Marie and her two children cuts to shots of a painting defaced with graffiti like "Queen of Debt!" and "Spending France into Ruin!" The director sketches lightly the downward trajectory—personal sadness in the death of a child, which we see indicated only by an oil painting that includes an empty crib, followed by a baby's funeral; the rising revolution; and the eventual loss of all whom Marie loved in France, her "girlfriends," as we would say. She goes out on the veranda and bows to the people, humbling herself before them. But this is not a queen trained in the governing arts of oratory and symbolism. This is not Garbo, appearing before her people, or Henry Fonda's Lincoln facing down a lynch mob. These little people in the palace, these "bunglers," don't get the absurdity and futility of continuing to eat lavish meals while the people outside demand a new regime. In showing a Marie who goes to the window and bows to the waist before the mob, Coppola foreshadows the end of Marie, her neck on the guillotine. Marie/Dunst, erect and alert, plays a junior version of the Great Lady. Marie, unlike Louis, harbors no illusions. As the carriage takes the Royal Family away from Versailles, he asks, "Are you admiring the Lime Avenue?" still making pleasantries. "I'm saying goodbye," she replies in resignation.

Marie Antoinette may be a textbook example of the postclassical Hollywood genre film. It complements forebears like *The Scarlet Empress, Queen Christina,* and the 1938 *Marie Antoinette.* Coppola makes a next-generation, this-is-not-your-father's-costume-biopic, rather than a film that breaks with tradition, in the manner of modernists such as Kubrick and Altman. This is similar to the way Francis Coppola's *The Godfather* (1972) showed a New Hollywood take on gangster film conventions, as opposed to the totally different direction for the genre presented by Scorsese's *Mean Streets* (1973).

Marie's friendship/affair with Count Fersen of Sweden was the main selling point of the MGM version, with Shearer and Tyrone Power, the budding matinee idol cast as Fersen, billed together above the title. The affair in Coppola's version is played similarly to the way Campion depicts Janet Frame's first affair, as a delicious sexual awakening that the heroine owns but that by no means defines her, and which cannot last. The MGM film has *l'affaire de Fersen* beginning just before Louis becomes king and Louis and Marie conceive their first child; thus it grows directly out of Marie's and Louis's sexual problems. Fraser's biography reports the affair as beginning no sooner than eight years after the coronation and soon after a miscarriage of what would have been Marie's third child. Coppola's film, although less certain about the time elapsed, begins the affair years after Marie and Louis have been having regular sexual relations. The marriage of the king and queen is complex, to put it simply. Once the consummation problem is solved, Coppola does not probe it. Fersen eventually disappears from Coppola's film, becoming for Marie a daydream with no substance. Marie, pining for her lover, however, looks out the window to see Fersen in a martial image modeled, ironically, after the Jacques-Louis David painting *Napoléon at St. Bernard* (1801), an anachronism that partakes of latter-day romance novels, but even more so of the coming of Napoleon. David himself was an ardent champion of the Revolution who, as a member of the National Convention, voted for the execution of Louis XVI and made a sketch, *Marie Antoinette on the Way to the Guillotine* (1793). Marie's late-film longings for love and life begin to be colored over, unbeknownst to her, by harbingers of death and the destruction of her way of life.

Thus the film moves through its dialectic of reality and dream. Coppola seems to have been interested in the passages of Fraser's book that show the queen, having misogynistically become the French public's scapegoat for the monarchy and the ruinous economy, refusing to leave Versailles first, declaring that "my place is with my husband." Here is an ownership of responsibility, taught to Marie by her mother, Maria Teresa, but also an acceptance of duty and responsibility that has as much to do with her new-found maturity as with her relationship with Louis, whatever it finally was.

49. The entire film is condensed in *Marie Antoinette*'s final shot. Digital frame enlargement.

Coppola therefore has Marie still learning and evolving as her end nears, and Marie cannot help it if no one else sees that.

The entire film is condensed in the last shot. Marie has asked for one last look at Versailles; we see it as she does, the site of her adult life. Cut to a static shot of her bedchamber in late afternoon light, ransacked, destroyed in a mob scene that Coppola allows to have happened offscreen. In this remarkable shot is everything: the morning dressing rituals, the early sexual failures with Louis, a metaphor for a woman's femininity played out in public and the symbol of it destroyed. It's also a symbolic imprisonment and execution, as every means by which Marie was defined by court and public is summed up in that bedchamber, and now it has been killed. At the same time, there is a sense of escape, that the queen's paraphernalia might be destroyed, but the woman herself finally eludes those who think they have defined her. The Revolution thinks it has killed the scapegoat Marie Antoinette, but all it has guillotined is the female role, the foreign femme fatale, the free-spender. Coppola has an affinity for showing the vacated domestic spaces of her female characters. The camera moves through the Michigan home of the Lisbon family in *The Virgin Suicides* after the girls are all gone and the parents have moved away, trying to make the rooms speak as they didn't when they hummed with life. The trashed bedroom in *Marie Antoinette* also speaks of the "familiar double-bind" to which Tania Modleski refers whereby patriarchy moves women to identify with "feminine" pursuits like fashion and then belittles and condemns them for it (73). Marie moves beyond the bedchamber; we rarely see it in the second half of the film, and yet the marriage bed was always her "destiny," no matter how far she may have moved beyond it.

In *Marie Antoinette* and *The Notorious Bettie Page* we see what appear to be deliberate attempts to rethink the female biopic, to eschew melodramatic situations, conflicts with individuals rather than with systems, and the external gaze. They also avoid the downward trajectory and the victimhood spiral, an approach that is especially obvious with biographical subjects that clearly would avail the wrong filmmakers of all the conventions. A problem with both films is that they might seem works of negative virtues, notable for what they do not do. At the point in the halting development of the female biopic when they were made, however, the avoidance of melodrama and the reappropriation of the gaze were no small accomplishments. They brought forth sincere, heartfelt films whose importance over time will grow.

18

I'm Not There

Some Conclusions on a Book Concerning Biopics

He was able to adopt a kind of theatre about himself. Actually, the first time I met
him he was acting, in a way. And that was good because you could go anywhere
when you're somebody else.
　　—MARK SPOELSTRA, WHO KNEW BOB DYLAN IN HIS EARLY DAYS IN
　　GREENWICH VILLAGE

I hope that this book has left little doubt that the biopic continues to matter
as a theatrical film genre. Biopics materialize out of a filmmaker's desire to
create drama out of the lives of someone he or she finds interesting. Biopics
are a form of celebrity culture. They are made not in order to tell what James
Welsh called "entertaining lies" (86), but to find truth out of invention, re-
creating the most dramatic and characteristic stretch(es) of a person's life
by creating a structure and scenes, hiring actors, building sets, and all the
other means of cinematic creation. It is very clear that the biopic is one of the
most divisive of genres for audiences and critics, with many people quick to
see the generic framework; this keeps them from identifying with truth in
the genre, while others find pleasure in the generic structure itself and are
curious to see what kind of alchemy will result from the engagement by a
particular filmmaker with a particular biographical subject.

Perhaps part of the point of film genres, however, is to divide certain
stories and audiences from each other. The search on the part of film companies for films with so-called universal appeal might be summarized as the

desire to overcome the audience-limiting boundaries of genre. Westerns, "chick flicks," horror films, crime films, romantic comedies—all invite audiences to be attracted or repelled, to identify themselves as those who will enjoy one kind of film or other; at its most constraining, genre permits the identification of oneself protected by a barrier that keeps us from having new experiences, from experiencing people and events outside our own self-identification.

The biopic is a form that itself is about self-identification and self-invention, but it is also about identification with others. The history of the biopic genre as female star vehicle shows especially that the biopic very often is an explicit acting out of human efforts to construct ourselves as characters, to play ourselves as personae. MGM and Greta Garbo, for instance, imagined Garbo's playing of Queen Christina differently—the studio seeing the role as the latest means of furthering the Garbo "brand"; the actress earnestly endeavoring to play as many aspects and qualities of the historical queen as she could. The best biopics, we've often seen, are about people who play roles and about how they feel within those roles: Queen Christina imagines herself as an ordinary woman (even while the film insists, visually, that Greta Garbo can never be ordinary); T. E. Lawrence is disturbed to the edge of madness by the effect that power over others has on him. Richard Nixon spends his life climbing to the top; once he's there he is both too insecure to be satisfied and too hardened to admit his insecurity. Susan Hayward's performance as Barbara Graham in *I Want to Live!* may live on as the best example of an exquisite self-fashioning. Hayward's Graham presents herself to the prying world as a dignified person in defiance, as it were, of all expectations.

The most misunderstood aspect of the biopic, after its mistaken conflation with documentary history, may be that it leads us to identify with people who strive to identify themselves—as artists, as writers, as statesmen. It follows that a culture that encourages individual ambition would produce stories about individuals who apparently were destined to distinguish themselves in the society. It is our personae that both open us up to the world and protect us, creating the mystery of humanity. We want to live as characters in a story to the extent that we want our lives to have shape, purpose, and meaning. And we watch biopics so as to plumb that mystery of humanness, the inability completely to know another person, and the absolute importance of knowing them and ourselves.

I'm Not There (2007) capsulates the public's attraction in the postmodern era to celebrities who not only fulfill our dream to make ourselves over and become what we'd like to be, but who themselves undergo the process of self-invention repeatedly, letting us live vicariously with them not as the role we would like to play, but as a series of roles. This book has been careful to favor the verb "dramatize" over "fictionalize" in explaining how biopics treat lives. *I'm Not There* (2007) *fictionalizes* Bob Dylan, despite the fact that Todd Haynes obtained the "music rights and life rights," as he put it, to make an authorized biopic of the singer-songwriter (IFC News). Haynes understands that in the life of a legendary person fiction might get closer to the truth of the person than do the so-called facts. Probing the literal facts of someone who made himself as much a creation as his music might be as naïve and fruitless as trying to explicate his songs. "You who're so good with words," Joan Baez wrote to Dylan in "Diamonds and Rust," "and at keeping things vague." In order to make a film about Dylan, Haynes makes *like* him, juxtaposing unconnected images, music styles, eras, influences, song lyrics, incidents in Dylan's life, film allusions, and in just one case a music video (of "Ballad of a Thin Man") with varying interpretations. For Haynes, therefore, Dylan is, or rather, Dylan *means* fictions, masks, and personae, each of them, in a grand paradox, genuine.

In succeeding decades it will appear that after the turn of the twenty-first century the biopic had its way with numerous baby boomer icons, none of whom is more of what Michael Gray called "a very famous minority taste fixation of an ageing generation" than Dylan ("It Ain't Me" 20). A "unitary" biopic of Bob Dylan might be feasible, but it would probably not be interesting, and ultimately would not be about Bob Dylan in a truthful way. Haynes celebrates his subject; vindication is there, but it is muted. *I'm Not There* is the logical next step in the *Citizen Kane* mode of deconstructive biopic. Haynes seems to concede that Bob Dylan's life does not in any way lend itself to the treatment accorded a unitary biopic—that Dylan's coherence is his incoherence.

Imagine this unitary plot: A young subject has a remarkable gift; he enters into the world to share his great talent and becomes established as an icon. The icon begins to be overwhelmed by the whirl of celebrity, the demands of fans, the temptations of sex and drugs; he veers out of control and self-destructs. The protagonist also enters into a romantic life with one woman, whom the film portrays as long-suffering and cast in the role of helpmeet and support. Eventually, she leaves him and he must see how hollow and unfulfilled his life has become. Finally, he faces the future and his legacy;

will his art outlive him? Will it transcend his earthly life? What contribution does the subject make to the culture? How does his art live on and how does the drama coexist in memory and culture with the actual subject?

I've described the Great Man biopic, as it has been revived in the 2000s in what I would call neoclassical form, in films such as *Ray, Walk the Line, Kinsey, The Aviator,* the HBO film *The Life and Death of Peter Sellers, Capote, Infamous, Talk to Me,* and *Breach.* These films synthesize, often quite smoothly, elements of the studio-era form, the warts-and-all film, and the deconstructive, investigative film. Reviewers of *Ray,* for example, while wondering at the film's conventionality, overlooked the fact that director Taylor Hackford cut between shots of Ray Charles's family-man home life and his girlfriends and drug use while on tour in a montage bridged together by one of his songs. A juxtaposition that would have been viewed as condemnatory of its subject in the times of *The Joker Is Wild* or *Lady Sings the Blues* is now viewed myopically as conventionally holistic, showing the subject in all his aspects, some of which happen not to be complementary. Those, however, will be worked out within the course of the narrative; they won't finally drag him down.

The queer biopic *Milk* (2008) demonstrates the continuing effectiveness of the minority appropriation. As with *Malcolm X,* those who complain that *Milk* falls into conventions of the genre miss the point. *Milk* reworks as a biopic an Academy Award–winning documentary, *The Times of Harvey Milk* (Rob Epstein, 1984). A cynic could say that the film makes itself safe for the mainstream. A known heterosexual actor, Sean Penn, plays the nation's first openly gay elected official. Harvey Milk dies, shot by Dan White (Josh Brolin), the archetypal disgruntled former employee, making the story of a gay person into the tragedy that it seems to have to become in order to pass into cultural mythology. On the other hand, *Milk* is positive and joyous in its celebration of its main character; the acclaim and awards for Penn centered more on the ease and relaxation of the usually intense Penn in the role of an upbeat character than on the courage of a straight actor playing a gay part in a homophobic industry.

The openly gay director Gus Van Sant deemphasizes Milk's death and victimization and stresses his political successes. Many reviewers noted the irony of the film's release three weeks after the November 2008 passage in California of Proposition 8, which made same-sex marriage illegal under the state constitution. Proposition 8 rendered Van Sant's film more poignant than it otherwise might have been. Its passage made even clearer

than earlier appropriational biopics the continuing relevance of a protagonist who lived, struggled, and died decades before. This desire to make a
minority subject of the past live for film audiences in the present is one of
the chief aims of the appropriation biopic. Ironically, in the case of *Milk* the
sad reality of continuing homophobia helped accomplish the goal; it's only
a movie indeed.

The neoclassical wave has predominated in the 2000s, however, and *I'm
Not There* is about as out of place within it as *Citizen Kane* was amid early
forties biopics such as *Sergeant York* and *The Pride of the Yankees*. Like *Kane*,
I'm Not There illustrates all the possibilities if not of cinema (what single
film, including *Citizen Kane*, can carry out that mandate?) then of the biopic.
Haynes critiques Hollywood genres as if from inside them; there is in *I'm
Not There* a tendency to enter the genre and interact with it. Haynes then
invites us to go outside his film and mentally reconstruct what the movie
would be like if it were a conventional biopic, and to see Bob Dylan from the
outside as a biopic would.

Dylan is the film's structuring absence. Often read out of culture during
his long career—a reviewer of Dylan's *Chronicles, Volume One* (2004) began
his column by stating that he "hadn't given a Flying Wallenda about Dylan
in years" (Carson)—Dylan is never anything other than there, even when
he isn't there. Similarly, while it seems unrecognizable in Haynes's film,
the biopic is present in every frame of it. *I'm Not There* stands as the fullest demonstration to date of the biopic's capacity for ongoing reinvention;
what the film maintains about its subject's slippery transformation goes just
as strongly for the genre on which it relies. Haynes has made a biopic in
reverse: Rather than start with the whole subject and analyze it in his/her
aspects, Haynes works with the parts and by the end gels them into a coherent person, using them to define and analyze Dylan the phenomenon.
Dylan the man remains someone "come in from the wilderness, a creature
void of form," as he sings in "Shelter from the Storm" (1975). *I'm Not There*
fragments the subject, viewing him as a collection of personae. It takes Bob
Dylan through the stages of warts-and-all, from promising youth, first blush
of success, the frenzy of fame, and the resultant decadence and private turmoil, through to middle-aged retrospection, vindication, and transcendence.
Haynes does all this in the postmodernist, déjà vu manner of *Superstar*.

Unlike a life for which a storyline needs to be devised, Dylan's life and career went beyond drama into legend well before he was out of his twenties—
indeed this was part of the legend. Haynes makes a film that cuts and pastes

the various dramas, positing them as objects for endless study. "Study" is surely the right word for a filmmaker who likens the effort to a "dissertation, probably the Ph.D.," who originally subtitled the film "Some Suppositions for a Film About Bob Dylan," and whose *New York Times Magazine* profile said about *Superstar:* "Academics loved it" (Sullivan). *I'm Not There* presents the apotheosis of the biopic as it has evolved to date. It breaks one of the hidden assumptions of the genre: it feels no need to prove Dylan's worth or to establish his mythology. Haynes assumes that the spectator already knows about Dylan's importance. Therefore, he can set about at once to dissect his myth and meaning. It is *Citizen Kane* without the newsreel.

Haynes splits Dylan into multiple characters. He appears to tell the same story as *No Direction Home* (2005), the three-and-a-half-hour documentary attributed to Martin Scorsese. Rich with historic footage, much of it not seen before publicly, and peppered with interviews, including material from a ten-hour sit-down with Dylan, *No Direction Home* covers the period from young Robert Zimmerman's upbringing in the Iron Range town of Hibbing, Minnesota, through his rise in the early and mid-1960s. Scorsese's film ends with the motorcycle crash near Dylan's home in Woodstock, New York, that temporarily halted Dylan's unprecedented influence and allowed him to change direction, not for the last time. Haynes's film begins as if the motorcycle crash had administered a mercy killing to the insane glare of the "Dylan Goes Electric" period, and allowed new lives to rise for the singer. "He gave up the limelight," as Haynes's *Superstar*-like narrator intones, "for a different kind of light." This new light is defined throughout the film variously—by Sara, his wife, whom the film names Claire, his children ("My family was my light," Dylan wrote in *Chronicles, Volume One,* his 2004 memoir [123]), and his Christian conversion. Haynes's subject (who is never named Bob Dylan) arises and withdraws, to emerge again and again in a series of career phases that continue as of this writing. Thus Haynes's film, technically, covers a period from the late 1950s past the accident to the breakup of Dylan's marriage to Sara Lownds Dylan in the mid-1970s, the Rolling Thunder Revue of the late 1970s, the born-again period of the early 1980s, and beyond. *I'm Not There* treats Dylan's life as a collection of fables. While the biopic genre makes a character out of an actual subject, this film has seven characters in search of the subject.

The title *I'm Not There* undercuts the customary function of the title in the musical biopic subtype, whose title often is that of a song with which the subject was identified. There is a familiar kind of show business communication with the public going on when a title such as *Yankee Doodle Dandy, La Bamba, Coal Miner's Daughter,* or *What's Love Got to Do with It?* is emblazoned across a marquee. By this token, a biopic of Dylan should announce itself as *Like a Rolling Stone* or *Blowin' in the Wind.* Surely filmmakers concerned for their commercial prospects would give their film such a title, which would amount to a brand, and would also appear to guarantee a certain kind of conventional biopic. *I'm Not There,* by contrast, is taken from the title of a song Dylan recorded with The Band in 1967. It was left out of the double-album culled from the sessions, *The Basement Tapes* (1975), and could be heard only in bootlegs right up until the day the film's sound track CD went on sale. That Haynes would use it as his title shows he's interested only in its thematic value, suggesting the biopic subject as absence, as well as Dylan's frequent movement from one position, one style, to another. By the time audiences, or anyone else, expected to find Dylan in a particular place, be it folk, or protest, or rock, or country . . . he was no longer there. He was somewhere else.

If Dylan was not "there," then where, or who, was he? "I am another," wrote Dylan's favorite poet, Arthur Rimbaud. Haynes's film shows one "other" on top of another and another. But with all these "others," who is the "self," the "I"? Jonathan Cott described an interview with Dylan near the release of the four-hour concert film-*cum*-fantasia, *Renaldo and Clara* (1978):

> "There's Renaldo, there's a guy in whiteface singing on the stage, and then there's Ronnie Hawkins [who incidentally weighed 300 pounds] playing Bob Dylan. Bob Dylan is listed in the credits as playing Renaldo, yet Ronnie Hawkins is listed as playing Bob Dylan." "So Bob Dylan," I surmised, "may or may not be in the film." "Exactly." "But Bob Dylan made the film." "Bob Dylan didn't make it," he told me. "I made it." (Cott x–xi; brackets in the original)

Wherever or whoever Bob Dylan is, *I'm Not There* exists in the personae, the fictions, each of which I will analyze at length.

1. *"Woody Guthrie" (Marcus Carl Franklin).* This is the prodigy, the nineteen-year-old baby-fat singer who showed up out of nowhere in Greenwich Village with a fantastic (and invented) personal background, a determination to emulate his hero Woody Guthrie, and an ability to sponge up musical and poetic styles and traditions. Played by a twelve-year-old African American

50. He contains multitudes, as perhaps do we all. Marcus Carl Franklin embodying the Woody Guthrie in Bob Dylan in *I'm Not There* (Todd Haynes, The Weinstein Co., 2007). Digital frame enlargement.

actor, Woody seems a magical figure, yet he is in truth none other than the visionary biopic subject, full of confidence, unable to keep from doing what he is doing. The archetypal subject is infused with childlike enthusiasm and faith, so why shouldn't Haynes make him a child? In a remarkable passage in *Chronicles, Vol. 1,* furthermore, Dylan describes seeing the Denzel Washington film *The Mighty Quinn* (1989), whose title came from one of Dylan's songs. "Denzel Washington. He must have been a fan of mine . . . I wondered if Denzel could play Woody Guthrie. In my dimension of reality, he certainly could have" (187). This is a peculiar comment, considering that Dylan himself turned down the role of Woody in *Bound for Glory* (1976) (McDougal 168). There is no Denzel in Haynes's film, but in Dylan's "dimension of reality" spirit transcends physical reality. Marcus Carl Franklin is perhaps Haynes's idea of Denzel Washington at twelve: poised, inspired, and self-assured. Woody, moreover, is the only one of the "Dylans" who sings in the actor's own voice. It is an amateur voice, in the tradition of child actors in folk musicals, such as Margaret O'Brien and Joan Carroll in *Meet Me in St. Louis* (1944). Dylan's songs, however, sound perfectly natural in Franklin's nicely phrased, untrained delivery. As each of the personae comes from certain album covers, with the iconography of certain stages or personae of Dylan, "Woody" is the baby-faced troubadour of the first LP, *Bob Dylan* (1962).

2. *Arthur (Ben Whishaw), the poet-philosopher.* Arthur is a repository of Dylan interviews and statements. As Haynes posited Oscar Wilde as the forebear of his David Bowie figure, Brian Slade (Jonathan Rhys-Meyers) in

Velvet Goldmine, so Arthur Rimbaud is nineteen or twenty, is garbed as a late-nineteenth-century bad boy, and faces an inquisition that looks like the star chamber in the dream sequences of *The Manchurian Candidate* (1962). While the fourth persona, Jude Quinn (Cate Blanchett), faces her/his inquisitors too, and is nearly undone by them, Arthur is less affected by their questions. Arthur is the only persona who does not interact dramatically with other characters, does not sing, and is static throughout.

3. *Jack Rollins (Christian Bale).* The sinewy, denim-wearing folksinger on the cover of *The Times They Are a-Changin'* (1964); the darling of the 1963 Newport Folk Festival. This is the Dylan who performed at the March on Washington later the same summer; the young performer whom Joan Baez (named "Alice Fabian" here and played by Haynes regular Julianne Moore) brought onstage with her and with whom she apparently fell in (unreciprocated) love; the singer of protest songs such as "Masters of War" and "With God on Our Side"; the "voice of a generation." Peculiarly, *I'm Not There* revitalizes the biopic as star vehicle, in ways that serve Haynes's purposes and enrich the various Dylan personae. Even though actors were attached and then became unavailable as Haynes's project wound its long trail toward production, the eventual actors are uncannily resonant of their personae and best-known films. For instance, Jack Rollins, the former child prodigy, Woody, is played by Bale, the former child star who proved his coming of age by starring in *American Psycho* (Mary Harron, 2000) and went on to play toughened characters personally tested outside society in *Rescue Dawn* (2006), *3:10 to Yuma* (2007), and even *Batman Begins* (2005), with its ascetic, battle-hardened Bruce Wayne. (The sequel, *The Dark Knight* [2008] paired as the Caped Crusader and The Joker—characters often portrayed as *doppelgangers*—Bale and another of Haynes's Dylan avatars, Heath Ledger.) "Jack Rollins" is earnest and weather-beaten. He looks like he has been riding the rails and pitching hay, even if he hasn't (which is surely the case). When Dylan enters his born-again Christian stage in 1979, Jack, unseen for fifteen years, resurfaces, converted into "Pastor John," crusading for Christ just as "Jack" once protested racism, greed, and war.

4. *Jude Quinn (Cate Blanchett).* The rock-and-roll heretic. The frizzy-haired speed freak who "went electric," the outrage of the 1965 Newport Folk Festival and the 1966 British tour, the author of the novel *Tarantula,* denizen of Andy Warhol's "Factory," jilter of Baez, and erstwhile lover of Edie Sedgwick.

The Jude section conflates the Dylans of the 1965 and 1966 British tours, even though they were perceived very differently, as Haynes concedes (IFC News). Tracing this Dylan through the three landmark albums he/she encompasses, released in one fourteen-month period—*Bringing It All Back Home* (March 1965), *Highway 61 Revisited* (August 1965), *Blonde on Blonde* (May 1966; the title is said to refer to Sedgwick and Warhol)—one realizes how incremental yet rapid was Dylan's change from acoustic folk to electric psychedelic rock. Jude is the dazed and bedazzled "thin wild mercury" singer shown out of focus and androgynous on the *Blonde on Blonde* cover. "He was bizarre," said Haynes.

> The way he would play piano in concert, which Cate . . . mimics in the film and which you see in the Scorsese documentary where his hand sort of flies up after every line and he would jump around the stage like a little speedy marionette. . . . The way he spoke, his gestures, everything about him from that one time is not evident in *Dont Look Back* from a year earlier and would never return again after his motorcycle crash. . . . It was such a complete immersion in this moment and it was androgynous. . . . His flamboyance and foppery during that time is really profound. (IFC News)

The character played by Blanchett, furthermore, sports by far the richest of Haynes's invented names: Quinn from "The Mighty Quinn," about Quinn the Eskimo, a cool customer; Jude, as in "Judas," as the "electric" Dylan was famously called by a heckler at Manchester Town Hall in 1966; also as in "Hey, Jude," indicating the mutual influence between Dylan and the Beatles at this time (Sounes 212). "Remember to let *her* under your skin," write Lennon and McCartney. The name also evokes Saint Jude, the patron of lost causes, summing up the way Dylan came to feel about folk protest music and about "causes" in general ("No one makes social change with a song," Jude tells an interviewer in the film).

In Cate Blanchett, Haynes has an actress best known for portraying queenly, indomitable legends like Elizabeth I (in *Elizabeth* [1998] and *Elizabeth: The Golden Age* [2007]) and Katharine Hepburn (in *The Aviator* [2004]). Haynes first met with the Australian actress to discuss the role in Los Angeles the morning of the Academy Awards ceremony in 2005, where she would win Best Supporting Actress for playing Hepburn, who strangely resonates in Blanchett's Jude. Jude Quinn enters at the point where rock stars began to eclipse movie stars at the apogee of fame, glitz, hype, and fan frenzy. Blanchett's portrayal of the Hepburn of the late 1930s who was branded "box office poison" actually parallels the exhausted rocker whose audiences pay to boo him for abandoning folk music (if they bought a ticket, Dylan blithely maintained, they had a right to express their opinion [Sounes 192]). Both Hepburn circa 1938 and Dylan in 1966 reach the end of one phase, after which they reinvent themselves, Hepburn following her retreat to Broadway to star triumphantly in *The Philadelphia Story,* the film rights to which she held and sold to Hollywood on her terms; Dylan who repaired to the countryside and emerged at the end of 1967 with *John Wesley Harding,* a record so unlike his previous album, *Blonde on Blonde,* as to be the work of a different artist, yet still recognizably Dylan. The analogy of the androgynous Quinn to the pants-wearing, gender-bending Hepburn of *Christopher Strong* (1933) and *Sylvia Scarlett* (1935) is apparent as well.

By playing the Jude part of the singer as a woman, Haynes subverts Dylan, or improves him, or both. "Jude Quinn" is like a two-sexed being, nearly a hermaphrodite. Cate Blanchett may have, as she says, worn a rolled-up sock in her costume trousers to feel more like a man, but that seems a jest in the vein of the drawn-on mustache Jude wears in a scene that is already a pastiche of a similar sequence in *Dont Look Back.* Jude still looks and acts like a lithe, loose-limbed woman. Blanchett is recognizable in the role, as if moguls had been nervously looking over Haynes's shoulder to make sure that the star still resembled herself. Haynes proposes that Dylan with an electric guitar was no less an outrage to the folk fans than if he'd had a sex change or, at least, gone onstage in a dress. In re-creations of the interviews from the 1966 British tour seen in *No Direction Home,* the jilted fans can only look at the camera and mourn. "He's changed. He's not the same as he was." The fans are in the situation of the bitter, outraged Barbara Covett (Judi Dench) in *Notes on a Scandal* (2006), disapproving of but also attracted to the affrontery of the transgressing Sheba Hart (Blanchett), who is just transfixingly, maddeningly female.

In Haynes's "garden party" scene, which draws on *8½* (1963) and *A Hard Day's Night* (1964) simultaneously (both films *are* about the chaos of celebrity), the "mighty Quinn" is fawned over and attended to like a head of state or a queenly film star. All the while s/he evinces Dylan's frequently inarticulate speech ("um, uh, I dig Shakespeare"), which is first established by the stammering, misspeaking Jack Rollins but is unexpected from such a poetic lyricist. By contrast, the brash young subjects, Woody and Arthur, are masterfully glib. The Blanchett scenes have the advantage of being set in the era of the best-documented Dylan, that of D. A. Pennebaker's 1967 documentary *Dont Look Back* (with its intentional lack of an apostrophe; geniuses cant be bothered with punctuation) and its informal, little seen sequel, *Eat the Document* (1971), which Dylan "directed." Even though Bale and Whishaw strongly suggest Dylan's speech patterns and pronunciations, Blanchett performs a fully fledged *Dont Look Back* Dylan. Because the Dylan of Pennebaker's Direct Cinema classic is mocking, self-effacing, arrogant, polite, cruel (to Joan Baez, whom he ignores and lets others in his entourage make fun of), focused (typing lyrics in the hotel room in the midst of all kinds of commotion), passionate, calm, passive-aggressive, and direct, Blanchett plays all these facets, but most of all the ducking, spinning-out-of-control Dylan who still tries to maintain at least her/his cool.

In the Blanchett scenes Haynes mashes together the British concert tour of spring 1965 that was made famous by *Dont Look Back* and the equally renowned return to Britain one year later. The second tour took place after the release of the all-electric *Highway 61 Revisited;* after the stormy and legendary Newport Folk Festival reception the previous summer, as the effect of the murderous number of shows manager Albert Grossman was booking took hold and as the entourage got increasingly into drugs; and indeed after Dylan's marriage to Sara in November 1965 (which, six months later, was still a secret to the public). Dylan and his band were jeered at nearly every stop. At Grossman's insistence, one half of each concert was performed by the singer alone on acoustic guitar and the other half by Dylan and his band, the Hawks (later The Band). As a result, the shows had a jagged, disorienting quality that exhausted Dylan and frustrated his fans.

Haynes audaciously portrays Jude Quinn the way Dylan's songs often portray women—as inconstant, unfaithful, shrill, flighty, unpredictable, deadly, and betraying. Jude machine-guns the crowd at the "New England Folk and Jazz Festival" ("Folk and Jazz?"), has flirtations with Beatles (even as he pokes fun at them in his lyrics, as in "Some Englishman said 'Fab'" in "Bob Dylan's 116th Dream" [1965]), is undependable—is in short, "Just Like a Woman." Hints of Haynes's past as the Queer Cinema insurrectionist of *Poison* rear up in the Jude section. The Dylan–Edie Sedgwick relationship, whatever it may have been, is queered here, defamiliarized as a pas-de-deux between two women. The shape-shifting Dylan turns here into Virginia Woolf's Orlando, a point that could have been clearer only if Tilda

Swinton had played Jude. Moreover, Edie, who is renamed "Coco," is played in a spot-on performance by Michelle Williams, best known as the spurned wife of the cowboy Ennis Del Mar in *Brokeback Mountain*. This continues the juxtaposition with the "Robbie" persona, since that philanderer behind the Foster-Grants is played by Heath Ledger, who in real life fathered a child with his *Brokeback* co-star and who acts "Robbie" in a low growl that recalls the lovesick Ennis as much as it does the Dylan of *Blood on the Tracks*. Thus one sees the way that biopics can still use the star system to generate resonances between real personages/characters and the actors who play them.

5. *"Robbie Clark" (Ledger)*, the actor, may be Haynes's richest and most imaginative conceit, even though the Blanchett portrayal attracted most of the attention when the film was released. As this was the last Heath Ledger film released before his untimely death in January 2008 at the age of twenty-eight, Ledger's portion, as the Dylan "in a coat he borrowed from James Dean," may well become iconic. The concept is that Dylan at the end of the 1960s became an impersonator of his early, unwanted "voice of a generation" image, with the electric Jude having "died" in the motorcycle crash. Here again Haynes notes the interchangeability of rock star and movie star. "Robbie," the actor, and "Billy" ("the Kid") refer to Dylan's persistent attraction to the movies, one that yielded felicitous song lyrics, as well as unfortunate films such as *Renaldo and Clara* and *Masked and Anonymous* (2003). Robbie is the private, relationship Dylan, the lover of Suze Rotolo and especially Sara Lownds Dylan, Bob's wife from 1965 to 1977, and the mother of four of his children. Haynes centers almost entirely on the period after Dylan began touring again during the first months of 1974, after seven and a half years off the road. Robbie is filming abroad, where, like Dylan on tour, he falls into most of his former vices, including infidelity. The "Robbie" scenes center on Claire, the Sara character, and the consequences of Robbie's inconsideration, his absences, and his casual cruelties. A concept of Haynes's film is that just as Dylan is not there in the film literally (but he is present figuratively), so by the time Dylan can be fixed as dwelling in one time and place, he's not there; he's somewhere else. This sounds like a fitting summation of the principle of transcendence, of spiritual permanence that is the biopic genre's fondest and most permanent hallmark. It also speaks of Dylan's elusiveness and how Haynes endeavors to associate that with the contradictions of presence and absence in cinema itself.

"Claire" is the "different kind of light" whom the narrator informs us the subject has left the spotlight in search of. Haynes foregrounds Claire's point of view. "Robbie" is distant but a loving father. He produces work of dubious worth (again from Claire's point of view)—this is the period of poorly received albums: *Self Portrait* (1970), *New Morning* (1970), *Planet Waves* (1974). Much of this section is rooted in domestic dramas and made in the style of films of the era. Haynes conflates Dylan's marriage to Sara with the years of America's deep involvement in Vietnam—1964–1973; the Gulf of Tonkin resolution, described in voiceover, is concurrent with images of Bob and Claire's idyll, taken from the streetside candid shot of the singer with Suze Rotolo on the cover of *The Freewheelin' Bob Dylan* (1963). In making Sara a Frenchwoman, Haynes gives this section a Godardian, the-personal-is-the-political tinge, which "Robbie" openly disputes. He tells a friend flatly that "there *are* no politics," contending that as an artist—like most Hollywood films and popular culture in general—Dylan separates art and entertainment from the political. This contested notion, to which even a socially committed Dylan song of the period such as "Hurricane" (1976) does not adhere, is placed at the center of a battle of sexes between "Robbie"/Bob and "Claire"/Sara. Their conflicts parallel the late-1960s cultural environment that Dylan, in his reclusive period, ignored, with the exception of a few well-chosen public appearances, such as his performances at the memorial concert for Woody Guthrie in 1968 and the Concert for Bangladesh at Madison Square Garden in 1971.

The macho Robbie, with his black leather jacket, his shades (a carryover from Jude Quinn), and his taciturn Method-actor demeanor, is the man's man Dylan, the one who, as Haynes put it, "is often associated as a 'guy's artist,' or a heterosexual kind of icon" (IFC News). The title of Robbie's movie is *A Grain of Sand*, prefiguring the song "Every Grain of Sand" (1981) from his "born again" period. With the focus on Claire, in a reversal of Godard's Franco-American pairing in *À Bout de souffle*, Dylan comes across as a gendered Ugly American, as men of the sixties counterculture learned (or didn't) that as males in patriarchy they were very much part of the Establishment they were resisting. "Robbie" is also as much Marlon Brando and James Dean as he is Dylan; in *No Direction Home* Dylan reminisces about the film *The Wild One* (1954), which introduced the icon of a leather-jacketed Brando as the anomic leader of a motorcycle gang. Claire at home is framed in one shot in front of a giant movie poster showing a shades-wearing Robbie in

51. The actor Robbie Clark (Heath Ledger). It is as if a Method-style actor played the sixties Dylan in a warts-and-all biopic made in the seventies. Note the two-faced shading on the actor's face. Digital frame enlargement.

"*Calico*," a reference to *Serpico* (1973), which starred Al Pacino, an actor who idolized Brando the way the young Dylan revered Guthrie.

In the film styles favored for each of the characters, the film in which Robbie Clark plays Jack Rollins is shot in the style of black-and-white Hollywood realist films like Robert Wise's *Odds Against Tomorrow* (1959), a Harry Belafonte vehicle for which Dylan expresses admiration in his memoir (68), John Cassavetes's *Too Late Blues*, Robert Rossen's *The Hustler*, and Martin Ritt's *Paris Blues* (all 1961). The production design of the "Robbie and Claire" scenes, their use of extreme wide-screen interior framing, and their faded, muted color brought back to me the looks of specific comedy-dramas of the 1970s: *Blume in Love* (1973), *Alice Doesn't Live Here Anymore* (1974), and *A Star Is Born* (1976). It dawned on me that all of those starred Kris Kristofferson, as of course did *Pat Garrett and Billy the Kid* (1973), the Sam Peckinpah western in which Dylan appeared, for which he wrote the score, and which is the taking-off point of the sequences with the aging Billy (Richard Gere).

Kristofferson, an aspiring singer-songwriter in the 1960s, was a floor sweeper at the Columbia Records studio in Nashville in 1966 when Dylan recorded *Blonde on Blonde* there, and he assisted in the recording of *Nashville Skyline* three years later (Gray 389; Sounes 237). The tall, rugged Ledger combines the coy indirectness of Dylan with the virile charm of Kristofferson. A singer-songwriter in his own right, Kristofferson was in no way as accomplished as Dylan, but Dylan did not have the charisma or the movie-star looks of the Rhodes scholar Kristofferson. To top off all this Kristoffersonalia, in reading the cast list after my second viewing (I somehow missed doing so on my first), I was stunned to find that the narrator of *I'm Not There*—I'd thought it was Gere—is Kris Kristofferson! Thus the "Billy the Kid" persona indeed pervades the film and by the end, after Billy has discovered the dust-covered guitar case of the youthful Woody in a freight train box car, brings the journey full circle and takes it down the line in that "slow train coming."

For all this, then, is Haynes in the Robbie Clark sequences playing Dylan as a Kris Kristofferson protagonist, the romantic lead in his own life? A movie star of no enormous range (if Kristofferson was no Dylan, he was also no Brando or Dean), Kristofferson onscreen romanced Susan Anspach, Sarah Miles, Ellen Burstyn, and Barbra Streisand (in *A Star Is Born,* whose male lead role was first offered to Elvis!); he often played the love object in actress-centered films.

Much of the section, especially as it details Robbie's casual betrayals and the destruction of the marriage, is accompanied by songs from *Blood on the Tracks* (1975). In a scene in which Robbie, at a party with Claire, diverts her attention and is seen from her point of view as she discovers him with a woman, only the legs of whom are visible, we hear Dylan's recording of "Simple Twist of Fate." In such scenes, the sense of Dylan's songs commenting on Dylan the man is profound. In another scene the camera comes in Claire's face, as Dylan's studio recording of "Visions of Johanna" is heard with the line, "The ghost of 'lectricity howls in the bones of her face." Claire, haunted, begins to think of Robbie, who at that moment is in Europe with his co-star, the actress Louise Pickering (Jennifer Rae Westley), with whom he is having an affair; in lines of the song, "Just Louise and her lover, so entwined / And these visions of Johanna that conquer my mind." This song, from *Blonde on Blonde,* has brought forth interpretations that "Johanna" is Joan Baez, or that it is not a woman's name at all but "Gehenna," an Old Testament equivalent of hell (Scobie 259). As Claire sees visions of the war in Vietnam while her marriage crumbles, so visions of torment, hell, and torture, images Stephen Scobie associates with Gehenna, are not far away. In Haynes's treatment, however, the lover with whom Louise is "entwined" is Dylan, or Robbie, making the first person of the song the one having the visions; this visibly for us is Claire. Johanna and the speaker are the same person.

Thus the decentering of the subject accomplished by *I'm Not There* often involves displacing heterosexual male subjectivity onto women, with Dylan having become one of the causes of the world on fire that he depicts in some of his songs. The treatment of the songs in the Robbie-Claire sequence also underlines how his music affords subjectivities wider than his own. It suggests another way in which Haynes deconstructs the inherent masculinism of Dylan's music and persona—using Dylan's songs to express his wife's feelings of betrayal and abandonment. Claire's television set nearly bursts into the war flames being shown on it, while blaring out "All Along the Watchtower" in a version by Eddie Vedder and the Million Dollar Bashers (an homage to The Band, who played "Million Dollar Bash" with Dylan on *The Basement Tapes*) that approximates Jimi Hendrix's famous cover version. Cut from Claire's point of view to Robbie as he returns from his trip, loaded down with baggage, literally and figuratively. With the nightmare images of songs like "Visions of Johanna" and "Desolation Row" and songs of betrayal and loss like "Simple Twist of Fate" and "Idiot Wind," shown from a woman's point of view while heard in Dylan's voice, Haynes subverts the male perspectives (and fan base) these songs have always assumed. He also reveals an unexpected depth, pliability, and universal applicability, outside time, space, and gender ("past, present, and future happening all at once," as Billy discovers at the epiphanic conclusion).

More directly, the Jude and Robbie sections both confront the downward trajectory of the female biopic. The Jude scenes turn Dylan into a transgressive female who dares take on the way things are supposed to be. Her/his consequence is the downward spiral, which Haynes makes into a visual metaphor in the scene at the Warhol factory, as Jude looks down a corkscrew-shaped spiral staircase. Jude spins in the whirlpool of his own ambitions, as Dian Fossey figuratively falls off Mount Kirasote and Frances Farmer tumbles from the heights of Hollywood. In making Dylan the victimizer

52. Jude Quinn (Cate Blanchett) stares into his own downward spiral. Digital frame enlargement.

and Claire the victim, Haynes indulges the gothic woman's film side of the genre, with Claire hemmed in by her realization of what a prisoner of the marriage-domesticity-war-the-plight-of-the-foreigner-in-America ("I pity the poor immigrant," as Dylan sings) she has become.

Haynes redistributes aspects of Dylan, sometimes displacing him onto other characters. For instance, Claire is a painter, but it was *Dylan* who was taught to paint by Bruce Dorfman, his neighbor in Woodstock (Sounes 230). Dylan's art work, modeled after Marc Chagall's, according to Dorfman, adorned several of his album covers, including *Self-Portrait* and *Planet Waves.* The singer later took formal lessons in New York and even attributed the breakup of his marriage to his studies: "I went home after that and my wife never did understand me ever since that day. . . . She never knew what I was talking about, what I was thinking about. And I couldn't possibly explain it" (Sounes 279). Thus Haynes suggests an insight and depth of feeling on the part of Dylan the artist that far exceeds his understanding of his own life as a man. Like the French New Wave and Fassbinder films that Dylan admires, *I'm Not There* deals with overlapping time, as the personae overlap each other. "Woody," who visits his ailing namesake in a New Jersey hospital, exists at the same time that "Jack Rollins" makes his name in Greenwich Village clubs and is signed to a recording contract, somewhat incongruously, by Columbia Records, the ultra-mainstream CBS-owned label known in the early 1960s for MOR recording artists such as Johnny Mathis, the Ray Conniff singers, and Mitch Miller, who was also an executive there. Robbie meets Claire in 1964, in the "Jack" era, and marries her in between "Jude's" two tumultuous concert tours. The American history-frontier-western fixation emerges with *John Wesley Harding,* after a year and a half of secluded family life in rural upstate New York and playing music with friends like The Band. The cosmopolitan Robbie and the desperado Billy coexist; Sara was in the Rolling Thunder Revue (1975–76), is the subject of a song in *Desire* (a year after *Blood on the Tracks,* which many have said depicts their breakup), and is in *Renaldo and Clara* (which came out of the tour).

6. *Billy (Richard Gere).* The flashback/flash-forward near the opening of the film begins with the older man, the grizzled Billy, opening his eyes from sleep as little Woody runs across a field to hop a railroad boxcar. The West as an American male state of mind rather than a historical milieu is animated in many Dylan lyrics, in albums that seem to cast him as a country-western desperado on the run, an artist who portrays himself as mythic

outlaw, aligning his own aging to frontier American myths, and dissociating himself from the upheavals of the 1960s, which, after 1966, never actually applied to him, even if his songs did provide the sound track for them.

The "Billy" persona stems from Dylan's role as "Alias" in *Pat Garrett and Billy the Kid,* the albums *The Basement Tapes, Desire,* and songs such as "Lily, Rosemary, and the Jack of Hearts," from *Blood on the Tracks.* That song, from the first time I heard it as a twenty-year-old college student in the winter of 1975, sounded like a dream Dylan had after seeing *The Life and Times of Judge Roy Bean* (1972), John Huston's western comedy with Paul Newman as the "hangin' judge" whose Achilles' heel is his infatuation with the real-life dance hall singer Lillie Langtry (Ava Gardner). Dylan's song is an ultra-elliptical western tale whose slippery protagonist might be a marauding trickster antihero, something like the Eastwood-Leone spaghetti western character, who leaves behind some kind of justice (rough, ironic, poetic) before stealing off into the distance ("The only person on the scene missing was the Jack of Hearts," a post-facto line that can be heard either as oxymoronic paradox or just imprecise usage). Or he could be the card up Dylan's sleeve, the right bower in a euchre game with hearts as trump; he could be a dream, a wish-fulfillment projection of each of the characters.

Billy discovers a bearded Robbie in whiteface makeup singing "Goin' to Acapulco" with "The Band" on a bandstand in the town of Riddle. This is a ghostly tableau, which also features Keenan Jones (Bruce Greenwood) from the Jude section, the composite of all of Dylan's media inquisitors (and who gets to be the "Mr. Jones" of "Ballad of a Thin Man") appearing as an ancient Sheriff Pat Garrett, as if Sam Peckinpah had ended his movie the way he reportedly wanted to, with Billy escaping Garrett and living on, contrary to history (Fine 251). The sequence with Billy in Riddle also carries overtones of the many Dylan bootleg recordings, *The Basement Tapes,* the Beatles' *Sgt. Pepper's* album cover, and even its egregious 1970s degradation, the Bee Gees movie of *Sgt. Pepper's,* which appeared the same year that Dylan hit bottom with his four-hour film *Renaldo and Clara.*

The Billy of the final chapter is no magician; even his dog won't listen to him. Emerging from his shack that opens from darkness onto the prairie as in the opening scene of *The Searchers,* he lives in a legend that is dated and faded, a fantasy ghost town/theme park—the burg of Riddle, the fictional hometown of the fictional huckster, Lonesome Rhodes (Andy Griffith) in Budd Schulberg's and Elia Kazan's *A Face in the Crowd* (1957), a place, as

Woody says, in dialogue lifted from Schulberg, that isn't a composite, but "a compost heap." The borrowings from *A Face in the Crowd* seem apt given the film's thematics in what Schulberg called "a certain quality of success in America," one in which the biopic certainly also deals, as Lonesome Rhodes starts out a vagrant in jail and ends up a TV superstar in a penthouse. Dylan after the motorcycle crash shunned the mantle of "voice of a generation" that many wanted to drape over him. Haynes allows Dylan to inhabit his own myth of origin. Billy, hiding out from social and personal apocalypse, enters the town of Riddle and finds that he has survived his various incarnations and inquisitors. Eventually he makes his way to Woody's boxcar and reconnects, in the language of the biopic, with his destiny.

Like the now harmless western protagonist still wanted by those with a score to settle, and calling to mind Barack Obama's 2008 campaign critique of graying baby boomers who continue to carry on debates from the barricades of their youth, Billy slips out of the territory. Richard Gere has probably never allowed a director to make him appear so disheveled onscreen; Gere, who has usually not been convincing in non-modern roles, is perfect for a role-playing Dylan who similarly never really wore frontier trappings and mythology naturally. Billy makes it to the boxcar of a train that seems to circle endlessly. Finding Woody's decades-old guitar, Billy picks it up and starts all over again, discovering "past, present, and future all at once." As in the ending image of Hal Ashby's Guthrie biopic, *Bound for Glory*, the freight train barrels back through time, the troubadour still on it. Survival, if not transcendence. But perhaps the transcendence is *in* the survival.

Haynes circumvents the "body too much" issue. In casting six actors of, shall we say, diverse physiogamy, he is conceding that his Dylan is a representation, or rather multiple interpretations, and implies that there could be other ways to suggest "Dylan" than what we see here; in fact, there was reportedly another persona, a Chaplinesque figure named "Charlie," abandoned in the planning stages (Sullivan). Therefore, when Haynes performs the biopic trope of closely re-creating a photograph or film footage (the film of Dylan in performing at a civil rights rally organized by folk singers Theodore Bikel and Pete Seeger in Greenwood, Mississippi, in 1963 that Pennebaker cut to, *verité*-style without explanation, in the middle of *Dont Look Back*, which depicted events taking place two years later) or album covers, he is calling attention to his frank fictionalization of original life models no less than he did in carving the face of a Barbie doll to suggest Karen Carpenter's emaciation. Indeed, in re-creating, with Bale, the Mississippi event, Haynes alters the (extremely well known) original enough as to leave his finger-prints, if not his signature. "Jack Rollins" plays not "Only a Pawn in Their Game," the song about the killer of Medgar Evers that Dylan wrote for the occasion, but the no less scathing "The Lonesome Death of Hattie Carroll," also about race relations. The events that song depicts, however, took place between February and September 1963 and the song was recorded in late October (Frazier). Dylan sang at the civil rights gathering in early July.

Thus Haynes, for the cognoscenti (and one might question who this film's audience is, beyond those in the know), tweaks once again the biopic conventions of "dramatic purposes." The overtone, curiously, is a sense of greater fidelity to the truth of Bob Dylan than if Haynes had stuck closer to actualities. Originals and interpretations are allowed to exist side by side, without a sense of the "body too much." Haynes maintains that Dylan is limitless, that there could never be too many Dylans—or too much Dylan (although many would debate that). In listening to certain consecutive Dylan albums one wonders at how he transformed himself into different styles and forms from one album to another, one year to another. Listen to the sequence *Blonde on Blonde* (1966), *John Wesley Harding* (1967), and *Nashville Skyline* (1969), or even more so the seventies sequence of *Blood on the Tracks* (1975), *Desire* (1976), *Street Legal* (1978), and *Slow Train Coming* (1979), to feel the sense of one persona lap-dissolving over the previous one. Contained in Dylan is a long range of American and human possibilities. His art lies in trying to release and express as many of them as he can.

An aspect of *I'm Not There* that has received less attention than the six actors playing Dylan are the even more multiple voices heard singing Dylan's songs. This is taken for granted since Dylan has been perhaps the songwriter of the rock-and-roll era most often covered by other artists. According to the web site, DylanCover.com, there were, as of 16 June 2009, 26,157 cover recordings of Dylan songs. In Haynes's film the actors lip-synch to the performances of various singers. Just as Colm Feore in *Thirty Two Short Films* never mimics Glenn Gould's hands at the keyboard, when Bale, Blanchett, and Ledger lip-synch, it's to Stephen Malkmus (Blanchett), Mason Jennings, John Doe (Bale), and Jim James (Ledger). Although more than half the music heard in *I'm Not There* is sung by Bob Dylan, *the actors never lip-synch to him,* again avoiding direct competition with the subject. The embodied Dylan is always a "cover," visually and vocally. Furthermore, just as the personae overlap in time, so Haynes often uses the music of one persona against action of another, even as the film stresses how different the

Dylans are from each other. For instance, the antic *8½*-style sequence that begins with Jude and the Fab Four exploding out of a cloud of steam and speaking in helium voices is scored to "The Nashville Skyline Rag" (1969). A rare Dylan instrumental, the song came from one of Dylan's later flirtations with country music. It was written and performed in the midst of his family seclusion period, after the not-so-lonesome and unlamented (by Dylan) death of Jude Quinn. (The same piece is first heard in the film under Woody's dialogue on the boxcar.) By consistently undermining the premise that "one Dylan can very often be seen turning into the next," Haynes subtly unifies the personae (Gray "It Ain't Me" 24). Out of the various, disparate personae, therefore, Haynes re-creates a unitary, transcendent artist.

Haynes deals on the level of myth rather than on a more realistic level in which a subject is brought down to earth. Dylan is never less than "uncommon" except in the Robbie section, where he is the "common" husband-as-schmuck. Haynes includes Dylan's remark that "folk music is a bunch of fat people" (Cott 98). Dylan, ever the movie fan (some of the most charming moments in *Chronicles, Vol. 1* have him slipping off to movies), could even have had Lawrence of Arabia's disdain for England—"fat country, fat people." "You are not fat?" "No, I'm different."—somewhere on his brainpan when he made the remark in 1966. Dylan may have sung "in a coat he borrowed from James Dean / And a voice that came from you and me," as Don McLean famously sang in "American Pie" (1972), his chart-topping lament about the onset of modern rock. The idea that Dylan came from the common people and somehow belonged to them was one that he fought all his life. Ronnie Gilbert of The Weavers introduced Dylan in 1964: "You know him. He's yours. Bob Dylan." "What a crazy thing to say," he wrote in *Chronicles*. ". . . As far as I knew, I didn't belong to anybody, then or now. My destiny lay down the road with whatever life invited" (115). "The idol of production rose on his merits," wrote Michael Rogin; "the idol of consumption rises through good fortune, through being in the right place at the right time. . . . The idol of consumption is the chosen not the chooser" (qtd. in Hagopian 221).

While Dylan certainly did rise on his merits, on being an extraordinary wordsmith and alchemist of musical styles, he arrived at the right place at a time when record companies and concert promoters sensed that there would be a huge market of baby boomers coming of age and that now was the time to take chances. But business practicalities in show business biopics frequently take a backseat to myths of predestination, and Haynes opts for the latter approach entirely. Dylan's manager Albert Grossman, who took him on after Dylan was already a success and with whom Dylan had a bitter falling-out after the motorcycle accident, is played here in the leechlike manner that several of Dylan's biographers also portray him. This places Dylan (in the Jude scenes) in the melodramatic position of the artist being milked dry by greedy businessmen. Dylan/Jack Rollins, being played by the actor Robbie in a movie scene, intones with actorish bravura a classic biopic line, "I don't pick my songs. They pick me." Remarks that Dylan probably intended to sound modest establish him instead as the artist as vessel, the ultimate in transcendence. "I don't think Dylan had a lot to do with it," said Bob Johnston, the producer of six Dylan albums, in *No Direction Home*. "I think God, instead of touching him on the shoulder, kicked him in the ass. Really. And that's where that came from. He can't help what he's doin.' I mean, he's got the Holy Spirit about him. You can look at him and tell that."

The most fundamental of artist myths, the myth of the absolute artist, would work its way into any film about Dylan (most untenably, in those he's made himself). What Haynes has done is neither to pretend that such a figure was ever a unitary human individual, refusing even to anchor him to a single corporeal being and personality. Dylan's human traits emerge, because we are invited to find them and make meaning from them. At the same time, because Haynes makes the film about a living artist, he expects us to get the joke in making transcendence out of someone who currently walks the earth.

I'm Not There asks whether a biopic can be about both the person and the great things the person did. By exhaustively exploring the public myths of Bob Dylan, Haynes indulges the part of Dylan that "belongs" to the public, while leaving Dylan himself his privacy. "I don't think one word can explain a man's life," says *Kane*'s Mr. Thompson. Neither can the "facts." More than the classical structure in which the end speaks back to the beginning (although the film does have that too), *I'm Not There* plays like a loop. It begins in grainy Direct Cinema–style black and white, with the subject laid out on a slab while everyone rushes to see it and take pictures. In a rapid-fire opening sequence, Haynes cuts to a panning shot from one chatting mouth to another, an allusion to *2001*, with the dead Jude Quinn positioned like the lip-reading HAL, ready for the rebound. Cued by the line, spoken by "Arthur," "A song is something that walks by itself," the film immediately asserts the transcendence of Dylan's music over his body and physical existence. *I'm Not There*'s opening resembles *Superstar*'s. The Karen Carpenter film had the archetypal opening with a discovered death, leading to a flashback that tells the story. *I'm Not There* begins with a "death" that is strictly symbolic and fictional, taking off from Bob Fosse's autobiographical fantasia, *All That Jazz* (1979), which ended with the director's own imagined death. Within that fiction lies the legend and mystery of Bob Dylan, as well as perhaps the singer's humanity. Accordingly, the film ends with the subject, glimpsed in a heap of mangled metal amid the bushes after the motorcycle accident, recalling not just the opening frame of *Lawrence of Arabia* (cue the flashback) but also the motorcycle cop laid to waste by the hero in *À bout de souffle* amid the jump cuts and 180-degree-line violations of what is now understood as the first postmodernist film.

Dylan had already faked his life story, as it were, waiting forty years, in Scorsese's documentary, Howard Sounes's biography, and his own memoir, to set the record straight. Why wouldn't he fake a near-death too? In *Chronicles, Volume One* he wrote,

> I had been in a motorcycle accident and I'd been hurt, but I recovered. Truth was that I wanted to get out of the rat race. Having children changed my life and segregated me from just about everything that was going on. Outside my family, nothing held any real interest for me and I was seeing everything through different glasses. Even the horrifying news items of the day, the gunning down of the Kennedys, King, Malcolm X . . . I didn't see them as leaders being shot down, but rather as fathers whose families had been left wounded. Being born and raised in America, the country of freedom and independence, I had always cherished the values and ideals of equality and liberty. I was determined to raise my children with those ideals. (114–115)

What a subject, presenting himself as biopic-ready whether he knows it or not. The reluctant hero, the star who retreats from the limelight, the regular person who protests "I just want to raise my family and be left alone," the conflict between fame and everyday life, but especially the view of the political as personal, the large-scale made small and intimate, the professed fealty to American ideals—Dylan in this passage is ready for his close-up *and* his long shots. The problem is all those other Dylans who contradict this one. Problematic for a conventional biopic though he may be, he is perfect for the jigsaw puzzle Dylan of Haynes's conception, inviting the inevitable reminders of *Citizen Kane* that arise from almost any biopic made innovatively. David Bordwell points out that "one problem facing contemporary

American filmmakers is their overwhelming awareness of the legacy of the classic studio era. They suffer from belatedness," after so many narrative and cinematic conventions have been mined ("Legacies"). This is the logic that leads many to write off the biopic, since all the makers of them can do supposedly is restage conventions and recycle stylistic devices that were false to begin with. This point does not take into account filmmakers like Todd Haynes and many others who, as we have seen, turn the conventions wrong-side-out.

Over "Jude Quinn's" dead body, the narrator intones that "a devouring public can now share his legacy—and his phone numbers." In place of the *Superstar* narrator's doomy question, "What happened," *I'm Not There* bounds into the harmonica wail that opens Dylan's recording of "Stuck Inside of Mobile with the Memphis Blues Again," from the Jude Quinn period. Opening credits are a film convention that contemporary directors often forgo, but which Haynes can't seem to do without, perhaps because of the sheer "movieness" of them. Haynes snakes one of his signature traveling pan shots along underneath the credits, as Ed Lachman's cinematography covers a low-lit urban sidewalk in dreamy, desaturated color. At first the denizens of the sidewalk literalize the lyrics: "Shakespeare, he's in the alley / With his pointed shoes and his bell / Talking to some French girl / Who says she knows me well." Soon the camera pans over more anonymous, even stereotyped ghetto-dwellers and street people, including the director in a cameo. Next we're on a subway with subterranean homesick commuters; they all look like photographs by Weegee. Next we find ourselves among coal miners and hard luck people on the railroad—the folk in folk music and in Woody Guthrie's world; they look at us in shots that seem part Barbara Kopple realism and part dream. Next is a moving shot, in color, of lush, green fields as seen from a train. Suddenly, a grizzled old man, in extreme close-up, opens his eyes from sleep and we see an African American boy, running across the field in a pastoral tableau. This is as close as Todd Haynes's authorized biopic disguised as a fictionalization disguised as a genuine biography comes to letting us know that we are going into the biopic-style flashback that motivates the rest of the film. A flashback, however, it is. From the point of view of someone who is "not there."

The final two images of *Superstar*—the family home and Karen onstage— summed up the subject's public/private legacy: the transcendent performer and the "No trespassing" sign that keeps her identity finally a secret even from herself. *I'm Not There* also ends with twin images. One is the overdetermined signifier of the freight train, which Dylan borrowed from Woody Guthrie, folk music, Depression imagery, and Hollywood westerns. The other is, startlingly, film footage of Dylan—the first image or mention of him in the entire 135-minute film—looking puckish and elusive, playing his harmonica, as if into eternity.

Early reviews drew the to-be-expected denials. Emanuel Levy wrote that "*I'm Not There* is not a biopic in any sense of the term.... Those familiar with Haynes's work should be able to detect recurrent themes and motifs [such as] the impossibility of capturing any life in a conventional narrative format, such as the Hollywood biopic." This is fair enough; later critiques saw more genre in the film, however. "The unexpected upshot," wrote Michael Gray in *Sight and Sound,* "is that while all the hype about the film shouts that this is as far from the tired old conventional biopic as possible, for the Dylan aficionado it works *exactly* like a biopic" ("It Ain't Me" 20). The most obsessional of films (just try writing about it)—Lisa Schwartzbaum recommended to the readers of *Entertainment Weekly* four viewings for a full understanding of it (110)—*I'm Not There* may do what any biopic is doomed to achieve, to leave its subject an enigma on the screen—an enigma, but not a cipher.

In treating Dylan as if he were a fictional character, Haynes brings us to the sharpest reality of a subject that a spectator can have. Far from feeling that we know nothing about Dylan, Haynes makes us feel we know everything about him, that it's all mythology rather than what the subject is "really like," and that somehow that is plenty. As Vincent LoBrutto says at the end of his Martin Scorsese biography, all the biographer of a living subject, such as Haynes, can say finally is "He's out there," which contradicts the

53. *I'm Not There* tells us everything and nothing about its subject as myth of artist and person. And that is its attraction. Digital frame enlargement.

narrower meaning of the movie's title. "He will pursue personal projects that are dear to his heart and reflect his honesty and humanity," LoBrutto wrote about Scorsese (387). One senses that the Dylan of Haynes's film would not want to be spoken for even this much. The film's last shot gives us Dylan: raw reality, continuing presence, and elusiveness.

Biopics, whether the subject is Marie Antoinette or Glenn Gould, Richard Nixon or Bob Dylan, make individuals who have lived public, large-scale lives understandable as people and as myths. "All the trouble in the world," "Jude Quinn" says, "comes from people caught in scenes." The successful biopic imagines people in scenes where they lived their lives, but also makes their lives into cinema, just as Bob Dylan makes life into music and po- etry. The point then is to release them from those scenes into some lasting meaning, into transcendence. As they find their meaning in life, so perhaps do we. We would love to imagine our own lives in story form, wouldn't we, ourselves as the subjects of our own biopics? Perhaps in cultures that most celebrate a myth of the individual, biopics are devoutly to be desired, for the same reasons that any hint of conventional generic form is deplored. Each of us has his or her own story and each is unique. As Susan Alexander says to Mr. Thompson at the end of his interview with her, "Come around and tell me the story of your life sometime."

WORKS CITED

Adler, Renata. "*Star!* Arrives." *New York Times* 23 October 1968, 23.

Aldington, Richard. *Lawrence of Arabia: A Biographical Inquiry.* 1955. Westport, Conn.: Greenwood, 1976.

Alexander, Scott, and Larry Karaszewski. *Man on the Moon: Screenplay and Notes.* New York: Newmarket, 1999.

———. *The People vs. Larry Flynt: Screenplay and Notes.* New York: Newmarket, 1996.

Alpert, Hollis. "Film Review: *Lawrence of Arabia.*" *Saturday Review* 29 December 1962, 29.

Als, Hilton. "Picture This: On the Set, the Street, and at Dinner with *X* Director Spike Lee." *Village Voice* 10 November 1992, 38+.

Altman, Rick. *Film//Genre.* London: BFI, 1999.

Anderegg, Michael. *David Lean.* New York: Twayne, 1984.

Anderson, Carolyn. "Biographical Film." *Handbook of American Film Genres.* Ed. Wes D. Gehring. New York: Greenwood, 1988. 331–352.

Andrew, Dudley. *Concepts in Film Theory.* Oxford: Oxford University Press, 1984.

An Angel at My Table. DVD. With audio commentaries by Jane Campion (2003), Stuart Dryburgh (2005), and Kerry Fox (2005). Los Angeles: Criterion Collection, 2005.

Ansen, David. "Invading His Spacey." *Newsweek* 13 December 2004, 64.

———. "Kevin Costner Rides Again." *Newsweek* 4 July 1994, 71.

Apted, Michael. *Amazing Grace.* Full Text, Links, and Reviews. www.landmarktheaters .com. February 2007. Accessed 16 February 2007.

Baldwin, James. *The Devil Finds Work.* New York: Dial, 1976.

———. *One Day When I Was Lost: A Scenario Based Upon "The Autobiography of Malcolm X."* 1972. New York: Vintage, 2007.

Baraka, Amiri. *Blues People: Negro Music in White America.* New York: Morrow, 1963.

———. "Malcolm as Ideology." *Malcolm X: In Our Own Image.* Ed. Joe Wood. New York: St. Martin's, 1992. 18–35.

————. "Spike Lee at the Movies." *Black American Cinema*. Ed. Manthia Diawara. New York: Routledge, 1993. 145–153.

Bazzana, Kevin. *Wondrous Strange: The Life and Art of Glenn Gould*. Oxford: Oxford UP, 2004.

Beaver, Frank. *Oliver Stone: Wakeup Cinema*. New York: Twayne, 1994.

Bernstein, Matthew. *Walter Wanger: Hollywood Independent*. Berkeley: U of California P, 1994.

Bernstein, Richard. "Books of the *Times:* Lumumba, the African Castro or a Dazzling Ray of Hope?" *New York Times* 3 August 2001. www.nytimes.com. Accessed 4 June 2008.

Bernstein, Nina. "A Free Speech Hero? It's Not That Simple." *New York Times* 22 December 1996, H1+.

Bingham, Dennis. "Kidman, Cruise, and Kubrick: A Brechtian Pastiche." *More Than a Method*. Ed. Cynthia Baron, Diane Carson, and Frank P. Tomasulo. Detroit: Wayne State UP, 2004. 247–274.

Bolt, Robert. "Clues to the Legend of Lawrence." *New York Times Magazine* 25 February 1962, 15+.

Bordwell, David. "Legacies." *David Bordwell's Website on Cinema*. www.davidbordwell.net/blog/?p=1261. 8 September 2007. Accessed 21 September 2007.

————. *The Way Hollywood Tells It: Story and Style in Modern Movies*. Berkeley: U of California P, 2006.

————, Janet Staiger, and Kristin Thompson. *The Classical Hollywood Cinema*. New York: Columbia UP, 1985.

Bradley, David. "Malcolm's Mythmaking." *Transition* 56 (1992): 20–46.

Breznican, Anthony. "*W.*: Not Quite Out of Left Field." *USA Today* 24 September 2008, 1D+.

Briley, Ron. Rev. of *Lumumba. Cineaste* 27.1 (Winter 2001): 37–39.

Brockovich, Erin. www.brockovich.com. Accessed 16 August 2007.

————, with Marc Eliot. *Take It from Me: Life's a Struggle But You Can Win*. New York: McGraw-Hill, 2002.

Brooks, Peter. *The Melodramatic Imagination, New Preface Edition*. New Haven: Yale UP, 1995.

Brown, Georgia. "Down Under and Dirty." *Village Voice* 21 May 1991, 58.

Brownlow, Kevin. *David Lean: A Biography*. New York: St. Martin's, 1996.

Burgoyne, Robert. *The Hollywood Historical Film*. Malden, Mass.: Blackwell, 2008.

"Bush Sr. Recalls His Days in the First College World Series." Associated Press. 14 June 2007. http://sports.espn.go.com/ncaa/news/story?id=2904554. Accessed 6 June 2009.

Byars, Jackie. *All That Hollywood Allows: Re-reading Gender in 1950s Melodrama*. Chapel Hill: U of North Carolina P, 1991.

————. "The Prime of Miss Kim Novak: Struggling over the Feminine in the Star Image." *The Other Fifties: Interrogating Midcentury American Icons*. Ed. Joel Foreman. Urbana: U of Illinois P, 1997. 197–223.

Calhoun, Dave. "50 Greatest Music Films Ever. Number One: *Superstar: The Karen Carpenter Story*." *Time Out London*. 4 October 2007. www.timeout.com/film/features/show-feature/3567/12. Accessed 14 October 2007.

Callow, Simon. *Charles Laughton: A Difficult Actor*. New York: Grove, 1987.

———. *Orson Welles: The Road to Xanadu*. New York: Penguin, 1995.

Cantwell, Mary. "Jane Campion's Lunatic Women." *New York Times Magazine* 19 September 1993, 44+.

"Carpenters—Now: The Definitive, Canonical Digital Discography." *The Carpenters at the White House*. www.famousfolk.com/carpenters/bootlegs/73-white-house.shtml. Accessed 14 September 2008.

Carringer, Robert. *The Making of "Citizen Kane."* Berkeley: U of California P, 1985.

Carson, Tom. "*Chronicles:* Zimmerman Unbound." *New York Times Book Review*. 24 October 2004. www.nytimes.com. Accessed 20 February 2008.

Casper, Drew. *Postwar Hollywood, 1946–1962*. Malden, Mass.: Blackwell, 2008.

Caton, Steven C. *Lawrence of Arabia: A Film's Anthropology*. Berkeley: U of Calfornia P, 1999.

Champlin, Charles. "*Star!* Depicts Life of Noted Actress." *Los Angeles Times* 1 November 1968, F1+.

Chisholm, Ann. "Missing Persons and Bodies of Evidence." *Camera Obscura* 15.1 (2000): 122–161.

Christie, Ian. "A Life on Film." *Mapping Lives: The Uses of Biography*. Ed. Peter France and William St. Clair. Oxford: Oxford UP, 2002. 283–301.

Citizen Kane. DVD. "Gallery of Storyboards, Rare Photos, Alternate Ad Campaigns, Studio Correspondence, Call Sheets, and Other Memorabilia." Burbank, Calif.: Warner Home Video, 2001.

Clark, Mike. "Scoring with True Life, 'True Lies' and 'Fiction.'" *USA Today* 28 December 1994, 05D+.

Coal Miner's Daughter. DVD. With audio commentary by Michael Apted and Sissy Spacek, an interview of Loretta Lynn by Michael Apted, and featurette, "Tommy Lee Jones Remembers *Coal Miner's Daughter*." Universal City, Calif.: Universal Home Video, 2003.

Cole, Benjamin J. "The Congo Question: Conflicting Visions of Independence." *Emporia State Research Studies* 43.1 (2006): 26–37.

Comolli, Jean-Louis. "Historical Fiction: A Body Too Much." *Screen* 19.2 (1978): 41–53.

Cook, Gale. "Barbara, Perkins, Santo Die; Woman 'Tortured.'" *Los Angeles Examiner* 4 June 1955, 1.

Corliss, Richard. "Battier and Better." *Time* 22 June 1992. www.time.com. Accessed 19 September 2008.

Cornell, Drucilla. *The Imaginary Domain: Abortion, Pornography, and Sexual Harassment*. New York: Routledge, 1995.

Cott, Jonathan, ed. *Bob Dylan: The Essential Interviews*. New York: Wenner Books, 2006.

Coupland, Douglas. "32 Thoughts about 32 Short Films." *New York Times* 1 May 1994, 2:1+.

Cripps, Thomas. *Hollywood's High Noon: Moviemaking and Society before Television*. Baltimore: Johns Hopkins University Press, 1997.

Crowdus, Gary, and Dan Georgakas. "Our Film Is Only a Starting Point: An Interview with Spike Lee." "By Any Reviews Necessary: A *Malcolm X* Symposium." *Cineaste* 19.4 (March 1993): 20–25. EBSCO Host. Accessed 30 March 2008.

Crowley, Monica. *Nixon in Winter*. New York: Random House, 1996.

Custen, George F. *Bio/Pics: How Hollywood Constructed Public History*. New Brunswick, N.J.: Rutgers UP, 1992.

————. *Twentieth Century's Fox: Darryl F. Zanuck and the Culture of Hollywood*. New York: Basic Books, 1997.

Daly, Steve. "*Frost/Nixon*." *Entertainment Weekly* 22–29 August 2008, 94.

Denby, David. Rev. of *Gorillas in the Mist*. *New York* 3 October 1988. Clipping file, Margaret Herrick Library, Academy of Motion Picture Arts and Sciences, Los Angeles.

Desjardins, Mary. "The Incredible Shrinking Star: Todd Haynes and the Case History of Karen Carpenter." *Camera Obscura* 19.3 (2004): 23–55.

De Witte, Ludo. *The Assassination of Lumumba*. Trans. Ann Wright and Renée Fenby. London: Verso, 2001.

Diawara, Manthia. "The 'I' Narrator in Black Diaspora Documentary." *Multiculturalism, Postcoloniality, and Transnational Media*. Ed. Ella Shohat and Robert Stam. New Brunswick, N.J.: Rutgers UP, 2003. 193–202.

Dickstein, Morris. "The Last Film of the 1930s, or, Nothing Fails Like Success." *Perspectives on "Citizen Kane."* Ed. Ronald Gottesman. New York: G. K. Hall, 1996. 82–93.

Dirga, Nik. "Music Review: I'm Not There Original Soundtrack." *Blog Critics Magazine* 22 November 2007. blogcritics.org/archives/2007/11/22/110114.php. Accessed 29 December 2007.

Dixon, Poppy. "The Bettie Page Story." *Adult Christianity*. www.jesus21.com/content/page/index.php?s=bettie_page. Accessed 29 February 2008.

Doane, Mary Ann. "Pathos and Pathology: The Cinema of Todd Haynes." *Camera Obscura* 19.3 (2004): 1–20.

Doherty, Thomas. Rev. of *Erin Brockovich*. *Cineaste* 40.3 (Fall 2000): 40–41.

————. "Malcolm X: In Print, On Screen." *Biography* 23.1 (Winter 2000): 29–48.

Doyle, Kegan. "Muhammad Goes to Hollywood: Michael Mann's *Ali* as Biopic." *Journal of Popular Culture* 39.3 (2006): 383–406.

Drucker, Elizabeth. Interview with Jane Campion. *American Film* July 1991, 52+.

Dylan, Bob. *Chronicles, Volume One*. New York: Simon & Schuster, 2004.

Dylan Covers Database. www.dylancover.com. Accessed 18 May 2008.

Dyson, Michael Eric. *Making Malcolm: The Myth and Meaning of Malcolm X*. Oxford: Oxford University Press, 1995.

Edelstein, David. "Readers' Picks for Best Biopics, Plus More on the Genre." *Slate.com* 24 November 2004. Accessed 23 December 2004.

————. "The Riot Grrrl Next Door." Rev. of *Erin Brockovich*. *Slate.com*. 17 March 2000. Accessed 5 September 2007.

Erin Brockovich. DVD. Universal City, Calif.: Universal Home Video, 2000.

"Ernie Pyle." *Indiana's Popular History*. www.indianahistory.org/pop_hist/people/pyle
.html. Indianapolis: Indiana Historical Society. Accessed 24 July 2008.

Fairchild, William. *The Gertrude Lawrence Story*. Notes on Revised Treatment, 10 December 1965. Robert Wise Collection, University of Southern California.

———. Letter to Robert Wise. 26 July 1965. Robert Wise Collection, University of Southern California.

———. Letter to Robert Wise. 19 June 1966. Robert Wise Collection, University of Southern California.

———. Memo to Saul Chaplin. 9 June 1966. Robert Wise Collection, University of Southern California.

———. *Star!* (script). 25 January 1967. Robert Wise Collection, University of Southern California.

Feeney, Mark. *Nixon at the Movies*. Chicago: U of Chicago P, 2004.

Ferguson, Niall. *Empire: The Rise and Demise of the British World Order and the Lessons for Global Power*. New York: Basic Books, 2003.

Fine, Marshall. *Bloody Sam: The Life and Films of Sam Peckinpah*. New York: Donald I. Fine, 1991.

Fossey, Dian. *Gorillas in the Mist*. Boston: Houghton Mifflin, 1983.

Fox-Genovese, Elizabeth. "To Write Myself: The Autobiographies of Afro-American Women." *Feminist Issues in Literary Scholarship*. Ed. Shari Benstock. Bloomington: Indiana UP, 1987. 161–180.

Frame, Janet. *An Autobiography*. New York: George Braziller, 1991.

Fraser, Antonia. *Marie Antoinette: The Journey*. New York: Doubleday, 2001.

Frazier, Ian. "Legacy of a Lonesome Death." *Mother Jones* November–December 2004. www.motherjones.com/commentary/slant/2004/11/10_200.html. Accessed 26 December 2007.

Friedrich, Otto. *Glenn Gould: A Life and Variations*. New York: Vintage, 1990.

Frow, John. *Time and Commodity Culture: Essays in Cultural Theory and Postmodernity*. Oxford: Oxford UP, 1997.

Fuchs, Cynthia. "Crass." Rev. of *Erin Brockovich*. popmatters.com. 17 March 2000. Accessed 3 August 2007.

Funny Girl. DVD. "This Is Streisand." Columbia Pictures, ca. 1968. Culver City, Calif.: Sony Pictures Home Entertainment, 2005.

Gates, David. "The Roles They Are A-Changin.'" *Newsweek* 26 November 2007, 68.

Giles, Jeff. "The $20 Million Woman." *Newsweek* 13 March 2000, 56+.

Gillett, Sue. "Angel from the Mirror City: Jane Campion's Janet Frame." *Senses of Cinema* October 2000. www.sensesofcinema.com. Accessed 7 November 2007.

"The Girl." *Time* (cover story) 10 April 1964. www.time.com/time/magazine/article/0,9171,875750,00.html. Accessed 16 October 2007.

Gledhill, Christine. "Signs of Melodrama." *Stardom: Industry of Desire*. Ed. Christine Gledhill. London: Routledge, 1991. 212.

Goldberg, Elizabeth Swanson. "Who Was Afraid of Patrice Lumumba? Terror and the Ethical Imagination in *Lumumba: La Mort du Prophet?*" *Terrorism, Media, Liberation.* Ed. J. David Slocum. New Brunswick, N.J.: Rutgers UP, 2005. 248–266.

Goldstein, Laurence. "The Spectacle of His Body." *Michigan Quarterly Review* 34.4 (Fall 1995): 681–702.

Gondola, Ch. Didier. "Prophet and Profit: Patrice Lumumba's Resurrection in Congolese 'Urban Art.'" Talk delivered for exhibit, "A Congo Chronicle: Patrice Lumumba in Urban Art." Miriam and Ira D. Wallach Art Gallery, Columbia University. New York, 2 March 2006.

Gorillas in the Mist. DVD. "Featurette." ca. 1988. No title credits. Universal City, Calif.: Universal Home Video, 1999.

Gould, Glenn. "Let's Ban Applause." *The Glenn Gould Reader.* Ed. Tim Page. New York: Knopf, 1984. 245–249.

Grady, Pam. "A Talk with Steven Soderbergh, The Man Behind *Erin Brockovich.*" Reel. com. February 2000. www.stevensoderbergh.net. Accessed 15 August 2007.

Graham, Barbara. Letter to Al Matthews. 8 March 1955. Walter Wanger Collection, State Historical Society of Wisconsin, Madison.

Grant, Susanna. *Erin Brockovich: A True Story.* First draft script. 1 February 1998. simply-scripts.com. Accessed 15 August 2007.

———. *Erin Brockovich: A True Story.* Revisions by Richard La Gravenese. Revised draft. 22 March 1999. www.simplyscripts.com. Accessed 15 August 2007.

———. *Erin Brockovich: Screenplay with Introduction.* New York: Newmarket, 2000.

Gray, Michael. *The Bob Dylan Encyclopedia.* New York: Continuum, 2006.

———. "It Ain't Me, Babe." *Sight and Sound* (January 2008): 18–24.

Greenberg, David. *Nixon's Shadow.* New York: W. W. Norton, 2003.

Greve, Frank. "Susan Hayward's Fight for Life." *Detroit Free Press* 12 October 1975: 1E.

Grey, Rudolph. *Nightmare of Ecstasy: The Life and Art of Edward D. Wood, Jr.* Portland, Ore.: Feral House, 1992.

Hafner, Katie. *A Romance on Three Legs: Glenn Gould's Obsessive Quest for the Perfect Piano.* New York: Bloomsbury USA, 2008.

Hagopian, Kevin Jack. "Hollywood Restoration: Genre and the American Film Industry in the Culture of American Affirmation, 1936–1945." Ph.D. diss., U of Wisconsin, Madison, 2006.

Hamilton, Ian. *Biography: A Brief History.* Cambridge, Mass.: Harvard UP, 2007.

Hancock, Brendan. *The Bettie Page Companion.* www.shamanalternative.com/bettiepage _com_page_1.htm. Accessed 29 February 2008.

Hardy, Ernest. "In Film Biographies: A Fuller Spectrum." *New York Times* 24 June 2001, AR 13+. www.nytimes.com. Accessed 15 October 2006.

Harron, Mary. Interview with Terry Gross. *Fresh Air.* National Public Radio. 12 April 2006. www.npr.com. Accessed 5 March 2008.

Hastings, Chris, and Fiona Govan. "Stars Vote *Lawrence of Arabia* the Best British Film of All Time." *Daily Telegraph.* 15 August 2004. www.telegraph.co.uk.

Hayes, Harold T. P. *The Dark Romance of Dian Fossey*. New York: Simon & Schuster, 1990.

Heart Like a Wheel. DVD. "Shirley Muldowney: Behind the Wheel." Troy, Mich.: Anchor Bay Entertainment, 2006.

Heffernan, Harold. "Susan Cries at Own Film (Just Like Other Movie Fans)." *Detroit News* 8 February 1959. Clipping file, Detroit Public Library.

———. "Susan Hayward Determined to Dodge 'Sweet Girl' Career." *Detroit News* 25 July 1943. Clipping file, Detroit Public Library.

Heilbrun, Carolyn. *Writing a Woman's Life*. New York: W. W. Norton, 1988.

Herman, Jan. *A Talent for Trouble: The Life of Hollywood's Most Acclaimed Director, William Wyler*. New York: G. P. Putnam's Sons, 1995.

"Heroine's Reel Life Outstripped by Real Version." *Times of London* 29 March 2000. Clipping File, Margaret Herrick Library, Academy of Motion Picture Arts and Sciences, Los Angeles.

Hilderbrand, Lucas. "Grainy Days and Mondays: *Superstar* and Bootleg Aesthetics." *Camera Obscura* 19.3 (2004): 56–91.

Hinson, Hal. "*Gorillas in the Mist*." *Washington Post* 23 September 1988. www.washingtonpost.com. Accessed 4 August 2005.

Hoberman, J. "Ed Wood . . . Not." *Sight and Sound* (May 1995): 10–12.

———. "Like a Complete Unknown: *I'm Not There* and the Changing Face of Bob Dylan on Film." *Village Voice* 20 November 2007. www.villagevoice.com. Accessed 21 November 2007.

———. "*Lumumba*." 26 June 2001. www.villagevoice.com. Accessed 10 April 2008.

Hodson, Joel C. *Lawrence of Arabia and American Culture: The Making of a Transatlantic Legend*. Westport, Conn.: Greenwood, 1995.

Holroyd, Michael. *Lytton Strachey: The New Biography*. New York: Noonday, 1995.

hooks, bell. "Male Heroes and Female Sex Objects: Sexism in Spike Lee's *Malcolm X*." "By Any Reviews Necessary: A *Malcolm X* Symposium." *Cineaste* 19.4 (March 1993): 13–14. EBSCO Host. Accessed 30 March 2008.

Horne, Gerald. "'Myth' and the Making of '*Malcolm X*.'" *American Historical Review* 98.2 (April 1993): 440–450.

Howard, Leslie. "How I Shall Play Lawrence." 1937. *Filming T. E. Lawrence: Korda's Lost Epics*. Ed. Andrew Kelly, Jeffrey Richards, and James Pepper. London: I. B. Tauris, 1997. 22–27.

Howe, Desson. "A Stirring '*Lumumba*.'" 13 July 2001. www.washingtonpost.com. Accessed 10 April 2008.

Hultkrans, Andrew. "Look Back in Angora: Tim Burton's Film on Filmmaker Ed Wood." *ArtForum* (December 1994). BNet. findarticles.com/p/articles/mi_m0268/is_n4_v33/ai_16547718/pg_1?tag=artBody;col1. Accessed 11 September 2008.

Hutcheon, Linda. "An Epilogue: Postmodern Parody: History, Subjectivity, and Ideology." *Quarterly Review of Film and Video* 4.12 (1990): 125–133.

Hynes, Samuel. "Court Gossip" (rev. of *Lytton Strachey: The New Biography*). *New Republic* 1 May 1995. 41–45.

IFC News. New York Film Festival Press Conference with Todd Haynes. 3 October 2007. www.youtube.com/watch?v=HBAsheMKyos. Accessed 28 December 2007.

Jackson, Kevin. *Lawrence of Arabia*. London: BFI, 2007.

Jameson, Fredric. *Postmodernism, or the Cultural Logic of Late Capitalism*. Durham, N.C.: Duke UP, 1991.

Jeffords, Susan. *The Remasculinization of America: Gender and the Vietnam War*. Bloomington: Indiana University Press, 1989.

Joannou, Mary, and Steve McIntyre. "Lust for Lives: Report from a Conference on the Biopic." *Screen* 24.2 (1983): 147.

Johnson, Erskine. "Susan Hayward Has Found Happiness in the Deep South." n.d. (ca. April 1958). Walter Wanger Collection, State Historical Society of Wisconsin, Madison.

Johnson, Robert Craig. "Heart of Darkness: The Tragedy of the Congo, 1960–67." 1997. worldatwar.net/chandelle/v2/v2n3/congo.html. Accessed 3 June 2008.

Johnston, Trevor. "Art of Gould." *Time Out (London)* 15 June 1994. Clipping file, Margaret Herrick Library, Academy of Motion Picture Arts and Sciences, Los Angeles.

Jones, Jacquie. "Spike Lee Presents Malcolm X: The New Black Nationalism." "By Any Reviews Necessary: A *Malcolm X* Symposium." *Cineaste* 19.4 (March 1993): 9–10. EBSCO Host. Accessed 30 March 2008.

Jost, Jon. "Some Notes on 'Political Cinema' Prompted by Seeing Raoul Peck's *Sometimes in April* in Competition at the Berlin Film Festival." *Senses of Cinema* no. 35 (April–June 2005). www.sensesofcinema.com. Accessed 26 May 2006.

"Julia: An Appreciation of the Last True Movie Star by, among Others, James Gandolfini, Roger Ebert, and, of course, Ralph Nader." *Esquire* April 2001, 122+.

"Julia Roberts: Personal Quotes." Internet Movie Database. Accessed 18 June 2009.

Kael, Pauline. "Bravo!" 29 September 1968. *Going Steady*. Boston: Little, Brown, 1970. 133–137.

———. "Cripes!" 26 October 1968. *Going Steady*. Boston: Little, Brown, 1970. 161–166.

———. "Hair." 14 November 1983. *State of the Art*. New York: Dutton, 1985. 79–85.

———. "Raising Kane." *The "Citizen Kane" Book*. Boston: Little, Brown, 1971. 3–84.

Kakutani, Michiko. "Who Was Dian Fossey and What Killed Her?" *New York Times* 29 June 1990, C23.

Kauffmann, Stanley. Rev. of *Nixon*. *New Republic* 22 January 1996, 26.

———. "*Funny Girl*." *New Republic* 9 November 1968, 22.

Kelly, Andrew, Jeffrey Richards, and James Pepper. *Filming T. E. Lawrence: Korda's Lost Epics*. London: I. B. Tauris, 1997.

Kenrick, John. "*Funny Girl* Debunked: The Truth about Fanny Brice." www.barbra-archives.com/articles/streisand_funnygirl_debunked.html Accessed 16 October 2007.

Kifner, John. "Remaking History: Britain Tried First. Iraq Was No Picnic Then." *New York Times* 20 July 2003, 4:1.

Kimmel, Michael. *Manhood in America: A Cultural History*. New York: Free Press, 1996.

Kinder, Marsha. "Back to the Future in the 80s with Fathers & Sons, Supermen & Pee-Wees, Gorillas & Toons." *Film Quarterly* 42.4 (Summer 1989): 2–11.

Klein, Andy. "32 Short Films about Glenn Gould." *L.A. Reader* 14 April 1994.

Korda, Michael. *Charmed Lives*. New York: Random House, 1979.

Kovacik, Karen. "Nixon on the Pleasures of Undressing a Woman." *Nixon and I*. Kent, Oh.: Kent State University Press, 1998.

Landy, Marcia. *British Genres: Cinema and Society, 1930–1960*. Princeton, N.J.: Princeton UP, 1991.

———. *Cinematic Uses of History*. Minneapolis: U of Minnesota P, 1996.

———. "Storytelling and Information in Todd Haynes' Films." *The Cinema of Todd Haynes: All That Heaven Allows*. Ed. James Morrison. London: Wallflower, 2007. 7–24.

———, and Amy Villarejo. *Queen Christina*. London: BFI, 1995.

Lawrence, T. E. *Seven Pillars of Wisdom: A Triumph*. 1926. New York: Doubleday Anchor, 1991.

Lawrence of Arabia. DVD. Columbia Tri-Star Home Video. 2001.

"Lawrence/Tussaud." *Time* 8 November 1968. www.time.com. Accessed 18 October 2007.

Lean, Tangye. Rev. of *Citizen Kane*. 1941. *Perspectives on "Citizen Kane."* Ed. Ronald Gottesman. New York: G. K. Hall, 1996. 49–53.

Lee, Spike, with Ralph Wiley. *By Any Means Necessary: The Trials and Tribulations of the Making of "Malcolm X."* New York: Hyperion, 1992.

Leemann, Sergio. *Robert Wise on His Films*. Hollywood, Calif.: Samuel French, 1995.

Lennart, Isobel. *Funny Girl* (scripts). 21 March 1967 and 24 July 1967. William Wyler Papers, UCLA Arts Library Special Collections, Los Angeles.

———.*Funny Girl: A New Musical*. Lyrics by Bob Merrill. New York: Random House, 1964.

———. *My Man* (script). 20 October 1960. William Wyler Papers, UCLA Arts Library Special Collections, Los Angeles.

Lessem, Don. "Saint Simeon." *GQ* September 1988, 414+.

Levy, Emanuel. Rev. of *I'm Not There*. www.emanuellevy.com. Accessed 13 November 2007.

———. Interview. *I'm Not There*. www.emanuellevy.com. Accessed 25 January 2008.

"Lily Morris, Gertrude Lawrence." Posted by jozefsterkens. 5 February 2007. www.youtube.com/watch?v=UIJOTsHSF_c. Accessed 12 October 2007.

Lim, Dennis. "After 50 Years, Still No Time for Cheap Sentiment." *New York Times* 21 October 2007, 23+.

Linet, Beverly. *Susan Hayward: Portrait of a Survivor*. New York: Atheneum, 1980.

LoBrutto, Vincent. *Martin Scorsese: A Biography*. Westport, Conn.: Praeger, 2008.

Lumumba. DVD. Liner Notes and Production Notes by Raoul Peck. New York: Zietgeist Video, 2002.

Macdonald, Dwight. *On Movies*. Englewood Cliffs, N.J.: Prentice-Hall, 1969.

Maio, Kathi. "A Flop about a Failure." *Fantasy & Science Fiction* 88.6 (June 1995): 74+.

Malcolm X, and Alex Haley. *The Autobiography of Malcolm X*. 1965. New York: Ballantine Books, 1993.

Malleson, Miles, Brian Desmond Hurst, and Duncan Guthrie. *Lawrence of Arabia.* In Kelly et al., *Filming T. E. Lawrence.* 29–129.

Maltby, Richard, and Ian Craven. *Hollywood Cinema.* Oxford: Blackwell, 1995.

Mankiewicz, Joseph L. Letter to Walter Wanger. 27 August 1957. Walter Wanger Collection, State Historical Society of Wisconsin, Madison.

Manners, Dorothy. "Wanger Betting—on a Murderess!" *Los Angeles Examiner* 10 August 1958, 11.

Marable, Manning. "Malcolm X." *Christianity and Crisis* 52.19 (4 January 1993): 432(3). Gale Group Academic OneFile. Accessed 29 May 2008.

Marie Antoinette. DVD. With special feature "The Making of *Marie Antoinette,*" written and directed by Eleanor Coppola. Culver City, Calif.: Sony Pictures Home Entertainment, 2007.

Marlowe, Leigh. "*Heart Like a Wheel.*" *Psychology of Women Quarterly* 11.2 (June 1987): 276.

Maslin, Janet. "Bonnie Bedelia as a Race-Car Driver." *New York Times* 6 October 1983, C30.

Matthews, Anne. "Rage in a Tenured Position." *New York Times Magazine* 8 November 1992, 46+.

Matthews, Chris. *Kennedy and Nixon: The Rivalry That Shaped Postwar America.* New York: Simon & Schuster, 1996.

May, Elaine Tyler. *Homeward Bound: American Families in the Cold War Era.* New York: Basic Books, 1988.

McCrisken, Trevor, and Andrew Pepper. *American History and Contemporary Hollywood Film.* New Brunswick, N.J.: Rutgers UP 2005.

McDonagh, Maitland. "Jane Campion's 'Angel' Is Another Quirky Soul." *New York Times* 19 May 1991, 2:22.

McDougal, Dennis. *Five Easy Decades: How Jack Nicholson Became the Biggest Movie Star in Modern Times.* New York: John Wiley, 2007.

McHugh, Kathleen. *Jane Campion.* Champaign: U of Illinois P, 2007.

Medovoi, Leerom. "Democracy, Capitalism, and American Literature: The Cold War Construction of J. D. Salinger's Paperback Hero." *The Other Fifties: Interrogating Midcentury American Icons.* Ed. Joel Foreman. Urbana: U of Illinois P, 1997. 255–287.

Mellencamp, Patricia. *A Fine Romance.* Philadelphia: Temple UP, 1995.

Mizejewski, Linda. *Ziegfeld Girl: Image and Icon in Culture and Cinema.* Durham, N.C.: Duke UP, 1999.

Modleski, Tania. *The Women Who Knew Too Much: Hitchcock and Feminist Theory.* Rev. ed. New York: Routledge, 2005.

Morgan, Peter. *Frost/Nixon.* London: Faber & Faber, 2006.

Morgenstern, Joseph. "Great Girl." *Newsweek* 30 September 1968, 96.

_____. "Superstar: The Streisand Story." *Newsweek* 5 January 1970, 36+. www.barbra-archives.com/MagazineArchives/streisand_newsweek.html. Accessed 15 October 2007.

Morris, L. Robert, and Lawrence Raskin. *Lawrence of Arabia: The 30th Anniversary Pictorial History.* New York: Anchor Books, 1992.

Morrison, James, ed. "Todd Haynes in Theory and Practice." *The Cinema of Todd Haynes: All That Heaven Allows.* Ed. James Morrison. London: Wallflower, 2007. 132–144.

Mulholland, Gerry. "*Raging Bull.*" *Time Out (London)* 15 November 2000. Clipping file, Margaret Herrick Library, Academy of Motion Picture Arts and Sciences, Los Angeles.

Mulvey, Laura. "*Citizen Kane.*" London: BFI Publishing, 1992.

Naremore, James. "The Director as Actor." *Perspectives on Orson Welles.* Ed. Morris Beja. New York: G. K. Hall, 1995. 273–280.

_____. *The Films of Vincente Minnelli.* New York: Cambridge UP, 1993.

Nixon, Richard. *RN: The Memoirs of Richard Nixon,* Volume 1. New York: Grosset & Dunlap, 1978.

Nixon. DVD. Supplemental material introduced by Oliver Stone. Burbank, Calif.: Walt Disney Home Video, 2003 (1996).

"No. 5: Shirley Muldowney." *50 Top Drivers NHRA.* www.nhra.com/50th/top50/S_Muldowney05.html. Accessed 18 September 2007.

Norman, Brian. "Reading a 'Closet Screenplay': Hollywood, James Baldwin's Malcolm X and the Threat of Historical Irrelevance." *African American Review* 39.2 (Spring/Summer 2005): 103–118.

The Notorious Bettie Page. DVD. With audio commentary by Gretchen Mol, Mary Harron, and Guinevere Turner. New York: Home Box Office Video, 2006.

Nugent, Frank S. "The Screen: A Worshipful Biography of Florence Nightingale Is *The White Angel,* at the Strand." *New York Times* 25 June 1936, 24.

Nutting, Anthony. *Lawrence of Arabia: The Man and the Motive.* New York: Bramhall, 1961.

O'Brien, Sharon. "Feminist Theory and Literary Biography." *Contesting the Subject: Essays in the Postmodern Theory and Practice of Biography and Biographical Criticism.* West Lafayette, Ind.: Purdue UP, 1991. 123–133.

"Oliver Stone Session." Meeting of the American Historical Association, New York, 4 January 1997. Cablecast on C-Span, 17 February 1997.

"One on One: Michael Apted and Alan Parker." *American Film* (September 1990): 42–45.

Ostwald, Peter F. *Glenn Gould: The Ecstasy and Tragedy of Genius.* New York: W. W. Norton, 1997.

Painter, Nell Irvin. "Malcolm X Across the Genres." *American Historical Review* 98.2 (April 1993): 432–439.

Parliamentary Committee of Enquiry in Charge of Determining the Exact Circumstances of the Assassination of Patrice Lumumba and the Possible Involvement of Belgian Politicians. Summary, Introduction, Conclusions. December 2001. africawithin.com/lumumba/murder_of_lumumba.htm. Accessed 4 November 2006.

Parke, Catherine. *Biography: Writing Lives.* New York: Twayne, 1996.

Peary, Danny. *Alternate Oscars.* New York: Delta, 1993.

Perlstein, Rick. *Nixonland: The Rise of a President and the Fracturing of America*. New York: Scribner, 2008.

Phelan, Anna Hamilton. *Gorillas in the Mist* (scripts). 29 September 1986, 6 April 1987, 11 May 1987, 16 May 1987, 23 June 1987, 2 July 1987. Arts Library Special Collections, UCLA.

Pickle, Betsy. "Forget Looks: Hopkins Portrays Inner Nixon." *Indianapolis Star* 31 December 1995, I-4.

Pizzitola, Louis. *Hearst over Hollywood: Power, Passion, and Propaganda in the Movies*. New York: Columbia UP, 2002.

Polan, Dana. *Jane Campion*. London: BFI, 2001.

"Powe." Review of *I Want to Live! Variety* 29 October 1958. Walter Wanger Collection, State Historical Society of Wisconsin, Madison.

Powers, Jessica. "An Obsession with Lumumba." 14 March 2004. www.suite101.com/article.cfm/african_history/107242. 1–3. Accessed 5 June 2008.

Radner, Hilary. "Pretty Is As Pretty Does: Free Enterprise and the Marriage Plot." *Film Theory Goes to the Movies*. Ed. Jim Collins, Hilary Radner, and Ava Preacher Collins. London: Routledge, 1993. 56–76.

Rattigan, Terence. *Ross: A Play in Two Acts*. London: Samuel French, 1960.

Reeves, Richard. *President Nixon: Alone in the White House*. New York: Simon & Schuster, 2001.

Ressner, Jeffrey. "The Odd Fellows." *Time* 31 December 1999, 225+. www.time.com/time/magazine/article/0,9171,993006,00.html. Accessed 29 September 2008.

Riding, Alan. "In a Mirror on Africa, A Hero Unfairly Tarnished." *New York Times* 24 June 2001, AR 13+ www.nytimes.com. Accessed 15 October 2006.

Rivele, Stephen J., Christopher Wilkinson, and Oliver Stone. "*Nixon:* The Original Annotated Screenplay." *"Nixon": An Oliver Stone Film*. Ed. Eric Hamburg. New York: Hyperion, 1995. 81–318.

Robbins, Bruce. *Upward Mobility and the Common Good: Toward a Literary History of the Welfare State*. Princeton, N.J.: Princeton UP, 2007.

Rodriguez, Robert. "Big Movies Made Cheap." *Spy Kids 2*. DVD. Burbank, Calif.: Miramax Home Entertainment, 2003.

Rogin, Michael. *Blackface, White Noise: Jewish Immigrants in the Hollywood Melting Pot*. Berkeley: U of California P, 1996.

———. *Ronald Reagan, the Movie: and Other Episodes in Political Demonology*. Berkeley: U of California P, 1987.

Rosenbaum, Jonathan. "Allusion Profusion." 21 October 1994. *Movies as Politics*. Berkeley: U of California P, 1997. 171–178.

———. "Hollywood Radical." 11 December 1992. *Movies as Politics*. Berkeley: U of California P, 1997. 145–153.

Rosenstone, Robert A. "In Praise of the Biopic." *Lights, Camera, History: Portraying the Past in Film*. Ed. Richard Francaviglia and Jerry Rodnitsky. College Station: Texas A & M UP, 2007. 11–29.

————. *Visions of the Past: The Challenge of Film to Our Idea of History.* Cambridge, Mass.: Harvard UP, 1995.

Routt, William D. "Bad for Good." *Intensities: The Journal of Cult Media* 2 (Novermber 2001). intensities.org. Accessed 22 March 2008.

Rubin, Jacob. "I'm Not Here." *New Republic Online.* 21 November 2007. www.tnr.com. Accessed 23 November 2007.

Rutherford, Jonathan. *Forever England: Reflections on Race, Masculinity, and Europe.* London: Lawrence & Wishart, 1997.

Salisbury, Harrison E. "Senators Start Morals Hearings." *New York Times* 25 May 1955. www.nytimes.com. Accessed 1 March 2008.

————. "Smut Held Cause of Delinquency." *New York Times* 1 June 1955. www.nytimes.com. Accessed 1 March 2008.

Sarris, Andrew. *The American Cinema: Directors and Directions 1929–1968.* 1968. New York: Da Capo, 1996.

————. "Notes on the Auteur Theory in 1962." *Film Theory and Criticism.* 6th ed. Ed. Leo Braudy and Marshall Cohen. Oxford: Oxford UP, 2004. 561–564.

Sartre, Jean-Paul. *Colonialism and Neo-Colonialism.* Trans. Azzedine Haddour, Steve Brewer, and Terry McWilliams. London: Routledge, 2001. 156–200.

Sawhill, Ray. "Malcolm Zzzzzzz." raysawhill.wordpress.com/writing-on-art-and- culture/ movies/malcolm-x/. 1992. Accessed 12 April 2008.

Scheer, Robert. "Foreword." *"Nixon": An Oliver Stone Film.* Ed. Eric Hamburg. New York: Hyperion, 1995. ix–xii.

Schickel, Richard. "Shootout at the ZZ Corral." *Time* 4 July 1994, 73.

Schultz, Rick. "Gould's Ghost. Director François Girard Reflects on the Enigmatic Canadian Pianist Glenn Gould." *L.A. Village View* 15–21 April 1994, 11+.

Scobie, Stephen. *Alias Bob Dylan Revisited.* Calgary: Red Deer, 2003.

Scott, A.O. "Francis Ford Coppola: A Kid to Watch." *New York Times* 9 September 2007. www.nytimes.com. Accessed 22 February 2008.

————. "Here's to the Ambitious and the Altmans." *New York Times* 24 December 2006. www.nytimes.com. Accessed 18 February 2008.

"She Wanted to Win." *New York Times* 8 April 1959, 41.

Sheehan, Henry. Rev. of *Gorillas in the Mist. Los Angeles Reader* 23 September 1988. Clipping file, Margaret Herrick Library, Academy of Motion Picture Arts and Sciences, Los Angeles.

Silberg, Jon. "Deconstructing Bob Dylan." *American Cinematographer* November 2007. www.ascmag.com/magazine_dynamic/November2007/ImNotThere/page1.php.   Accessed 3 January 2008.

Simkins, David. "Episode 9a: Larry Karaszewski and Scott Alexander." *The Zicree Simkins Podcasts.* 10 March 2008. zicreesimkins.wordpress.com/2008/03/10/episode-9a-larry-karaszewski-and-scott-alexander-11020-repost. Accessed 29 June 2008.

The Sound of Music. DVD. Beverly Hills, Calif.: Twentieth Century Fox Home Entertainment, 2000.

Sounes, Howard. *Down the Highway: The Life of Bob Dylan*. New York: Grove, 2001.

Soussloff, Catherine M. *The Absolute Artist: The Historiography of a Concept*. Minneapolis: U of Minnesota P, 1997.

"Special Trailer" for *I Want to Live!* Interview with Al Matthews. 1 July 1958. Wisconsin Center for Film and Theater Research, Madison.

Staggs, Sam. *All About "All About Eve."* New York: St. Martin's, 2001.

Stam, Robert. *Film Theory: An Introduction*. Malden, Mass.: Blackwell, 2000.

Star! DVD. With running audio commentary by Julie Andrews, Robert Wise, Saul Chaplin et al, and featurettes "The Saga of *Star!*" and "Silver *Star!*" Beverly Hills, Calif.: Twentieth Century Fox Home Entertainment, 2004.

Star! Publicity Manual. Hollywood, Calif.: Twentieth Century Fox, 1968. Robert Wise Collection, University of Southern California.

"The Star." *American Cinema*. Vol. 1, Part 2. PBS-TV. Los Angeles: Fox Video, 1995.

Stevens, Maurice E. "Subject to Countermemory: Disavowal and Black Manhood in Spike Lee's *Malcolm X*." *Signs* 28.1 (Autumn 2002): 277–301.

Storhoff, Gary. "Icon and History in *Frances*." *Literature/Film Quarterly* 23.4 (1995): 266–272.

Strachey, Lytton. *Eminent Victorians*. 1918. New York: Modern Library, 1999.

Strober, Gerald S., and Deborah Hart Strober. *Nixon: An Oral History of His Presidency*. New York: HarperCollins, 1994.

Sullivan, Robert. "This Is (Not) a Bob Dylan Movie." *New York Times Magazine* 7 October 2007. www.nytimes.com. Accessed 14 December 2007.

Superstar: The Karen Carpenter Story. Internet Movie Database. www.imdb.com. Message board post by mhearn. 11 August 2006. Accessed 12 September 2007.

Superstar: The Karen Carpenter Story (description). Google Video. n.d. video.google.com/videoplay?docid=622130510713940545. Accessed 9 February 2007.

Svetkey, Benjamin. "First Look: *W.*, Oliver Stone's Bush Biopic." *Entertainment Weekly* 16 May 2008. www.ew.com. Accessed 6 June 2009.

Swenson, Karen. "The Making of *Funny Girl*." *Barbra Magazine* 2.3 (1982): 33–47.

Taubin, Amy. "Notes on Campion." *Village Voice* 28 May 1991, 62.

Thomas, Kevin. "*Funny Girl*." *Los Angeles Times* 31 August 2001. Clipping file, Margaret Herrick Library, Academy of Motion Picture Arts and Sciences, Los Angeles.

Thomson, David. *Rosebud*. New York: Vintage, 1996.

Tibbetts, John C. "Robert Altman: After 35 Years, Still the 'Action Painter' of American Cinema." *Film/Literature Quarterly* 20.1 (1992): 36–42.

Toplin, Robert Brent. *Reel History: In Defense of Hollywood*. Lawrence: UP of Kansas, 2002.

Turan, Kenneth. "Baby, It's All Right." *Los Angeles Times* 29 October 2004, E1+.

United Artists Publicity Department. *I Want to Live!* (press release). n.d. (ca. November 1958). Walter Wanger Collection, State Historical Society of Wisconsin, Madison.

Van Gelder, Lawrence. "A Life Like the Movies." *New York Times* 15 March 1975, 30.

Volkan, Vamik D., Norman Itzkowitz, and Andrew W. Dod. *Richard Nixon: A Psychobiography.* New York: Columbia UP, 1997.

Wagner-Martin, Linda. *Telling Women's Lives: The New Biography.* New Brunswick, N.J.: Rutgers UP, 1994.

Waites, Kathleen J. "Graeme Clifford's Biopic, *Frances* (1982): Once a Failed Lady, Twice Indicted." *Literature/Film Quarterly* 33.1 (2005): 12–19.

Waldron, D'Lynn. www.dlynnwaldron.com/Lumumba.html. Accessed 3 June 2008.

Wanger, Walter. Letter to Mrs. Eaton Chalkley (Susan Hayward). 12 March 1957. Walter Wanger Collection, State Historical Society of Wisconsin, Madison.

———. Letter to Joseph L. Mankiewicz. 29 October 1957. Walter Wanger Collection, State Historical Society of Wisconsin, Madison.

———. Letter to Joseph L. Mankiewicz. 22 November 1957. Walter Wanger Collection, State Historical Society of Wisconsin, Madison.

Watson, Julia. "Raoul Peck's *Lumumba:* A Film for Our Times." *Research in African Literatures* 33.2 (2002): 230–235.

Weissman, Stephen R. "Opening the Secret Files on Lumumba's Murder." *Washington Post* 21 July 2002. www.africawithin.com/lumumba/murder_of_lumumba.htm. Accessed 4 November 2006.

Welsh, James. "Musical Biography and Film: John Tibbetts Interviewed by Jim Welsh." *Film and History* 35.2 (2005): 86–91.

White, Armond. "Malcolm X'd Again." 2 December 1992. *American Movie Critics: An Anthology from the Silents until Now.* Ed. Phillip Lopate. New York: Library of America, 2006. 574–578.

White, Theodore H. *Breach of Faith: The Fall of Richard Nixon.* New York: Atheneum, 1975.

White-Stanley, Debra. "Case Study: Julia Roberts." Unpublished manuscript, ca. 1998.

Wicker, Tom. *One of Us: Richard Nixon and the American Dream.* Rev. ed. New York: Random House, 1995.

Wills, Garry. *Nixon Agonistes: The Crisis of the Self-Made Man.* Boston: Houghton Mifflin, 1970.

Wilson, Earl. "Susan Hayward Pulls a Switch." *Detroit Free Press* 9 October 1950. Clipping file, Detroit Public Library.

Wilson, Jeremy. *Lawrence of Arabia: The Authorized Biography of T. E. Lawrence.* New York: Atheneum, 1990.

Winn, J. Emmett. "Challenges and Compromises in Spike Lee's *Malcolm X.*" *Critical Studies in Media Communications* 18.4 (December 2001): 452–465.

Wise, Robert. Letter to [Fox executive] David Raphel. 19 March 1968. Robert Wise Collection, University of Southern California.

———. Letter to Saul Chaplin. 12 August 1965. Robert Wise Collection, University of Southern California.

Wood, Thomas. "Unlazy Susan." *Colliers* 18 (August 1951): 20.

Woodward, Bob. *Plan of Attack.* New York: Simon & Schuster, 2004.

Wyles, David. *"W.": The Film Guide.* Supervised by Oliver Stone and Stanley Weiser. www
.wthefilm.com/guide. Accessed 20 October 2008.

Young, James O. *Cultural Appropriation and the Arts.* Malden, Mass.: Blackwell, 2008.

Ziff, Bruce, and Pratima V. Rao. "Introduction to Cultural Appropriation: A Framework
for Analysis." *Borrowed Power: Essays on Cultural Appropriation.* Ed. Bruce Ziff and
Pratima V. Rao. New Brunswick, N.J.: Rutgers UP, 1997. 1–27.

INDEX

ABOUT THE AUTHOR

Dennis Bingham teaches English at the IU School of Liberal Arts at Indiana University Purdue University Indianapolis, where he directs the Film Studies Program. He is the author of *Acting Male: Masculinities in the Films of James Stewart, Jack Nicholson, and Clint Eastwood* (Rutgers University Press) and many articles on gender, genre, acting, and stardom.